The Frontiers of Catholicism

For this we are gathered together
For this we are united

Seeds of violence remain within each of us
We must be vigilant that these seeds don't
overwhelm us

Star Trek, next generation

New Directions in Cultural Analysis
Edited by Robert Wuthnow

The Frontiers of Catholicism

The Politics of Ideology in a Liberal World

GENE BURNS

University of California Press

BERKELEY   LOS ANGELES   LONDON

University of California Press
Berkeley and Los Angeles, California

University of California Press, Ltd.
London, England

First Paperback Printing 1994

© 1992 by
The Regents of the University of California

Library of Congress Cataloging-in-Publication Data

Burns, Gene, 1958-
    The frontiers of Catholicism : the politics of ideology in a liberal
world / Gene Burns.
        p.   cm. — (New directions in cultural analysis ; 1)
    Includes bibliographical references and index.
    ISBN 0-520-08922-7
    1. Catholic Church—United States. 2. Ideology—Religious
aspects—Christianity. I. Title. II. Series.
    BX1406.2.B8651992
    282'.73—dc20   914-6039
                                                                    CIP

Printed in the United States of America

9 8 7 6 5 4 3 2 1

The paper used in this publication meets the minimum requirements
of American National Standard for Information Sciences—Permanence
of Paper for Printed Library Materials, ANSI Z39.48-1984. ♾

For Alison and for my parents

Contents

Acknowledgments

My thanks first to those who have been with this research from its inception. Elizabeth McLean Petras, Ewa Morawska, and John Noakes helped me to pursue this research and to clarify my thoughts. Braulio Muñoz first suggested this case study, one of the many ways that he has aided me over the years. Most important, Fred Block has been an invaluable teacher and friend. Not only is he almost foolishly generous with his time; his insight, warmth, and humor are always more than one has a right to expect.

The stimulating environments of the Sociology Departments of both the University of Pennsylvania and Princeton University have also been most beneficial. Jean-Guy Vaillancourt, Stephen Chiu, Libby Schweber, Paul DiMaggio, Wade Clark Roof, R. Stephen Warner, the members of Princeton's Culture Seminar of 1988–1989, and an anonymous reviewer have read the manuscript, in whole or in part, in its various forms and made very helpful comments. Naomi Schneider of the University of California Press has been a most encouraging and dependable editor. Amy Klatzkin guided the manuscript through publication, and Anne Canright's copyediting significantly improved it. I am indebted as well to Wendy Clauson Schlereth, Sharon Sumpter, Kevin Cawley, and especially Charles Lamb, all of the University of Notre Dame Archives, for bringing to my attention the archival collections that are the basis of chapter 6 and for aiding me in their use. The Most Reverend Paul M. Boyle, CP, and the Leadership Conference of Women Religious were generous in allowing me access to their papers in those collections. A number of Catholic sisters and bishops have been generous in granting interviews or sharing informal comments.

Quotations from *The Documents of Vatican II*, edited by Walter M. Abbott, are reprinted with permission of America Press, Inc., 106 West 56th Street, New York, NY 10019. Copyright 1966, all rights reserved.

Chapter 2 appeared in a similar form as "The Politics of Ideology: The Papal Struggle with Liberalism," in the *American Journal of Sociology*, vol. 95, 1990. May I also thank the anonymous reviewers of that paper.

I dedicate the book to Alison Hirschel, to whom I am married, and to my parents, Paul and Kathleen Burns. They always help remind me what is important.

Popes, Councils, and Selected Documents since Vatican I

Pope Pius IX, 1846–1878

Syllabus of Errors (an appendix to the encyclical *Quanta Cura* [Condemning Current Errors]), 1864

First Vatican Council (Vatican I), 1869–1870

Pope Leo XIII, 1878–1903

Rerum Novarum (On the Condition of Labor), 1891

Pope Pius X, 1903–1914

Pope Benedict XV, 1914–1922

Pope Pius XI, 1922–1939

Quadragesimo Anno (Commemorating the fortieth anniversary of Leo XIII's *Rerum Novarum*: On Reconstruction of the Social Order), 1931

Pope Pius XII, 1939–1958

Mystici Corporis Christi (On the Mystical Body of Christ), 1943

Humani Generis (Concerning Some False Opinions Threatening to Undermine the Foundations of Catholic Doctrine), 1950

Pope John XXIII, 1958–1963

Mater et Magistra (On Christianity and Social Progress), 1961

Pacem in Terris (On Establishing Universal Peace in Truth, Justice, Charity, and Liberty), 1963

Abbreviations

AIDS	acquired immune deficiency syndrome
CELAM	Consejo Episcopal Latinoamericano (Latin American Episcopal Conference)
CNBB	Conferência Nacional dos Bispos do Brasil (National Conference of Brazilian Bishops)
CMSM	Conference of Major Superiors of Men
CMSW	Conference of Major Superiors of Women (in 1971, renamed the Leadership Conference of Women Religious)
LCWR	Leadership Conference of Women Religious
NCCB	National Conference of Catholic Bishops (succeeded the National Catholic Welfare Conference)
NCWC	National Catholic Welfare Conference
SCR	Sacred Congregation for Religious (renamed in 1967 the Sacred Congregation for Religious and Secular Institutes; after 1985, "Sacred" was dropped from the name)

1 Introduction: Catholic Ideology

By the 1960s, American Catholics had become part of the American mainstream. They had made it. While it is true that there was, and remains, great variety in the experiences and lifestyles of American Catholics, anti-Catholic prejudice had greatly receded, Catholics had made enough socio-economic gains that they no longer looked very different from other Americans, and one of their own had even been elected president.

But the Catholic Church as an institution did not simply blend into the mainstream. Especially to non-Catholics, the opinions of institutional representatives and personnel of the Catholic Church could appear strikingly provocative and, in many eyes, extreme.[1] The U.S. Church did not become a complacent institution, internally content with its successes and ready to adulate the American dream.

Instead, American sisters (commonly known as nuns) rebelled against patriarchal authority within the Church; American bishops became vocal critics of U.S. government policies and occasionally clashed with the Vatican. But had not sisters voluntarily taken a vow of obedience? Why such tumult precisely when the Catholic Church seemed to be stronger than ever? And had not bishops been good American patriots for two centuries? Why would they become such "leftists" just as their laity had finally escaped poverty and discrimination and had begun an apparent ideological shift to the right? A cursory glance at history—at Iberian colonialism in the Americas, at the French Revolution—suggests that the bishops' opinions did not appear to be very "Catholic." Did not the Church internationally have a long history of alliance with conservative elites and governments?

Perhaps the most immediately sensible explanation is that put forward by Catholics labeled "traditionalists" or "conservatives": the decline of traditional deference to the central, spiritual authority of Rome has allowed

1

divergent groups to import ideas from outside the Church and thus Balkan-
ize and politicize Catholicism. (Some critics, however, even say that Rome's
social and political views have become tainted.) Feminism, the peace
movement, socialism, Protestantism—these are among the apparent
sources of alien ideas.[2] An overly radical interpretation of Vatican II
(1962–1965) was the beginning of a completely different Church;[3] or, as
the followers of French Archbishop Marcel Lefebvre would argue,[4] Vatican
II itself was the problem, for it turned away from true Catholicism in favor
of secular ideals. Even supporters of the new directions of Catholicism
would agree with much of this description, if phrased in a more positive
light: the Church has boldly and bravely entered the modern world, secure
enough in its own message to leave its ethnic ghetto and to champion
pluralism and the rights of the oppressed.

There is a shade of truth in most of these descriptions, save for one: as I
will demonstrate in the following pages, it is historically and sociologically
inaccurate to argue that the politicization of the Church is without precedent and that reform-minded and politicized Catholics developed their
concerns simply by absorbing non-Catholic ideologies. (By "ideologies," I
mean belief systems with implications for social interaction.)[5] There has
been some borrowing, but the borrowing has been as much a result as a
cause of political and ideological processes internal to the Church. Although it is not the sociologist's place to judge what doctrinally qualifies as
Catholicism, historically it is quite clear that Rome, Catholic conservatives,
Catholic socialists, and Catholic feminists all inherit a truly Catholic legacy.
They emphasize different aspects of that legacy, but because the legacy is
multifaceted and partly ambiguous, they all can point to true historical
precedents for their beliefs.

Without an appropriate sociological and historical perspective, we can
misunderstand the context of current ideological and political change
within the Catholic Church. First, we might not realize that even a century
ago (and perhaps especially a century ago), it was not true that concerns
with spirituality and papal supremacy were divorced from concerns with
temporal politics. Second, we might not see that many of the perspectives
now labeled as alien to Catholicism continue to be framed within peculiarly
Catholic worldviews; in some cases, such supposedly alien perspectives
actually appeared within the Church before they were popular in the
secular world. For example, feminist challenges among American sisters
appeared too early to be considered the products of contemporary secular
feminism. And we cannot understand American bishops' "leftist" positions
on economic and nuclear policy without understanding the very Catholic

nature of their perspective and the origins of their interests in such issues in internal processes of Church politics.

In fact, once we understand the variety of past precedents as well as the current potential volatility within Catholicism itself, we can begin to answer a question that has puzzled so many observers of the Church: why can representatives of the Church, even popes and bishops, appear at times so clearly to be on the left side of the political spectrum and at other times—when it comes to such issues as abortion or sexual orientation—so clearly on the right? The most common resolution of this paradox is to treat the left and right opinions as completely separate, with separate origins. There is a kernel of truth to this resolution, but it is only a half-truth and thus can be extremely misleading. In fact, although Catholicism's "left" and "right," to a great extent, concern different types of issues with different historical importance to the Church, the "left" is not complete, and not understandable, except in relation to the "right." Indeed, one of the major topics of this book is the process by which the Catholic hierarchy of the last century defined issues of "faith and morals," on the one hand, and issues of politics and social problems, on the other, by attempting to distinguish the two types of issues *in relation to each other*. We can understand much of the change in Catholic ideology of the last century by analyzing the hierarchy's (not fully successful) attempt to separate issues of "faith and morals," where the institutional Church appears to be conservative, from social and political issues, where the Church sometimes even appears to be on the radical left.

The categories of right and left politics are taken from secular analyses. In fact, the political labels of "left" and "right" began as references to the seating patterns of political blocs in continental European legislatures (originally in the National Assembly of the French Revolution) of the last two centuries—the more reform-minded blocs customarily sat to the left.[6] But the political changes of revolution and republicanism in eighteenth- and nineteenth-century Europe commonly included hostility toward Church influence in politics. It is, therefore, not surprising that conceptual categories that originated among the Church's antagonists do not correspond to those of Catholic ideology. It is legitimate to ask what implications Catholic ideology might have for secular politics. But to understand the origins and dynamics of Catholic ideology itself, we cannot begin by classifying its components according to such categories as "left" or "right," as if Catholicism were just another secular party platform. It is true that we have to look at the politics of Catholic ideology, but much of the relevant "politics" is internal to the Church and does not reflect secular debates.

For popes and bishops understand the world through a perspective learned and developed within the Church. The more the lives of individual Catholics are encompassed by participation in the Church, the more important will Catholic perspectives be to their ideology. Indeed, this book argues that we can understand ideological change only by understanding the subtleties of the specific, relevant social structures within which ideologies develop.

As Catholics reflect and argue about the implications of their faith, they talk with each other, they negotiate with each other, they challenge each other. Sometimes their focus and their challenges also involve forces outside the Church, for example, modern states. Not surprisingly, in the case of conflict, powerful organizations and persons are often able to suppress the ideas and challenges of others.

The chapters that follow are an analysis of how various groups within the Catholic Church have developed different ideological positions depending on how much and what type of power they have within the Church. The title's reference to Catholicism's "frontiers" refers not only to the new paths that many Catholics have forged, but also to the internal and external boundaries that define the politics of contemporary Catholicism. Central to the analysis is the Catholic hierarchy's particular way of distinguishing its own authority from secular authority and the ideological and political boundaries that many groups within the Church attempt to draw so as to define their distinctive identities and their religious priorities.

The U.S. Church is the primary case study, but it is not really possible to understand the U.S. Church without first understanding the ideological and political inheritance that the U.S. Church receives from the international Church. That is, the most powerful persons in the Church will have the greatest ability to structure Catholic ideology, and so it is essential to begin with the papacy, which is the subject of chapter 2. In the nineteenth-century, the papacy lost a political battle with European liberalism that forced Rome to restructure its ideological priorities. (I refer here to *classical* liberalism.)[7] To avoid persistent conflict, Rome, although quite resistant at first, eventually abandoned its insistence that Catholicism have a special, legally enforced political status within European society. Thus a new boundary between church and state emerged.

Nevertheless, the papacy's adjustment to a changing social and political landscape in Europe was neither rapid nor without complications. Such an adjustment had implications for the distribution of authority within the Church; for example, several European states had traditionally been quite involved in determining the makeup of the Church's hierarchy, but liberal states generally abandoned such direct interference. Somewhat suddenly, the papacy had more internal institutional control, but over a more restricted set of issues. The rest of the book concerns the difficulties and opportunities that emerged within the context of this political and ideological reconstruction. Some of these complications, examined in the discussion of Vatican II in chapter 3, were inherent in Rome's ambiguous, hesitant approach to a restructuring it had not originally welcomed. But problems also emerged as the traditions of different national Churches either reinforced or clashed with the newly emerging boundary between church and state as well as the new distribution of institutional power.

Chapters 4, 5, and 6 follow the ideological history of the U.S. Catholic Church. Chapter 4 describes the somewhat special social context of the American Church; as a minority church experiencing discrimination, it had long been more receptive than Rome to a liberal approach to church-state issues. Thus American bishops, the topic of chapter 5, welcomed Rome's ideological reconstruction. But the attempt by Rome to centralize institutional authority as well as the changing place of the Catholic Church in twentieth-century America led to new tensions between Rome and American Catholicism as well as between American Catholicism and U.S. secular society. The church-state boundary remains today a contentious issue not only within Catholic doctrine, but within American society.

Chapter 6 is a detailed analysis of the ideological transformation of a group excluded from the center of institutional power, namely, American sisters. American sisters, with a quite different set of priorities than the bishops, are an excellent example of the power of the powerless to turn their exclusion into the asset of autonomy. But they also demonstrate the costs of exclusion.

Chapter 7, an overview of ideological changes in Latin American Catholicism, brings into focus the comparative differences among national Churches with different histories of church-state relations and internal institutional politics. The book then concludes with a discussion of the implications of this analysis for the general study of ideological change as well as a discussion of ideological trends we might expect in the future of the Catholic Church.

Social Structures and Ideologies

SOCIAL STRUCTURES

This book, then, attempts to explain a perplexing pattern of ideological change within the Catholic Church, focusing on the specific, relevant social structures within which a particular ideology has developed. The discussion so far should be sufficient to provide a general sense of the argument. But a complete understanding of why struggles within the Church take a particular shape requires a full theoretical discussion of the sociology and politics of ideology. The casual reader interested, for example, more in the history of Catholicism than in the validity of the sociological argument could probably skip this section and still understand most of the book. But explaining exactly what I mean by "relevant social structures within which an ideology develops" requires a greater level of conceptual sophistication.

By "structures," I mean impersonal organizational and social patterns that constrain our freedom of movement. It is not altogether unreasonable that nonsociologists would, at first, feel an irresistible urge to flee from jargon about social structures. But the concept is a useful one and not as abstract as it first seems: a structure is much like a building. In our social life, we are constantly constructing and altering patterns much like we construct buildings; while they stand, these patterns, like buildings, have a certain permanence and to some degree are more solid than are those who built them.

A building is not alive, and so its relation to us is impersonal, although much life takes place within it. It constrains us, for we cannot walk through bricks and walls. But it also allows us to do things that we could not have easily done otherwise:[8] it gives us a place to interact with others, and it helps us conduct and organize our lives (our work lives in an office building or home lives in an apartment building). And even though it constrains and, to some extent, organizes, our lives and is impersonal, people planned it and built it. Of course, it may not always work the way we intended; perhaps we did not anticipate some design problems. Or perhaps we were forced for various reasons to live or work in a building designed for someone else's needs (e.g., a landlord's need to keep costs down), so the building is a constant source of frustration. Buildings can have weak points as well, where there may be danger of collapse. In some cases, we can alter the building, but usually only in cooperation with others and often at great expense.

We create, use, and are constrained by social structures in much the same way. Social life has patterns; it depends on social organization. People create those patterns and organization, but the structures are impersonal to the extent that those patterns take on a life of their own, and challenging them involves costs. Thus to take an everyday trivial example: although Americans could certainly have developed their habits and planned their roads so that they drove on the left rather than the right, this social convention could not now easily be changed.[9] Our road signs and some exits and entrances (e.g., for parking garages or jug-handle turns) are designed for driving on the right, and we are used to it; millions of people participate in, and thus re-create, this convention every day. While those who do not drive are less affected, individual drivers have to organize their habits in some mutually compatible way, and driving on the right is a fundamental part of that organization. An individual American could, of course, drive on the left. At best, however, she will end up with a ticket; at worst, she will have a horrible collision. A city could have a little more success challenging this convention but would have trouble controlling patterns outside the city borders; the U.S. government could have even greater success (although it would still face the problem of those roads that connect to Canada and Mexico; it is no accident that driving on the left is associated with *island* nations). Even if the U.S. government opted for driving on the left, however, there would be enormous obstacles: the need to rebuild many exits and entrances and to change thousands or millions of road signs, street maps, and driving manuals; the facts of (at least temporary) chaos, resentment, and resistance; and so on. Driving on the right is, then, a social pattern that impersonally structures our lives, partly via our collective, everyday participation, and partly via its material manifestations (e.g., in road signs; not all social structures, however, have tangible manifestations). Visitors from Ireland or Britain or Australia may find this pattern frustrating, but they have little choice but to conform.

Notice, in this example, that American driving patterns affect different people differently. They have different relevance and meaning for American drivers, American nondrivers, and non-Americans. In general, indeed, different people experience, and participate in, social structures differently.

SOCIAL STRUCTURES AND POWER

Ultimately, I argue, different aspects of power, broadly conceived, most determine how people differentially experience and participate in social structures.[10] There are varying ways this is true. Let us begin with a simple one: most individuals have essentially no power to alter social patterns of driving, while high government officials have considerably more. Barriers to changing laws, or even social conventions, are greater obstacles to the average citizen than they are to the president.

To extend this example, we must first ask a simple question: what *is* power? A standard sociological definition of power comes from Max Weber: power is the high "probability that one actor within a social relationship will be in a position to carry out his own will despite resistance, regardless of the basis on which this probability rests."[11] In this definition, then, power is the ability, if necessary, to enforce one's will. But as Peter

Bachrach and Morton Baratz as well as Steven Lukes have pointed out,[12] sometimes power includes preventing resistance to begin with. Power, then, includes the ability to control the agenda and prevent undesirable issues or problems (e.g., resistance) from arising in the first place.

What, then, are the *sources* of power? I argue that there are basically two sources. One is *resources*, which can include money, weapons, effective supporting organizations (e.g., a bureaucracy or party)—anything that can be used to make oneself a decision-maker (i.e., outcompete others) or to pressure other decision-makers. A second source of power is *autonomy*—that is, the state of being unaffected by the actions or decisions of others.

To some extent, people with large amounts of resources are by definition autonomous of the structural conditions that constrain others.[13] In this way, autonomy is very much a positive source of power: one can change the patterns that constrain others and thus re-form, reduce, or increase the social constraints others face.

But autonomy can often be more a negative source of power over only a limited portion of one's own life; it can involve freedom from constraints without any corresponding ability to change the constraints that govern the lives of other people. Thus nondrivers are relatively unconstrained by the American pattern of driving or by *any* pattern of driving. They need know only where to look for oncoming cars and what side of the street to catch the bus. Because they are free of a constraint relevant to the lives of others, we can say that in that aspect of their lives—even if a trivial one—they do have more autonomy, and thus some small amount of power over their lives, that drivers do not. (Remember, this is true only in a limited, negative sense; whether they have more autonomy in their lives as a whole is a different question.) But they hardly have much ability to change the patterns that govern American driving as a whole; their autonomy is thus of a different sort than the autonomy that the U.S. government has vis-à-vis those patterns.[14]

These two faces of autonomy have interesting implications for the ways that power shapes how people experience, and participate in, particular social structures. To the extent that a particular social structure is irrelevant to one's life, one is autonomous of that social structure. As long as they stay at home, Irish or British or Australians are not constrained by American driving patterns. But suppose, through American pressure (e.g., so that American tourists would always feel comfortable driving abroad), these countries suddenly instituted the American way of driving. (This is only a hypothetical example; I am not saying this is empirically realistic.) To suddenly be integrated into a pattern of behavior formerly irrelevant to one's life can mean the creation of relative powerlessness and, perhaps, resentment. Suddenly, these drivers will be less competent and less comfortable on the road than they used to be. On a smaller level, a similar situation arises when, for example, an Irish person visits the United States and rents a car. That person is relatively disadvantaged driving on American roads and quite likely will feel some difficulty in having to participate in an unfamiliar system. The point of this discussion is that lack of participation in a social structure—or, alternatively, the relevance of social structures to one's life—is an aspect of autonomy and thus of power.

POWER AND IDEOLOGY

Power is a complex thing. First, as Otto Maduro has pointed out, no one is all-powerful.[15] Second, the exercise of power can actually create new spaces of autonomy for dissenting groups. Third, as sociologists studying agenda-setting have demonstrated, power often means control over the relative *priorities* of issues more than control over the *content* of every belief that people have.[16] After we examine these three aspects of power, which have important implications for the study of ideology, it will become clear that ideologies are actually special types of social structures.

The first point, then, is simply that in no institution or social structure will anyone have a monopoly of power. This is important because no one has total ideological control over others. There will always be areas of contest, compromise, and unresolved tensions. There will also be issues that powerful people will simply not care about. If I am your political superior, and you are an obedient subject, it is unlikely that I will care about beliefs irrelevant to your behavior as a subject. For example, I may not care what your religious beliefs are as long as you restrict the application of those beliefs so that they do not have (what I consider to be) political implications.[17] If I am an American president running for reelection, I will care much more about whether you vote Democratic or Republican than about whether we belong to the same religious denomination. (If I am a member of the clergy in your church, however, my ideological priorities will likely be reversed.)

Second, it is possible to exercise power by controlling the agenda and excluding people from participation in political structures, but this can create new spaces of political and ideological autonomy. For example, suppose a monarch expels from the kingdom people who participate in rebellion. Or a pope excommunicates dissenters (like Archbishop Lefebvre, a French bishop who rejected most of the changes within the Catholic Church of the last three decades) who, in that pope's eyes, go too far in rejecting Vatican authority. In the case of Lefebvre, especially important in his excommunication was his decision to ordain bishops—something Rome had explicitly forbidden—which set up a structure to continue his movement. If Lefebvre had died without ordaining bishops (chosen from among the priests who supported his dissent from the post–Vatican II papacy), his movement would have lacked leadership and the ability to self-reproduce. Because Lefebvre saw himself as a representative of true (i.e., pre–Vatican II) Catholicism, in which only existing bishops could ordain new bishops, his having died without new bishops to replace him would have meant death to the movement.

This type of exercise of power, exemplified by monarch and pope, has some interesting implications. To begin, it makes very clear that the control of ideology involves the exercise of power.[18] The pope decisively punished this flagrant act of disobedience, an act creating new bishops claiming authority to teach and perpetuate Lefebvre's view of Catholicism. If those bishops remained part of the institutional Church, the pope would lose control of part of that institution: the new bishops could continue to propagate their perspective by, for example, controlling the seminary education of new priests. And Catholics might perceive them to be a legitimate part of the Church. And so, by expelling Lefebvre and his followers, the pope made clear that he did not consider them part of the institutional Church. (Controlling ideology through the exercise of power can also be indirect: more powerful persons or groups can shape the social institutions that socialize others.)[19]

But there is also an additional, quite different implication. In some sense, those who are expelled from participation in a social institution, or a social structure in general, have attained an autonomy they did not have before. In practice this might mean that they can become less guarded in their pronouncements now that compromise is not worth pursuing. Or in the case of physical expulsion from a country, they may now be beyond the coercive reach of the ruler they opposed.

While expulsion is an extreme example of forced nonparticipation in a political structure, a similar type of autonomy exists, in part, for people still acting within an institution but whose political participation is restricted. Groups forbidden to participate in certain practices or decisions have, in a negative sense, a certain autonomy. Let us consider the example of Catholic sisters. Women are excluded from ordination to the priesthood, but ordination is a prerequisite to most significant decision-making authority. Women, then, do not generally participate in seminary education of priests, in the hierarchy's decisions on important official Church policy or doctrine, in the interpretation of canon law, and so forth.[20] This means that the activities in which sisters *do* participate are necessarily devalued within the political processes of the Church; the lives and decisions of sisters are, politically and ideologically speaking, peripheral issues.

In the chapters that follow, we see that this type of autonomy—which to a great extent is simply equivalent to powerlessness—has more complex implications than we would expect. We see that autonomy that results from political *exclusion* is not simply a trivial form of autonomy; it can be the basis of rebellion. In the case of sisters, in practice autonomy meant that the hierarchy did not fully attend to the processes of social and organizational interaction among sisters. Because the details of sisters' lives were relatively devalued ideologically, sisters—if they had adequate resources—could take control of those processes. This was especially true in the wake of Vatican II, as the hierarchy was preoccupied with refining the "more important" policies and doctrines of the Church. It also meant that sisters, once they had the resources to develop ideological independence (after Vatican II), quickly rejected dominant ideological perspectives—that is, the perspectives of the hierarchy. Their lack of participation in the politics that reinforced those perspectives resulted in a weaker commitment than we might have expected, given their lack of rebellion before Vatican II.

This example brings us to the final point about power, a point implied in the previous paragraphs. That is, power often means control over the relative *priorities* of issues more than control over the *content* of every belief that people have. Thus it can be more important to a political ruler that subjects stay out of politics in general than that the ruler know and control every political belief that every subject has. If the subject never expresses or acts on political beliefs, the ruler may not care about the content of those beliefs. Of course, content is not completely irrelevant, either for ruler or subject. Rulers will care more about the content of beliefs they consider to have political implications than about beliefs concerning nonpolitical domains. And it may be the case that ideological content unimportant to a ruler may be important to the subject: perhaps, as subject, you care about your religious freedom but not about sharing political power. In both cases, however, the priority of issues is central. Whether particular contents (of beliefs) are important depends on one's hierarchy of issues. Within the larger social context (as opposed to the idiosyncratic preferences of individuals), content will usually be more important for those issues that are the concern of powerful persons or for issues that become objects of social struggle.

At this point the theoretical discussion has come full circle; it should now be clear that an ideology is a form of social structure. We started by examining some general aspects of social structures: they are social creations, and yet they constrain the people who participate in them. We can try to overcome those constraints but can succeed only by incurring some significant costs. Structures will have more relevance to the lives of some people than others. And resources and autonomy are essential aspects of our power within social structures as well as our ability to change them.

All these characteristics of social structures are true of ideologies, which are systems of belief developed and maintained through social interaction. What, then, does an ideology look like? An ideology is not simply a list of beliefs. It is more a hierarchy of issues; people with the greatest power within the ideological structure will attempt to control the content of those issues at the top of their hierarchy more than those issues they place at the bottom. An ideology is a hierarchy of issues enforced through the exercise of power, but it always includes various spaces of autonomy and is always potentially an object of political struggle. An ideology can exist only if social interaction (including political interaction) continuously reinforces its hierarchy of issues. It is, however, empirically not static, as the very exercise of power can alter patterns of autonomy and the distribution of resources.

IDEOLOGIES AS SOCIAL STRUCTURES

A major theme of this book is the relationship between political interaction and ideological change. But we must keep in mind that ideology is not completely determined by the exercise of power; in fact, given the spaces of autonomy that necessarily exist within political interaction, to say that ideology is completely determined by the exercise of power is a contradiction in terms. Let us remember, then, that ideologies also have other properties of social structures. Like buildings, they not only constrain us. They also enable us to do things: we must participate in ideologies to communicate with others not only to survive socially, but even to enjoy life. If we belong to a particular social circle or any group at all—a society, a work group, a religious congregation, a clique in school—we will share certain attitudes, perspectives, even in-jokes.[21] Of course, the larger and less encompassing the group is, generally the less comprehensive is the shared ideology. But within any group, if I share almost no assumptions about the world, use terminology that other people do not understand, or pepper my speech with references to literature or stories unknown to other members of the group, I cannot participate very adeptly. Others will not understand me and will feel uncomfortable around me. My social interaction—a fundamental component of social structures—will either be extremely limited or extremely ineffective. Of course, that does not mean that the structure of beliefs and attitudes in a given society or group is unchanging rules. They change, and they are the creations and re-creations of members of that group. But they take on a life of their own, and (especially in larger groups) individuals will have minimal ability to change them.

Ideologies, then, sound a lot like social structures. They include understandings and priorities that pattern our social participation. In some cases, sanctions very directly shape ideology: for example, we express an opinion and learn that our family or peers or superiors feel that certain beliefs are wrong or strange. So we internalize their negative perspective. But the patterning of social life is not only about sanctions; it involves active participation.

Granted, it is very difficult to say a priori what the ideological structures are in any given society; indeed, this book takes several hundred pages to demonstrate the existence and nature of such a structure within Catholicism. It would be a grave mistake to take the approach of some sociologists of several decades ago, confidently beginning the task of social analysis by identifying a list of static beliefs and values that supposedly guide a society.[22] Instead, we cannot effectively identify the ideological structures within an institution or a society unless we understand its politics because, this book argues, distributions of power shape ideological structures. *Changes* in power distributions are thus fundamental channels of ideological change.

Indeed, one of the reasons identification of ideological structures *is* problematic is that social structures do not affect everyone's life in the same way, or to the same degree, because any institution or society contains groups and persons with different amounts and kinds of resources and autonomy. If we identify the content of beliefs of just one group or another, we will not understand the *pattern* of beliefs that links those groups together. When we talk of structures, we mean social patterns that organize the lives (or beliefs) of many people; it is not possible to identify a social structure in the actions or beliefs of just one group or one individual.[23] Although, for example, we may learn a lot about class relations in a society by examining one class, our understanding will be limited; by its nature, a class *structure* is a pattern of relationships among all classes in the society. Only by studying the patterns of political interaction among different participants in the social and ideological structures will we come truly to understand those structures. Even though the claim that any perspective on the world will have varying interpretations is, in principle, generally uncontroversial, there are few empirical sociological analyses, and even fewer developed theories of ideology, that adequately apply this fact.

It is best to hold discussion of the implications of this study for specific theories of ideology until the concluding chapter. For now, let it suffice to summarize the approach of this book as one that focuses on the influence of power structures on ideological change. I do not argue that power is the only variable that affects the dynamics of Catholic ideologies, but I do believe it is the most important one. In general, I argue that (not only in the Catholic Church) we can understand the likely ideological directions that people will take according to where they stand in distributions of power—that is, power structures. Thus we have to examine the resources they have and the degree and type of autonomy they have within those structures. Developing an independent perspective (what William Sewell would call an "ideological variant" within a larger ideological structure)[24] requires social interaction, the development of a sense of a community. Without sufficient resources groups will be unable to develop their own social communities and their own understandings of the world and (if they are relatively powerless) to challenge those distributions of power.

Usually people excluded from power in social institutions are also excluded from, and unable to develop, sufficient independent resources to develop ideological independence. As Paul M. Harrison and Henry J. Pratt have demonstrated, the centralization of resources is a prime component of the ideological dominance associated with power.[25] But occasionally, often inadvertently, they do develop such resources. Thus as an example, the Catholic hierarchy itself had inadvertently encouraged communities of American sisters to develop their own educational and organizational strengths in the 1950s and 1960s, with the result that this relatively powerless group came very quickly to reject some dominant patriarchal themes of Vatican ideology and develop their own, independent visions of the Church. The ideological history of the Catholic Church, in fact, is most interesting when social changes widen or constrain the autonomy or the resources available to particular groups, thus widening or constraining the possibility of their developing ever more distinctive worldviews. As Robert Wuthnow has pointed out, ideological change quite often develops quickly during relatively short periods, rather than occurring only gradually.[26]

As Wuthnow has also pointed out, ideological change is not a neat, functional process. We become committed to particular perspectives and may have difficulty reconciling the old and the new; or perhaps a change in our autonomy makes it difficult to continue participating in the same social structures. Ideological structures, like any kind of social structure and any kind of building, may have points of stress or weakness where problems are unresolved. Precisely because there will always be struggles over power and there will always be various autonomous spaces within any power struc-ture, ideological change will not always develop in a way consistent with the goals of any one person or group. There will always be unresolved political struggles and unresolved ideological disputes. Particularly difficult political times will result in attempts to restructure an ideology—change the priorities of, or boundaries between, particular issues. (By perceptively analyzing how scientists have at times been forced to draw public boundaries between science and what they consider pseudoscience, Thomas Gieryn and his colleagues have identified this process as "boundary work.")[27] Indeed, one of the more interesting developments in Catholicism since the Second Vatican Council has been the ambiguous conciliar doctrine on Church decision-making authority and Church commitment to social and political issues, leading different sectors of the Church to question different parts of the ideological structure. Ideologically, the last quarter century has been a particularly ambiguous and contentious period in the Church's history, partly due to the legacy left by the council and partly due to the development of new resources and greater autonomy by Catholic groups challenging Vatican dominance. Let us now briefly summarize the argument of the following chapters before turning to a specific, sociohistorical analysis.

Ideology and the Catholic Church

As becomes clear later, among the most important issues in the ideological politics of the modern Catholic Church is the relationship between issues concerning the faith and morals of individuals and families, on the one hand, and what I call sociopolitical issues (or, synonymously, temporal issues), on the other. By "sociopolitical issues," I mean macroeconomic and macropolitical questions. Throughout this book, when I refer to "faith and morals" I mean Catholic ideology concerning the faith and morals of individuals and families. Starting in the late nineteenth century, the Church gradually widened the distinction between these issues and more "macro," sociopolitical issues having to do with macropolitics, economics, and state policy.

When officials and theologians of the contemporary Catholic Church speak of avoiding "politicization" of the faith, they mean avoiding emphasis on sociopolitical issues. I do not mean to argue that one can always cleanly distinguish faith and morals from such sociopolitical issues. The important point is that the hierarchy has tried to do so. Indeed, one of the interesting ideological tensions that has emerged in modern Catholic ideology is the difficulty of drawing an exact boundary between these two types of issues.

Ideological debates involve conflicts over the distribution of decision-making power in the Church. Not all Catholic groups are equally involved in or affected by every debate or conflict, although all Catholics are affected to some degree. It is important in this study to focus on groups within the

Church that can teach us the most about the political dynamics of Catholic ideology. This is especially the case given that the Catholic Church is an enormous institution; it is questionable whether any one book can truly talk about the Catholic Church, or even just the U.S. Catholic Church, in its entirety. Indeed, in studying ideological change, we must look in some detail at the ideological history of particular groups because the most interesting variables—resources and autonomy—differ greatly from group to group. To understand what Catholicism really is socially and historically, we must study its divergent interpretations.

Popes, bishops, and, in the United States, sisters are, I argue, the most interesting groups for this study. Given the position each holds in the power structure of the Church, some degree of autonomy combined with significant political resources has led each to take strong, persistent ideological stands at the center of the difficult and unresolved legacy of Vatican II. Examination of these three levels of the Church allows us to study a very wide range of the most important ideological changes and conflicts within the Church. This is not to say that other groups are not important, only that these particular groups allow us to examine the largest range of ideological change. Adding many more groups would require readers to deal with an inordinately long book.

It is worth noting at this point that the Catholic laity in particular is not the most fruitful focus in a study of the patterns of ideological change within the institutional Church. The laity's power in the Church is weak and almost wholly indirect. Whether the laity considers Church leaders' opinions legitimate, then, a topic that James R. Wood investigated in Protestant churches,[28] is not necessarily relevant in the very hierarchical Catholic Church. Thus for example, interest group activism[29] is not as significant in determining Catholic ideology as is the case in many other political and religious institutions. Within what can specifically be called Catholic ideology, the laity are more acted on than they are actors.

Furthermore, as Wood has pointed out, the Catholic laity is composed of many different types of groups existing in a complex matrix of ideological influences, especially in a country with some religious diversity, such as the United States. Not only would Catholicism influence their beliefs, but in addition class, regional, ethnic, and other influences would be much stronger than they would be for Church personnel.[30]

Catholicism may be just as important to members of the laity, but they are less committed to the complex theological and other matters that have a strong influence on those whose entire lives and careers are committed to working within the institutional Church. Thus, as has already been noted, U.S. bishops' sociopolitical opinions simply do not reflect the opinions of the American Catholic laity. The bishops' opinions are shaped much more by internal Church ideology.

Lay Catholicism is likely to be considerably more diffuse, as these Catholics are often even unaware of debates within Catholic ideology. An example of this comes from (almost unbelievable) survey data that by 1979 only about half of the English Catholic laity had heard of the Second Vatican Council and few took strong positions either for or against the results of the council.[31] This is despite the fact that the meaning of Vatican II is one of the most politicized issues within the Church.[32] In general, some of the most interesting ideological tensions within the U.S. Church are barely even issues for the laity. For example, the attempt to distinguish sociopolitical issues from issues of faith and morals is primarily of importance for the hierarchy but not necessarily of great concern for much of the rest of the Church.[33]

This book, then, examines the main sources of change in modern Catholic ideology and examines how different groups have struggled within the institutional Church to restructure Catholic ideology. The ideological history of the modern Catholic Church begins with social changes in which the papacy lost some of its power to secular forces, which altered the means by which it asserted ideological dominance over other parts of the Church. That process originated with the decline of feudal social structures, in which the Church had been a central beneficiary.

Liberal, anticlerical states, particularly in Italy and France, were resentful of the Church's historical influence and had the power to suppress its operations in their countries; indeed, the pope lost his kingdom to the newly unified republic of Italy. To avoid conflict, the papacy came to gradually deemphasize doctrine that had specific, controversial implications for state policy. Instead, Rome increased emphasis on the faith and morals of Catholic individuals and families as the basis of its religious authority. Faith and morals were ideologically peripheral issues for secular states, mostly irrelevant to their own power. Thus they were happy to allow the Church autonomy over such concerns.

What had happened, then, is that simultaneously the papacy had obtained increased autonomy over one category of issues (more purely "religious" issues) while becoming politically excluded from another category of issues ("temporal" issues). The papacy actually had more latitude over internal Church affairs and doctrine, given the decline of secular state meddling. And even though Rome had to avoid controversial specifics of state policy, it also gained some new autonomy, albeit negative, over sociopolitical issues. Rome no longer had any political reason to participate actively in the legitimation of state policy.

This had interesting implications for papal ideology on temporal issues. Such ideology, most of which fell under the category of social doctrine, became a less binding level of doctrine.[34] It also addressed the topic of state policy only in vague terms, in contrast to the Church's style while it still had temporal power. By avoiding specificity, Rome avoided ever condemning particular state policies.[35]

Nevertheless, in developing the content of social doctrine, Rome drew on centuries-old Catholic conceptions of corporatist society and rejected the legitimacy of liberalism. This was true even though the critique of liberalism was vague and subordinated in importance to issues of faith and morals. Within the limits of liberal Europe, Rome became fairly oppositional ideologically.

But the reconstruction of Catholic ideology, a political process, had implications for the distribution of power within the Church. For example, Rome's inability to assert temporal political rights meant that the hierarchy gradually abandoned attempts to control the political opinions and activities of Catholics. Nevertheless, Rome was slow to fully abandon the model of church-state alliance through which it had prospered in medieval times. The Second Vatican Council implemented important doctrinal reforms that addressed the centralization of power in the Church and the Church's role in a secular world in which its status was very different than it had been in the nineteenth century. The council touched on several crucial issues: the centralization of authority in Rome, the Church's relation to temporal power, the nature of unchanging doctrine, and the Church's perspective on social reform.

In reaction to Roman centralization of ideological control, the desire among theologians and bishops for decentralization effected the council declaration that the Church is ruled "collegially" by pope and bishops. There was also a more general, ambiguous statement that all Catholics, as "the People of God," share in the Church's authority. Nevertheless, the significance of collegiality was ambiguous. On the one hand, the council affirmed Rome's ideological control over faith and morals. On the other hand, the council granted increased organizational autonomy and legitimacy to national conferences of bishops, even if it did not grant those conferences any new authority.

Two other important reforms both evolved from Vatican II's attempt to abandon the doctrinal legacy that still formally valued church-state alliance, although such doctrine had been deemphasized for much of the previous century. For the first time, the council formally declared that the Church should not be involved in temporal government and that state or other coercion of religious beliefs is illegitimate. These were both positions that nineteenth-century popes had rejected.

This declaration had some interesting implications. First, it had to be explained. The need to justify the abandonment of doctrine that a century before had been part of Catholicism's ideological core led the council also to declare that doctrine can develop with the times. Such a declaration gives important ideological ammunition to any group that argues that Catholic doctrine needs to develop even further—for example, toward a more pluralist and/or socially active Church. Exactly how one determines when doctrine needs to develop was not addressed.

The new view of church-state relations also had some interesting implications for the boundary between central religious concerns (faith and morals) and sociopolitical concerns. The council incorporated a basically liberal view of politics into its ideology, although it did not accept a liberal view of morality. With Vatican II, the Church implicitly treated "moral" issues as outside the bounds of politics. Thus in the United States, bishops declare that the government should uphold the moral prohibition on abortion and yet see such declarations as moral, not political, statements. Much as conflict had emerged when the pre–Vatican II Church defined the boundary between church and state differently than did secular states, conflict has emerged as the Church attempts to retain its own ideological boundary between the moral and the political.

And yet the council also suggested that the Church needed to be concerned not only with spirituality. In attempting to abandon a century of withdrawal from the world—partially forced by liberal states and partly a result of Rome's increasing emphasis on Catholic faith and morals, in opposition to secular influences—the council also declared a renewed commitment to political and social reform and thus to social doctrine and sociopolitical issues in general. Yet the council did not explain how the Church, on the one hand, had different realms of authority than did states but, on the other hand, should actively be involved in temporal issues. The implications of these reforms were, then, both ambiguous and potentially far-reaching.

Focusing in detail on one branch of the Church allows us to see the effects of Rome's forced ideological adjustment on less powerful sectors of the Church. The U.S. case is especially interesting because the particular church-state relations that it experienced led it to favor a reconstruction of Catholic ideology along the lines of some of the Vatican II reforms decades before Rome or before the actual council did. As a minority church, it could only benefit from a wide separation of church and state, as Alexis de Tocqueville observed about 150 years ago.[36]

Through most of its history, the U.S. Church existed on the periphery of both the international Church and of U.S. society. Interestingly, then, it did not absorb either the Vatican or the American perspective on liberal society. As a minority church occasionally experiencing discrimination, the U.S. Catholic Church generally avoided sociopolitical controversy. With Vatican II, however, the Roman and U.S. Catholic perspectives on the fundamental issue of church-state relations came to resemble each other. Once, then, the American episcopacy had attained a more secure place in both the international Church and in American society, it applied papal sociopolitical ideology with a new vigor.

U.S. bishops are a particularly interesting group because nearly all the dilemmas and ambiguities of Vatican II's attempt to resolve the legacy of the nineteenth-century ideological restructuring have affected the bishops. Their particular dilemma emerges from the fact that they are relatively high in the power structure (and thus their power depends on the maintenance of a substantial degree of orthodoxy) and yet their power vis-à-vis Rome is fairly limited, given how ideologically centralized are the core issues of faith and morals.

The fact that, ideologically, collegiality was only partly implemented spurred U.S. bishops to increase their commitment to the one level of ideology where they could be fairly independent of Rome—issues with direct implications for state policy. But this increased commitment does not actually give them increased authority within the Church's power structure, for they are reluctant to question the ideological structure that subordinates such issues to faith and morals. At the same time, their increased commitment to these sociopolitical issues has made more explicit the tension involved in attempting simultaneously to influence state policy, avoid specific policy commitments, and distinguish binding doctrine on faith and morals from nonbinding social doctrine.

The ideological dynamics of Catholic political structure are quite different at lower levels of the Church's power structure. As a fairly powerless group, American sisters had few political resources in the Church before the 1950s. But with the development of both intellectual and organizational resources, the unintended result of initiatives by both Pope Pius XII (1939–1958) and Vatican II, it became clear that U.S. sisters' commitment to the hierarchical, patriarchal ideology of Rome was quite vulnerable to change. They quickly challenged Rome's control of their daily lives and developed a most decentralizing interpretation of the meaning of Vatican II. Thus as a group less powerful than the bishops, they were less committed to dominant ideology and developed a more radical ideological challenge (once they had the resources to do so).

A brief comparison with the Latin American Church provides a different political context in which to examine the effects of Catholic ideological reconstruction. Unlike the U.S. Church, historically the Latin American Church has been closely linked with ruling secular elites and with state powers. Its relationship to social and state power has been much more similar to the situation of the papacy in medieval times than to the U.S. Church.

U.S. bishops do not have among themselves much of a political culture that looks to lay alliance as a part of sociopolitical ideology. Perhaps they are in the midst of developing such a tradition; but the national Churches of Latin America have long depended on links with powerful secular forces as the basis of their institutional strength. Historically, however, their ties to the poorer masses of Catholics have been weak. Having experienced a sharing of power with such forces, the Church shared the ideology of privilege and authoritarian power.

The episcopacy of all the Latin American Churches has historically focused primarily on the institutional strength of the Church; in this respect they are similar to U.S. bishops. For some in Latin America, that strength is still founded on alliance with the state and with powerful, wealthy elites; consequently, in such countries the episcopacy has not been receptive to Vatican II themes emphasizing social reform and, of course, even less so to liberation Catholicism. In other countries, a widened church-state separation has developed in this century, but the episcopacy has been unwilling or unable to be ideologically innovative, either because of continued close ties with wealthy and/or powerful, conservative, secular groups or because of a lack of organizational strength.

Yet in other national Churches, namely, Chile and Brazil, the Church has at different times been forced into an adversarial role with the state and has loosened ties with secular elites. Only in Brazil, in which an organizationally strong Church is faced with strong competition from other religions, has the episcopacy chosen and been able to build links with poorer Catholics and given some legitimacy to liberation Catholicism.

In all Latin American national Churches, as in all social institutions throughout the world, the patterns of ideological conflict depend on the patterns of political conflict. Thus even in Brazil, once relations with the state improved, the episcopacy began to withdraw from sociopolitical issues and thus from its commitment to liberation Catholicism. A stronger commitment to liberation themes exists throughout the region among minority groups of priests, religious, and laity.

Let us now turn to the church-state conflicts that sparked the modern reconstruction of Catholic ideology.

2 The Papal Struggle with Liberalism

The Church ought to be separated from the State, and the State from the Church.

Among the beliefs *condemned* in Pope Pius IX's *Syllabus of Errors*, 1864, in Henry Denzinger, ed., *The Sources of Catholic Dogma*, p. 440.

Founded to build the kingdom of heaven on earth rather than to acquire temporal power, the Church openly avows that the two powers—Church and State—are distinct from one another; that each is supreme in its own sphere of competency.

Pope Paul VI, *Populorum Progressio*, 1967, in Claudia Carlen, IHM, ed., *The Papal Encyclicals. Vol. 5: 1958–1981*, p. 185.

The road from the Rome that served as capital of Pius IX's Papal States to the Rome where Paul VI presided over the Second Vatican Council was a long one. But considering the institution's long and conservative history, the Catholic Church traversed that distance relatively quickly. In the process, many Catholics became unsure of their sense of direction, while others were certain that there could be even brighter paths ahead.

In the nineteenth century, the papacy had a reputation for being a prime reactionary force in European politics. Popes defined and declared the official Church opinion on such liberal principles as freedom of the press, separation of church and state, and freedom of religion. That opinion was decidedly negative. The strongly argued papal position was that the pope's religious independence depended on his being the ruler of his own temporal kingdom. The Church was allied with authoritarian governments, and until 1859 the pope himself was absolute monarch not only of the Church itself, but of his temporal kingdom, known as the Papal States, in central Italy.

Today Pope John Paul II (1978–) is forbidding priests and nuns to hold political office;[1] in his view, holding such office detracts from their spiritual concerns. He bases this prohibition on a particular reading of a declaration of the Second Vatican Council according to which the Church's role in the world does not include temporal government.[2] John Paul II, like Paul VI (1963–1978), inherited the legacy of the Second Vatican Council, which changed the official Church position on a variety of issues. The hierarchy accepted, for example, the principle of freedom of religion and a widened separation of church and state, opinions of those whom Pius IX (1846–1878) had declared "wretches."[3] Furthermore, the post–Vatican II Church, from Rome to the United States to Asia to Latin America, has produced deep criticisms of social injustice and has even been accused of too easily accepting Marxist political opinions.

The origins and implications of these dramatic changes are the topics of this chapter and the next. This chapter follows the seeds of ideological change planted by popes in response to changes in European politics in the century or so preceding Vatican II. Chapter 3 discusses Vatican II, which, on the one hand, reversed many of the positions formerly associated with papal reaction and, on the other, introduced new ambiguities into Catholic ideology. By doing so, the council opened new possibilities for divergent interpretations of Catholic ideology.

This chapter, then, attempts to explain the political dynamics whereby the papal struggle with liberalism in the late nineteenth and early twentieth centuries led to change in both the structure and the content of Catholic ideology. That is, there was change in the boundaries between, and relative priorities of, different issues as well as a change in the content of particular beliefs. There would have been little reason for the content to change if changing European politics had not forced a modification of the ideological structure. The structural change—a greater distinction between faith and morals, on the one hand, and sociopolitical issues, on the other—was forced on Rome by changes in European society and politics beyond the papacy's control. Rome opposed this change but had to subordinate sociopolitical concerns to avoid dangerous conflict with European states.

The change in content—namely, the development of antiliberal "social doctrine"—was the papacy's ideological reconstruction of Catholicism within the constraints of that new ideological structure.[4] Even the losers in an ideological battle are not completely passive in the process of ideological reconstruction. The new perspective of social doctrine is interesting because the papacy avoided conflict with liberal states by devaluing doctrine on social and political issues and making it vague enough to avoid specific policy commitments. Yet the retention of precapitalist organic views of society perpetuated an independence from liberal ideologies. This reconstruction of Catholicism took advantage of the autonomy that the pope did have within this new ideological structure and at the same time reflected the political alliances and hostilities within which the papacy acted. In the complicated way that structural change occurs, popes had become more constrained in determining the Church's ideological structure but less constrained from centralizing their internal Church power over "faith and morals" and from determining the ideological content of Catholicism.

Through most of the nineteenth century, the ideological boundary between spiritual and temporal concerns was not as sharp as it is today. The absolute primacy of the spiritual mission of the Church is today a fundamental tenet of Rome and of Catholic conservatives, in opposition to Church reformers and radicals who want to emphasize the Church's obligation to transform political and social structures. But a century ago, the political division in the Church was almost completely reversed; popes and conservatives condemned those who argued that the Church had no role in temporal government, most famously in Pope Pius IX's *Syllabus of Errors*.[5]

The reversal occurred because the rights that the Church still possesses, and thus is able to conserve, have changed in response to modern political forces that came to exclude the Church from its former privileged role in the European political economy. The old feudal order declined, and an increasing secularization of politics also grew to threaten the Church's role. Although the Church did not welcome such a process, the actions of even conservative popes could not stop—in fact, at times, even aided—a changing political context whereby it was easiest for Rome to increase control over central doctrinal issues within the Church while deemphasizing Catholic participation in modern European politics. New constraints forced the papacy to engage in "boundary work":[6] the papacy had to widen the distinction between "politics" and "religion" (even though that distinction could never be completely unambiguous). The Church faced a world that was hostile to Catholicism's role in the ancien régime and that had already removed many of the Church's feudal economic privileges. But secular opponents were willing to trade the Church religious autonomy in exchange for a withdrawal from temporal politics.[7] Interestingly, however, the papacy used the opportunity of autonomy to further centralize power within the Church as well as to develop a clear ideological autonomy from temporal forces.

The Catholic Church never participated in the liberal social order as it had in the medieval social order; thus it never absorbed liberal ideology, the ideology of its perceived enemies. The papacy therefore filled the newly emerging social doctrine with a content derived from the Church's traditional neofeudal perspective. Ideologically, nineteenth-century social doctrine opposed liberalism from the right.

Politically, popes consistently failed whenever they attempted to reintegrate the Church into European state politics, while they were quite successful in expanding their own internal Church authority in a way that took advantage of the Church's increased autonomy from European states. Ideologically, they could not avoid the restructuring of Catholic ideology that made sociopolitical issues more distinct from, and more subordinate to, faith and morals. But they successfully took advantage of the opportunity to fill sociopolitical ideology with a new antiliberal content. The papacy, then, lost a political battle with liberalism; but as a result, it had a newfound autonomy from liberal society. The widened separation of church and state had been forced on Rome by changing European political structures; Rome's own attempts to circumvent those changes thus, ironically, failed so badly that they served only to reinforce the Church's isolation from secular politics. But as long as Rome remained within its politically determined ideological boundaries, it had the autonomy to develop new ideological forms and even expand its authority over what had been politically defined as religious issues. An understanding of the constraints on and opportunities of the papacy's ideological reformulations lies in the history of the Church's conflict with modern states, to which we now turn.

The Papacy's Temporal Power

At least from the conversion to Christianity of the emperor Constantine in A.D. 312 until approximately 1870, the Catholic Church was a distinct part of the European sociopolitical order. Although doctrinally it always emphasized the importance of the spiritual over the temporal, in fact the Church's own religious authority was heavily intertwined with the temporal order. Major European Catholic powers heavily influenced not only papal policies, but even papal elections. France, Spain, and Austria even possessed the officially accepted right to veto any candidate in a papal conclave, until 1903, when Pope Pius X (1903–1914) declared the veto invalid. (Use of the veto was common in the eighteenth and nineteenth centuries.) Popes were heavily dependent on such nations to conduct their policies, and Catholic sovereigns occasionally had to fear the loss of their thrones should the pope come to oppose them.[8] As another example of the intertwining of spiritual and temporal authority, the central role of the Church in European feudalism of course hardly needs mention.

As a result of the Church's status in the European order, Catholic doctrine and practice very much valued and sanctioned the temporal prerogatives of the Church. For example, into the nineteenth century it was not uncommon for the papal secretary of state, second in rank in Rome only to the pope himself, to be a layman with experience and ability in managing the pope's kingdom in central Italy, even though the holder of the office was automatically a cardinal. The very powerful secretary of state during most of Pius IX's reign, Giacomo Cardinal Antonelli, for instance, was never a priest. It is of course impossible to imagine a layperson holding such a high Vatican post today because papal authority is centered much more on purely religious concerns, rather than those of state management. (Into the nineteenth century, it had even been acceptable for unordained Roman bureaucrats to wear clerical clothing as professional uniforms.)[9]

Perhaps a more important indication of the intertwined relationship of temporal and religious authority is the fact that the papacy and its supporters argued fervently through the nineteenth century that the religious sovereignty and independence of the pope very much depended on his having his own temporal kingdom, so that he would be the subject of no other ruler.[10] Likewise, popes insisted that in any truly Christian nation, Catholicism was to be enforced by the state, as Pius IX argued in his 1864 encyclical, *Quanta Cura*:

> For you well know, venerable brethren, that at this time men
> are found not a few who...against the doctrine of Scripture, of
> the Church, and of the Holy Fathers...do not hesitate to assert
> that "that is the best condition of civil society, in which no
> duty is recognized, as attached to the civil power, of restraining
> by enacted penalties, offenders against the Catholic religion, ex-
> cept so far as public peace may require." From which totally
> false idea of social government they do not fear to foster that
> erroneous opinion, most fatal in its effects on the Catholic
> Church and the salvation of souls, called by Our Predecessor,
> [Pope] Gregory XVI, *an insanity*, viz., that "liberty of con-
> science and worship is each man's personal right."[11]

This general perspective on the alliance of throne and altar dominated Church ideology from the French Revolution to the early twentieth century. The perspective had existed long before 1789, but it became the central axis of Catholic ideology once political change threatened Rome's place in the European sociopolitical order.

With the French Revolution, one of the most powerful European states attempted to destroy the influence of Christianity, not only ideologically, but, probably more important, institutionally. The Church was to suffer a number of defeats and humiliations. In a country whose monarch had long claimed the title of "Eldest Son of the Church," Church lands were confiscated, and the early years of the revolution seemed to promise the extinction of all clerical presence, let alone privileges. Eventually Napoleon made peace with the Church, the Church was granted control over most primary education, and priests became employees of the state. But in the meantime Napoleon's forces had taken over the Papal States, Pope Pius VI (1775–1799) died in French exile, and Napoleon had imprisoned Pope Pius VII (1800–1823) from 1809 to 1814. Closer relations with the state after the fall of Napoleon in 1815 were to be reversed again in 1830.[12]

Reacting against the revolutionary threat, Pope Pius VI officially condemned the events and principles of the revolution as early as 1791;[13] that the Church would take such a position is hardly surprising. The legacy of the revolution, from the Church's point of view, was that liberal politics not only threatened the Church's role in any specific society—a role that seemed so natural to priests, bishops, and popes of the time—but threatened the very existence of the Church. In papal eyes, liberal political principles of rationalism, freedom of thought, freedom of religion, and so on were nothing but declarations of war on the Catholic faith, both as belief system and as institution. And the imprisonment of two popes seemed good evidence to Church conservatives that the papacy needed temporal independence.

Events in the nineteenth century did little to reconcile the Church to liberalism. Interested nations as well as political forces within the Papal States of central Italy pressured Rome to institute the kind of constitutional system gaining favor in other countries.[14] Such popes as Gregory XVI (1831–1846) were hardly receptive. A few weeks after his election, Gregory called on Austrian troops to help him suppress a liberal revolt in his dominion. In 1832, in an explicit rejection of great-power recommendations that he reform the Papal States, Gregory published the encyclical *Mirari Vos*,[15] which condemned the principles of separation of church and state, freedom of the press, and freedom of religion.[16] Despite some minor concessions, Gregory made no moves toward separating the papacy's religious rights from its temporal control of central Italy.

Gregory's successor was Pius IX, whom we have already encountered. As a bishop, the future Pius IX showed conduct that was less authoritarian than Gregory's,[17] but despite European hopes that a liberal pope had finally come to power, it is unlikely that Pius IX had ever been a liberal.[18] For example, his first encyclical, *Qui Pluribus*, criticized the Enlightenment championing of reason over faith.[19]

Nevertheless, in response to pressure within the Papal States, Pius IX instituted in his kingdom a short-lived division of jurisdiction between secular and religious ministries. The political goals of the papacy and of Italian republicans of the secular cabinet, however, were hopelessly contradictory: the Papal States were, of course, a major impediment to Italian unification. The results of the power sharing were thus disastrous, as the secular cabinet wanted to wage an Italian war of unification on Austria, an important papal ally. Pius, having initiated the secular ministries in May 1848 abolished them in August.[20]

As if this experiment in dividing religious from temporal sovereignty were not enough to sour Pius IX on liberalism, toward the end of 1848 Rome, like much of Europe around the same time, experienced a republican uprising. The pope fled the city, fearing for his life. Although restored to power by an enemy of Italian republicanism (French emperor Napoleon III), in 1859 the emerging Italian republic took from Pius all the papal territories except for Rome itself. On the withdrawal of French troops to fight in the Franco-Prussian War in 1870, the Italian republic annexed Rome, leaving the pope only the Vatican and a few small properties in and around Rome.[21]

It is possible but unlikely that another pope might have chosen a more conciliatory posture, but Pius IX, declaring himself a prisoner of the Vatican, opted for intransigence in the face of modern political forces that boded ill for the Church. He ignored those who argued that by identifying itself with an archaic political order, the Church would lose the people, as he hoped for what Italian republicans feared[22]—foreign intervention to restore his kingdom.

In reaction to his losses, Pius IX issued in December 1864 the famed *Syllabus of Errors* condemning most of the tenets popularly associated with liberalism, including freedom of worship and, as we saw in the beginning of this chapter, the separation of church and state. The *Syllabus* was an appendix to the encyclical *Quanta Cura*,[23] which insisted on the evils of the separation of church and state and of tolerating any but "the true religion." In 1870 came the *nonexpedit*—the papal prohibition of Catholics voting in the republican elections—which remained in force until Pope Benedict XV (1914–1922) lifted it in 1919 (though by that time it had been increasingly disregarded for at least a couple of decades).

Beginning a pattern that lasted through Pope Pius XI (1922–1939), Pius IX's own attempts to oppose liberalism ironically reinforced the separation of church and state. Although the *nonexpedit* was consistent with the view that the Italian republic had grievously sinned against the papacy, it prevented those most faithful to the cause of the pope from having any influence on the government that was to legislate the future relationship between the republic and the Church. Italian nationalists who still considered themselves devout Catholics, despite disagreements with the pope, still voted and held office. But political participation by the staunchest supporters of the papacy, those who obeyed the *nonexpedit*, might have exerted pressure toward a compromise more favorable to Pius IX's position.[24] The papacy could not prevent church-state separation; attempts to oppose the widening of that separation only reinforced it.

Despite Pius IX's opposition, the 1871 Law of Guarantees was not unreasonable; it offered the papacy greater autonomy in religious affairs in exchange for noninterference in temporal politics. The law, whose validity the Vatican never formally accepted, granted the pope sovereign status so that he could not be prosecuted under Italian law and allowed him to conduct international diplomacy. He was to receive a stipend from the Italian government (which Pius IX refused) and to have complete freedom of international communication; control of communication of domestic decrees and such, which was not uncommon throughout Europe, was liberalized but not completely eliminated. Participants in papal conclaves, even if from nations hostile to Italy, were guaranteed freedom of assembly. The state was no longer to nominate candidates for the Italian episcopacy, and bishops no longer had to take an oath of allegiance to the king. Nevertheless, Pius IX and his secretary of state, Cardinal Antonelli, treated the Law of Guarantees as essentially blasphemous. Although Pius IX's successors were less openly hostile, disputes continued, in some cases for decades, especially over the place of the Church in Italian education, the property and privileges of religious orders, and marriage laws.[25]

Many anticlericals as well as devout liberal Catholics had hoped that widening the separation of church and state would also liberalize the Church, thereby giving the papacy less to be autocratic about. The irony was, that liberal attack on the Church (which, in Italy, took his kingdom) internationally had the opposite effect. It increased Pius IX's autonomy within the institutional Church, allowing him to further centralize and increase internal papal power: episcopacies no longer institutionally intertwined with the state became more dependent on the Vatican's protection against hostile governments than they did on the state's protection against the papacy.[26] The papacy became less dependent on, or hampered by, the privileges that states had controlled (e.g., in many countries, the nomination of episcopal candidates)[27] for perhaps centuries, allowing it to exert further control. Ironically, then, just as the papacy's resistance to liberalism contributed to the separation of church and state, liberal states' attacks on Catholicism made the Church internally even more Roman and less liberal.

We can describe this process in terms of those social structures in which the papacy most directly participated: liberalism ushered in a rupture between Church and society, and so their reciprocal influence lessened. "The Church had entered the decade of the 1850's in close collaboration with all the dominant interests in society; in the 1870's she stood isolated and alone."[28]

In extending his internal Church control, Pius IX could use the argument that it was essential to close ranks when the Church was under attack. Thus he began the Church's period of greatest centralization, which was to last at least until the Second Vatican Council and which in some respects continues. Pius concentrated decision-making in the Curia, the Vatican's bureaucracy,[29] but the most important centralizing accomplishment was the formal declaration of the doctrine of papal infallibility. This doctrine involved a shifting of power away from the episcopacy in favor of the papacy; a serious challenge would not come until Vatican II. To make this fundamental doctrinal declaration, Pius IX called (and dominated) Vatican I, the first ecumenical council since the sixteenth-century Council of Trent met to inaugurate the Counter-Reformation.

On the one hand, the doctrine of infallibility reflects the ideological priority of the faith and morals of individuals and families over concerns of temporal politics and economics, a prioritization that legitimately can be said to have a long history.[30] Thus infallibility—while it lends an aura to all papal statements—officially applies only when formally invoked for fundamental doctrinal declarations of faith and morals.[31] In practice this means specific religious and moral doctrines distinct (in papal eyes) from macropolitical or economic issues.[32] Nevertheless, although there has always been *some* distinction between faith and morals and more temporal issues, at the time of Vatican I (1869–1870) the two were much less distinct in Catholic ideology than they are today. Thus the interesting fact about the declaration of infallibility is that Pius IX felt the need to declare it precisely when his temporal authority was crumbling. Thus primary (and controversial) on the Vatican I agenda were two issues: the formal declaration of infallibility and church-state relations in the wake of Italian unification.[33]

Rome was trying to keep both issues under control, but it was all the more easy to centralize on religious questions as the Church was being forced out of temporal government, thus gaining an (unwanted but) increased autonomy from states. Pius IX himself, however, was unwilling to accept a widened separation of church and state, with the result that Vatican I's approach to church-state relations was one of total hostility to liberalism.[34] Politically, church and state were separating, but popes would only gradually become ideologically receptive to that structural reality. Contemplating the end of Pius IX's reign, Catholic powers considered using their veto to prevent the election of another pope as intransigent as him to make sure the papacy would accept the autonomy it had so far rejected.[35]

The Church would continue to encounter states trying to limit its involvement in temporal politics in turn-of-the-century France, revolutionary Mexico, Fascist Italy, and Nazi Germany, among others. Pius IX's successors, dealing with the aftermath, would gradually sharpen the boundary between religious and temporal issues, decentralizing sociopolitical issues—where the Church's formerly large influence had receded—away from the ideological core. Without necessarily intending to widen the distinction between religious and temporal matters, such popes increasingly differentiated their authority on matters of faith and morals from their authority on sociopolitical matters.

Ideological Boundaries and the Loss of Temporal Power

The world had changed, the alliance of throne and altar had gone forever, but the papacy did not fully accept this fact until Vatican II. With the possible exception of Benedict XV, the Church between Vatican I and Vatican II was ruled by a series of popes with little sympathy for the modern separation of church and state. Leo XIII (1878–1903), Pius IX's immediate successor, had a personal preference for monarchical government,[36] and an ancien régime perspective was clear in his views of the obligation of the state to protect no religion but Catholicism and to repress error and immorality in the press.[37] As pope, although he recognized that the U.S. Church had prospered by the separation of church and state there, he told Americans that it was much preferable, and beneficial for the Church, for Catholicism to enjoy the protection and patronage of the state.[38]

Unsurprisingly, then, Leo was authoritarian on religious matters. In a move that some have interpreted as an effort to stimulate Catholic philosophical studies,[39] he mandated that only Thomism was to be studied, an action that was fairly repressive.[40] As a bishop, the future pope had been a very important inspiration for the *Syllabus* and the dogma of papal infallibility.[41] Furthermore, in 1899 Pope Leo condemned doctrines of "Americanism," which argued for greater religious toleration and a more liberal view of the Church's role in society. Such doctrines were generally popular in the United States but were just as much a product of European (especially French) liberal Catholics who exaggerated American Catholic outlooks. In any case, in Leo's mind such views were threatening because they affirmed church-state separation and attempted to legitimate freedom of religion.[42]

And yet Leo was more conciliatory than Pius IX on the matter of temporal sovereignty. In Belgium, France, and Spain, he was willing to exchange the local Churches' stepping out of overt political agitation in return for peaceful church-state relations, even when this entailed prohibiting clergy from actively advocating a return to monarchy, despite his own personal preference for monarchy.[43] In Italy, while he continued to argue that temporal power was essential to his independence, he spoke only of recovering the city of Rome, implicitly accepting the 1859 losses as a fait accompli.[44] Thus Leo had no interest in democratizing the papacy's religious authority, but he began a slow, halting withdrawal of the Church's temporal claims.

The most interesting aspect of Leo's pontificate, however, is the birth of what was, in effect, a new branch of doctrine, known as social doctrine, with his 1891 encyclical, *Rerum Novarum*.[45] The actual term *social doctrine* apparently did not become common until the pontificate of Pius XI, and some recent popes and other Catholics have preferred the term *social teaching*. But in any case, it was not until Leo XIII that "the Church's social concerns were given a systematic philosophical and theological justification" separate from that of other doctrine.[46] And Catholics interested in such issues universally cite Leo as the parent of such concerns.[47] Social doctrine deals generally with questions of politics and economics on the societal level, as opposed to the religious and moral obligations of individuals and families. And although social doctrine implied a new Catholic view of the moral standards for conduct in modern society, the hierarchy has always regarded it as the least binding level of doctrine, one allowing disagreement at the specific level of policy, considered outside of the Church's competence.[48] (The more recent, common preference for the term *social teaching* demonstrates the progressive trend to make social doctrine even more flexible and nondogmatic.[49] This is in great contrast to doctrine that concerns the faith and morals of individuals and families, such as sexual morality, which deals very much in particulars within binding, supposedly unchanging doctrinal requirements.)[50] *Rerum Novarum*—and papal ideology on social and political issues ever since—avoids specific policy questions, arguing instead that the Church's role is to teach a moral outlook that transcends historical and political particulars.[51]

Thus Leo stated that social doctrine does not address economic issues per se but their moral dimensions and that Catholic political parties derive their Catholic identification from their moral principles, which do not imply any preference for a system of government.[52] Whereas Pius IX had attempted very much to retain the connections between obligatory political opinions and religious devotion, Leo had begun to separate them.

It would not be until the reign of Pius XII (1939–1958) that ideological reconstruction would progress to the point that the Church's religious authority would come to be defined as virtually separate from the temporal realm. In the period between Leo XIII and Pius XII, such reconstruction of ideological boundaries would develop haltingly; nevertheless, papal policy gradually contributed to the Church's withdrawal from temporal prerogatives, even when the opposite result was intended. Simultaneously, popes increased Vatican control over "faith and morals." Let us examine this process in the pontificates of Pius X, Benedict XV, and Pius XI.

Leo's successor, Pius X, very much saw his role as one of silencing dissent. Pius X condemned some of the same views designated by Leo to be aspects of "Americanism," but Pius X's dragnet was wider and more vicious. Eager to exterminate a partly imaginary conspiracy of theological dissenters grouped under the heading of "modernism," he had no qualms about ruining scores of ecclesiastical careers in the process.[53]

Interestingly, however, Pius X's attempt to control *all* aspects of Catholic life could be successful only on these more purely religious and theological matters. The inquisition against modernism can be understood as a part of the Vatican reaction against the loss of its standing within European social structure, a reaction that served to further consolidate the centralization of institutional power in Rome.[54] But European party politics was beyond papal grasp; thus Pius X's attempts to control Catholic political groups only served to reinforce the separation of church and state.

Part of the mythology about Pius X is that he was little concerned with politics, feeling that the Church should concentrate on spiritual concerns.[55] Although a partial truth, this myth is fairly misleading; it is a misunderstanding of the nature of the Church's involvement in secular politics at the time. In fact, Pius X wanted primarily to prevent the emergence of a *liberal* Catholic politics. Like previous popes, he sympathized with the ancien régime perspective. Compared to his condemnations of liberal groups, then, Pius X was fairly lenient with the semifascist Action Française because its royalism was compatible with his idealization of the ancien régime.[56] But the interesting aspect of Pius X's approach to Catholic participation in politics is that in a world in which even the Catholic laity desired freedom from the hierarchy on matters of temporal politics, refusal to grant that freedom was in practice nearly equivalent to the prohibition of all explicitly Catholic political participation.

Pius X prohibited the reformist Sillon in France and the Christian Democrats in Italy, and he prohibited Christian Democratic priests from serving in legislatures or in general from being active politically.[57] Thus in a world where Catholic lay groups were interested in political organization only if allowed some autonomy from hierarchical control, Pius X's refusal to sanction such groups simply meant that there would be little or no organized, political participation explicitly oriented toward furthering Catholic goals.

Christian Democratic groups throughout Europe were explicitly attempting to differentiate secular political activities, even when inspired by Catholic principles, from moral or religious issues that came under the jurisdiction of the hierarchy.[58] Pius X's response was to force political withdrawal. There resulted, then, the irony that Pius X in practice contributed to the separation of church and state by prohibiting precisely those groups attempting to distinguish religious from political concerns. Similarly, in France, his hostility to liberalism contributed to the withdrawal of the Church from politics. Much less conciliatory than Leo XIII toward France in church-state disputes, his refusal to deal with the French government de facto reinforced the Church's exclusion from political influence.

But outside the realm of sociopolitical issues, Pius X—like all popes since Pius IX—was able to strengthen Church autonomy in those matters that did not challenge the widening separation of church and state. In fact, he could increase Church autonomy by contributing to that separation. Thus in reaction to Austria's exercising a veto in the 1903 conclave, he quickly acted to eliminate the privilege, thus extracting the Church from one aspect of state domination.[59]

Yet Pius X was not hostile toward the Italian republic; he was basically inactive on the "Roman Question," although he did feel it needed to be settled; even a conservative like Pius X perhaps began to recognize that only "in the realm of fantasy or dreams" did anyone expect the Church's temporal power to be restored.[60] Perhaps this explains why he did not seem troubled by the lack of political effectiveness that resulted from his refusal to allow Catholics freedom of ideological movement around political questions. In any case, Pius X himself tended to focus his energy on purely religious issues, such as liturgy, Church music, and canon law,[61] issues over which, of course, he had almost complete control.

Pius X, then, without necessarily intending so, contributed to a Church withdrawal from politics while emphasizing the religious authority of the papacy. His withdrawal, however, did not increase individual Catholics' freedom of movement around social and political questions, as Leo XIII had begun to do. Nevertheless, by the early twentieth century, the stage was set for further sharpening of the boundary between religious and temporal concerns, the latter expressed doctrinally in an increasingly distinct, and less binding, way. Secular politicians came to care less about the internal workings of a Church rapidly losing its temporal power base, and even

Church conservatives began to see some clear advantages, such as a new-found autonomy from interfering states, that came with the loss of temporal power.[62]

Later popes continued to ease the official hostility toward Italy, and they went further than Pius X in seeking to resolve the situation. Benedict XV, despite the brevity of his reign and the fact that it was dominated by World War I, did make a conciliatory gesture in setting aside the papal policy of refusing to meet with Catholic heads of state who implicitly recognized Italy's sovereignty over Rome by meeting with the king in that city. Benedict also encouraged official discussions to settle the Roman Question.[63]

Benedict was followed by a conservative pope who ruled with an iron hand. But because of the changed status of the Roman Question, we find that with Pius XI the nature of conservatism in the Church changed. Pius XI retained an antidemocratic view of the world, and his clear preference—as we see in his dealings with Benito Mussolini—was for a church-state alliance over liberal arrangements. Yet circumstances had developed to the point where he saw the unrealistic pretensions toward temporal sovereignty as obstacles to be eliminated; he had little patience with fellow prelates who echoed Pius IX's intransigence. He aimed, then, for an alliance with an Italian state that had sovereignty over Rome, rather than attempt to establish papal rule over the city. But this was still a basically ancien régime arrangement. When Pius XI did try to reestablish a church-state alliance, his actions backfired, demonstrating how it was no longer possible for the Church to hope to enforce its religious authority via temporal, political means. Pius XI's failed policy made clear that the Church would be wiser to protect its autonomy than romanticize its past.

Pius XI had no commitment to church-state separation in principle; quite the opposite was the case. He settled the Roman Question by signing the Lateran Treaty with Mussolini in 1929, and yet he did so because his sole interest was the practical protection of the institutional Church, preferably via protection from a confessional state.[64]

Pius XI clearly admired Mussolini from early on as a man who could not only guarantee the Church's independence in a way, so Pius XI thought, that unpredictable democratic governments could not, but as "a man who lacked the prejudices of the liberal school"—that is, hostility toward the Church.[65] On paper, the Lateran Treaty and the accompanying concordat seemed highly favorable to the Church; the Italian state in practice had had sovereignty over the former papal territories for over half a century, and yet the papacy conceded little more than formal recognition of that sovereignty and a guarantee of noninterference. In return, the state granted the primacy of religious over civil marriage, freedom for religious orders, a large money settlement, and the presence of religion in education. Mussolini even agreed that persons in official disrepute with the Church (e.g., defrocked priests) would lose civil rights and that the state would recognize and enforce canon law (i.e., the internal rules of discipline and procedure in the Church). At the time, it seemed that Pius XI was indeed correct that fascism could offer what a liberal government could not—a return to the confessional state.[66]

In his eagerness to reach an agreement with the Church's apparent temporal savior, Pius XI bargained away the existence of the Catholic political party, the Popular Party, thereby guaranteeing that the Church would not interfere with the Fascist state. He preferred groups directly under hierarchical control, such as Catholic Action, over the Popular Party in any case.[67] Under Pius XI, the Vatican secretariat of state became a flurry of activity in negotiating concordats with authoritarian governments. But in Italy at least, he did not realize that without any real temporal power base, the Church was in reality bargaining away its ability to counter political suppression, its ability to defend itself should the Fascists not uphold the confessional state.[68]

Pius XI had surrendered the right of any Catholic organizations to challenge fascism and, more important, had agreed to dismantle those organizations in exchange for an agreement that Mussolini, like Adolf Hitler, had no intention of keeping when it became inconvenient. The dictators signed to gain international prestige and, at least temporarily, to remove the Catholic Church from the ranks of the domestic opposition. This complete bad faith in signing explains why Mussolini, like Hitler, would assent to an accord that on paper seemed so favorable to the Church. Although after the war the Church would receive state protection of its privileges concerning education, marriage laws, and de facto civil recognition, a full return to the confessional state, especially a truly authoritarian alliance, was unrealistic in Western Europe. The government that Pius XI thought would rebuild the church-state alliance could persecute the Church much more viciously than liberals ever had, for the Church had already lost the means to retaliate effectively. Pius XI was not a medieval pope who could force Mussolini to abdicate, and the failure of Pius's attempt at a church-state authoritarian alliance only demonstrated how outdated such policy was.

The pontificate of Pius XI, then, somewhat repeated the pattern of Pius X's but—given the Fascist context—with much graver results. Like his papal namesake, Pius XI held an authoritarian control over matters of faith and morals, and he preferred hierarchical control over Catholic lay organizations. But there was a contrast with Pius IX that points to the political reality of a sharpened boundary between religious and temporal matters.

While it is true that Pius IX and Pius XI were similarly interested primarily in defending the Church's religious and institutional prerogatives and thought that an alliance of throne and altar was the best method of doing so, Pius XI (as well as, to a lesser degree, Pius X before him) took a much more strategic, rather than doctrinaire, approach to relations with modern states. He was willing to assure that the Church would withdraw from overt political activity if, in particular nations such as France, that was the only option by which the Church could escape state hostility.[69] Church-state alliance remained only an ideal, one that he mistakenly believed he could achieve in Fascist Italy.

Thus the reign of Pius XI, who quite clearly had no sympathy for liberalism, either as it pertained to church-state separation or to republican forms of government, demonstrates the emergence of a new Catholic ideological structure, one that subordinated sociopolitical issues to faith and morals. His important contribution to social doctrine, the 1931 encyclical *Quadragesimo Anno*,[70] states that the Church is interested in presenting the moral principles of social order, not in dealing with temporal particulars. Unlike Pius IX, Pius XI's own preferences for church-state alliance remained *preferences*, rather than doctrinal obligations, because his social doctrine argues that it is not within the Church's competence to advocate a particular state arrangement. In addition, the encyclical continues Leo's criticism of capitalism from a neofeudal perspective, emphasizing the glories of the old guild system. But before we address the particulars of the neofeudal content of that social doctrine, we must examine the pontificate of Pius XI's successor, in which the distinction between the Church's religious authority and temporal involvement reached a new extreme.

Pius XI's secretary of state, Eugenio Pacelli, succeeded him as Pius XII. Pius XII's embattled reign during World War II remains a controversial one, especially over his attitudes and actions concerning the Holocaust.[71] But of main interest here is that under Pius XII, the Catholic faith reached perhaps its highest level of separation from the temporal world.

Pius XII's conception of the Church as the Mystical Body of Christ (in his encyclical, *Mystici Corporis Christi*)[72] emphasizes a Church that is very distinct from the world around it by virtue of that divine presence. For Pius XII's conception of the Church's purpose primarily concerned spiritual matters as well as moral matters, especially those affecting the family.[73] But this otherworldly spirituality was to be under the firm authority of a hierarchical Church. So his emphasis on the Church as physical institution was not an emphasis on temporal involvement, strange as that may seem to non-Catholics. The hierarchy, then, was to be in firm control of spiritual matters, whereas such issues as the specifics of the social order, although

Pius XII certainly referred to them, were simply not high priorities. Even Pius XII's acceptance of democracy in the fight against communism seemed to be less an absolute moral commitment than a strategic, realistic acceptance of the best option available at the time. Thus for example, he did not display any great concern for the specifics of democratic processes.[74]

Even when he argued explicitly that social and economic matters are within the domain of the Church, Pius XII implicitly recognized the hierarchy of ideological levels that harks back to Leo XIII, in that such matters are of concern only insofar as they have moral implications.[75] That is, the Catholic view of the world is through the lens of morality, not focusing much on issues that have no clear moral implications within Catholic moral theology. In general, Pius XII did not emphasize these social concerns in any case.

Carlo Falconi likens Pius XII's encyclical *Humani Generis* to Pius X's campaign against modernism because it aimed to restrict new developments in theological and biblical research.[76] In this encyclical, Pius XII argued that because human intellect is often hampered by desire and must be properly trained, the hierarchy's pronouncements on faith and morals had to be the starting point of all theology and Catholic philosophy, thereby implying infallibility.[77] In fact, he stated, citing Pius IX, that the job of theologians was to demonstrate the sources in revelation of doctrine already defined by the Church (meaning the hierarchy). So as not to leave any ambiguity, *Humani Generis* also states explicitly that encyclicals— many of which Catholic theologians treat more as points of discussion than as inalterable truth—have dogmatic status.[78] *Mystici Corporis Christi* had earlier clearly implied that the Church never makes a doctrinal error, whether or not the hierarchy formally invokes infallibility.[79] Yet implicitly acknowledging a hierarchy of ideological priorities, *Humani Generis* notes that there is much in philosophical investigation "that neither directly nor indirectly touches faith or morals, and which consequently the Church leaves to the free discussion of experts."[80] Thus he very clearly distinguished Roman authority over matters of faith and morals, which cannot be questioned, from other issues that are much more open to debate. Among those were issues of social reform, which, at least under Pius XII, were not often papal concerns.

Arguably, there were contradictions within Pius XII's approach to the boundary between religion and politics. As I noted, Pius XII clearly allied the Church politically with the West and was obsessed by his anticommunism.[81] He was similar as well to his immediate predecessor, Pius XI, insofar as he almost surely preferred a Church protected by and allied with the state; in fact, in post–World War II Italy he worked hard and successfully to guarantee Church privileges under the Christian Democrats.[82]

That a widened church-state separation was forced on the papacy, however, explains why popes themselves did not always prefer the new boundary. Even today, although Pope John Paul II generally enforces a very strict boundary separating faith and morals from sociopolitical issues, he has not always been consistent. Anticommunist activism among priests in his native Poland, for example, seemed more acceptable than activism among Latin American Church personnel. We should remember, however, first, that these examples are notable mainly because, by the mid-twentieth century, they had so clearly become exceptions rather than the rule. (Interestingly, for both Pius XII and John Paul II, it is difficult to find exceptions outside their native lands, where, perhaps, their personal sentiments overwhelmed their usual predilections.) Second, anticommunism is a somewhat special case. From the papal point of view, communism is evil mainly for its atheism, and thus denies a fundamental tenet of faith. This position is quite consistent with Catholic ideological structure. John XXIII (1958–1963) and Paul VI, for example, were more tolerant in dealing with communist parties and leaders, "distinguishing between an atheistic ideology that had to be condemned, and the historical evolution of an economic and political structure that the Church could tolerate."[83]

Even when we look at postwar Italy, Pius XII, unlike Pius IX, did not give formal doctrinal sanction to his political ideals and activities. His concern with communism and his political alliance with the West are best understood as means to protect the Catholic Church and contain what he saw as the evils of atheism, rather than intertwining church and state functions. Thus even though he made infrequent references to (especially Leo XIII's) social doctrine, his concern with temporal issues such as social reform, democratic participation, or particular state policies did not go beyond the advocacy of a general political alliance with Western democracy. That is to say, the Church was to ally itself with the West so good Christians could carry on their religious mission, not so that the Church itself could focus on temporal issues. Thus Pius XII, while concerned with geopolitics, did not pay much attention to social doctrine. Pius XII conceived the Church as a more purely religious, hierarchical institution than did perhaps any other modern pope.

The papacy of Pius XII is therefore of most interest for culminating the centralization of religious authority that had begun with Vatican I. Pius XII was the first, and so far only, pope to formally invoke the infallibility formally defined at Vatican I, in his 1950 declaration of the dogma of the bodily Assumption of Mary into heaven. It is interesting to note how often, in at least five separate encyclicals, Pius XII cited Vatican I, the council of infallibility and centralization.[84] Pius XII in fact emphasized the divine nature of the papacy and of the Church more than any pope since at least Pius IX.

In outlook, Pius XII, born two years before Pius IX died, was very much a twentieth-century version of his papal namesake in terms of the desire to centralize authority in the papacy. But the world had changed, forging a different context and a different meaning for the same institutional authoritarianism. Pius IX increased theological and institutional centralization in reaction to temporal threats. By the mid-twentieth century, defending papal temporal power was no longer a concern, and so centralization meant making the papacy, and the Church, even more divine and less worldly.

Structural Autonomy and the Struggle with Liberalism: A Neofeudal Social Doctrine

The ideological history of the Catholic Church confirms Mary Fulbrook's finding that a church's perspective on the temporal world very much depends on whether that church is allied with or alienated from state structures.[85] Having been very much a part of the feudal social order, the medieval Church granted doctrinal sanction to the economic and social hierarchies of the age. Being politically and economically intertwined with the medieval social order, the Church ideologically reflected a very close affinity with temporal sovereigns and ruling elites.

But with the emergence of the modern state system and industrial capitalism, the Church gradually became excluded from its former political and economic power. It never was an important partner in liberal politics or liberal economics. This process of exclusion, we have seen, led to a sharpening of the boundary between sociopolitical issues and more central religious beliefs. But while forced into a restructuring of Catholic ideology, popes did not simply passively accept that they were losing the battle with liberalism. They developed new ideological content in the form of the new social doctrine, or social teaching, from a perspective that simultaneously kept alive their opposition to liberalism, avoided church-state conflict, and opened the door to a new Catholic approach toward society and politics.

As already noted, Leo XIII, who founded social doctrine as a distinct ideological category, was certainly no liberal, and he did not abandon the claim that temporal sovereignty (his own kingdom) was necessary to assure his religious independence.[86] Interestingly, although it is contemporary moderate and left-leaning Catholics who most often emphasize social doctrine, the two most important (pre–Vatican II) contributors to social doctrine were Leo XIII (in his 1891 encyclical, *Rerum Novarum*), the monarchist, and Pius XI, the pope eager to form an alliance with fascism. Modern reform-minded Catholics have often assumed that the development of social doctrine as a distinct ideological category meant that the papacy was heightening the value of reforming the world. But nearly the opposite was the case because social doctrine became distinct by becoming ideologically subordinate to faith and morals. Thus some popes (e.g., Pius X, Pius XII) put little effort into refining social doctrine, while none, of course, neglected faith and morals.[87]

But the content of social doctrine was a novel development. It allowed the papacy to give a general analysis of social issues that remained ideologically independent of liberalism without addressing specific, controversial policy issues. Leo's paternalistic discussion of the plight of workers in industrial society was, despite its basic conservatism, a great contrast to previous Church approaches to social issues. It opened the door to Catholic advocacy of proletarian causes. It is interesting to note in this context that Leo was the first modern pope not to rule central Italy and thus the first for whom the attempt to gain the allegiance of the working class would not encounter the fundamental contradiction that the Church was closely intertwined with the ruling elites and ruling sovereigns of Europe. Thus Leo made small moves toward a new political alliance, given that the Church had been forced out of its old alliance with preliberal states and social elites.

Leo's advisers on the ideas that influenced *Rerum Novarum* might initially appear to have been progressive social reformers;[88] and within a paternalistic worldview, they did advocate social reform. But they appear more accurately to be characterized as conservative aristocrats, critical of capitalism from the right, not the left.[89] Leo himself came from an aristocratic background likely to emphasize preindustrial values and lived in a relatively undeveloped country; his personal style was likewise aristocratic, sometimes even snobbish.[90]

Although there was a true, paternalistic concern for the plight of the working class, *Rerum Novarum* was an attempt to apply to the contemporary world (a somewhat romanticized view of) medieval social organization,[91] in which the Church was a crucial link. The "lessons" of that social organization still have an important legacy in Catholic social doctrine, a fact that contemporary observers of the Church often miss. Liberalism, a force perceived as so hostile to the Church, could not, in a pope's eyes, provide answers to modern social problems; would not the days when the Church was at its zenith—at the center of European civilization, the days of guilds, before church-state separation—provide a better model?

Thus we find that essential to Leo's approach was the interventionist role of the institutional Church and religious morality in the social order. *Rerum Novarum* argues that modern social problems are the result of the decline of religion, an argument he had been making for decades[92] and one that, not too surprisingly, remains a strong influence on Catholic social doctrine: "Public institutions and laws set aside the ancient religion. Hence by degrees it has come to pass that working men have been given over, isolated and defenceless, to the callousness of employers and the greed of unrestrained competition."[93]

To someone outside the Catholic worldview, the second sentence may not follow from the first as clearly and convincingly as it does for Leo; this logic, however, remains important in Catholic social doctrine.[94] The solution to industrial and social conflict, the argument goes, begins with a return to religion.[95] Religious devotion, reflecting the modern structure of Catholic ideology, is always primary to technical questions of policy; the Church, so the argument goes, leaves the details of policy—where disagreement is allowed because such details are not very important—to temporal authorities. Thus *Rerum Novarum*, and social doctrine in general, avoids questions of policy and often exhorts society to return to religion.

While avoiding such specific issues, social doctrine is, however, clearly opposed to libertarian views of the market. It is not up to owners to do whatever they wish with property;[96] the interests of society must be kept in mind. Employers are to pay a fair wage, enough to support a worker and family; Leo rejected a purely market wage.[97]

Continuing the essentially neofeudal perspective, Leo argued that the wealthy are obliged to practice Christian charity to aid workers; the continued amassing of profits as well as usury are immoral.[98] Social reform, then, is to occur paternalistically, via charity, via noblesse oblige, although preferably in a more regular, dependable manner than simply alms-giving.[99] Denying that class conflict was inevitable, and assuming that the class structure of society was natural, Leo argued that the state is to work to the benefit of all classes.[100] The state is to intervene if necessary to protect the workers' welfare, including the workers' ability (e.g., being physically healthy) to practice religion. It is the moral duty of all classes to work together in harmony. Pre–Vatican II social doctrine, having no direct experience in managing modern liberal economies or states, argued a simplistic and romantic social theory that saw state partisanship toward particular classes as well as class conflict in general as purely moral failings. Such doctrine made little reference to the structural complexity of modern society.

Thus Leo in fact legitimated few concrete means—other than increasing religious devotion[101]—by which the working class could improve its position, although he was supposedly championing the workers' cause. He argued that the conditions that led workers to strike should be removed, but in practice he did not seem to approve of strikes.[102] He pronounced on the moral obligations of owners but was not specific on exactly how the state should regulate the market.

After Leo, political developments, as we have already seen, continued to contribute to the church-state separation that opened the ideological room for social doctrine. But given the low ideological priority of that category of doctrine, popes did not necessarily attend to it; there were few significant contributions to social doctrine until Pius XI's *Quadragesimo Anno* in 1931.[103] *Quadragesimo Anno* was more reform-minded than *Rerum Novarum*—for example, in its insistence that charity is essential but not enough to achieve justice, and that opposition to unions is criminal.[104] Pius XI even hinted that the developing world (not, of course, his term) is poor because of exploitation by colonial industry.[105]

How was it that a pope with such apparent right-wing sympathies could produce such a document? Pius XI inherited Leo's neofeudal perspective, which was critical of capitalism and the laissez-faire state, but he updated it. And by Pius XI's time, the Church in Europe was even more distant from liberalism socially and politically than it had been under Leo. Leo had still hoped to win some concessions from the Italian republic, but Pius XI more optimistically hoped for the end of liberalism and had definite admiration for the corporatist critiques of capitalism that had become quite common (e.g., among fascists) and that merged rather well with romanticized notions of medieval guilds. (Pius XI, however, was no revolutionary and so urged the reform, not the abolition, of capitalism.)[106]

Like Leo, Pius XI was insistent that no solution could be found without the Church,[107] specifically via a religious and moral reform to precede social reform, even within unions.[108] He even stated that a source of the social problem was that people were *too* preoccupied with temporal matters.[109] He was quite self-conscious that Catholic social doctrine is born of an opposition to both political and economic liberalism.[110] He stated, following the corporatist perspective, that unions were only one form of desired association, which should not be restricted to just one class.[111]

Like Leo, Pius XI argued for the inviolability of property while stressing the social obligations of ownership, again rejecting the notion that property is simply a commodity to produce profits. Thus Pius, like Leo, distinguished between rights of ownership and rights of use. The state has a right to assure that use of property has social benefit and to control property whose domination by individuals would lead to social harm.[112] An important reform is that all be able to acquire property.[113] Seeming to imply that class differences are inevitable and just, he repeated Leo's argument that no one is morally entitled to income "which he does not need in order to live as becomes his station."[114] He argued a theme, later repeated by Pope John Paul II, that both capital and labor are essential, each deserving a just but not total share, the worker's being enough to support a family.[115] But Pius XI seemed more attuned than Leo to the requirements of the market.[116]

As far as ideological boundaries are concerned, again Pius XI was more explicit than Leo in noting that the Church's authority concerns not technical matters, but the moral aspects of social and economic questions, clearly rejecting, however, the notion that it is possible to talk of technical matters completely independently of moral questions.[117]

What Pius XI presented in *Quadragesimo Anno* was a vision of a corporatist social order[118] in which workers share in ownership[119] yet are forbidden to strike because the state would prevent class conflict,[120] an order that he explicitly asserted once existed (in medieval times).[121] Members of society were to be joined in ways that cut across class divisions; thus once again papal social doctrine was arguing that market/class divisions do not necessarily become social and moral divisions.[122] This pope, then, attempted to reinstitute the ancien régime in an alliance with fascism—but, as we have seen, failed—and continued the critique of capitalism from the ancien régime perspective.

Reconstructing Catholic Ideology

Ideological change in the modern Catholic Church involved a political process in which the struggle with liberalism actually allowed popes to increase the centralization of authority within the Church itself as well as to develop an antiliberal social doctrine. Studies by Lester Kurtz and Stephen Lyng of the modernist heresy have noted the relationship between the papacy's defensive posture and centralization.[123] But the papacy's actions were not *only* defensive, and popes could not define orthodoxy and centralize ideological control any way they chose. The papacy could not control the changing political structure of Europe, but it successfully augmented its own power within the constraints of that structure. That is, it concentrated its control over internal Church matters now that it had gained greater autonomy from European states within the institution. But it had to tread carefully around sociopolitical issues and thus subordinated doctrine on such issues and made it quite vague.

Thus the papacy unwittingly participated in an ideological restructuring that it had, in fact, initially resisted. Some of its own resistance contributed to the widened separation of church and state, which ultimately effected a sharpened ideological boundary between faith and morals, on the one hand, and sociopolitical issues, on the other. But as long as Rome avoided specific denunciations of European (especially Italian) state policy (thus accounting for the vagueness of social doctrine), it could fill its newly created social doctrine with preliberal and antiliberal themes. Those themes of course held great appeal for popes who perceived a harsh political climate filled with liberal persecutors. As was pointed out in chapter 1, the structure of the ideology was ultimately more important than its content. That is, social doctrine's oppositional perspective, despite its antiliberal content, was structurally weakened by its ideological subordination to faith and morals. Nevertheless, the content was not insignificant: it resulted from the papacy's active development of an antiliberal posture within the constraints of a new European sociopolitical structure. We shall see later that some groups within the post–Vatican II Church attempted to reinterpret social doctrine in a socialist direction. Interestingly, this reinterpretation was possible because of that doctrine's anticapitalist perspective, its relative vagueness, and its nonbinding character, so that Rome could not easily prohibit variant interpretations. (In general, we can expect that ideology concerning less important issues will become more vague and will not be enforced as strongly as is the case with more important issues.)

Thus ideological restructuring was a complex process of political interaction. To some degree the papacy was highly constrained in its political and ideological options: therefore the strategy of reestablishing the central role of the Church hierarchy in secular politics consistently failed. In fact, as we can see most clearly during the pontificates of Pius X and Pius XI, such attempts ironically served to reinforce a widening separation of church and state. The papacy fought the newly emerging structure of Catholic ideology in which sociopolitical issues became more separate from, and subordinate to, the faith and morals of individuals and families. But Rome ultimately took part in reconstructing Catholic ideology in a way that respected the liberal separation of church and state while simultaneously maintaining—and to some extent even strengthening—ideological autonomy from liberalism. Here it is important to remember that the papacy had significantly less control over the structure of boundaries and priorities within Church ideology than it did over the content of that ideology. But the content was not arbitrarily, or perhaps even freely, chosen: it reflected the history of ideological commitments the papacy had made, which in turn reflected Rome's political relationships with forces within and outside the Church. The papacy reconstructed Catholic ideology in a way that was still very consistent with a nineteenth-century Vatican understanding of the world.

In doing so, however, Rome opened the possibility that Catholic views on society could become more critical than justificationist. Important to remember here is that people develop their perspectives on the world with reference to the social structures that most directly affect their lives. This fact was significant in a number of ways: first, within liberal social structures, Rome had some degree of autonomy, which it avidly protected. But it did not absorb liberal perspectives: its autonomy was very much tied to its exclusion from liberal society. The Church simply was no longer a central part of the dominant power structures of European secular society. Second, and related to this development, the papacy's own political decline followed from the decline of the medieval social order. With that decline, there was the potential that papal ideology on sociopolitical issues would be neofeudal in orientation and yet have no neofeudal social groups or social order to defend. That did not mean that the neofeudal ideological content would necessarily decline; it had become part of Catholic ideology itself, making sense of the world to the hierarchy and becoming part of their socialization within the institution. But it could mean that the Church had the potential to step *around* liberalism, moving from right to left in its criticism of capitalism, as the "right" position increasingly had little social reality to defend. The Church remained critical of capitalism and of modern state policy: it had never absorbed the secular ideologies associated with either. We see this potential within Catholic sociopolitical ideology in the following chapters.

3 Change and Ambiguity at Vatican II

The truth cannot impose itself except by virtue of its own truth, as it makes its entrance into the mind at once quietly and with power. Religious freedom, in turn, which men demand as necessary to fulfill their duty to worship God, has to do with immunity from coercion in civil society. Therefore, it leaves untouched traditional Catholic doctrine on the moral duty of men and societies toward the true religion and toward the one Church of Christ.

> Vatican II's "Declaration on Religious Freedom," in Walter M. Abbott, S.J., ed., *The Documents of Vatican II*, p. 677.

Within this statement are the fundamentals of much of the ideology of the post–Vatican II hierarchy. Most obviously, the statement rejects the long-standing papal doctrine that states should enforce the priority of Catholicism over other religions. Thus the council sanctioned a wider separation between Church authority and state authority and accepted the liberal principle of religious freedom. The statement also asserts that Catholic doctrine on moral duties is left "untouched." Even though Gregory XVI or Pius IX would have disagreed, this statement was true from the perspective of those conciliar reformers who felt that the Church itself had been in error to think that its *true* moral doctrine necessitated a union of church and state. (The council also claimed that "the doctrine of the Church that no one is to be coerced into faith has always stood firm," even though the Church had long opposed religious freedom.)[1]

One might ask whether much of pre-twentieth-century Catholicism remains, however; the statement insists on the "*moral*" obligation to follow the "true religion," a phrase describing Catholicism that, at least in nineteenth-century papal usage, was decidedly antiliberal and antiecumenical.[2] Nevertheless, there is implicit change here as well, as other council documents acknowledged that there was value in, and some degree of Catholic unity with, Protestant religions and even non-Christian religions.[3] All

47

Christians, not just Catholics, were part of the Church of Christ, and even non-Christian religions often shared religious truth. True, the council did declare that Protestants "do not profess the faith in its entirety,"[4] and even though the council's statements on non-Christian religions were quite positive and respectful in tone, there was no acknowledgment, for example, of the history of Church-sponsored anti-Semitism. Nevertheless, compared to preconciliar Church pronouncements, Catholicism had come a long way.

There remain, however, some questions about this statement: how exactly are "societies" morally bound by the principles of "the true religion"? Does this not contradict papal statements that "technical," state policy matters are outside the Church's competence? And even if popes such as Gregory XVI and Pius IX had been wrong about such issues as religious freedom, they had indeed rejected a whole host of liberal freedoms with a clear doctrinal certainty. Is it not simply historically incorrect for the council to have implied that doctrine had not changed?

This statement is just one of the examples of the ambiguities of Vatican II: the legacy of Vatican II is unclear and contested. The hierarchy's efforts at furthering a reconstruction of Catholic ideology that in some ways began with Leo XIII and in many other ways went much further has increased the possibility of ideological divergence.

Ideological reconstruction does not happen automatically; for example, pre–Vatican II popes continued to idealize church-state alliance even as they were gradually forced into accepting a sharper ideological boundary separating faith and morals from sociopolitical issues. Nor does it necessarily develop functionally. It involves people committed to particular understandings of the world acting within the social structures relevant to their lives, sometimes acting within the autonomy they have, to contribute to changes in those structures. Ideological reconstruction can involve political compromises and resistance to the rejection of long-standing commitments, thus resulting in ambiguity and the potential for ideological divergence. And, indeed, ideological structures themselves can allow enough freedom of movement on some issues so that no one can control diverse interpretations.

In sum, the politics of ideology can be complicated and can involve halting, even problematic, change. This becomes very clear as we look more closely at Vatican II. It is important to realize, first, that we cannot understand the meaning of Vatican II for the political and ideological history of Catholicism without remembering that the Church's loss of direct temporal power, the papal centralization of authority over matters of faith and morals, a sharpened ideological boundary between such matters and sociopolitical issues, and the birth of modern social doctrine were all intricately connected developments. Doctrinally, the Vatican gradually lost interest in its temporal claims, devaluing doctrine pertaining to macropolitics and economics. But the newfound autonomy from temporal powers made it all the easier, and perhaps more necessary, for the Vatican to concentrate power over more important doctrine (that of faith and morals) in the papacy. States no longer stood between the papacy and its control over bishops, and Rome acted to preserve what authority it retained as it attempted to rally the Church into a united front against liberalism.

To some extent Vatican II involved the hierarchy's ratification of these changes, but the council added new dimensions of its own. The present chapter addresses those changes instituted by the council that were most important for the political and ideological structure of the Church.[5] These changes were numerous. First, through the council, the Church finally and officially abandoned the ancien régime model of church-state relations, declaring that the Church does not belong in temporal government and, as we have seen, that all individuals have a right to be free from any coercion to belong to and believe in a particular faith. Second, the council reacted against the extreme centralization of power within the Church that had begun with Vatican I and that had been a particular emphasis of Pius XII. Third, the council reacted against the ideological withdrawal from the temporal world that, again, reached its culmination during the papacy of Pius XII and was expressed ideologically in the subordination of sociopolitical issues to faith and morals.

Each of these council reforms, however, lent a certain tension or ambiguity to Church ideology. Taking them in order, we can observe first that the end of the idealization of church-state alliance entailed a partial acceptance of political liberalism. The Church essentially endorsed liberal democracy as the preferable form of government. Nevertheless, it was not the case that the Church accepted liberalism wholesale: it continued to oppose economic liberalism and a liberal view of morality. As always, the ideological change accepting political liberalism was a result of the Church's own institutional experience: its position internationally had come more and more to resemble that of the U.S. Church (as discussed in chapter 4). In a world in which the Church could not depend on church-state alliance (as was clear from Pius XI's disastrous flirtation with fascism), liberal politics was the best guarantee of the Church's institutional integrity. At least liberalism allowed the Church a certain autonomy on religious matters, even if it required that the Church accept a certain degree of church-state separation.

But the partial ideological incorporation of liberalism had two important consequences. First, it was indeed *partial*; the Church had not simply adopted liberal ideology wholesale. The Church's definition of what parts of society were protected by liberal freedoms did not fully accept secular boundaries. Even though religious practice and freedom were to be protected, the Church still claimed that there were absolute, binding morals; thus governments as well as individuals could not violate fundamental moral prescriptions. The Church was thereby defining some issues as moral that others would define as political. We see in later chapters (especially chapter 5) that this boundary dispute became particularly inflamed around sexual issues because by the mid-twentieth century it was no longer necessarily the case that secular society took for granted the same traditional, patriarchal morality endorsed by the Church. To some degree, then, "morals" became an even higher ideological priority than "faith" (while both remained a higher priority than sociopolitical issues) given that Vatican II accepted the relevance of liberal freedoms to the practice of faith but not to the practice of binding morals.

N.B.⟶

The second consequence of the acceptance of political liberalism was that such a drastic disavowal of the Church's own past could not be papered over easily. The Church does not have means of coercive power, and so its own institutional stability depends on maintaining strong ideological allegiance among Church personnel. But, as we see later, once central doctrines were rejected, it would become difficult to control calls for further change. The council itself seemed to legitimate further change in pronouncing that doctrine could develop with the times.

In regard to the second conciliar innovation, that of reaction against centralization, the problem here was that the council instituted only a partial and ambiguous decentralization, one almost sure to provoke conflict among different sectors of the Church. The council granted new organizational resources to important sectors of the Church, such as bishops and religious, that were an effort to decentralize organizational decision-making. But because the council did not question Rome's control of important ideological matters of faith and morals, it actually gave these lower levels of the power structure little new authority. The result was that some sectors of the Church would fight for more independence, and they had enough organizational autonomy and strength to do so (as we see in chapters 5 and 6).

Third, the opening up to participation in the modern world was again only partial and so sent mixed ideological signals. On the one hand, the council called for a greater Church commitment to promoting social reform. On the other, the council did not question the ideological subordination of sociopolitical issues to faith and morals.

These ideological tensions, of course, emerged as political conflicts over Catholic ideology in the post–Vatican II period, conflicts likely to remain with the Church for some time. To understand how these changes and tensions came about, let us first analyze the origins of the council and then discuss the ideological implications of the acceptance of liberal politics. Following are an analysis of the partial decentralization of the Church power structure and an examination of the council's ambiguous ideological approach to the Church's involvement in the temporal world. The chapter closes with a discussion of the political tensions that emerged from the council's complex ideological legacy.

Vatican II

THE CONTEXT OF THE COUNCIL

The Catholic Church all over the world is still debating and pondering the exact meaning of the Second Vatican Council; most important debates over theology as well as the current boundaries of dissent depend on various interpretations and applications of the conciliar decrees and spirit. It was a monumental event, probably ultimately more important than even Vatican I.

The council is generally regarded in Catholic intellectual circles as an immensely liberating experience; it is difficult to remain part of the mainstream Church and disavow the council, as demonstrated by the 1988 excommunication of French Archbishop Marcel Lefebvre, a contemporary disciple of Pius X's antimodernism. (The proximate cause of Lefebvre's excommunication was his ordination of bishops in defiance of Rome, but his rejection of modern papal authority originated in his rejection of the legitimacy of Vatican II.)[6] There are, of course, many traditionalists, in the Vatican and elsewhere, who insist on a conservative reading of the council, which, we shall see, is quite feasible. But it is nearly impossible for a mainstream Church official or theologian fervently to criticize the council itself.

The council was the most successful individual papal initiative to change the course of the Church's relations to the temporal world since the days of Leo XIII. The history of the council begins with the 1958 papal conclave, which effected a compromise between supporters and critics of the style and policies of Pius XII in electing Angelo Roncalli, who, at just under seventy-seven years, was expected to leave an insignificant legacy.[7] And although one must go back well over a century before John XXIII, the name Roncalli took as pontiff, to find a pope with a shorter reign, and though he died after the completion of only one of the four sessions of the council (in June 1963), John XXIII changed the Church irrevocably.

John apparently struck a cord in his call for an updating of the Church, so that the Church would attempt to carve out a role in the modern world so as to supersede the moralistic withdrawal that began with Pius IX's declaration that he was a "prisoner of the Vatican." That moralistic withdrawal culminated in Pius XII's policy of emphasizing the spiritual supremacy of the Church and of the papacy, implying, in most countries, a suspicion and near-condemnation of the corrupting influence of the material world.[8] John, in contrast, attempted to orient the Church toward dialogue with the secular world. For example, John abandoned his predecessor's policy of complete intransigence toward the Soviet bloc, beginning a controversial "opening to the left."[9] John's call to rejoin the world probably ultimately sparked the council's call for a greater commitment to social justice.

The initial calling of the council met with great surprise and uncertainty,[10] but it provided the occasion, as the pope apparently intended,[11] for the world's bishops to question the extreme centralization of authority, dogmatic rigidity, and rejection of the modern world that the Church had practiced since Vatican I. John declared the mission of the council to be pastoral, rather than dogmatic, and in his opening speech to the council, he rejected the attempts to deal with the modern world by condemning it and identifying the Church only with "the time of former Councils," presumably referring to Vatican I and the Council of Trent.[12] Referring to errors the Church has opposed, John declared, "Frequently she has condemned them with the greatest severity. Nowadays, however, the Spouse of Christ [the Church] prefers to make use of the medicine of mercy rather than that of severity."[13]

Even the very calling of a council of bishops, just months after John assumed leadership of a Church in which the supremacy of the papacy could hardly be more emphasized,[14] almost necessarily meant questioning that centralization. John was implicitly raising as problematic the power and the perspective of the office he held, perhaps reflecting the humility of his personality that still evokes such warmth in the memories of many Catholics. It is likely that the enthusiasm for change at the council resulted partially from a resentment of Pius XII's extreme centralization.[15]

Rome, whether or not aware of the problem, had never fully absorbed the changes ushered in by the decline of the ancien régime. But the council tackled many of these issues head-on.

THE CATHOLIC CHURCH AND LIBERAL POLITICS

The council faced a daunting task in developing what quickly became a major goal of the assembled prelates: to update and reform the Church's approach to the modern world.[16] Up until the council, the view from Rome of the modern world had been one of hostility, especially given the Church's experience with liberalism.

Nevertheless, the defense of ancien régime privileges had become increasingly irrelevant after those privileges were lost. Indeed, in those parts of the world that contributed the vast majority of the participants in Vatican II—Western Europe and North America—liberal church-state relations were probably the best situation the institutional Church could hope for. Without the protection of, and alliance with, the state, autonomy from potentially interfering states was the best guarantee of the Church's strength.

The council, then, rejected the notion that any religion deserved special political privileges. Toward that end, the council, following John's lead, opened wider the door to ecumenism; it accepted the freedom of the individual to choose and practice a faith;[17] and it stated that the Church's role in the world does not lie in participation in temporal government.[18] It even showed a clear preference for liberal democracy.[19] (The hierarchy, however, has continued at times to appeal to the traditional claim that the Church prefers no particular type of government, a claim that is diplomatic but was probably never really true.)[20]

Perhaps because it faced the fact that some countries still recognize Catholicism as the official religion, the council did not condemn the establishment of an official church. Nevertheless, even in cases of establishment, "it is at the same time imperative that the right of all citizens and religious bodies to religious freedom should be recognized and made effective in practice."[21] The council thus attempted to reconcile the diverse histories of national Churches with a modern acceptance of religious freedom.

The very title of one of the most important documents the council produced, "The Pastoral Constitution on the Church in the Modern World" (*Gaudium et Spes*), indicates the importance that reconciliation with the modern world had for the council. The term *constitution* usually applies to a document defining or declaring dogma, not one relating to pastoral concerns. Thus the council was underscoring the importance of the Church's relation to the modern world by using a title normally applying just to fundamental dogma. And in contrast to many papal documents on modern life from Pius IX to Pius XII, Vatican II's relative openness to intellectual and social developments in the modern world is striking (even inviting a dialogue with atheists).[22]

It is interesting to note that the American delegation was a liberalizing force at the council. When we take a closer look at the U.S. Church (in chapter 4), we will see that such positions as the idealization of church-state alliance were embarrassing in the American context. Catholics were accused of valuing subservience to the pope over loyalty to the American system of government, including the separation of church and state. In contrast to its situation at Vatican I, the American episcopacy was an important force at Vatican II. It was a large, vocal delegation (second in size only to Italy's), especially influential in the adoption of *Dignitatis Humanae*, the "Declaration on Religious Freedom." This declaration shows the heavy influence of American theologian and Jesuit John Courtney Murray, although European theologians had also made similar arguments. Murray was probably the first American Catholic theologian of lasting international importance. He was eager to go beyond the traditional view in which "error has no rights," implying that Catholicism is obliged when possible to repress the propaganda of other faiths. He wanted to end forever the view of church-state relations that implied a lack of Catholic respect for democratic institutions.[23]

Thus, as already noted, Vatican II accepted three premises of liberal politics: first, that the Church does not belong in temporal government; second, that liberal democracy is the most preferable form of government; and third, that all individuals have the right to religious freedom. Implicitly, however, the council's acceptance of liberal politics was only partial; for the Church, the realm of issues to be decided in the public give-and-take of politics was more circumscribed than it would be in the view of most politicians operating in a liberal state. Although the Church was not to involve itself in government and recognized that legitimate disagreements about policy might arise, there were some outer limits on policy options defined by binding moral obligations. Thus for example, while governments have a right and duty to concern themselves with overpopulation problems, they are not to promote birth control and abortion.[24]

> Political authority, whether in the community as such or in institutions representing the state, must always be exercised within the limits of morality and on behalf of the dynamically conceived common good....Where public authority oversteps its competence and oppresses the people,...it is lawful for them to defend their own rights and those of their fellow citizens against any abuse of this authority, provided that in so doing they observe the limits imposed by natural law and the gospel.[25]

> Government is not to act in arbitrary fashion or in an unfair spirit of partisanship. Its action is to be controlled by judicial norms which are in conformity with the objective moral order.[26]

[The Church] has the right to pass moral judgments, even on
matters touching the political order, whenever basic personal
rights or the salvation of souls make such judgments necessary.[27]

The Church thus had partly accepted liberalism's drawing of a new
ideological boundary between church and state; the state was not to
enforce or restrict religion. But the Catholic Church did not redraw the
boundary exactly the way liberalism had; for the Church, there was a
moral order that was divine and objective and thus not subject to political
negotiation and compromise. There was, then, a possible tension in that the
Church was accepting that in a liberal political order, it did not belong in
government; and yet it reserved for itself authority over some issues that
liberal governments would not willingly abdicate. We see in later chapters
that this tension became a political and ideological problem for American
bishops, both within the Church and within American society. This was
especially true concerning sexual and reproductive issues; in the nineteenth
century, the Church could assume that most secular elites, and most
governments, accepted the Church's traditional, patriarchal view of sex
and reproduction. But in the twentieth century that was no longer true.

LIBERAL POLITICS AND THE DEVELOPMENT OF DOCTRINE

Popes from Leo XIII to Pius XII had increasingly distinguished the
Church's authority on faith and morals from temporal authority, but not
until Vatican II did the Church attempt the official revision of doctrine
necessary to explain this distinction. Quite aware of the doctrinal complex-
ities involved in legitimating religious freedom, John Courtney Murray
made the following comments on *Dignitatis Humanae*:

It was, of course, the most controversial document of the
whole Council, largely because it raised with sharp emphasis
the issue that lay continually below the surface of all the conciliar debates—the issue of the development of doctrine. The notion of development, not the notion of religious freedom, was
the real sticking-point for many of those who opposed the Declaration even to the end. The course of the development between the *Syllabus of Errors* (1864) and *Dignitatis Humanae
Personae* (1965) still remains to be explained by theologians.
But the Council formally sanctioned the validity of the development itself; and this was a doctrinal event of high importance
for theological thought in many other areas.[28]

Murray's comments make clear that Vatican II, despite the fact that it
failed to modify drastically the Church's power structure or ideological

structure, contained an undercurrent of potentially radical change. The situation of a Church long associated with monarchy and feudalism now attempting to deal with the aftermath of liberalism was indeed a radical challenge. The world was not what it used to be politically and economically, and neither could the Church be. But it was perhaps less difficult to actually join the modern world—the Church had come a long way in a relatively short period of its history—than to admit that it was rejecting former doctrine to do so. Consider comments on such matters in the documents of Vatican I: "Meaning of the sacred dogmas is perpetually to be retained which our Holy Mother the Church has once declared; nor is that meaning ever to be departed from, under the pretense or pretext of a deeper comprehension of them."[29]

But Vatican II broke with the triumphalism of the past and went so far as to acknowledge that, although "the Church has kept safe and handed on the doctrine received from the Master and from the apostles...., there have at times appeared ways of acting [within the Church] which were less in accord with the spirit of the gospel and even opposed to it."[30] The council did not specify the Church's past errors and did not elaborate on the topic in general, but this was one more example in which conciliar pronouncements could be applied to argue the fallibility of the hierarchy's pronouncements.

Perhaps even more important, however, was the discussion of the need for the Church to attend to the "signs of the times," an image invoked by John XXIII in summoning the council and one that entered one of the main council documents.[31] This image, closely related to the notion of the development of doctrine, has been institutionalized within Catholic ideology and perhaps even within Catholic doctrine. Pope Paul VI, for example, invoked it in his major pronouncement of social doctrine, *Populorum Progressio* (1967),[32] and the American bishops cited it in justifying their increased attention to the morality of nuclear policy in the 1980s.[33] By implicitly accepting the principle of the development of doctrine, John and the council had opened up a number of new ideological options, for it is not surprising that many Catholics interpreted the council as a call to "develop" further outdated doctrines in light of the "signs of the times." Since Vatican II, Rome has fought to control such movements. But the council, if it had not accepted this principle, could not easily have legitimated rejecting embarrassing doctrine such as the view that "error has no rights"—that is, that non-Catholics are not entitled to the same degree of religious freedom as Catholics.[34]

DECENTRALIZATION?

As we continue analyzing the changes wrought by Vatican II, it is important to recall that the liberal attack on papal power led not only to a rejection of the modern, liberal world, but also to a greater papal centralization of authority over matters of faith and morals. The Vatican had centralized both in developing a united Catholic opposition to liberalism and, once European states were less involved with the Church, by concentrating decision-making power in Rome, a move that was in part an attack on the autonomy of bishops. Pius IX's most important concerns in the calling of Vatican I were defending his temporal sovereignty and formally declaring the doctrine of papal infallibility. That is, he was concerned simultaneously with the liberal political threat and the centralization of religious authority. It is not surprising, then, that Vatican II would take (at least partial) measures to reverse the Vatican I legacy on both of these matters. Church-state relations and centralization of authority had been linked historically; consequently, Vatican II linked a new view of church-state relations with *de*centralization.

One of the more frequently cited acts of the council was the declaration that the bishops rule the Church collegially with the pope,[35] which served to question the extreme centralization practiced in the period between the two Vatican councils. The concept of collegiality has served as a very important rallying point for those Catholics urging a continuing decentralization of power in the Church—even though in *Lumen Gentium* collegiality clearly refers only to the pope's relations with the episcopacy, not with any other members of the Church.

The attempt to further decentralization beyond the episcopacy does, however, have some precedent in the model of the Church that the council evoked. Catholics who want to continue the process of decentralizing power often cite the vision of the Church community as "the People of God" in which all parts of the Church share in some way "in the one priesthood of Christ."[36] Thus Sister Mary Luke Tobin, the only American sister invited as an official observer of the council proceedings, reflected in 1966: "It is true that the direct application of this doctrine [collegiality] falls on the bishops, but the principle of shared government and of mutual responsibility affects all those exercising any function of leadership in the community of the Church."[37] Liberation theologians join sisters and other Catholics who favor a reform-minded interpretation of Vatican II in citing the images of a collegial People of God responding to the signs of the times.[38]

But if we look more concretely and specifically at the changes that Vatican II legitimated, we can see that the attempt to reverse the centralizing tendencies of the Church since Vatican I was in some ways only partial, more symbolic than substantive. Ultimately, its partial nature would precipitate increasing political conflict in the Church.

Perhaps one of the most sociologically inflammatory methods of democratizing is to claim to decentralize power, and even create new, internally strong institutional organs (such as national episcopal conferences), but in fact to grant these new organs little or no new authority. This allows disgruntled groups the organizational resources by which to become more active, thereby giving them the social space in which to notice that they in fact have been granted little or no power. This is what Vatican II and the subsequent implementation under Pope Paul VI did for both the episcopacy (see also chapter 5) and for religious orders (see chapter 6).[39] The council never named specific realms of authority that the pope must abdicate in this supposedly more decentralized power structure. Thus how much collegiality would truly be a reform was questionable. This was particularly a problem because the council encouraged the formation of episcopal conferences, usually at the national level, that would serve as forums within which to practice collegiality.

Note how the "Dogmatic Constitution of the Church" (*Lumen Gentium*) addresses the relations between pope and bishops:

> Although the individual bishops do not enjoy the prerogative
> of infallibility, they can nevertheless proclaim Christ's doctrine
> infallibly. This is so, even when they are dispersed around the
> world, provided that while maintaining the bond of unity
> among themselves and with Peter's successor, and while teaching authentically on a matter of faith or morals, they concur in
> a single viewpoint as the one which must be held conclusively.[40]

> The infallibility promised to the Church resides also in the
> body of bishops when that body exercises supreme teaching authority with the successor of Peter. To the resultant definition
> the assent of the Church can never be wanting, on account of
> the activity of that same Holy Spirit, whereby the whole flock
> of Christ is preserved and progresses in unity of faith.[41]

In stating that individual bishops do not enjoy infallibility but can "proclaim Christ's doctrine infallibly," the first passage explicitly refers to matters of faith and morals that the Church has already accepted as valid, for there can be only one viewpoint. (Unstated here is that the pope, not the bishops, has the right to define the one proper viewpoint.) The second passage likewise states that although infallibility "resides also in the body of bishops," symbolically a very important statement especially when contrasted with Vatican I, it is defined as impossible for bishops to disagree with the pope on matters within the realm of "supreme teaching authority," that is, faith and morals. An appendix of clarification affixed by the document's drafting commission removes any possibility of interpreting collegiality to mean that the bishops collectively (let alone individually) could ever question a papal pronouncement on faith or morals or define such doctrine independently of the pope.[42]

Likewise, the People of God image of the Church is a symbolic, rather than a substantive, change; it does not question papal control over doctrine of faith and morals. As in the case of collegiality, one might initially interpret substantial change in the statement that the People of God cannot err in matters of belief because of supernatural inspiration. But this is true only "when it shows universal agreement in matters of faith and morals,"[43] again leaving no possibility of independent initiative to the laity on primary issues.

But we should not therefore dismiss the council or even more specifically the particular images of collegiality and the People of God. For example, although in practice the People of God image does not allow independent lay initiative on matters of faith and morals, symbolically it was important, especially because this particular passage speaks of universal agreement among the bishops and the laity, not mentioning the pope. Indeed, we see in later chapters that these concepts haunted Rome in the postconciliar period. Before discussing the political tensions that Vatican II produced, however, let us continue to examine the important ideological innovations of the council.

THE COUNCIL AND IDEOLOGICAL STRUCTURE: SOCIOPOLITICAL ISSUES

Chapter 2 discussed the twin developments of a more subordinate position for (macro) sociopolitical issues and the late nineteenth-century birth of a new doctrinal category covering (but not exhausting) such issues. Social doctrine could emerge not because the Church was granting sociopolitical issues a new importance, but more nearly the opposite: social doctrine became more clearly differentiated from other doctrine because it became more explicitly subordinate, leading a number of popes virtually to ignore it.

Vatican II officially accepted the sharpened boundary subordinating sociopolitical issues to the religious sphere (faith and morals). Rome allows little room for Catholics to dissent on faith and morals; but ideology on sociopolitical issues, while informed by Catholic ethical principles,[44] is much less specific in application. This lack of specificity allows the hierarchy to avoid the difficulties of continually challenging particular state policies, which in many countries would result in charges of Church interference. Because of the lack of specificity, doctrine on sociopolitical issues does not bind individuals to specific beliefs or courses of action.

It is also the case that the lack of specificity is essential in upholding the ideological boundary between binding morals and nonbinding doctrine on sociopolitical matters. The morals are binding, but the Church's view on sociopolitical, macro issues—although inspired by Catholic ethical principles—is not specific enough to be binding. In such a hierarchical institution, where the laity is doctrinally obliged to follow the moral teaching of popes and bishops, it would be very difficult for the papacy and hierarchy to address the validity of specific policies and yet claim that their interpretations are not binding. That is, to argue too specifically that particular policies violate Catholic ethical principles would make problematic the claim that there is a distinction to be made between the Church's moral authority and its authority over sociopolitical matters. The weakness of such an approach, however, is that it may blunt the political effectiveness of social doctrine, a problem examined in more detail in chapter 5.

For now, let us note that the ideological subordination of issues of macropolitics and economics left open some new possibilities for ideological change. Ideology on sociopolitical issues had two interesting qualities: first, it demonstrated that the Church had (originally, involuntarily) gained ideological autonomy from secular powers and thus could take a more critical perspective on sociopolitical issues; second, Catholic ideology was devaluing precisely those types of issues. If one were interested in moving Catholicism to the left of the secular political spectrum, an excellent strategy would be to emphasize the first quality and deemphasize the second. If one instead were interested in retaining papal control and focusing on the strength of the institution (and thus the need to avoid conflicts with states and powerful social classes), it would be more sensible to deemphasize the first quality and emphasize the second. But it would not be easy for anyone in the Church to prevent, or even greatly control, alternative spins given to Catholic ideology on sociopolitical issues, precisely because it was a devalued level of ideology, meaning it was nonbinding doctrine around which there was a fair degree of freedom of movement.[45]

There is, then, a possible tension: as a relatively uncontrolled level of ideology, the content of Catholic ideology on sociopolitical issues could become the basis of a reformist politics. But structurally an important feature of this level of ideology is precisely that it is ideologically devalued.

Vatican II, paradoxically, dealt with this tension by reinforcing the importance of the both the content and the relative ideological priority of social doctrine; it called for an increased commitment to social justice, yet it reaffirmed the ideological dominance of faith and morals.

I noted previously that the very title of *Gaudium et Spes* indicated the importance that the council attached to the Church's relationship to the modern world. The document, which with *Lumen Gentium* was one of the two most important of the council, emphasizes social issues. Through the prominence attached to *Gaudium et Spes* (which is the longest conciliar document), the council sent a clear message that the Church needed to emphasize more strongly its commitment to social change. That message had a broad impact throughout the Church, as we see especially in chapters 5 and 7.

Nevertheless, *Gaudium et Spes* did not specifically change dogma. The document's significance does not lie in any innovative approach to the principles of Catholic social doctrine, which it mostly simply reiterates. And an explanatory note appended by the council explains, in a way consistent with the less definitive nature of ideology on sociopolitical themes, that "interpreters must bear in mind—especially in part two [which deals with specific applications of ideology on sociopolitical issues]—the changeable circumstances which the subject matter, by its very nature, involves."[46]

This document addressed "to the whole of humanity"[47] is actually, therefore, quite consistent with the ideological structure we have encountered. It does not question the basic principle of social doctrine that the Church is not competent in specific matters of policy,[48] other passages noting, however, that policy cannot contradict Catholic morals, which are at a higher level ideologically. *Lumen Gentium* designates the question of political and social change in the temporal world the domain of the laity,[49] the least powerful branch of the Church granted authority over the least spiritually significant activity. Likewise, *Gaudium et Spes* grants freedom of inquiry and of thought to all, clerics and laity, in "those matters in which they enjoy competence," the context clearly excluding fundamental doctrine on which the hierarchy has already pronounced.[50]

It was not clear, then, that the council legitimated the hopes of those most receptive to social doctrine—reformers interested in Catholic alliance with popular social classes and in issues of social reform. Starting with Leo XIII's *Rerum Novarum* in 1891, social doctrine appears to have been an attempt to reach out to the working class. Yet the vagueness of social doctrine allowed the avoidance of any advocacy of particular social changes; remember that Leo XIII, for example, advocated few, if any, legitimate actions that the working class could take to improve its situation. In fact, no matter whether we look to the papacy (chapter 2), the U.S. episcopacy (chapter 4), or the Latin American episcopacy (chapter 7), we see that in the pre–Vatican II period, in practice most prelates were not active promoters of social change. Some even used the principles of social doctrine to justify quite conservative politics. Not only could a bishop or other Catholic emphasize Leo's defense of property or stay at a level of generality and thus avoid the specifics of social change, but he or she could even emphasize the corporatist element of social doctrine to legitimate support of fascism. This latter emphasis emerged, for example, among Chilean fascists and, of course, during the papacy of Pius XI.

It is not, however, altogether surprising that the "council fathers," as some Catholics refer to the participants at Vatican II, would fail to challenge the ideological subordination of sociopolitical issues. There were fundamental reasons social concerns remained subordinate to faith and morals. Eliminating that subordination would involve either elevating ideology on sociopolitical issues to the level of binding doctrine or making faith and morals nonbinding as well. To make sociopolitical doctrine binding would lead to renewed battles with states, and with secular society, that the Church had lost in the nineteenth century. To make all doctrine nonbinding, however, would entail Rome's surrendering most of its remaining authority.

There is, then, no easy solution to the council's ideological ambiguity. Perhaps the only "third" option would be to cease addressing sociopolitical issues at all; but that would entail abandonment of a distinct Catholic tradition and an implicit declaration that Catholicism is of only partial relevance to the modern world. The council's ambiguity, ultimately, reflected the complex nature of the relationship between Catholicism and liberalism in the last century: the ideological restructuring that began under Leo XIII ultimately entailed a forced acceptance of the liberal widening of the separation of church and state. And yet the papacy, somewhat ingeniously, expanded its ideological autonomy and continued to oppose liberalism through its social doctrine. In so doing, it could, in theory, attain the allegiance of Catholics regardless of their political views.

By Vatican II, however, the hierarchy—which at the council rejected a Church role in temporal government and even stated a preference for liberal democracy—had become somewhat of a partner in liberal politics. But it attempted to maintain, or even expand, the Church's sociopolitical importance and independence by calling for renewed commitment to social justice, based on a social doctrine opposed to liberal economics.

THE COUNCIL AND IDEOLOGICAL STRUCTURE: MORAL ISSUES

The complex implications of the council do not stop with macro sociopolitical issues. Nor are such issues the only areas where the Church encounters controversy, in American society and elsewhere. The boundary subordinating such issues was not the only ideological boundary addressed by the council. At Vatican II the hierarchy, perhaps unintentionally, also somewhat separated the significance of moral doctrine from doctrine on the fundamentals of faith because fundamental morals were to bind states, while the specific doctrines of Christian faith were not. That is, the Church reserved the right to condemn state actions that it considered fundamental violations of the "objective moral order," especially "whenever basic personal rights or the salvation of souls" were involved. Thus from the Church's point of view, the state had to respect moral doctrine on individuals and families, while Church views on what we might call more macro sociopolitical issues (equivalent to social doctrine, more or less) did not bind states.

Thus the council created a three-tiered ideological structure: there was first the level of individual and family morality as defined by the hierarchy, which was binding on both individuals and states; second there was faith, binding on Catholic individuals but (because of the newfound acceptance of religious freedom) not a matter of state concern; and then there were sociopolitical issues (embodied especially in social doctrine), a concern of the Church but of lower priority and thus binding on no one.

The twentieth-century ideological reconstruction lessened but did not completely remove the possibilities of church-state conflict. In hindsight, indeed, we can see that Vatican II somewhat invited conflict both between church and state over moral issues and within the Church over the importance of sociopolitical issues. It is interesting to note that the post–Vatican II Catholic Church—doctrinally defined as the church founded by God in the form of Jesus Christ—can become embroiled in state conflict over laws on birth control and abortion ("moral" issues) and yet can accept that states themselves need not be Christian (or perhaps even specifically very religious) or do anything particular to advance Christianity. In the era of religious freedom, "faith" issues pertain only to individual Catholics. From the ultramontane position (favoring papal supremacy and thus opposing liberalism) in the era of Vatican I, that would probably have seemed a strange set of priorities.

I argue that such possibility for state conflict around moral issues—so that, in effect, moral issues became a higher priority than faith issues in terms of what doctrine the hierarchy would attempt to enforce in the temporal sphere—developed because the Church was forced into liberal church-state relationships but not into a liberal view of morality. For both external reasons and internal institutional reasons, the hierarchy is more resistant to liberal views of morality.

Rome was forced out of macro policy issues at a time when issues it would consider individual and family issues, such as sexual orientation and abortion, were significantly less controversial. Not only in the United States, but also in Europe, such moral issues simply were not great areas of conflict in the nineteenth century—the traditional, patriarchal morality the Church taught was not in conflict with dominant secular ideas.[51] When public debates over "moral" issues did arise, Church involvement in the debate did not entail particularly adverse consequences. The Catholic Church was of course a prime opponent in Europe and the United States of early twentieth-century movements to legalize contraception, but here the Church was not arguing a minority position and was not surrounded by hostile adversaries. Those who wanted to liberalize the legal regulation of sexuality and reproduction faced an uphill battle; the Catholic Church's position was consistent with that of many secular elites. Furthermore, such controversies were more sporadic than controversies over the basic Catholic view of church-state relationships. If we look at the American example, Roman views of church-state relations and religious tolerance were controversial long before the Church's position on "moral" issues such as abortion became a central focus of public debate, as it is today.

Since that time, the Catholic Church has had to become an active participant in liberal church-state relationships but not in the lifestyles associated with liberalized morality. Remember from chapter 1 the argument that we can understand ideological change only by understanding the subtleties of the specific, relevant social structures within which ideologies develop. After the papacy lost its partnership with European states—a reality strongly reinforced by Pius XI's disastrous attempt to wed the Church to Italian fascism—the Church operated in a world in which church-state alliance was disappearing. Even in countries whose politics were far from classically liberal, a widened separation of church and state became more common in the nineteenth and twentieth centuries. (Indeed, in the twentieth century, the church has been under attack from the state much more in nonliberal political systems than in liberal ones.) Starting with the loss of the Papal States to the emerging Italian republic, the papacy had no choice but to participate in a liberal church-state relationship: the ancien régime relationship had come to a violent end. By the 1960s, the Catholic Church internationally was more a participant in, than an enemy of, liberal church-state relations. It stood to gain, rather than lose, from liberal political arrangements. A church that cannot have a partnership with the state can maintain its institutional strength best by protecting its autonomy. And so with Vatican II the hierarchy had for the most part come to welcome the new relationship (although this is not true in every national Church, as we see, for example, in chapter 7).

But the pressure on the Church to accept liberal views of morality has not been so strong or direct. Indeed, liberal views of morality have taken much longer to gain acceptance in Western society as a whole than have liberal views of politics. It is questionable whether a live-and-let-live tolerance of homosexuality, for example, could become predominant in American society any time in the near future. Furthermore, once the Church gained a certain amount of institutional freedom, it did not really need to worry about state attacks on the Church over Catholic moral ideology; the institution of liberal church-state relationships to some extent actually helped the Church maintain its nonliberal views of morality. And moral issues remain a central component of Vatican centralization of authority within the Church. There is little reason for Rome suddenly to allow greater tolerance and pluralism on such issues—that is, to decentralize Church ideological control. Or, at least, as the policies of such nineteenth-century popes as Gregory XVI and Pius IX would suggest, we can expect the papacy will put up a good fight before altering its views of what it considers religious issues.

The Post–Vatican II Church: Ideological Change and Political Tensions

Readers may wonder whether the pronouncements of Vatican II really changed the way Rome interacted with the rest of the Church. It is worth reviewing some of the major postconciliar developments that demonstrate that Vatican II's innovations and tensions were not simply matters of abstract theology.

THE INCORPORATION OF LIBERAL POLITICAL PRINCIPLES

For Gregory XVI and Pius IX, liberalism in all its forms was the greatest enemy of the Church. The papacy viewed liberalism as a conspiratorial, pervasive force of secularism that had to be opposed at all costs. (There is somewhat of a pattern in the uncompromising way the pre–Vatican II papacy perceived the evils of its enemies, exemplified in a number of popes' opposition to Freemasonry, Pius X's approach to modernism, and Pius

XII's view of communism.)[52] To some extent this view of liberalism was true of the papacy through at least the reign of Pius XI, who was obviously hostile to liberal politics, and perhaps even Pius XII. But beginning with John XXIII and Vatican II, there was an acceptance of liberal political rights and liberal separation of powers, so that, in effect, the Catholic opposition to liberalism became restricted primarily to a liberal view of morality and economics.

We have already encountered the most important manifestations of the ideological incorporation of liberal political principles—namely, in the rejection of a church role in temporal government, the endorsement of liberal democracy, and the acceptance of freedom of religion. In addition, interestingly, there has been an acceptance within social doctrine of a social and political individualism that is quite novel within an ideology so committed to institutional authority over individual morality and communal notions of social life, as exemplified by the corporatism of social doctrine. Starting with John XXIII's important social encyclical, *Mater et Magistra*, a new emphasis is the notion of human dignity.[53] *Mater et Magistra* was promulgated in 1961; *Pacem in Terris*,[54] promulgated in 1963 after Vatican II had begun (and just about a month before John XXIII died), specifies further a *personal* dignity that is the foundation of human freedom:

> Any well-regulated and productive association of men in society demands the acceptance of one fundamental principle: that each individual man is truly a person. His is a nature, that is, endowed with intelligence and free will. As such he has rights and duties, which together flow as a direct consequence from his nature. These rights and duties are universal and inviolable, and therefore altogether inalienable.[55]

This was perhaps the first time the political views of a pope could have been confused with those of Thomas Jefferson. Of course, Pope John emphasized that the individual has universal, inalienable duties as well as rights, so his is not a discourse solely on individual freedom. But the important point is that since the early 1960s, social doctrine has reflected some degree of political liberalism. Given how long individual popes can be in office and how slowly Catholic doctrine can change, it is difficult to tell whether there has begun a radical transformation of social doctrine. Paul VI did not explicitly emphasize liberal rights as much as did John XXIII; indeed, in *Populorum Progressio*, although referring to economic, not political principles, Paul twice criticized liberalism by name,[56] which by the 1960s could be taken as a strong, pointed objection. John Paul II, however, has made human dignity a major theme of his social pronouncements. (It is worth remembering, incidentally, that the Vatican II document on religious freedom was titled *Dignitatis Humanae*, literally, Human Dignity.)

But even though the post–Vatican II Church's acceptance of political liberalism is quite extensive, reflecting the Church's participation in liberal political structures, the Church is not an important participant in capitalism. Certainly it has investments (the value of which critics often inflate enormously), and perhaps a concern with such investments could ultimately lead the Church to be more favorable toward liberal economics.[57] But the power of the hierarchy is not based on popularity or investments; it is based on the control of faith and morals and on the maintenance of the institution more or less in its current form. The hierarchy, although quite slow to adjust to liberal politics, ultimately has made choices that reflect the political structure of the Church and the political and ideological autonomy that liberal politics forced on it. Again, this is not necessarily a functional, automatic process, as demonstrated by the slow adjustment to liberal politics. It may be that the hierarchy's approach to maintenance of the institution is shortsighted and, in the long run, self-defeating. (Of course, the Catholic Church's track record in maintaining the institution over long periods of time is unsurpassed.) But given the basis of the hierarchy's power within the Church, the acceptance of liberal political principles combined with the continuing opposition to liberal morals and economics is quite understandable.

Contemporary Catholic ideology is partly a product of the historical forces of liberalism. But the ideology itself is only partly liberal; structurally Catholic ideology accepts a boundary between its sphere of authority and that of secular society, reflecting a liberal boundary between church and state as well as church and society. But the Church's specific ideological structure implies a boundary between church and state drawn in a way sure to displease a true, classical liberal, given the approach to issues the Church calls "morals." In a further difference with liberalism, we can look at the content of Catholic ideology, especially its critical view of liberal economics.

POLITICAL TENSIONS IN THE POST–VATICAN II CHURCH

Roman control over moral issues remains a prime concern of the papacy. Thus for example, within a few years after Vatican II, Paul VI reaffirmed the increasingly unpopular, traditional teachings on birth control.[58] Indeed, Paul's widely disobeyed moral policy on birth control has become a symbol of Vatican intransigence and traditionalism. The pope decided against the majority recommendation of a papal advisory commission to modify the Church view of contraception; a number of Catholic theologians had already argued that the ban on contraception was theologically unjustified. Paul VI had been associated with the procollegiality forces at Vatican II; consequently, many active theologians, clergy, and others were surprised by, and objected to, his manner of dealing with this issue. The majority report (as well as the minority report) of the advisory commission was leaked to the press, further undermining Paul's views that contraception was a sin. On 31 July 1968, eighty-seven Catholics, including some prominent (ordained) theologians, dissented from the teaching in a statement published in the *New York Times*. The list of signers grew as the statement later appeared in additional publications. Catholic laity as well as a large number of Catholic clergy in the United States and elsewhere widely disregard *Humanae Vitae*, Paul's encyclical on birth control.[59] Nevertheless, birth control remains a high priority within Catholic ideological structure; dissent can mean serious sanctions. Thus for example, there has been relatively little public objection to this teaching among Church personnel in recent years.

The insistence that moral doctrine remains binding has meant that church-state conflicts increasingly concern "moral" issues. American bishops, for example, are structurally constrained to emphasize the binding, inflexible nature of moral doctrine. But when American bishops speak to moral issues that have become politicized in American society, they participate in two social structures—the American polity and the Catholic Church—that draw conflicting boundaries between church and state. The Catholic hierarchy claims that abortion, for example, is a moral, not a political, issue.

Of course, in addition to moral issues, bishops and other Catholics are also constrained to follow doctrine on faith, and Rome resists modification of any traditional Church religious beliefs, institutional structures, and so on.[60] But issues of faith are unlikely to lead to external conflicts. First, without acceptance of at least some basic doctrines of faith, why remain a Catholic? Of course, as we see especially in chapter 6, some aspects of faith, such as belief in the legitimacy of the Church's hierarchical structure, have become objects of dispute for some parts of the Church. But even when there are such disputes, they are likely to remain conflicts solely within the Church; since Vatican II's acceptance of religious freedom, the Church has had little reason to make faith issues controversial in the temporal world.

The priority of sociopolitical issues has also been a source of internal conflict. To see why, let us first note the path of social doctrine since Vatican II. Within social doctrine, there remains to a significant extent the legacy of the romanticization of the social order of medieval Christendom. Notably, even though some Catholics (e.g., in Latin America) have revised and extended Catholic social doctrine to argue an ethical need to oppose exploitative, repressive states, the papacy has continued to see states as, ideally, paternalistic protectors of society. States are to stand above social conflict, although there does seem to be increasing recognition of the dangers of too much centralization of power in the state.[61] In fact, with *Gaudium et Spes* and Paul VI's *Populorum Progressio*, the Church applied its neofeudal view of states to the international order—in a way that some might consider quite innovative—placing high hopes on the ability of the United Nations to resolve disagreements in a cooperative, paternalistic way.[62] Papal social doctrine thus continues to insist implicitly that members of the Church should not be involved in political conflict; social doctrine treats such conflict as unfortunate but not necessary.

As I have noted, the suspicions of liberal economics remain. If anything, under Paul VI social doctrine became even more critical of capitalism. Parts of the influential encyclical *Populorum Progressio* argued that the poverty of the developing world was the result of international capitalist dominance. Indeed, *Gaudium et Spes* and *Populorum Progressio* were central inspirations for Latin American proponents of liberation theology (discussed in chapter 7).

John Paul II's pronouncements have not inspired as much social radicalism as did *Populorum Progressio*, but to the consternation of Catholics who would like to see the same "conservatism" in his social pronouncements as his moral pronouncements, he very much continues the anticapitalist tradition of Leo XIII, Pius XI, John XXIII (in *Mater et Magistra*), and Paul VI.[63]

A focus, then, on the content of social doctrine could easily be taken to imply that active critique of the injustices of capitalism is very Catholic. Liberation Catholics, for example, see themselves as faithful followers of Vatican II and of *Populorum Progressio* as well as all the Church's social teaching. They can easily argue that doctrine has developed in accordance with the signs of the times; indeed, while the hierarchy may proclaim that doctrine on faith and morals is timeless, it does not say the same about social doctrine.

Nevertheless, John Paul II has shown exceptional interest in enforcing the ideological priority of faith and morals over sociopolitical issues. His 1988 encyclical, *Sollicitudo Rei Socialis*, certainly is strongly anti-laissez-faire. But it is also quite clear in asserting that the Church does not prefer particular political or economic systems and does not propose technical, policy solutions to social problems; it provides a general ethical perspective. The discussion here is particularly interesting because it explicitly insists that the Church's lack of preference for particular political and economic systems is contingent on the Church being "allowed the room she needs to exercise her ministry in the world."[64] That is, the ideological priorities and Church autonomy from secular powers are intimately related, reflecting the history of Church relations with liberalism.

John Paul II has insisted that, in conformity with the Code of Canon Law, Church personnel not hold political office. Such a prohibition, which John Paul seems to apply reasonably consistently, would follow from the Vatican II declaration that the Church does not belong in temporal government. We have seen that *Lumen Gentium* designated temporal government to be the domain of the laity. (Moral issues are also relevant here, however; John Paul has been especially adamant on this issue when there is a question of violation of Catholic moral doctrine—for example, when Church personnel administer public programs that involve funding for abortions in the United States.)[65]

There are places where we might question the consistency of John Paul's separation of religion from politics—for example, in his apparent support for priests' involvement in Solidarity activism in Poland in the early 1980s. Interestingly, however, on one occasion when the communist government became particularly distressed over comments the pope made in support of Solidarity during his 1983 visit to Poland, the Vatican press secretary blamed Western journalists for the politicization of the pope's "exclusively religious and moral" visit. Indeed, the general tenor of John Paul's papacy has been an insistence on religious piety and moral fundamentals that transcend the specifics of politics. The Church is not competent to address those specifics.[66]

More important than the interpretations of one pope, however, are inherent tensions in the place of sociopolitical issues in Catholic ideological structure itself. To set the stage for the chapters that follow, let us review this complex, ambiguous legacy of Vatican II.

We have examined a number of sources of tension that emerged from the council. First, in accepting political liberalism, the council reserved for the Church the right to condemn actions and beliefs that it considers "moral" violations, even though others might consider some such actions and beliefs "political." Second, it legitimated a view that doctrine can develop, or evolve, according to the "signs of the times." Third, it legitimated a decentralization of the Church power structure and gave new organizational resources to some sectors of the Church. But it did not institute a true ideological decentralization. In fact, as we saw, with the fourth source of tension—the call for greater commitment to social reform without a questioning of the ideological subordination of sociopolitical issues—the council upheld the ideological structure that had begun to emerge with Pope Leo XIII. But there was the problem that the council practically invited Catholic social activists to challenge the hierarchy of ideological priorities.

I noted in the beginning of this chapter that a number of important changes in the Church have been historically connected. We saw in chapter 2 that the Church's loss of direct temporal power, the papal centralization of authority over faith and morals, a sharpened ideological boundary separating sociopolitical issues from faith and morals, and the birth of modern social doctrine were all intricately connected developments. As a result, the redefinition of church-state relations, the questioning of the centralization of power, and the attempt to increase the Church's commitment to social reform have all been intimately connected as well.

That partial decentralization has greatly encouraged ideological challenges is a primary topic of chapters 5 and 6. Sometimes such challenges involve questioning the structure of ideological priorities; sometimes they involve questioning the legitimacy of the Church power structure. American bishops, for example, have encountered some problems with the boundary between morals and politics. Can one increasingly specify social doctrine without making it equivalent in importance to moral doctrine? Alternatively, can one insist on the right to disagree on political opinions but declare that certain moral issues, such as abortion, are not within the realm of pluralist politics?

The conciliar innovation of appealing to the signs of the times can make it difficult for Rome to control emphases on sociopolitical issues as well as calls for ideological reform in general. At the time of the council there were criticisms that the appeal to "the signs of the times" was quite vague: which signs were to be significant? Who would identify these signs?[67] Yet it is nearly impossible for Rome, or anyone else in the Church, to disavow this ambiguous conciliar appeal. It is no accident that an ambiguous concept would be the center of political conflict in the Church: political conflict usually surrounds ideological ambiguity precisely because ambiguity means lack of clear structural constraints. In this case, the conflict involves the distribution of power in the Church and the Church's social mission. Let us now turn to a detailed study of the U.S. Church to understand the history of such conflict.

4 Ideological Boundaries in a Minority Church

U.S. bishops, sisters, and laity in the contemporary world sometimes complain that Rome cannot understand the traditions of American Catholicism and American culture. Since Vatican II, given that conciliar documents made references to a greater respect for cultural divergence, African and other Church leaders have also stressed the importance and validity of religious traditions specific to particular cultures. But in the United States such assertions have a particularly long history; they are also especially significant in Church history because through the Second Vatican Council, the American hierarchy (as we saw in chapter 3) helped bring Catholic doctrine closer to the American view of Catholicism.

While there is and always has been diversity within U.S. Catholicism, there has also been a clear tendency for American Catholicism, in comparison to most European national Churches, to emphasize church-state separation and a greater tolerance of other religions. Pope Leo XIII condemned such "Americanism," and Rome exerted increased control over the U.S. Church earlier this century, but tensions between Rome and the U.S. episcopacy over church-state issues and religious freedom persisted.

The current chapter traces the development of that distinctively American Catholicism, especially as espoused by the American episcopacy. Catholicism in the United States developed quite differently than it did in Europe. In the United States, Catholicism had never been a majority religion, had never experienced church-state alliance, and had always had a fairly positive experience with a wide separation of church and state.

Neither dependent on nor restrained by state entanglements, the U.S. Church managed to build a strong organization with close religious ties to its immigrant, working-class laity.

The particular experience of the pre–Vatican II U.S. Church made American bishops significantly more receptive than was the papacy to the ideological reconstruction that began to take form under Leo XIII. That included a strong commitment to a hierarchical view of the Church where issues of faith and morals were concerned as well as a view that church-state separation and religious toleration were in the interest of the Church as long as state and society respected fundamental moral principles. The U.S. bishops, as a group at a high level of the power structure, saw the Church in strictly hierarchical terms, but the circumstances of the Church in the United States led them to see their ideological authority in terms of a narrower range of issues than did the European Church. They never shared secular power and so never absorbed the content of secular ideologies; instead, they were primarily interested in autonomy to lead what to outsiders seemed a peculiar religious institution. American Catholics in fact experienced a good deal of discrimination, which led U.S. bishops to avoid any behavior that might suggest political interference. They emphasized a strong, if amorphous, patriotism, to prove their loyalty and prevent inflammation of further discrimination. At times, protecting the security and independence of their own national Church required deemphasis of ideological themes popular in European Catholicism, especially the Vatican I perspective on church-state relations.

Unlike (as we see in chapter 7) the Latin American episcopacy, the U.S. bishops did not have the luxury of subordinating concerns about the internal strength of the institution to an emphasis on the Church's links with the state and powerful secular groups. As a result, the Church in the United States devoted itself to internal organizational concerns, developing a rich institutional network of schools and hospitals, ministering to and supported by a devout laity. As we see in chapter 5, this institutional strength allowed American bishops to take new directions after Vatican II once their insecurity as leaders of a minority church had faded.

The U.S. Church concerned itself with maintaining close relations with the average Catholic layperson more than was true in Europe and Latin America. The American hierarchy's bonds to its laity, however, were centered strictly on religious issues. American bishops did not want to take sociopolitical positions that would alienate large numbers of the laity (a generally less central concern of the European and Latin American hierarchies), but that did not mean that they avidly promoted the laity's political causes. Instead, they preferred to avoid sociopolitical issues as much as possible. Let us now examine the history of the U.S. Church in greater detail.[1]

An Immigrant Church, a Minority Church

The Catholic Church in the United States, with Baltimore as its ecclesiastical center, began as a tiny, unassertive minority. Despite some definite suspicions that Catholics were loyal to a foreign power,[2] through the early nineteenth century the Church fit relatively easily into American society as it was really too small to be of much concern to anyone else. But the waves of nineteenth- and twentieth-century immigration radically altered the composition and experiences of the Church here. Catholics became much more numerous, and American Catholicism became almost exclusively a religion of poor farmers and, especially, proletarians. In contrast to the aristocratic episcopacies more common in Europe, even U.S. bishops usually came from such backgrounds, especially that of Irish-American, conservative, working-class Catholicism. The unprivileged background of U.S. bishops held true into the twentieth century.[3]

The immigrant, lower-class Catholics in this country experienced sporadic nativist attacks (e.g., anti-Catholic riots and burnings of churches) into the early twentieth century, sometimes inspired by groups such as the Know-Nothings and the Ku Klux Klan. Obviously the vast majority of Catholics never experienced violent bigotry personally, but the American episcopacy and Catholics in general were aware that in some respects they were not fully welcome, not fully trusted as loyal Americans (both because of their religion and because of their status as recent immigrants). One of the most common accusations was that they could not be true patriots because their allegiance to a foreign pope necessarily took precedence over their allegiance to the United States.[4]

Because of the threat of discrimination, the papacy's views on church-state relations were problematic for the U.S. Church. Vatican I's endorsement of church-state alliance and insistence on papal infallibility were exactly the kind of doctrines that could fuel accusations that Catholics were bound to follow Rome blindly in an opposition to American democracy and religious freedom. Within the U.S. episcopacy, there was a tension between loyalty to Rome—which, after all, was an essential component of the religion—and the ideological difficulties that Rome presented. The result was that the American episcopacy was doctrinally conservative on faith and morals issues and thus loyal to the pope, with the exception that they avoided commitment on doctrine directly or indirectly related to church-state relations. Rome occasionally took the U.S. episcopacy to task for its independent thinking on such matters.

There were a number of reasons U.S. bishops would diverge ideologically from the papacy on issues of church-state relations and religious tolerance (freedom of worship). First, it could only be to the U.S. Church's disadvantage to claim that the Church deserved a role in secular politics and state policy. Whereas Rome was interested in reclaiming a lost kingdom and special privileges in Catholic Europe, the U.S. bishops were primarily interested in the survival of their national Church.[5]

Second, the Catholic Church in the United States never encountered the kind of heated political disputes with the state itself that had led the papacy and much of the European episcopacy to declare liberalism the enemy. A minority church that experienced some discrimination indeed benefited from the particular separation of church and state found in the U.S. political system, a separation much wider than that which existed in Europe. A reversal of separation would mean an officially Protestant United States, while the constitutional system protected the Catholic minority and allowed them to practice their religion mostly free from interference. And so American bishops were quite conscious of the advantages of the First Amendment, even though Pope Leo XIII specifically cautioned them against believing that separation was the most desirable church-state relationship.

Third, the U.S. Church was quite isolated from the mainstream, as well as from the controversies of European theology and religious politics. Until the second third of this century at least, the U.S. Church was a theological backwater, relatively ignorant of innovative Catholic intellectual currents. The hierarchy, clergy, and religious found the assimilation of immigrants into, and the simultaneous building of, the quickly growing American Church plenty to occupy them. A relatively young national Church had not developed its own theological traditions and did not have the luxury of developing scholarly theological concerns. It was distant from the concerns of European Catholic ideology.

Fourth, the foregoing factors combined with a general process of maneuvering for limited autonomy that is part of the politics of any organization. Bishops command a great deal of power in the Church because they are monarchs of their own dioceses. But ties to Rome constitute both the source of that power and restrictions on it (in that power structures, like all social structures, are simultaneously enabling and constraining). In most regions of the world, there are bishops who emphasize strong ties to Rome and others who maneuver for independence. In the United States, while there was no questioning of fundamental doctrine outside of church-state issues and religious tolerance, the balance leaned toward attempts to keep Rome at arm's length. And the U.S. bishops had a fairly strong collective identity, the result, in part, of their distance from European Catholicism and their common experience of having to deal with uncomfortable Roman doctrine. A collegiality fostered by Americanism persisted to some degree in the entire period before Vatican II, although it was stronger after that council and did periodically weaken, given occasionally strong ethnic divisions, regional divisions, a period of tightening Roman control over the U.S. Church in the early twentieth century, and disagreements over that Romanization. American bishops tried to keep under their control decisions about such matters as discipline in the American Church, and they generally attempted to prevent having Vatican representatives resident in the United States.[6]

An important example of the contrast between the American Church and the Vatican, or European Catholicism in general, is the First Vatican Council of 1869–1870. Many U.S. bishops attempted to be excused from attendance at Vatican I; the council did not seem to them a higher priority than administration of their dioceses. Then, once there, many were without a clue what to expect, quite unaware of the urgency of the infallibility issue for many Europeans, or of other theological debates. Very few Americans spoke at the council rostrum.[7] Likewise, the American bishops, though they knew that the Vatican's church-state doctrines caused them problems, may have been so distant from Vatican ideology that they did not generally understand until the 1890s the connection between those doctrines and the papacy's concern about temporal sovereignty over Rome.[8]

Vatican I demonstrated not only the ideological isolation of the U.S. Church, but also the divergence between its and Rome's political experience with church-state relations. Thus U.S. bishops, although not a powerful presence at the council, were in general quite anxious about the infallibility dogma, sure that it would cause them great problems in their home country. While respecting the papacy, they saw the authority of the Church based more in the episcopacy than Pius IX's vision of the Church would allow. A good number of American bishops were not present at the final vote so as not to have to vote against the pope, and one of two bishops who actually did cast a negative vote was an American. American bishops, and American Catholics in general, also showed little sympathy for the papacy's loss of its temporal kingdom, to the chagrin of the Vatican.[9]

Yet the U.S. bishops were ideologically selective in their approach to papal doctrine; they did not reject the authority of the papacy as a whole, and they never questioned the hierarchical structure of the Church domestically or internationally.[10] For example, within the U.S. Church itself,

American bishops were quite intolerant of dissension from their priests; Rome, in response to the many complaints that the Vatican received from American priests about their bishops' authoritarianism, even chastised U.S. bishops for dealing inequitably with priests.[11] But U.S. bishops' respect for Church hierarchy included acceptance of their own subordination to Rome. The Irish-American Catholicism of much of the U.S. episcopacy had a tradition of papal loyalty, as did the Catholicism of the second largest Catholic immigrant group, German-Americans. And such loyalty was probably also a reaction to anti-Catholic hostility. Just as nineteenth-century liberal and socialist anticlericalism had placed European episcopacies in the situation of greater dependence on the papacy for protection, the American Church identified with Rome when more locally it did not feel completely at home. Pre–Vatican II American Catholicism never substantially, actively challenged the authority of the Vatican in any areas but sought instead to ignore and work around a troublesome doctrine. There were in the U.S. episcopacy traditionalists opposed to the more openly pro-American (and pro–church-state separation) faction. But ideologically most U.S. bishops could not swallow the papal perspective on church-state alliance, given how troublesome adherence to such doctrine would be to the American Church.

Rather than rejecting Roman authority as a whole, then, U.S. bishops were receptive to an ideological boundary separating faith and morals from temporal affairs far earlier than was the European Church (as early as the first American bishop in the late eighteenth century).[12] Faith and morals were to remain authoritative doctrine defined and enforced by the Church hierarchy but in a way that was to avoid conflict with states and powerful (non-Catholic) social groups. The U.S. Church appreciated its autonomy from the state, whereas the Vatican had not yet embraced the advantages. The American Church was hesitant to take actions that might appear to be interference in politics, but a liberal political context had only minor effect on its authoritarian approach to religious issues within its own institutional structure.

It is important to note that simply because the U.S. bishops diverged ideologically from Rome, it does not follow that they would instead adopt the content of secular political and economic ideologies. U.S. bishops simply did not care much about economic and political issues that had no direct bearing on their ability to build and administer the Church. That is, sociopolitical issues were so far from their central religious concerns that they would have liked to see such issues essentially excluded from Catholic ideological structure. More important to them than the content of any sociopolitical opinions was the subordination of such issues to religious concerns. Unlike in parts of Europe and in Latin America (as we see in chapter 7), the U.S. Church was not ideologically influenced by powerful secular groups—because those groups contained few Catholics—and was not involved in sociopolitical issues in general. The U.S. Church was composed of poor, working-class immigrants; the hierarchy aimed solely to be autonomous of the state and of powerful secular forces and thus did not absorb the content of their ideologies. Within the international Church, some of the content of the sociopolitical views of the European hierarchy could indeed be problematic for the U.S. episcopacy, which wanted to avoid alienating the working-class laity. Generally, then, the hierarchy tried to avoid sociopolitical content altogether.

It is reasonable to argue that the U.S. Church actually grew stronger than many of the European and Latin American national Churches as a result of its unprivileged position in society. We see in chapter 7 that the Latin American Church has historically suffered weak ties to the laity because it both depended on and was restricted by its ties to the Iberian empires and then to authoritarian states as well as to ruling elites. The U.S. Church, which did not have the luxury of such alliances, instead devoted its energies to such goals as the founding of new parishes and the establishment of systems of Catholic schools and hospitals, services that immigrant Catholics wanted and needed.[13]

In such endeavors, the American Catholic Church strengthened itself and thus its autonomy, or even isolation, from the state and larger society, living somewhat in a ghetto subculture until at least World War II. Such a subculture was the result not only of discrimination, but also of the Church's own concern with keeping its members and their children part of the Church. Separate schools, for example, had been a major concern since the Third Plenary Council, an official, national meeting of the episcopacy in 1884. The emphasis on Catholic schools in this country and the founding of new parishes were perhaps the major preoccupation of the Church in the late nineteenth century and through much of the twentieth. The large majority of Catholic sisters have worked as schoolteachers. The schools contributed greatly to lay identification with the Church and probably helped lessen the impact of secular ideologies on Catholics.

The U.S. Church greatly valued its autonomy and the institutional benefits of its networks of parishes and schools. The devotion to Catholic schools was most responsible for the few clear, concrete church-state conflicts that actually emerged. The U.S. episcopacy fought a law in Oregon to ban such schools in the 1920s, and it continually provoked charges of violating church-state separation in its attempts to receive local government support of Catholic education.[14] We see in chapter 5 that partial public funding of Catholic schools remains a concern of U.S. bishops and an issue where they feel they have received an unfair deal.

(The American perspective on the benefits of church-state separation for the Catholic Church in the United States, however, led some bishops initially to oppose setting up separate Catholic schools. The prominent archbishop John Ireland, who headed the diocese of St. Paul, Minnesota, from 1884 until his death in 1918, was particularly eager to extol the virtues of the public schools. Ireland was a proponent of cooperative arrangements with public authorities in the use of buildings, with the state responsible for most of the child's education and religious instruction taking place after regular school hours. The controversy over Archbishop Ireland's views on schools in the 1890s was just one of many incidents that raised Vatican suspicions about his orthodoxy.)[15]

Naturally such schools as well as the tendency of Catholics to cluster in urban areas contributed to the development of an American Catholic subculture.[16] A national Church such as that of Italy, where Catholics were a majority, could of course emphasize Catholic schools and social groups and discourage intermarriage without removing Catholics from the larger culture. But the existence of an American Catholic subculture meant that those heavily involved in the Church were socially rather distant from larger secular ideologies. The effects of their existing in a subculture would be most pronounced on those most involved in the institutional Church—that is, on bishops more than laity. Lay Catholics could be affected by secular ideologies in the workplace and at home more than would bishops or even priests and sisters, whose activity and ideology would be more wholly oriented toward the Church.

The worldview of American bishops, then, was almost completely focused on the institutional Church in the United States. While this emphasis contributed to the growth and strengthening of the institution, it also led to an important conflict with Rome. I have already mentioned that there was some tension between loyalty to Rome and the ideological difficulties that papal doctrine presented. This tension was perhaps most clear at Vatican I, where the U.S. delegation initially opposed the declaration of papal infallibility. But once the delegates returned home, even the opponents remained loyal to this newly defined dogma thrust on them by a higher level of the Church power structure.[17] It probably helped that, even though papal ideology as a whole had yet to subordinate sociopolitical issues strongly to faith and morals, the dogma of infallibility per se applied only to faith and morals.[18] But the U.S. episcopacy, and U.S. Church in general, never showed inclination to support the papacy's temporal claims—quite the contrary. Because differences in ideology are tied to differences in power, this tension led to Roman attempts to assert its own authority by disciplining the U.S. Church.

This process began in the late nineteenth century, when the Vatican made moves toward bringing the American Church closer into its orbit, reflecting the increased centralization of religious authority in the Church that began with Vatican I. It is true that this was not a complete crackdown on the U.S. Church; the Vatican did not concern itself enough with America to make U.S. Catholic dissent a central concern.[19] Through at least the papacy of Pius XII, the Vatican clearly thought of the Church mostly in terms of Europe, although the financial contributions and size of the American Church made it increasingly important in this century.[20] But Pope Leo XIII did send an apostolic delegate (a resident papal representative) to the United States for the first time in 1892, a move resented by a number of American bishops.[21]

Nevertheless, the establishment of a permanent papal delegation was the beginning of increased Roman control over the American Church.[22] By the end of the decade, the papal delegate (Francesco Satolli and after 1897, his successor, Sebastian Martinelli) and the Vatican as a whole had come to exert some mild discipline on those parts of the U.S. Church that emphasized independence from Rome.[23] For example, Satolli showed concern about bishops participating in ecumenical efforts. A tenet of pre–Vatican II Roman faith was that only Catholicism held religious truth; to participate with other denominations could be an erroneous, implicit recognition of partial truth in their religions.[24]

In 1895, Leo XIII addressed an encyclical, *Longinqua*, to the U.S. Church.[25] Leo expressed positive evaluations of the general health of the U.S. Church, but he also implicitly rebuked those bishops who had opposed the establishment of an apostolic delegate.[26] Some of his concerns, such as those about marriage and divorce, could have applied anywhere, but his comment that Catholics in general, especially workers, needed to avoid association with non-Catholics certainly was especially ominous for American bishops attempting not to alienate their laity or non-Catholics. Furthermore, Leo reiterated orthodox church-state doctrine, after first acknowledging that the U.S. Church benefited from "the equity of the laws" of "the well-ordered Republic":

> For the Church amongst you, unopposed by the Constitution
> and government of your nation, fettered by no hostile legisla-
> tion, protected against violence by the common laws and the
> impartiality of the tribunals, is free to live and act without hin-
> drance. Yet, though all this is true, it would be very erroneous
> to draw the conclusion that in America is to be sought the type

of the most desirable status of the Church, or that it would be universally lawful or expedient for State and Church to be, as in America, dissevered and divorced.... [The U.S. Church] would bring forth more abundant fruits if, in addition to liberty, she enjoyed the favor of the laws and the patronage of the public authority.[27]

This interesting statement demonstrates that Leo could not appreciate the relationship between religious liberty and church-state separation, nor could he appreciate the realities and necessities of national churches that compose a religious minority. In the United States, church-state union would have meant the establishment of an official *Protestant* religion. In response to *Longinqua*, Archbishop Ireland, one of the best-known American bishops at home and abroad, lamented: "That unfortunate allusion to Church & State cannot be explained to Americans."[28]

The U.S. bishops' difficulties with papal ideology did not stop with *Longinqua*; they worsened with the Americanism controversy, which concerned a body of doctrines that Leo condemned in 1899. In general, the Americanist outlook was one full of optimism about the health of the Catholic Church under the American political system. Thus there was little sympathy for papal claims of temporal sovereignty. Americanism, then, may be described as a position in favor of church-state separation along the U.S. model. Even though historians have argued that Americanism was not really a clear body of specific principles, Archbishop Ireland and a few American allies with positions in Rome, whether because of ignorance or boldness, showed open disregard for the Vatican's temporal claims.[29]

Americanism was more ecumenical than European Catholic positions because a need to get along with the Protestant majority and an optimistic evangelical attitude emphasized a slow and tolerant approach toward convincing non-Catholics of the validity of Catholic doctrine.[30] Traditionalists charged that such an approach illegitimately compromised doctrinal integrity.[31] In Rome's eyes, Americanists looked dangerously like liberal European Catholics, with whom the Americans did indeed cultivate alliances.

When Leo condemned Americanism in 1899, exactly which beliefs were included was a source of controversy after the condemnation. In his statement, Leo implicitly recognized a distinction between "religious" and "political" Americanism, a distinction the archbishop of Baltimore, Cardinal James Gibbons, among others, had made to a sympathetic curial official. Leo and Gibbons probably did not have exactly the same distinction in mind, but "political Americanism" apparently meant a pragmatic acceptance of the general situation of the U.S. Church, including its church-state relations and relations with non-Catholics, without any doctrinal implications. "Religious Americanism," however, meant a questioning of the hierarchical structure of the Church and of official doctrine on freedom of religion and church-state relations.[32] The defense of Americanism thus included an appeal to some sort of ideological boundary between religious belief and practical politics, and Leo was at least partly persuaded.

American bishops were never schismatic, and so they never openly attacked Roman doctrine the way some European liberal Catholics did. But at the level of moderate advocacy of a liberalization of views of church-state separation, Americanism is interesting because such advocacy was more mainstream in the United States than in Europe. It also is interesting to note that Americanism resembled modernism in emphasizing the need for the Church to pragmatically adjust to the world as well as emphasizing a more immanent view of God's presence through the Holy Ghost,[33] the third and generally least emphasized part of the Trinity. Thus Leo XIII's condemnation of Americanism, a prelude to Pius X's condemnation of modernism, indicated a similar conservatism and theological authoritarianism despite important differences between the two popes.

Leo did not claim that any particular American prelates held to Americanism; his style was not as uncompromising as that of Pius X, who was eager to exorcise modernism by ruining scores of ecclesiastical careers. But the Americanist point of view was generally associated with the more proassimilation and reforming sector of the American clergy, particularly Archbishop Ireland.[34] Even with the distinction between religious and political Americanism, after the controversy the Vatican demonstrated increased suspicion of American bishops' views on papal temporal sovereignty, religious liberty, and ecumenicism.[35] It is true the U.S. Church was too isolated to really be part of European modernism, and the condemnation of Americanism was ambiguous. But the two condemnations together stifled for decades what little theological originality had begun to emerge in American Catholicism in the late nineteenth century in the thought of such distinctively American Catholics as the convert priest Isaac Hecker, inspiration for many Americanist ideas.[36]

The fear of being labeled a dissenter or heretic thus reinforced the basic theological conservatism of the U.S. Church. It appears that Vatican suspicions about Archbishop John Ireland's Americanist views pressured him to declare in favor of papal sovereignty over the city of Rome and may have cost him elevation to the status of cardinal.[37] But the evidence does not suggest that U.S. prelates abandoned their views in favor of church-state separation; more likely, they simply became more discreet in addressing the matter. It does seem that the collegial identity that American bishops possessed before the Americanism controversy weakened a bit as Rome instituted greater control over the U.S. episcopacy in the earlier twentieth century.[38] But even papal discipline could not overcome the fact that for the U.S. Church, Americanism was a political necessity.

In the twentieth century, then, the U.S. Church on the one hand retained its distinctive character and on the other did come increasingly within the Roman orbit. The Vatican became more vigilant in appointing American bishops sympathetic to increased Romanization of the U.S. Church, which meant more frequently passing over candidates recommended by American bishops and priests. A prime example was the appointment of William O'Connell to be archbishop of Boston in 1906. (In 1911, Pius X made O'Connell a cardinal, once again passing over John Ireland.) O'Connell became a prime exponent of Roman control. But Romanization of the U.S. Church did not quite continue the momentum begun under the papacies of Leo XIII and Pius X.[39] It is true that the Americanism controversy and its aftermath partly weakened the autonomy of the American Church: as I have already noted, a budding theological originality disappeared for decades, and collegiality among American bishops was temporarily weakened. Nevertheless, the other side of Roman interest in the U.S. Church was an increased importance of the American Church to Rome, which coincided with a slow improvement in the status of the Church in American society. The American Church came to be less of a distant oddity among the branches of the Catholic Church internationally, and the episcopacy came to participate more in American society. In the following decades, some American cardinals would be important avenues of communication between Rome and the U.S. government, and the bishops would rebuild their collegiality by testing the waters of increased involvement in American society. Before detailing these developments, we must first examine the history of the American episcopal perspective on U.S. society.

The U.S. Bishops and Sociopolitical Issues

We have already seen that to avoid domestic controversy, it was important for the U.S. Church to avoid the appearance of interfering in secular matters. Only on an issue that was central to its task of incorporating immigrant Catholics into the institution, that is, the building of Catholic schools, did it risk state conflict. U.S. bishops' primary concern was the strength and growth of the American Church.

For most of its history, then, issues of social reform were not important concerns in themselves. Nevertheless, there was a negative concern with such issues in the sense that the American episcopacy generally wanted to avoid actions that would alienate its own laity.[40] On social issues, as with church-state issues, the authority of U.S. bishops—whose laity consisted not of the powerful and wealthy, but of farmers and the working class—depended on preventing the strict application of Roman perspectives to the American context. And on issues of social doctrine, American bishops did not have to silently dissent (as they did on church-state issues) but could maneuver for influence in Rome.

In 1887, the actions of Cardinal James Gibbons of Baltimore, the unofficial primate of the American Church,[41] were instrumental in preventing the Vatican from condemning the Knights of Labor, a majority of whose members were Catholic. The basis of the consideration of condemnation was the allegedly socialist tendencies and prohibited secret-society characteristics of the Knights. The Vatican saw all secret societies as variants of Freemasonry, which (as noted in chapter 3) popes condemned as a vast conspiracy out to destroy the Church. Leo XIII, pope at the time of the proposed condemnation of the Knights of Labor, was particularly concerned with Freemasonry. Leo, a prolific encyclical writer in general, devoted several encyclicals entirely to the Freemasons.[42]

At the time, of course, when the state very much sided with employers, unions had little option but to attempt to hide their organizing from employers. That the Vatican under Leo XIII could consider condemning the fairly moderate Knights of Labor just four years before *Rerum Novarum* is an example of how Catholic doctrine of the time did not really sanction any specific prolabor practices. At the time of Gibbons's intervention, the Vatican had already condemned the activity of the Knights in the province of Quebec, at the urging of Quebec's ultraconservative Archbishop Elzéar Taschereau. (Some American bishops also strongly disapproved of the Knights.)[43]

Gibbons appears to have been motivated as much or more by a concern that the Church would lose the working class as by a genuine prolabor sympathy. One of his arguments against condemnation was that it was not really necessary because the Knights were in decline.[44] It is important to note, however, that as early as 1884 Gibbons was among a number of bishops who wanted to discourage clerical and episcopal blanket condemnations of labor unions by ruling at the Third Plenary Council (mentioned previously in connection with the establishment of parochial schools) that any condemnations of societies had to be approved by a special committee of bishops.[45]

But condemnations of individuals could still be a problem. In 1887, Archbishop Michael Corrigan of New York succeeded in securing from Rome the excommunication of a popular priest in his diocese, Father

Edward McGlynn, for McGlynn's avid support of social reformer Henry George.[46] Although it appears that Father McGlynn's disobedience toward his bishop was the immediate cause for his excommunication, Archbishop Corrigan raised the whole issue of disobedience because McGlynn did not recognize Corrigan's right to prohibit him from publicly supporting George's egalitarian view of property use and ownership. Furthermore, Corrigan also worked hard at having the theories of Henry George condemned. Here the Vatican was more hesitant to cooperate, resulting in the strange decision to condemn those theories but not to tell anyone, as a compromise between proponents of the condemnation and opponents, like Cardinal Gibbons, concerned about alienating working-class Catholics.[47]

Even moderate, more tolerant bishops—those for whom the Americanist label might have been especially appropriate—were hesitant to criticize Corrigan's hasty and questionable condemnation of McGlynn.[48] American bishops were generally very authoritarian and thus worried about encouraging insubordination, even though Corrigan's approach was unpopular within the American episcopacy as a whole. Nevertheless, behind the scenes, Cardinal Gibbons of Baltimore and Archbishop Ireland of St. Paul worked to reverse McGlynn's excommunication. Both prelates were concerned about the effect the McGlynn case would have on the U.S. Church's relations with its laity. Cardinal Gibbons especially was concerned about the message that McGlynn's excommunication and condemnation of Henry George's ideas could send to poor Catholics.[49]

Ultimately, in 1892, McGlynn was reinstated as a priest, with the help of Gibbons, Ireland, and the recently arrived apostolic delegate to the United States, Francesco Satolli.[50] Satolli was initially an ally of Gibbons and Ireland, but within a year (Gerald Fogarty believed as a result of Gibbons's defense of such "socialist" organizations as the Knights of Labor),[51] the apostolic delegate had begun to ally himself with the minority of bishops interested in further Romanizing the American Church.[52]

Despite representing a minority opinion within the American episcopacy, the condemnations of McGlynn and George are instructive. Together with the Knights of Labor episode, they demonstrate that American bishops were concerned with social issues primarily in a negative fashion so as to avoid alienation of their laity. Although Corrigan was an example of a bishop who wanted ideological control over sociopolitical issues, most bishops were content to avoid such issues, even though they almost certainly abhorred Henry George's politics.[53] The bishops did not approach sociopolitical issues as representatives of the laity; their own political ideology probably did not reflect the laity's. They simply were interested in the health of the institutional Church.[54]

That interest was very compatible with ideological boundaries that placed sociopolitical issues outside of the core interests of the Church. Thus for example, Gibbons and his allies saw the question of disciplining McGlynn for insubordination as separate from, and more legitimate than, deciding to condemn the actual content of the social theories he espoused.[55] From quite early, the hierarchy in this country feared accusations of religious interference in government and thus left most political organization and lobbying to the laity.[56] They were hesitant to condemn working-class groups—those precisely that European prelates were most eager to condemn[57]—not because they were champions of working-class causes, but because they wanted to avoid alienating their laity.[58] Had they been interested in promoting working-class economic interests, they would not have ignored Leo XIII's *Rerum Novarum*, the 1891 encyclical that launched modern papal social doctrine.[59]

The U.S. bishops, then, had in practice developed a perspective that was still only beginning to emerge in papal thought. Nevertheless, both within the international Church and within U.S. society, the American Church had learned the dangers of asserting ideological independence because it did not have the power to enforce its views within the international Church. (Catholic ideological structure as a whole, then, was closer to the papal perspective; ideological constraints originating in Rome involved somewhat effective sanctions against those who objected.) Within the Church, U.S. bishops faced the condemnation of Americanism, and within the United States, they faced anti-Catholic sentiment. Within American society, although they avoided specific political issues,[60] Catholic bishops, and Catholics in general, tended to overcompensate for the suspicions on their loyalty by being ultrapatriotic. Thus the American episcopacy exhorted Catholics to be scrupulously obedient citizens—for example, in pastoral letters and statements from 1852, 1919, 1933, and 1941.[61]

But the bishops did not simply absorb secular perspectives on church and state. For example, the bishops in this country never gave up the notion that there are moral principles for which the church is the authority and the state is under obligation to respect.[62] This perspective is consistent with modern Catholic ideological structure, which emphasizes that there are specific moral principles concerning families and individuals that the state must respect but that sociopolitical issues are subject only to broad moral guidelines that themselves are subject to interpretation. But through most of its history, the U.S. Church could probably have argued that most such fundamental principles were respected in this country. As in Europe, while governments and much of secular society did not fundamentally disagree with the Catholic patriarchal view of families and conservative view of sexuality, the episcopacy had little reason to question the moral principles of the state and secular society.

The pre–Vatican II episcopacy, then, had no trouble identifying as patriotic Americans. U.S. bishops did not hesitate to support every American war effort enthusiastically until a late questioning of the Vietnam War. Such patriotism is a not uncommon immigrant reaction (that is, not just among Catholics), reinforced in this case by appreciation of the relative benefits the American system offered to a minority church.

The peripheral position of the U.S. Church, within both the international Church and American society, then, heavily influenced U.S. episcopal ideology. As the twentieth century progressed, however, new conditions placed the American bishops, gradually and haltingly, on a more confident course, but one that would not result in substantial ideological change until after Vatican II.

World War I had an important effect on the relations of the U.S. episcopacy to both the U.S. polity and the Vatican. The war provided an opportunity to prove Catholic loyalty to the United States; the Catholic episcopacy was careful to assure that it was involved in raising money for the home front by establishing an organization of its member bishops, the National Catholic War Council.[63]

The American episcopacy had for decades found some reason or other for groups of bishops, especially archbishops, to meet annually, subtly building a fraternal social network independent of Rome (which opposed frequent meetings).[64] But the success of the War Council in establishing closer relations with the U.S. government and demonstrating Catholic patriotism led to an even more effective basis of collective identity. After the war, the now-confident episcopacy established a successor organization, the National Catholic Welfare Council (NCWC), to protect Catholic interests. Although Pope Benedict XV initially approved the establishment of the Welfare Council, almost immediately a minority of American bishops (led by the Romanizer Cardinal O'Connell of Boston) caught the Vatican's ear in complaining that the organization would be legislating national ecclesiastical policy, thus interfering with a bishop's sovereign rights in his own diocese. This could also be a concern to the Vatican if it had to deal with a united and organized national episcopacy instead of individual bishops.

In response, Pope Benedict XV prepared to reverse his initial approval of the organization but died (in 1922) before announcing its suppression. His successor, Pius XI, soon notified the American hierarchy of that suppression; surprised and stunned, the Welfare Council's Administrative Board of seven bishops quickly protested the Vatican decision in an unusually vehement tone. Ninety percent of the American bishops signed a petition presented to the pope in favor of the NCWC. In response, Pius XI reversed the suppression but reiterated that the council did not have canonical status and thus was completely voluntary and could not interfere in the diocesan jurisdiction of any bishop. In response to Vatican directive, the NCWC removed the word *council* from its title because in canon law the word implies an official meeting with powers to make obligatory policy. (The NCWC was thereafter called the National Catholic Welfare Conference.)[65]

Before Vatican II, the NCWC had limited authority; it was a less participatory organization than its post–Vatican II successor, the National Conference of Catholic Bishops (NCCB), and the NCCB has elicited more membership commitment than did the NCWC. The NCWC's small Administrative Board, not the whole membership, actually wrote and issued statements. It also appears that before Vatican II, the U.S. episcopacy was very regionally oriented, so that bishops separated by great distances were not in close communication. Indeed, Fogarty saw the U.S. episcopacy of the 1920s and 1930s, even after the establishment of the NCWC, as clearly less collegial than was true in the nineteenth century.[66] But in fact the inability of Romanizers like O'Connell to organize much opposition to the NCWC suggests that collegiality, although not yet at the level it would reach in the NCCB period, suffered only a temporary setback in the early twentieth century.

Although the NCWC had no formal authority in the Church, the existence of such an organization did begin to build both new institutional strength and a stronger collective identity among the bishops. The objection to Benedict XV's suppression order itself suggested that the organization could become a vehicle of establishing greater independence from Rome, although that independence would remain more potential than real until after Vatican II. And perhaps because the NCWC was the child of an episcopacy more confident of its place in American society following World War I (and one that could build on its strong institutional network of schools, hospitals, and a devout laity),[67] it became the vehicle for the first important U.S. episcopal initiative on issues of social policy.

The Administrative Board of the NCWC published a document on social policy in the wake of World War I that reflected Leo XIII's social doctrine.[68] In itself, and in comparison to the bishops' historical fear of appearing to interfere in politics, the document was bold and impressive. The bishops urged a guaranteed living wage, social security insurance, equal pay for working women (with the preference that women not work at all), and spending on public housing. They defended the right of workers to organize unions. The prominent, socially progressive priest John Ryan, who had been the first to really apply and publicize Leo XIII's social doctrine in this country,[69] authored this 1919 "Program of Social Reconstruction." Throughout his career, which included direction of the Social Action Department of the NCWC and close relations with prominent, secular supporters of Franklin Roosevelt's New Deal, Ryan had argued the need for a living wage, enough to support a family.

But despite this initiative, the bishops did not then make social issues a high priority. The 1919 statement was quickly ignored. Although it is difficult to be absolutely certain, it appears in hindsight that the particular social conditions of the period immediately following World War I, when combined with the newly available resources of the NCWC, may have led the bishops to address issues that otherwise would have been low priorities. The period immediately following the war was one of social unrest in which there developed nationally a crisis mentality in attempts to deal with race riots, strikes, bombings, and political demonstrations.[70] The bishops' 1919 statement may have been fueled by that feeling of crisis, of the necessity to *do* something.[71] With the onset of political reaction, specifically the Red Scare in American society of 1919–1920, it appears the bishops did not object to their proposals' gathering dust. During times of "stability," the bishops saw no need to be controversial.

The American episcopacy thus remained tentative in addressing sociopolitical issues; events between the world wars reinforced their caution. An important dispute in the 1920s indeed reminded Catholics that many Americans remained suspicious of their loyalties. This dispute concerned the Catholic view of church-state relations as explained by Father John Ryan, author of the 1919 NCWC statement. In a 1922 book, *The State and the Church*, Ryan argued that should Catholics ever become predominant in the U.S., they would be obliged to change the Constitution and suppress other religions. Ryan's book further argued that this possibility was so remote that it was not even worth considering and so should not influence how non-Catholics perceived Catholic political views. (Note the similarity with Leo XIII's view of Americanism: pragmatically, the reality of U.S. church-state relations [political Americanism] was acceptable as long as doctrinally one rejected religious Americanism.) Ryan was apparently sincerely bewildered that non-Catholics would take such offense at his remarks, given that they would almost surely never be implemented.

Ryan is himself an interesting example of the boundaries of Catholic ideology. He stood on the left when it came to social reform; in the 1930s he would earn the nickname "the Right Reverend New Dealer." And yet his views of church-state issues struck many Americans as medieval and repressive. But he saw himself as a loyal papalist on all issues; indeed, he was much more familiar with papal social doctrine than were most bishops. He was essentially taking the position that Cardinal Gibbons had urged upon Leo XIII, that is, that one could accept American church-state relations on pragmatic grounds without doctrinally sanctioning such an arrangement.[72]

The consequent controversy over Catholic views of church-state relations, in which non-Catholics could cite embarrassing Vatican pronouncements, may have hurt the 1928 Democratic presidential campaign of Alfred Smith, a Catholic. During that campaign, the ultimate loyalties of Smith were a major issue. Smith himself was a typical American Catholic who, having had no experience or familiarity with papal involvement in temporal politics, could not see why his loyalty as an American would be such an important issue to many non-Catholics.[73] It is said that when asked about Leo XIII's views of church and state in the encyclical *Immortale Dei,* Smith responded, "Will somebody please tell me what in hell an encyclical is?"[74] The history of the American Church justified Smith's bewilderment as a layperson on encountering doubts about his national loyalty or even encountering expectations that he would be familiar with papal views of church-state relations or papal social pronouncements in general. The fine points of theology of any kind had not been an American Catholic concern, and the episcopacy had purposely deemphasized church-state doctrine—the American Catholic laity certainly had no active commitment to such doctrine. Much of the opposition to Smith was simple prejudice; but he also had to contend with what was indeed Catholic doctrine. Non-Catholics' objections to Ryan's remarks were not surprising and not unreasonable;[75] even the Catholic episcopacy quietly opposed the official doctrine.

Coming just a decade after the Catholic hierarchy's and populace's very enthusiastic support of American involvement in World War I, the treatment Smith received embittered some Catholics. When combined with the revival of the Ku Klux Klan in the 1920s, the experience of Smith's candidacy may have led the U.S. bishops, after their 1919 statement, to return to their fear of appearing to interfere in secular politics and thus fuel anti-Catholic prejudice.

The hesitation to address sociopolitical issues was probably reinforced by the infamous career of Father Charles Coughlin. Coughlin's radio broadcasts, which lasted from 1931 to 1942, originally urged social reform and supported the goals of the New Deal instituted with Franklin Roosevelt's election in 1932. But he displayed increasingly fascist and anti-Semitic sympathies mixed together with strong criticism of President Roosevelt. The link that many Americans might have perceived between Catholicism and Coughlin's social and political views was a delicate embarrassment and a difficult problem for the U.S. hierarchy. This was especially the case because several prominent bishops were allies of Roosevelt's, while the bishop who had jurisdiction over Coughlin until the bishop's death in 1937 was sympathetic to the radio priest. Even though the Vatican also showed concern about Coughlin engendering hostility toward the Church from the U.S. government, it was not easy for the episcopacy to silence Coughlin without giving fuel to those who saw the Church as an opponent of freedom of speech. There was explicit concern within the hierarchy that Coughlin would have to be silenced if he ever violated doctrine on faith and morals, but it would take the national unity of World War II to allow Coughlin's new bishop to forbid the priest's political rantings. Apparently the silencing of Coughlin in 1942 formally avoided judgment of his specific opinions by using the criterion that Pope John Paul II has used—that priests can be forbidden from nonreligious activities in general, given that their religious functions are ideologically more central.[76]

Bishops continued, then, to worry about how non-Catholics might perceive the U.S. Church. Anti-Catholic prejudice in fact continued to flare up occasionally at least into the 1950s.[77] For a brief period after World War I, social doctrine may have seemed safe, a way to enter the nation's polity without reviving anti-Catholic feelings. But perhaps the bishops felt that this safety was elusive and thus withdrew once again into internal Church concerns.

Structurally, social doctrine is of low priority; especially before Vatican II, one could be committed to the content of social doctrine while also having only a weak commitment to concrete social reform. Despite appeals to the rights of workers, it is not clear that U.S. bishops as a whole were any more committed to increasing real union power than was Leo XIII. In fact, there was every reason for U.S. bishops to be sympathetic to both the content of papal social doctrine and its place in the structure of Catholic ideology: they did not participate in American secular ideologies and so did not absorb them; social doctrine's birth represented the beginning of an ideological reconstruction of which they were eager proponents; and the emergent ideological structure that devalued sociopolitical issues was much in keeping with their attempts to decentralize such issues away from the ideological core of Catholicism.

Consequently, although American clerics and bishops did not generally make social issues a high priority until after Vatican II, when they did address such issues they generally adopted the content of Leo XIII's social doctrine wholesale.[78] But like Rome, the U.S. bishops did not make social issues a high priority. And like Rome, in actual practice the bishops did not appear to advocate a great degree of concrete social change, despite moralistic pronouncements.

Indeed, throughout the late nineteenth and early twentieth centuries, when it came to actual, specific practice the hierarchy for the most part was suspicious of labor unions and very anxious about what it perceived as militancy and socialism.[79] Uncomfortable with strikes, the hierarchy recommended binding arbitration without addressing what should be done when an employer refuses to submit to arbitration.[80]

The bishops' emphasis on ethics, rather than on concrete solutions, was itself quite consistent with papal social doctrine. The U.S. bishops, that is, were consistent in the application of the emerging ideological structure of Catholicism (including its internal boundaries) in viewing social issues through a primarily ethical lens: they saw moral failings as prior to and more significant than empirical socioeconomic questions. Catholics in the public eye initially judged the Depression as ultimately caused by ethical weakness,[81] a view that would be consistent with papal analysis of socioeconomic problems.

There was developing, however, the possibility that receptivity to social change could emerge from social doctrine. It was the case that conditions in the United States gradually brought Catholics into the mainstream of political and economic life, apparently breaking down the bishops' fear of addressing sociopolitical issues. Some of the same processes also changed the nature of the American episcopacy's relationship with Rome.

Even though it was the case that Archbishop John Ireland had had good relationships with Republican Party leaders, the political alliance between Franklin Roosevelt and some American bishops, especially Cardinals Francis Spellman of New York and George Mundelein of Chicago, was more significant. The New Deal was a crucial period in the social and political integration of American Catholics; in Ireland's time Catholics were politically much more marginal. In both periods the politically involved bishop was much more the exception than the rule, but this was especially true in Ireland's time. Franklin Roosevelt cultivated Catholic support, and New Deal aid to the working class benefited many Catholics. Catholics became more a part of the national polity, a process that had begun at least by World War I (through the National Catholic War Council). Catholic bishops, priests, and media discussed and lauded the New Deal, eager especially to compare it with Pope Pius XI's new social encyclical, *Quadragesimo Anno* (promulgated in 1931). Many Catholic bishops, clergy, and intellectuals heartily welcomed the National Recovery Administration as a guildlike, cooperative solution to the Depression, in conformity with that encyclical. That *Quadragesimo Anno* received more attention in the United States than had Leo XIII's *Rerum Novarum* indicates that by 1931 Catholic bishops and intellectuals were more willing to address social issues.[82]

Roosevelt voiced support for those bishops with similar social views, but ultimately the importance of the New Deal for the American episcopacy lay less in the advocacy of particular social programs than in the improved position of Catholics in American society in general by the end of that period. The bishops' commitment to particular social policies was weak compared to their concern with the institutional Church. In the period from the 1920s through the 1940s, the American episcopacy took advantage of a number of opportunities to improve the position of the U.S. Church not only within American society, but within the international Church. To begin with, the bishops, through NCWC statements and communications with the press and the U.S. government, lobbied to defend Catholic interests during and after the Mexican Revolution. The Vatican appreciated such efforts and also relied on NCWC officers to serve as liaisons to the U.S. government and to Mexican bishops in exile in the United States.[83]

Cardinals Spellman and Mundelein both had important friends in Rome and served as liaisons between the Vatican and Washington, which did not have official diplomatic relations. This was especially true of Spellman during World War II. Spellman's friend in the Vatican was Eugenio Pacelli, Pius XI's secretary of state who in 1939 became Pope Pius XII. With the approach of the war, Pius XII established closer communications with Roosevelt through Spellman. Roosevelt even established a special diplomatic mission to the Vatican (of a semiofficial status that did not require congressional action; congressional debate would have provided a forum for charges of violation of the separation of church and state). Throughout the war, American bishops faced the difficult, delicate task of showing themselves to be patriotic Americans while still maintaining close ties with, and to some extent representing, the Vatican, which remained neutral and occasionally made statements that seemed to favor the Axis powers. But the bishops were fairly successful at balancing the two, partially because the Vatican recognized the importance of the United States in world affairs and thus depended on the influence and communications of the American episcopacy. In the process, the Vatican came to treat the NCWC as the official voice of the American hierarchy, not just a forum for unofficial meetings, and it appears that in 1944–1945 Pius XII even came close to naming Spellman his secretary of state. After the war, the Vatican relied more on American bishops' recommendations in filling episcopal vacancies, thus lessening the Romanization of the American Church that had begun under Leo XIII.[84]

But despite the U.S. Church's growing influence under Roosevelt's presidency, the American episcopacy as a whole became wary of supporting social reform. The strength and status of the institution were higher priorities than particular commitments on sociopolitical issues. After the first few years of the Roosevelt administration, the interests and ideology of the episcopacy once again diverged from its own laity, who appear to have continued to support Roosevelt by enthusiastic margins. Among both Catholic bishops and media, fundamental Catholic conservatism returned, suspicious of widening state jurisdiction even in social causes the Church supposedly supported.[85] Perhaps once again the interest in social reform could be sustained only by the sense of a need to address social crisis, as characterized the early New Deal years.

So we find that even after the advent of the New Deal, the pre–Vatican II American hierarchy opposed child labor laws, the predominant view being that the government might next interfere with the education of Catholic children.[86] The hierarchy distrusted government motives, finding, for example, the courts more reliable than legislatures in the protection of First Amendment religious rights.[87] Such suspicions were fed by the hierarchy's perception that the U.S. government was not interested in the persecution of the Catholic Church especially in Mexico but later also in Spain and the Soviet bloc.[88]

Granted, the hierarchy continued to show sporadic interest in social doctrine, notably in a 1940 pastoral letter that dealt with such themes, titled "Church and Social Order."[89] It is true that as we approach the Vatican II era, Catholic support of union rights increased, for example, in a widespread Catholic opposition to right-to-work laws in the 1950s.[90] Some Catholic organizations (e.g., the German Catholic Central Verein)[91] and perhaps a good number of priests were involved in prolabor social reform activity.[92] But the hierarchy, despite its positions, was not very active in its moderate prolabor stands, partially because of a strong emphasis on anticommunism. Such hypersensitivity to communism, usually claimed to be not just a radical politics, but also an antireligious philosophy, pervaded all levels of the Church and led to a good deal of Catholic support for Father Charles Coughlin, Senator Joseph McCarthy, and Francisco Franco's Nationalists in Spain as well as to hostility toward militancy within the Congress of Industrial Organizations.[93] American bishops were more likely to cite *Rerum Novarum* in defense of private property than in defense of workers.[94] The NCWC declined to work closely with Peter Dietz, a prolabor priest from the Central Verein, at least partially because of his close association with unions, even though Dietz's unionism was of a relatively conservative variety.[95]

In addition, the Church was commonly associated with other conservative causes; for example, although many bishops had earlier in the century avoided official commitment on women's suffrage, the hierarchy and clergy probably generally opposed it, given their commitment to the traditional family.[96] Although there were individual exceptions, and a 1942 bishops' statement addressed racial injustice, for the most part the Church ignored the problems of segregation until the U.S. Supreme Court's *Brown* decision of 1954.[97]

There was more concern for religious persecution and other protests of communism in Eastern Europe and Asia as well as traditional Catholic concerns such as family life and secularism. Perhaps had it not been living under the very spiritual, devotional approach to Catholicism that predominated under Pope Pius XII, the American episcopacy would have participated in the political arena more forcefully in this period. Pius XII discouraged the notion that Catholicism meant an active approach to the secular world, which was seen as corrupt, materialistic, and dangerous to the faith.[98]

Nevertheless, there were emerging changes in the position of Catholics in American society that encouraged a more confident approach among the episcopacy. As always, the hierarchy avidly supported the American war effort in World War II; lay Catholics demonstrated their patriotism with disproportionately high enlistments. After the war, Catholics began a period of rapid socioeconomic progress and thus within decades were no longer a poor, fairly powerless minority.

Consequently, there did develop in the 1950s mild signs of a greater confidence and eagerness in addressing political affairs. The NCWC issued a pastoral letter in 1951 that discussed morality in government in general and questioned corruption in American government of the time in particular; the letter also made brief references to the issue of morality in other spheres such as economics and racism.[99] Continuing a long-standing concern, the NCWC also issued a controversial 1955 letter on the subject of Catholic schools, urging government assistance to Catholic pupils and a reduction of the tax burden for public school support paid by Catholics whose children did not attend such schools.[100] The letter aroused accusations that the Church was violating the church-state boundary. A 1958 letter protested segregation and racism.[101] Eager to oppose government violations of Catholic morals, the NCWC in 1959 opposed movements for the government to promote birth control internationally.[102] In 1963, on the eve of Vatican II, the NCWC produced a statement on racism as well as a general discussion of American freedoms.

There were beginning, then, new directions in the ideology of the American episcopacy. Further changes came about after Vatican II because of important transformations both in the international Church and in the position of Catholics in U.S. society.

Within the Church, Vatican II proclaimed collegiality and brought about partially decentralizing organizational changes but with a certain ideological ambiguity, as we saw in chapter 3. Ultimately, as we see in chapter 5, U.S. bishops attempted to fill collegiality with some content by developing their own approach to sociopolitical issues. Indeed, Vatican II, despite its ambiguous message, seemed to call for a greater emphasis on social reform.

Within American society, the socioeconomic position of Catholics continued to improve. Finally, the election of John F. Kennedy to the presidency was symbolically very important to American Catholics, who felt they had finally been accepted as mainstream members of society. As a result, American bishops felt able to address sociopolitical issues. Because they had never been closely linked ideologically with the laity's political and social views, their own perspectives were innovative applications of institutional Catholic ideology, not of secular ideologies. Now let us examine these ideological paths of American bishops after Vatican II.

5 Collegiality and Catholic Social Teaching in the American Context

From the vantage point of the American public, after Vatican II, especially in the last decade, American bishops appear to have awakened from a long dormancy. As if they had already slept through half the day and needed to accomplish their work quickly, they have burst on the public scene, asserting themselves in U.S. society.

To many observers, the bishops appear to have radically changed their outlook on American life, sounding criticisms of U.S. government policies and of the ethics of American capitalism, in contrast to their long-standing patriotism and conservatism. But the U.S. government is a modern government in a society that commentators from Karl Marx to Hernando de Soto have described as quintessentially capitalist and a major player in a world of geopolitics that long ago left the Catholic Church behind.[1] There is clearly precedent for officials of the Church to distance themselves from capitalism and from modern state policies. American bishops always had a tenuous relationship with the government and with secular society, and now they have more actively adopted the critical social views that pervade Catholic ideology.

The phenomenon of the bishops' publicly taking controversial stands on American political and social issues is both less and more than it seems. It is less because, although they have produced a number of original interpretations, generally the bases of those positions are thoroughly understandable within Catholic doctrine and indeed are to some extent elaborations of their own earlier, less publicly visible statements. It is more because this could not have happened if the American episcopacy had not also developed a new view of its place in the Church as a whole. That there has been occasional disagreement with Rome is not in itself new or surprising, as chapter 4 has made clear. Yet the possibility of heated controversy with Rome over doctrine has increased recently, as the bishops' own agenda sometimes conflicts with Catholic ideological structure.

The current chapter deals with the origins and development of two related changes in the ideological politics of the U.S. episcopacy: first, by the time of Vatican II, American bishops had become much more receptive to applying the ethical outlook of Church ideology to sociopolitical issues. Thus they tended to take an increasingly critical view of U.S. government policy and of U.S. socioeconomic trends. Second, in emphasizing Church ideology on such topics, they encountered the ideological and political tensions of Vatican II, whose origins we examined in chapter 3.

It is possible to summarize these developments briefly by stating that by the time of Vatican II, the reasons that Catholic bishops had been fearful about addressing sociopolitical issues in American society had largely dissipated. And then, of course, the council itself gave an important impetus to a concern with such issues in two ways. First, it had called directly for a greater emphasis on social justice. Second, there was an effect of selection in that the council had expanded the organizational resources of episcopal conferences without giving them increased authority over the fundamental ideological issues of faith and morals; thus sociopolitical issues were among the few areas where such conferences could turn their attention without unduly trespassing on Roman authority.

The consequent concern with sociopolitical issues itself has two important ideological aspects. First, it is the case, for reasons to be made clear during this chapter, that U.S. bishops' ethical perspectives on such issues were very much grounded in internal Church ideology. That ideology was not particularly oriented toward legitimating twentieth-century secular politics and social policy, and so the bishops have taken a more critical view of U.S. government policy and of the U.S. economy than they have in the past. Second, the attempt to heighten such concern can subvert, or at least run into difficulties as a result of, Catholic ideological structure. Catholic ideological structure distinguishes the specific, binding moral principles relevant to individuals and families from the more flexible, less specific ethical principles relevant to sociopolitical issues. The bishops are in the interesting position of a group located fairly high in the power structure that cannot continue to advance its own concerns (on sociopolitical issues) without undermining the ideological structure that justifies that very hierarchy of power.

Unfortunately for the bishops, they are also faced with the continuing problem that the secular world is not organized according to Catholic ideological boundaries. Thus just as nineteenth-century European secular society did not respect the papacy's right to intervene in its politics, so the American bishops of today face a world that does not recognize that certain "moral" absolutes, as defined by the Catholic hierarchy, are beyond political negotiation. In contemporary American society, the issue of abortion—in Church eyes, a moral, not a political, question—has become particularly controversial. Thus from within the Church and without, the boundary separating faith and morals from sociopolitical issues continues to be the center of ideological dispute.

In discussing these issues, I first address the changes in the social position of Catholics in the United States that led to a reduced episcopal fear of addressing sociopolitical issues. I then discuss the influence of Vatican II on concern with such issues. Following that is an analysis of the reasons that U.S. bishops' approach to sociopolitical issues tends to be so critical of U.S. politics and economics. Finally, I address the ideological and political tensions that result from the bishops' concerns.

Origins of a Changed Perspective

THE DECLINE OF THE CATHOLIC GHETTO

The 1960s saw an interesting coincidence of influences on the American episcopacy. There were, first of all, important domestic developments that opened the space for U.S. bishops, and American Catholics in general, to play a new role in U.S. society.

We saw in chapter 4 that the U.S. Church, through most of its history, felt somewhat insecure as a minority church; consequently, it generally attempted to avoid controversy. But in the twentieth century, it had gradually become more of a part of mainstream American society.

This process greatly accelerated in the post–World War II era. American Catholics had enlisted in the war effort in disproportionate numbers; after the war they made a dramatic ascent into the middle class, leaving behind their poor, immigrant status. By the time of Vatican II, Catholics were at least equal to Protestants in educational preparation and, according to most indices, socioeconomic status. Since then, they have clearly surpassed Protestants.[2] Catholics had become politically more influential during the New Deal; although it is easy for popular accounts to overestimate the legacy left by John F. Kennedy, it certainly was the case that his election as president in 1960 signaled to many Catholics that they had unequivocally entered the American mainstream. Non-Catholics could no longer reasonably suspect that a Catholic politician would sacrifice American interests to those of Rome.[3]

THE NATIONAL CONFERENCE OF CATHOLIC BISHOPS

We saw in chapter 3 that Vatican II left a legacy of a number of unresolved tensions—for example, the problem of emphasizing social justice activity while devaluing sociopolitical issues, and of implementing a partial organizational decentralization without decentralizing ideological control. The most important tension affecting bishops lay in the council's promising collegiality but not decentralizing Rome's control over faith and morals. The idea of collegiality might have had little effect if it had not been for the organizational decentralization that emerged from the council's emphasis on episcopal conferences.[4] The council underlined the importance of such conferences by stating that bishops needed to work more in concert with each other,[5] somewhat questioning the traditional arrangement in which individual bishops answered only to Rome. The council encouraged the formation of episcopal conferences where they did not already exist.[6]

The U.S. bishops already had a conference, the National Catholic Welfare Conference (renamed the National Conference of Catholic Bishops in 1966),[7] but after Vatican II all such conferences could with a two-thirds vote set Church policy for the country or region they represented.[8] The juridical status of the NCCB's pronouncements remains somewhat ambiguous, given that Vatican II did not make clear, specific changes in the authority structure of the Church. The problem is that although conference pronouncements have the "force of law,"[9] they in fact do not bind particular bishops, whose authority within their own dioceses remains under the jurisdiction of Rome only. In addition, conferences—like individual bishops—cannot actually change doctrine. Cardinal Joseph Ratzinger, prefect of the Vatican's crucial Congregation for the Doctrine of the Faith (which enforces orthodoxy), has claimed that the conferences do not have independent teaching authority.[10] In 1988 the Vatican proposed formal adoption of a strictly limiting interpretation of the role of such conferences, but it backed down in 1990 as the result of objections from the episcopacies of many countries. The American bishops had denounced the document. The head of Rome's Congregation for Bishops noted that there was disagreement about "the open theological issues."[11]

In practice, however, although the parameters of collegiality remain ambiguous, the activities and pronouncements of the NCCB have grown in importance. The increased status of episcopal conferences, and the NCCB's own efforts to include its members in its activities, fostered the growth of an important resource, a strengthened collective identity among American bishops.[12] The NCCB became a more participatory organization than the NCWC under the early leadership of Cardinal John Dearden of Detroit. An auxiliary bishop of that archdiocese reports that, symbolizing the more democratic deliberations, Dearden eliminated the seating pattern of NCWC meetings in which the few American cardinals sat facing the rest of the episcopacy, which became the cardinals' audience.[13]

But what would be the NCCB's role in implementing collegiality? Bishops were not about to openly challenge Rome's control of faith and morals. The American episcopacy is an interesting social body given that it has, on the one hand, been heavily influenced by decentralizing tendencies within the Church yet, on the other hand, must deal with those tendencies as problems of management and Church politics.[14] If less powerful segments of the Church emphasize a People of God model of the Church, the right to experiment, and the questioning of hierarchical authority, they implicitly challenge bishops' control over their dioceses. Experiments in liturgy, attempts to limit hierarchical control over Catholic schools, efforts of priests to increase their autonomy, and so on necessarily threaten episcopal control.

On such issues, bishops' power is aligned with that of Rome. In addition, of course, individual bishops are weak in relation to Rome should they try to take an independent path. They are monarchs in their own dioceses, but offending Rome on the central issues of faith and morals will make their lives difficult and put that power in jeopardy.

In dealing with threats to orthodoxy, Pope Paul VI was more vacillating and, at times, more lenient than John Paul II has been. But it is accurate to say that on the whole the post–Vatican II papacy has shown little sign of voluntarily decentralizing control, to bishops or anyone else, over faith and morals of individuals and families. Paul's strident defense of the ban on contraception in his 1968 encyclical, *Humanae Vitae*,[15] against the recommendation of a commission of theologians that he himself had established, quickly became a symbol of Roman intransigence over such issues.

John Paul II has, if anything, attempted to tighten control in a number of ways, giving even bishops little room to maneuver. His prefect of the Congregation for the Doctrine of the Faith, Cardinal Ratzinger, voices opinions not radically different from the old dictum that "error has no rights."[16] The Vatican has been sending particularly strong messages on the importance of orthodoxy to the American Church, which, like the Dutch Catholic Church, is one of Catholicism's most rebellious branches. In the United States, the laity largely ignores prescriptions against birth control, and some Church personnel (e.g., sisters) have questioned the legitimacy of the Church power structure. The pope ordered in 1983 a study of American religious life, with the obvious implication that American religious were too rebellious.[17] In 1986, Rome disciplined the Reverend Charles Curran for his dissent on sexual teachings, removing him from the theology faculty of the Catholic University of America.[18] (Catholic University is the only American Catholic university with a pontifical charter—that is, theoretically under the direct supervision of Rome rather than of a university board.) The major theme of the papal visit to the United States in September 1987 was that American Catholics cannot be selective in their obedience to Church doctrine.

John Paul has generally appointed very loyal bishops, who are uncompromising in asserting the primacy of Rome and the absolute necessity of obedience on faith and morals, to the most important dioceses—for example, John O'Connor in New York, Bernard Law in Boston, and Anthony Bevilacqua in Philadelphia. Episcopal appointments are an area in which a pope creates as much as responds to political, structural constraints within the Church. Many popes are not in office long enough to radically change the character of a large nation's episcopacy, but John Paul II may be an exception. He was a relatively young fifty-eight years old when he became pope. The recommendations of a country's bishops, and especially of the papal representative in a particular country, will also have some influence. Given the sheer number of dioceses internationally, the pope must depend on consultation.

Under Paul VI, and especially while his appointee, Jean Jadot, was apostolic delegate to the United States (1973–1980), appointments generally reinforced the U.S. episcopacy's moderately reformist receptivity to Vatican II themes—that is, decentralization, commitment to social justice, and the development of doctrine. (Paul himself vacillated in his commitment to decentralization.) The first two major appointments under John Paul's representative and Jadot's successor, Pio Laghi, were those of Law to Boston and O'Connor to New York.[19]

That Rome's tight control over faith and morals makes problematic the concept of collegiality is especially clear when bishops themselves are disciplined for departures from orthodoxy as defined by the Vatican. Under John Paul II, Walter Sullivan of Richmond, Virginia, and Raymond Hunthausen of Seattle have encountered Vatican investigations for alleged permissiveness toward beliefs and practices contrary to Catholic faith and morals. In 1986, Rome forced Hunthausen to share authority in his archdiocese for a little over a year, citing his permissiveness toward sterilization in Catholic hospitals, marital annulments, homosexual groups, and employment of ex-priests in liturgical functions, among other issues.[20]

There are signs that Rome has been policing episcopal approval of Catholic publications (i.e., granting of the imprimatur, indicating that a publication contains no doctrinal errors).[21]

It is not surprising, then, that bishops have been receptive to some of the messages of Vatican II; a decentralizing collegiality would free them of some of Rome's control. In the mid- and late 1980s, a number of American bishops, most prominently Archbishop Rembert Weakland of Milwaukee, publicly objected to Vatican heavy-handedness, objections made continually by other American Catholics.[22] Yet an overly direct challenge to Rome is a risky strategy. Most bishops, at least at this point, are not receptive to a radically decentralizing interpretation of Vatican II. They are in a difficult position, and ideological ambivalence has been the result. An illuminating example of their ambivalence is contained in "The Church in Our Day," the NCCB's pastoral letter of 1967, just two years after the council ended.[23] After a strained argument that Vatican II's notion of collegiality did not contradict Vatican I's concept of papal primacy, the letter implicitly invoked the notion of the development of doctrine (in light of changed circumstances) to explain the different emphases of the two councils. But the hierarchy at the time of Vatican I would not have accepted the notion of the development of doctrine, which "The Church in Our Day" invoked precisely to claim consistency with that nineteenth-century council.

It is true that American bishops have at times been hesitant to suppress efforts to widen Catholic pluralism; Eric Hanson has noted that they have occasionally been effective in resisting Rome by leaking messages to the press portraying Rome as dictatorial and secretive.[24] Nevertheless, although some American bishops have resented and opposed Roman control on some matters of faith and morals, they have usually done so over more minor matters, such as the timing of children's first confession. They have been considerably more hesitant to challenge the basic power structure and ideological structure of the Church. For example, they overrode the more reforming, decentralizing tendencies of the writing commission for a national catechetical directory (a religious teaching guide). At the 1977 NCCB annual meeting, the bishops voted editions that emphasized the hierarchical structure of the Church and the limits of dissent, angering members of the writing commission.[25] As another example of loyalty to Rome over faith and morals issues, there is little obvious dissent over reproductive issues, especially abortion. In 1987 the NCCB was quick to support the Vatican prohibition on certain reproductive technologies, a prohibition whose justification would be considered an issue of binding moral doctrine.[26]

In the 1980s, however, there seemed to develop increased dissatisfaction within the American episcopacy over, for example, the Vatican's disciplinary procedures[27] and the Church view of women. At a 1987 synod of bishops in Rome, Americans argued for an expanded role for women in the Church short of priesthood, but the proposal met with opposition from bishops from nations with weaker commitments to feminism.[28]

Bishops are cautious expressing such views, however, because Rome retains important power over them. For instance, we cannot know the personal preferences of most bishops on such issues as the ordination of women, but they are constrained from challenging the Vatican position on the issue; in 1983 Pope John Paul II essentially forbade them even to discuss it publicly.[29] At the 1986 annual NCCB meeting in Washington, the bishops endorsed the Vatican's disciplining of Raymond Hunthausen,[30] although influential prelates were probably important in behind-the-scenes efforts to have Hunthausen's full episcopal authority restored in a little over a year.[31] That is, it may have been the case that publicly the bishops felt unable to break with the Vatican, while privately they opposed Rome's heavy-handedness. Publicly, indeed, it is very difficult for the bishops to challenge Rome. But there is one level of ideology—sociopolitical issues— where bishops, like anyone else in the Church, can develop a fair amount of independence. Here the NCCB has devoted increasing attention.

We have already seen that there was a convergence of factors that pulled and pushed the bishops toward increasing their emphasis on such issues. The emphasis on sociopolitical issues is the result of what might be called "ideological selection" (or perhaps political selection). That is, bishops did not necessarily consciously choose an emphasis on social issues because that would free them of Roman control; indeed, it would be nearly impossible to keep such a conspiracy among several hundred men secret, especially when among them are bishops who would strongly oppose any challenge to Rome. Instead, they simply did not focus as much attention on faith and moral questions because there was nothing new they could say; under John Paul II especially, it is very risky even to try. Thus the attention of the NCCB became focused on those issues about which study and deliberation were possible and that had become more acceptable topics in the American context in the last few decades. Although such an emphasis is not in itself a challenge to the current ideological structure, it becomes one if bishops start to value this new sociopolitical focus as much as their commitments to faith and morals, a quite conceivable possibility given their lack of autonomy on the latter. It is only natural that once bishops increasingly based their own domestic authority on sociopolitical issues, they attempted, through the NCCB, to expand that authority by a tentative effort to become more of a part of public policy debates.

The Bishops and Public Policy

A NEW ATTENTION TO SOCIAL ISSUES

In the 1960s, the NCWC (and after 1966, the NCCB), while continuing concern with internal Church matters and moral doctrine, exhibited increased attention to such issues as racial justice, war and peace in the Middle East and Vietnam, justice for farm workers, and prisoners of war.[32] In November 1971, for the first time, the bishops' conference criticized American involvement in a war. Although the statement that the Vietnam War was no longer morally justified came rather late, following years of vacillation, it was a milestone in the NCCB's approach to the U.S. government.[33]

In the same time period, another issue, that of abortion, increased bishops' interest in social issues and bishops' distance from state policies. Kristin Luker's excellent study of the history of the politics of abortion in this country demonstrated that abortion's political visibility grew in the 1960s largely because ambiguities about the prevalence and legality of abortion became increasingly evident and because women's position in American society was changing.[34] As Luker would expect, the U.S. bishops' attention to abortion as well as to birth control greatly increased in the 1960s and early 1970s.[35] Presumably before this time, bishops, like many Americans, had assumed that there was a greater moral consensus about abortion—and thus less need to condemn it—than there really was.[36] Some of the bishops' concern in this period was with government programs that encouraged what they saw as immoral practices (birth control).

With the 1973 *Roe v. Wade* Supreme Court decision, the bishops' concern with legal encouragement of immorality turned to outrage. Within a month of the decision, they had sanctioned disobeying civil laws "that may require abortion."[37] It was a truly radical change, given their patriotic history, for bishops to encourage civil disobedience (the NCWC had, for example, avoided the issue during the civil rights movement). The bishops continued to denounce legal abortion and specifically organized episcopal direction of efforts to pressure the government and politicians to outlaw it via constitutional amendment.[38]

A year after the Supreme Court decision, in a document prepared for a synod of bishops in Rome, the NCCB presented a disillusioned view of the state of public morals in the United States. While they bemoaned the declining levels of obedience and devotion among American Catholics in general, probably more significant for the episcopacy's own outlook toward American society was their complaint that the society made it increasingly difficult for observant Catholics to feel comfortable. They blamed the *Roe v. Wade* decision as well as other Supreme Court decisions dooming the effort to secure public financing of Catholic schools.[39] The former decision was certainly the more important, however, in the bishops' view; the question of educational funding has not received nearly as much NCCB attention as has abortion, an issue of fundamental moral doctrine.

The bishops' outrage at the Court decision led to the American Church's most sustained, uncompromising effort (at the national, diocesan, and parish levels) ever to change particular U.S. laws. Historically, only episcopal efforts to obtain public funding of Catholic schools approaches the level of this prolife activism, but the abortion issue clearly is a significantly higher priority even than religious education. As a result, bishops have at times been charged with political interference and violations of the separation of church and state, most notably Archbishop (now Cardinal) John O'Connor's and Cardinal Bernard Law's criticism of 1984 vice-presidential candidate Geraldine Ferraro's stand on abortion. Theirs was a more doctrinaire stand than most bishops were willing to take publicly because O'Connor and Law did not believe Catholics could vote for a candidate unwilling to outlaw abortion. But their position was not clearly outside the episcopal mainstream. The bishops' conference did issue a statement written by the NCCB president, Bishop James Malone of Youngstown, Ohio, that opposed taking stands on particular candidates. But the statement (without mentioning particular politicians) rejected the view held by such prominent Catholics as Ferraro, Senator Edward Kennedy of Massachusetts, and Governor Mario Cuomo of New York that an observant Catholic official could oppose abortion privately but not work to outlaw it.[40]

It is easy to misinterpret the relationship between the bishops' position on abortion and their positions on foreign and economic policy issues, the latter being left-leaning by mainstream American standards. Most commonly, it is easy to see the two positions as unrelated, an odd mixture of right and left.[41] Such a treatment is misleading, if partially accurate, because the commitment to opposing abortion has different origins (in moral doctrine) than sociopolitical ideology does. Nevertheless, all the bishops' positions must be understood in light of the political history and structural unity of Catholic ideology. It is not accurate to say that the Catholic position on economic issues came from the "left" and the position on abortion from the "right." Both ultimately derive from the Church's alienation from liberal ideologies. And in the bishops' minds, their positions all reflect a coherent, Catholic perspective.

The positions on abortion and on social doctrine also both involve an oppositional approach to government policy. Although it may appear paradoxical from a secular perspective, it appears that the bishops' "conservative" opposition to laws on abortion contributed to their willingness to criticize U.S. foreign and economic policy from the "left." In both cases the American episcopacy shows disillusionment with the morals of American state policy, especially compared to the episcopacy's ultrapatriotism of the past. Since 1973, the bishops have even resorted to lawsuits to prevent government action violating Catholic moral doctrine. In 1979, the bishops' conference filed a class action suit challenging legal requirements that employers pay health benefits used for abortions. In 1984, John O'Connor of New York sued the City of New York over legislation barring discrimination against homosexuals in city-financed programs.[42]

A new phase of the NCCB's approach to its role in the American Church came with the Call to Action in the mid-1970s, also known as the Bicentennial Program because it was portrayed as the Catholic Church's program of participation in the nation's bicentennial celebration.[43] Cardinal Dearden of Detroit, the influential former NCCB president, was the main promoter of the Call to Action, which involved a series of regional meetings, and then a national meeting, of delegates chosen from within dioceses. Some emphases of Pope Paul VI on the Church's role in social justice inspired the title and themes of the Call to Action, a program that involved primarily persons heavily involved in the American Church (not only clerics and sisters, for example, but also diocesan employees and laity involved in Catholic organizations).

The Call to Action solicited recommendations for goals that the American Church should consider. The program, in the view of traditionalists, quickly grew out of control because there were many recommendations that would require changes in issues of faith and moral doctrine. Among such recommendations were the ordination of women, the election of bishops, and moral acceptance of gay lifestyles.[44] The reaction of the episcopacy was to state that there could be no change on such fundamental issues, but recommendations in areas of social justice could involve useful collaboration with the laity.[45]

Only those American Catholics heavily involved in Church activities beyond the parish level would have known about Call to Action; others were almost certainly unaware of it. Because doctrine on sociopolitical issues remains ideologically subordinate, there were only weak attempts to implement the message of the conferences.[46]

But the program must have impressed the bishops. Although tradition-alists thought the Call to Action was out of control, the most significant products of the NCCB in the 1980s—namely, the letters on peace and nuclear strategy and on the economy[47]—also emphasized consultation processes in the writing and revision of successive drafts. The difference is that these later consultation processes consisted of controlled series of hearings conducted by writing committees of five bishops and their staffs. Nothing similar to the Call to Action, which allowed organized reforming Catholics to control the agenda and thus publicly question doctrine on faith and morals, has been held since. The more recent consultations, however, are similar to the Call to Action in soliciting the opinions of elites rather than actively organizing parish-level contributions. In addition to Church employees and personnel, the 1980s letters solicited testimony from both Catholic and non-Catholic intellectuals and policy-makers.[48]

This process of consultation, which began with the Call to Action, has had a number of important effects. For one, the public, accessible nature of this process seems partially to account for the extended coverage of the letters on peace and on the economy in the secular media, as Cardinal Joseph Bernardin of Chicago has noted.[49] It has also led to a greater commitment to the issues involved as well as to more detailed analysis in the bishops' pastoral letters because they have been dealing with a large amount of information at a sophisticated level. Opponents of the NCCB's critical approach to U.S. economic and nuclear policy have claimed that the bishops have no expertise in such matters,[50] but in fact the writing commit-tees spent a considerable amount of time and energy studying the issues and consulting with experts.

The pastoral letters on peace and on the economy, titled *The Challenge of Peace* (published in 1983) and *Economic Justice for All* (1986), are a new stage of U.S. episcopal discussions of sociopolitical issues. Many of their themes are not new but instead are based on papal encyclicals and on the documents of Vatican II. Nevertheless, the letters are bolder and more specific critiques of Western government policy and economic ethics than anything that has come from the hierarchy, whether in Rome or in the United States. Ultimately, they may challenge the ideological structure of Catholicism.

THE 1986 PASTORAL LETTER ON ECONOMICS

We have already seen that the American Church accepted the legitimacy of liberal politics as early as two centuries ago: a minority church of fairly powerless citizens could only benefit from the liberal separation of church and state. With Vatican II, official Church doctrine on such matters became basically equivalent to the American Catholic perspective as throughout the world Catholic alliance with the state became increasingly uncommon.[51]

But the American hierarchy has little commitment to other types of liberalism, such as liberal economics or moral relativism.[52] The American episcopacy, and the institutional Church in general, derives its power primarily from its religious and moral authority. It of course participates necessarily in a capitalist economy in which it is not a significant actor; but the Church's power structure and ideological commitments do not have a necessary, strong commitment to capitalist economics. And moral relativism is fundamentally problematic in Catholic ideology.

Whereas the Catholic laity are as much involved in liberal society as they are in Catholic subculture, bishops' own social and ideological orientations are much more thoroughly directed toward the Church. This is a result of their high position in the Church power structure; their power and social status are based on, and they are well socialized into, dominant themes of Catholic ideology. Historically, there has simply been little reason for the American Church to pay much attention to liberal American ideology concerning economics. Thus we find the NCWC and NCCB over the decades making a number of statements rejecting a strongly free-market, individualist ideology. Chapter 4 already discussed the NCWC's 1919 "Program for Social Reconstruction." And many of the same themes of papal social doctrine appear in, among other statements and pastoral letters, "Church and Social Order" (1940), "Man's Dignity" (1953), and the most recent, *Economic Justice for All* (1986).[53] For example, from "Church and Social Order":

> No absolute or unlimited ownership...can be claimed by man as if he were free to follow his own selfish interests without regard to the necessity of others.[54]

> The first claim of labor, which takes priority over any claim of the owners to profits, respects the right to a living wage. By the term *living wage* we understand a wage sufficient not merely for the decent support of the workingman himself but also of his family.[55]

And from *Economic Justice for All*:

> The basis for all that the Church believes about the moral dimensions of economic life is its vision of the transcendent worth—the sacredness—of human beings. *The dignity of the human person, realized in community with others, is the criterion against which all aspects of economic life must be measured.*

...Similarly, all economic institutions must support the bonds of community and solidarity that are essential to the dignity of persons.[56]

But the more recent pastoral letters go much further than the bishops have ever been willing to go. The letters present extended critiques of what the bishops see as the ethical underpinnings of nuclear defense policies and American economic life. Both letters are departures from previous NCWC and NCCB statements because they are at a much higher level of sophistication and specificity, including extended citations not only of Church documents, but also of secular scholarship. These "letters," titled *The Challenge of Peace* and *Economic Justice for All*, weigh in at 111 and 204 pages, respectively. This includes an eight-page summary at the beginning of each, which the bishops apparently felt was necessary given the length and level of detail. (Although the letter on the economy was published in 1986, three years after *The Challenge of Peace*, I discuss it first because we have already encountered many of its themes in previous chapters.)

After summarizing its basic perspective, explicitly grounding itself in papal and Vatican II social doctrine, the letter discusses extensively the ethical principles for the economy that, for the bishops, are clearly implicit in scripture. Certain of these principles guide the entire letter. The bishops argue that the criterion for judging every economic decision and institution is its contribution to human dignity, which can be fulfilled only in community. Society as a whole has an ethical obligation to fulfill all people's rights to social (and thus economic) participation, especially the rights of the poorer members of society. Indeed, economic decisions must reflect a "preferential option for the poor."

The letter includes extensive discussion of specific problems in important policy areas, such as employment, poverty, agriculture, and international economic relations. The bishops recommend orienting fiscal and monetary policy toward a goal of full employment, as the current levels of unemployment are "intolerable";[57] the disproportionate number of minority unemployed is particularly "scandalous."[58] The letter supports efforts to save family farms and to resist concentration of agricultural ownership. Drawing on discussions in papal social doctrine (especially from John XXIII and Paul VI) of the existence of global interdependence and necessity for international cooperation, the bishops recommend shifts away from foreign military and security aid and toward development aid. In discussing the problem of Third World debt, the letter essentially declares current international financial and trade arrangements (the General Agreement on Tariffs and Trade, the International Monetary Fund, and the World Bank) to be outmoded.[59] It reiterates social doctrine's support for the rights of workers to unionize and to engage in collective bargaining as well as the right to private property with accompanying responsibility to use that property for the common good.

All the major themes of the letter—the internationalist outlook, the perspective on private property and labor relations, the emphasis on participation, the urging of the expansion of government welfare programs—clearly derive from papal social doctrine, not only that of Leo XIII and Pius XI, but also more recent statements such as John XXIII's *Mater et Magistra* of 1961 and Paul VI's *Populorum Progressio* of 1967. The emphasis on individual human dignity began with John, and Paul especially emphasized new themes of international economic obligation (discussed further in chapter 7).

But it is not the case that there is nothing new in *Economic Justice for All*. First, the letter demonstrates that the political and ideological space for the Church to address the concerns of the poorer sectors of society has grown considerably. That space began to emerge with the Church's loss of secular power in European society and with Leo XIII's encyclical founding modern social doctrine, *Rerum Novarum*. But note how much further *Economic Justice for All* takes the opening toward the poorer, nonelite parts of society. There is a stronger tone—for instance, in discussion of the need to "empower" the poor[60]—that contrasts with the image of poor people as passive objects of charity common in the encyclicals of pre–Vatican II popes.

But there is something even newer, perhaps bolder, and more important in *Economic Justice for All*: there is a new level of detail and thus of controversy, so that the bishops, for example, are willing to cite hard data to reject the view that people who receive welfare assistance do not want to work or that such assistance encourages people to have children at public expense.[61]

As a result, there is some implicit questioning of the ideological structure that makes discussions of sociopolitical problems more vague and subordinate to discussions of faith and morals. *Economic Justice for All* does make clear distinctions between matters of ethical principle (which have varying interpretations in practice and according to changing circumstances), and specific policies, and claims to have religious authority only over the former.[62] Yet, as already noted, the bishops devote much of the letter to discussions of specific policies. It is not entirely clear how exactly one should reconcile the following statements:

> The pastoral letter is not a blueprint for the American econ-omy. It does not embrace any particular theory of how the economy works, nor does it attempt to resolve the disputes between different schools of economic thought.[63]

> The Church's teaching opposes collectivist and statist economic approaches. But it also rejects the notion that a free market automatically produces justice.[64]

> We know that some of our specific recommendations are controversial. As bishops, we do not claim to make these prudential judgments with the same kind of authority that marks our declarations of principle. But, we feel obliged to teach by example how Christians can undertake concrete analysis and make specific judgments on economic issues. The Church's teachings cannot be left at the level of appealing generalities.[65]

Can one "not embrace any particular theory of how the economy works" while specifically rejecting collectivist and free-market approaches? Are the bishops suggesting that even though specific judgments are not currently part of the Church's teachings, those teachings "cannot be left" at their current "level of appealing generalities"? And what exactly would constitute a "blueprint for the American economy," if authoritative "declarations of principle" combined with "specific judgments on economic issues" do not?

THE 1983 PEACE PASTORAL

Similar questions emerge even more forcefully if one examines *The Challenge of Peace*, which the NCCB published in 1983. In fact, the "peace pastoral," as it is often called, may provide even stronger and more complex challenges to the structure of Catholic ideology than does *Economic Justice for All*. Before we address those challenges, let us examine the ideological bases of *The Challenge of Peace*.

The pre–Vatican II American episcopacy was willing to actively support U.S. war efforts against Roman preferences, especially in the Spanish-American War.[66] During World War II, the bishops displayed vocal patriotism as Pius XII made some statements criticizing Allied actions, statements difficult for American Catholics to defend. But Franklin Roosevelt was more friendly to the Vatican than had been previous presidents (this was partly due to his courting of Catholic voters),[67] so that it became easier to support both Vatican and American government ideology on foreign policy issues because the two overlapped considerably. In the late 1940s and 1950s, the U.S. government and Rome were both obsessed with anticommunism. The United States, of course, was fighting the cold war, and Pius XII, despite his Eurocentric view of the world, knew the United States was an important ally for his strongly anticommunist policy. The U.S. episcopacy, in turn, echoed many of Pius's themes, issuing at least nine statements in the 1950s protesting religious persecution in communist countries.[68]

After Vatican II, the foreign policy outlook of the American episcopacy began to diverge more from the U.S. government, as the bishops became increasingly multilateral in perspective as well as receptive to doubts about the moral basis of modern warfare. These doubts reflected a loyal consideration of the internationalist, cooperative views of war and peace that emerged with Pope John XXIII's *Pacem in Terris* of 1963 and Vatican II's *Gaudium et Spes*.[69] Paul VI echoed many of the same themes and gave explicit support for strengthened, cooperative, global decision-making in the form of the United Nations. John XXIII and Vatican II began the process of doubting the moral status of threatening to use nuclear weapons (but did not totally resolve the issue).[70] The American bishops' increased commitment to multilateral peace-making thus made them more hesitant to take the American government's perspective on, for example, Vietnam or Central America.[71] Likewise, the American episcopacy gained the confidence to apply Church ideology on sociopolitical issues to a critique of U.S. economic policy (incidentally, again, emphasizing an American international moral obligation, especially to the Third World).

At times, of course, bishops' positions converge with government policies. For example, in the late 1970s Father J. Bryan Hehir of the bishops' office for international justice and peace testified on behalf of the bishops in favor of the Panama Canal treaties.[72] Here the bishops addressed a specific, controversial legislative issue that did not have immediate implications for the Church, an action they had been hesitant to take until the previous few decades. Their view of development and of the Third World is inspired by Pope Paul VI's *Populorum Progressio*.[73] The point is not that they always choose to oppose the state but that they are oriented primarily toward applying Church ethics—regardless of whether those ethics stand in opposition to U.S. government policies—rather than toward accommodating state policy.

The U.S. Church has become, then, at least on sociopolitical matters, less parochially *American* and more *Roman* in its outlook. A recent, very well-informed analysis of the American Church and the international Church made the understandable mistake of seeing the bishops' perspective on social issues as deriving from their 1919 "Program of Social Reconstruction" and Catholic association with the New Deal.[74] In fact, the bishops' interest in the 1919 statement was short-lived, and their fear of government interference with families and schools eventually overrode their commitment to New Deal social programs, as we saw in chapter 4.[75] Although the 1919 statement has much in common with *Economic Justice for All*, largely because each is based on Church social doctrine, the bishops of the 1980s certainly paid much more attention to recent Church documents than to the 1919 statement when they wrote their pastoral letter on economics. And in many ways the U.S. bishops' strong commitment to social issues after Vatican II is more a break with their past than a continuation of it, although they retain many of the themes of their earlier statements.

The important point here is to remember that structures constrain selectively; the ability of the U.S. episcopacy to address social and political issues became *less* constrained because of a combination of influences—some from Vatican II and some from changes within the United States. Thus the bishops could look more to themselves and to the Catholic ideology in which they were socialized to produce their messages.

This Romanization of the American episcopacy's sociopolitical views is ironic given that critics have charged that in *The Challenge of Peace* and *Economic Justice for All*, the bishops too easily accepted leftist secular critiques of American society and government.[76] Because such critics judge the letters' recommendations to mirror the social and political policies of the 1960s civil rights and peace movements, they have misunderstood the origins of the bishops' approach. It is true that the bishops have become more receptive to critical political perspectives, and they may have absorbed some ideas from movements of the 1960s, but their perspectives originate primarily from within Catholic ideology. The appearance of an early 1988 encyclical by Pope John Paul II, for example, demonstrated that the concerns of U.S. episcopal social doctrine are not unorthodox. The encyclical, titled *Sollicitudo Rei Socialis*, continued the papacy's antiliberal perspective on capitalism and emphasis on international cooperation to establish peace. But as in the case of *Economic Justice for All*, *The Challenge of Peace*, while drawing very much on papal statements and especially on *Gaudium et Spes*, goes beyond the more general pronouncements of popes and of Vatican II.

Catholic ideology on war and peace (i.e., the just war doctrine, which originated with St. Augustine) is a combination of specific moral prohibitions, such as the prohibition of directing attacks on noncombatants, and flexible applications to macroscopic situations. In practice, the just war view has a long history of being applied in ways that justify and accommodate state policy, even to justify the purposes of both sides to a conflict, despite the fact that it prohibits offensive war. For example, Catholic bishops from the United States and Spain each supported their country's cause in the Spanish-American War. In the American Civil War, southern bishops did not object to the Confederate cause, while northern bishops did not object to the Union cause.

Indeed, Catholic ideology is structured so that applying perspectives on sociopolitical issues overly specifically undermines that ideological structure and thus causes political problems within the Church. Let us look at *The Challenge of Peace* closely to examine that process.

To summarize the letter, *The Challenge of Peace* was concerned primarily with nuclear weapons, with a good deal of discussion of the policy of nuclear deterrence—a policy aimed at discouraging enemy attacks by threatening nuclear annihilation in return. The bishops stated that "the first imperative is to prevent any use of nuclear weapons,"[77] implying, for example, that containing communism was a subordinate priority. They could foresee no legitimate reason to begin nuclear war on any scale,[78] and they expressed "profound skepticism about the moral acceptability of any use of nuclear weapons."[79] Like the economics pastoral of 1986, the peace pastoral examined what the bishops saw as relevant biblical discussions of war and peace and cited some relevant ethical guidelines,[80] but there is a difference because the bishops found no specific scriptural guidelines on war and peace.[81] But they did frame much of the discussion in terms of the just war tradition, focusing especially on the "legitimate principle of self-defense" and the morally binding principles of discrimination and proportionality. Acts of war must not be made indiscriminately; one must not target or unreasonably endanger noncombatants. By proportionality, they meant "that the damage to be inflicted and the costs incurred by war must be proportionate to the good expected by taking up arms."[82]

There were a variety of topics about peace and war that the letter discussed, including the need to build positive steps toward peace. For example, the bishops repeatedly called "for the establishment of some form of global authority"—that is, a stronger United Nations—to safeguard justice and peace.[83] But the burning issue of the letter, and the source of great controversy, was American policy on nuclear weapons, especially the strategy of nuclear deterrence, which they found inherently ethically problematic. It is impossible, they argued, to be confident that any use of nuclear weapons could be controlled and limited in a way that would meet the principles of proportionality and discrimination (or could be controlled in any way at all). Deterrence even involves explicit threats against civilian areas, which is unacceptable.[84]

In applying the principles of just war doctrine, the letter repeatedly distinguished binding, general principles from specific policy *recommendations*.[85] The bishops clearly did not claim that they had the final word on all issues.[86] But they certainly insisted that it was not enough to state general moral principles and that the Church must involve itself in politics because of the ethical dimensions of political decisions.[87] The bishops explicitly framed their letter as part of a process of increasing specificity in Catholic doctrine on rights and duties within "a moral order of international relations."[88] For example, they included very specific analysis of the value of particular treaties and policy initiatives.[89] The bishops accepted deterrence only as a transitional policy on the way toward more effective arms control; in the absence of such efforts, deterrence is unacceptable.[90] "Immoral means can never be justified by the end sought; no objective, however worthy of [*sic*] good in itself, can justify sinful acts or policies."[91]

Because of the emphasis on ethical purity, the letter, while explicitly emphasizing criteria from the just war tradition, partly steps away from that tradition by treating the just war approach and nonviolent resistance (i.e., civil disobedience) as equally valid Christian traditions.[92] This is a major innovation in Catholic social teaching. Vatican II legitimated conscientious objector status for Catholics,[93] in contrast to previous arguments that military duty was a moral obligation in a just war. The U.S. Church as an institution gave no support for conscientious objectors in World War II or any previous wars; the lay Catholic Worker movement provided the only such assistance in World War II.[94] *The Challenge of Peace*, however, essentially declared that there are two very different but equally valid ethical judgments of war: just war theory and "Christian non-violence."

It is interesting to see that this increased emphasis on a strict application of ethical criteria, resulting from a weakened institutional need to accommodate state policy, makes bishops' perspectives more similar to those of Catholics outside the hierarchy who have opposed American military policy—for example, Dorothy Day, Thomas Merton, and Daniel and Philip Berrigan. The "Catholic left" of the Vietnam War era took a very ethically oriented approach to the issue of war.[95]

Nevertheless, the bishops arrived at their position by a very different route than the Catholic left had; there is little or no evidence that the political opinions of such activists suddenly converted the bishops. Although the bishops did state that conscientious objection was a valid Christian tradition, most of the letter is in fact a very strict application of the ethical principles of the traditional just war doctrine.[96] But previously, that doctrine had been applied only loosely and, commonly, to justify Church support for particular state military actions and policies. But strict application undermines Catholic ideological structure because it leads to judgments on particular policies. With such an approach, it is extremely difficult to judge modern war strategies to be "just"; indeed, as the bishops argued, nuclear weapons and nuclear strategy inherently violate the principles of discrimination and proportionality.

The views of Thomas Gumbleton, the auxiliary bishop of Detroit who was perhaps the most important proponent of *The Challenge of Peace*, are a clear example of the emphasis on ethical purity. (Gumbleton, incidentally, seems to see the just war doctrine as inhibiting forceful Church opposition to nuclear weapons.)[97] In a 1982 interview with *U.S. News and World Report*, when asked whether the United States should disarm even if the Soviet Union were not willing to do so, Gumbleton responded, "When you make judgments about what is morally right or morally wrong, you can never base your judgment on what someone else does. You teach your children not to steal, because it's wrong. You don't say, 'Don't steal unless you see somebody else stealing.'"[98]

Church doctrine on war and peace has developed in a context analogous to that which produced its view of capitalist economics. That is, the Church stopped participating in temporal power long enough ago that Catholic ideology does not reflect the ideology of states, or of the most powerful groups in secular society, on such issues. It has not, then, developed any systematic defense of nuclear deployment, despite previous centuries of legitimating military initiatives. An example of this autonomy from state policy is the reinterpretation of the just war requirement that war be declared by a "competent authority," usually construed to mean that only governments can legitimately sponsor war. But *The Challenge of Peace* calls for further analysis of "the moral issues of revolutionary warfare" after stating that "the just-war tradition has been open to a 'just revolution' position, recognizing that an oppressive government may lose its claim to legitimacy."[99]

And so it is from the lay Catholic right, which does not have the historical autonomy from secular politics that the bishops have, that opposition to the bishops' positions was most forceful. Prominent critics of both *Economic Justice for All*[100] and *The Challenge of Peace* were Michael Novak and William F. Buckley, Jr., who are associated with the conservative magazine *National Review*. Very much emphasizing that the bishops' opinions on sociopolitical issues, in contrast to faith and morals, are not binding doctrine,[101] this group published *Moral Clarity in the Nuclear Age*, a "Letter from Catholic Clergy and Laity," about the same time as *The Challenge of Peace*. These authors also applied and extended just war doctrine but to argue that nuclear deterrence is an ethical imperative to assure justice and freedom in the world. (Interestingly, they also stated that the meaning of just war doctrine is not entirely clear in a nuclear world and needs to be reinterpreted.)[102]

It is, arguably, logically possible to use just war doctrine to defend modern military policies, but the bishops were not interested in doing so.[103] The lay Catholic right argued that in a nuclear world, deterrence is the only policy that allows self-defense—and just war doctrine clearly recognizes the right of self-defense. And one does not *intend* to kill noncombatants; instead, one intends to deter the use of nuclear weapons precisely so that noncombatants remain alive and free.[104] The point is not that this logic is airtight or that the bishops' logic is better or worse. Instead, the point is that defending state policy was simply not the bishops' top priority. Rather than allowing flexible interpretations of just war doctrine, as the Church has done in the past, they emphasized ethical clarity and specificity in a context of openness to views very critical of government policy. They rejected the ambiguity of Church ideology on war and peace, an ambiguity that was essential in leaving Catholic ideology flexible enough to justify a variety of state policies.

THE BISHOPS AND IDEOLOGICAL BOUNDARIES

Because the modern ideological structure of Catholicism sharpened the boundary between specific, "moral" rules and vague, less important sociopolitical principles, making sociopolitical ideology more critical of modern states is politically problematic within the Church. The Vatican is more hesitant than are American bishops to apply doctrine on war and peace so specifically, for Rome must concern itself with preventing state hostility against the Church in many different international contexts. In the 1980s, John Paul II seemed to be groping toward a yet ambiguous reconciliation of the attempt to guarantee Church independence of communist governments—requiring Western state protection—with the problematic moral implications of nuclear deterrence.[105] It is more important for the Vatican than the U.S. episcopacy to keep doctrine on war and peace somewhat vague. The Vatican actually intervened after the second draft (the third was the final) of *The Challenge of Peace* to ensure that the letter clearly distinguished between binding moral principles—such as the prohibition against attacking noncombatants—and particular policy preferences.[106]

Even American bishops, partly because of the Vatican's intervention, remained ambivalent about prohibiting or endorsing specific policy initiatives. In the NCCB debates over the letter, there was extended discussion over whether to endorse a nuclear "freeze"; ultimately the bishops decided to use the synonymous term *halt*, given that many feared the "freeze" language would be seen as an endorsement of a particular political movement known as the "nuclear freeze" movement.[107] The extended debate over what may seem a trivial difference in language demonstrates their ambivalence about addressing particular policy options.

Yet the bishops wanted to make very specific judgments—otherwise the letter would have consisted of uncontroversial platitudes. They clearly stated that certain policies can be unequivocally judged to be impermissible.[108] Nuclear deterrence itself, a number of passages unambiguously implied, is inherently unethical and unacceptable.[109]

Bishops face a dilemma in attempting to increase their commitment to sociopolitical issues. The basic choice is to respect the ideological structure of the Church, which means not delving into such issues too much (so as to avoid specification) and thus having little influence on American policy and little latitude for their own initiatives, or to devote considerably more attention, which could lead to a challenge to Catholic ideological structure.

If they continue to emphasize that their views on specific issues are subordinate to their views on "universal moral principles and formal church teaching,"[110] the bishops will be acknowledging that sociopolitical concerns are not as important as faith and morals. Even though it is of interest to the Church to specify in great detail what types of reproductive technology are impermissible, for example, they would be admitting that the Church is not willing to make the same commitment to matters of social ethics.[111] They could make only abstract ethical pronouncements on social issues; most likely, the greater the abstraction, the more difficult it will be to have an impact on the Church or on U.S. society.

How to deal with the relationship between moral doctrine and sociopolitical issues is an unresolved, central issue among the body of U.S. bishops. It is, of course, a delicate and difficult issue, both within the Church and within American society. Within the Church, such questions necessarily have implications for the centralization of ideological control— that is, the relationship between Roman authority and episcopal authority. Within U.S. society, the priority and specificity of sociopolitical issues versus moral issues would be considerably less difficult if Catholic moral stands were generally accepted by Americans, at least by those most politically active. This was the case in many nineteenth-century societies in which the Catholic Church was an important social force; the nineteenth-century hierarchy could proclaim the inviolability of a traditional, patriarchal morality that generally went unchallenged. Indeed, at that time, the Catholic Church concerned itself mainly with societies where a large majority of the population was at least nominally Catholic; but even non-Catholic European elites accepted some form of a patriarchal morality. Church moral absolutes in such a context were uncontroversial and thus did not require political advocacy to have them legally respected as binding on governments.

But contemporary U.S. bishops participate in a society and a polity that do not respect the Catholic boundary between moral and political. The law of the land does not necessarily accommodate Catholic morals, and so it is the people secularly known as "politicians" who have the direct ability to end any legal violation of what Catholic doctrine considers God-given moral rules that everyone must obey. According to Catholic ideology, such moral rules are not political issues. Bishops across the spectrum of sociopolitical opinion agree that abortion, a prime example, is not a political issue. True, binding morals (part of God's "natural law" and thus not simply a sectarian Catholic position) have political implications, but that does not put them in the sphere of politics, where there is legitimate room for disagreement. Indeed, binding morals limit political decisions precisely because they are of higher priority and importance than politics; politics is the realm of strategy and discussion within moral (nonpolitical) boundaries.[112] Of course, to most Americans, the issue of abortion is very political. Thus bishops themselves must engage in activities that look an awful lot like politics to have their moral doctrine heard.

The prominence of the issue of abortion in U.S. politics in the 1970s and 1980s has accelerated debate among American bishops about the relationship between their commitment to inflexible moral commitments and their sociopolitical commitments. Abortion is, to the pope and to the U.S. episcopacy, of such overwhelming moral importance that it is a prime public concern. A central axis of debate—usually an implicit, rather than explicit, debate (at least publicly)—that emerged among the American episcopacy in the 1980s was the question of how narrowly the moral teaching on abortion circumscribes the options of Catholic politicians. (The options of Catholic voters were also a topic of debate, although less so.) The more Romanizing bishops—most prominently, Cardinals Bernard Law and John O'Connor—insist that Catholic morals are absolute, inflexible doctrinal requirements to which Catholic politicians absolutely must adhere. In this position, they have considerable ideological capital on which to draw, even though they most likely are far from constituting a majority of the American episcopacy.

Thus when, beginning in 1989, a few bishops raised the possibility of sanctions as severe as excommunication against particular Catholic politicians, they could point to the inflexible, binding moral doctrine on abortion. (In at least one case, in San Diego, a bishop barred a prochoice

Catholic politician from communion.) As the 1990s began, there loomed on the horizon the specter of a few bishops increasingly denouncing, and even instructing Catholics not to vote for, Catholic politicians who decline to stake their careers on strong opposition to legal abortion, a stand apparently unpopular with the majority of voters in most states. Cardinal O'Connor warned of excommunication and condoned a fellow bishop's public declaration that Governor Mario Cuomo's stance on abortion placed him in serious risk of going to hell.[113] (Cuomo, like a number of Catholic politicians, has claimed that he is personally opposed to abortion but does not feel he should legally impose his views in the absence of a popular consensus.) It is certainly the case as well that John Paul II approves—his own public statements have shown no willingness to compromise on the legality of abortion.

Such an uncompromising position almost certainly characterizes only a minority of the American episcopacy, but such a position is easier to construct and defend within Catholic ideological structure than is the position that sociopolitical concerns are as important as moral issues. As long as bishops can excommunicate Catholics for their stands on abortion, yet they only *recommend* sociopolitical reform, they may have trouble establishing a reputation as luminaries rather than reactionaries. The legal status of abortion is to the American bishops of the late twentieth century what separation of church and state was to Gregory XVI and Pius IX: it is an issue that puts the Church on a collision course with secular politics. As in the nineteenth century, many non-Catholics (and even many Catholics) feel that the hierarchy's position on abortion is imperious and no less hostile to the separation of church and state than was the nineteenth-century papal condemnation of freedom of religion. Ironically, it is the opinion that the Church's primary mission concerns faith and morals (including the morality of abortion), rather than (what the Church considers) politics, that in a liberal world evokes the strongest cries that the Church needs to stick to religion and stay out of (what the secular world considers) politics.

THE ABSOLUTES OF MORAL DOCTRINE

Can U.S. bishops, then, increase their commitment to sociopolitical issues, or will those who favor the priority of moral issues always dominate? Even those who favor commitment to sociopolitical issues have their hesitations. For example, they are hesitant to organize support for their positions (presumably among Catholic laity), which may be necessary to be an effective force within American politics and policy-making.[114] This is not to say the bishops themselves intentionally undermine their sociopolitical commitments. Clearly, the bishops do want to have an impact, as they regularly make public statements on a range of issues from the plight of farm workers, to aid to refugees, to whether "Star Wars" can be ethically justified. They remain willing to take unpopular positions—for example, in opposing the Persian Gulf War in late 1990 and early 1991.[115] There have been attempts to raise ethical issues about nuclear weaponry and the economy within Catholic education and parish life.[116]

But these efforts have been of questionable success and do not compare with the episcopal involvement in the national debate over abortion, their most persistent, uncompromising involvement in public policy. The NCCB's 1990 controversial decision to hire the nation's second largest public relations firm to promote their views on abortion—a considerably more active step than they have taken in regard to the economics or peace pastorals—was apparently broadly supported among the bishops.[117] The bishops' own actions thus sometimes reinforce the view that Catholicism is primarily about restricting the moral options of individuals and families.

If the NCCB continues on its current course, over the years the public may grow accustomed to its making "leftist" pronouncements on sociopolitical issues, and it may have some influence, even as it continues implicitly to send the message that abortion, the prohibition of homosexuality, and so on are fundamentally more important than military adventurism or other violations of social ethics. It is true that shifting course, to attempt more aggressively to counter the image that Catholicism ultimately is about conservative sexual morality, would require some challenge to Catholicism's ideological structure. The bishops would have to argue either that both moral and sociopolitical pronouncements are binding on all political actors or that both are positions that Catholics should advance but are subject to political negotiation and compromise.

To insist that specific applications of social ethics are as binding as the specifics of faith and morals would mean that participation in certain government policies (such as nuclear deterrence) is inherently sinful. This type of challenge would involve a challenge to Rome's power to define what type of doctrine is binding, a challenge whose success would be extremely unlikely. (We can expect Rome to continue to centralize control over binding doctrine and to avoid issues that could elicit state hostility.) As it now stands, the pronouncements of episcopal conferences do not even bind individual bishops who belong to those conferences. It would be nearly impossible to maintain confidence among the laity in challenging what is considered a fundamental tenet of the faith—Roman dominance. Furthermore, they are unlikely to influence public policy if they insist that their ethical positions must be accepted absolutely and universally.

While theoretically possible, this, then, is an unlikely path, perhaps especially in the American context. We have seen that historically concern with innovation in sociopolitical ideology has been associated with the decentralization of doctrinal control away from Rome and thus with a narrowing of the scope of binding doctrine. It is unlikely that American bishops, who overall have been in favor of such a trend, would prefer to make more doctrine binding; indeed, such an approach could backfire because arguing to make more doctrine binding could easily be transformed into an argument that *Rome's* authority should be expanded, given that Rome has long decided on binding doctrine. So, not surprisingly, there has been little evidence that American bishops would favor such a change.

The other type of challenge, then, would involve extending the liberalization of Vatican II in arguing both that sociopolitical issues are not thoroughly subordinate to faith and morals and that if Catholics want to inject either faith and morals or social ethics into politics, they must act in a truly liberal, democratic fashion.[118] No longer could the Church insist that Catholic morals must be respected absolutely and universally. Such an approach would in some sense revive and extend the Americanist deemphasis of pre–Vatican II doctrine hostile to political pluralism. Again, this is a risky challenge because it means treating binding (and thus Roman) doctrine as subject to political negotiation.

There are, however, signs that some bishops will explore this path. The dilemma of attempting to be part of a pluralist public policy debate while accepting Roman control of faith and morals was especially clear in the December 1987 NCCB statement on AIDS (acquired immune deficiency syndrome) education and prevention. Supporters of the statement have said that it was not ready for consideration at the conference's annual meeting in November, but the Administrative Board of the NCCB—which has authority when the full membership is not in session—felt there was an urgent need to attempt to contribute to public consideration of the issue. It had been increasingly clear that the stand most consistent with Catholic moral doctrine—that the only legitimate prevention of AIDS is the absence of sex outside of heterosexual marriage—was not taken seriously by most health professionals and many government officials. The NCCB statement thus tentatively accepted instruction about condom use in public education as the lesser of two evils, the realistic alternative being continued spread of the disease. The statement insisted that such instruction had to be coupled with education about the moral requirements of abstinence outside of marriage. To receive a hearing on its insistence of abstinence, then, the NCCB was willing to allow a policy compromise that ran partly contrary to its own moral doctrine. In their own words: "Because we live in a pluralistic society, we acknowledge that some will not agree with our understanding of human sexuality."[119]

But ambivalence within the body of bishops expressed itself as conflict over this particular statement. A few more traditionalist bishops, led by Cardinal John O'Connor of New York, disavowed the statement (raising, incidentally, the problem that the NCCB cannot enforce its policies); bishops resorted to public squabbling. Cardinal Joseph Ratzinger, the Vatican official in charge of enforcing doctrinal orthodoxy, wrote to the bishops before their next meeting, suggesting that they should consult with the Vatican before addressing such important matters in public. Ratzinger also indicated that the bishops' acceptance of instruction about the use of prophylactics was contrary to Catholic moral doctrine. In November 1989 at the annual NCCB meeting, the bishops approved a new statement that continued to emphasize compassion for those suffering with AIDS but that eliminated the acceptance of instruction on condom use.

Nevertheless, the possibility of what we might call a "new Americanism" continued through the 1980s under the leadership of Cardinal Joseph Bernardin, archbishop of Chicago. Bernardin, beginning in the period of the writing of *The Challenge of Peace* (drafted in the early 1980s and published in 1983), has argued for a "consistent ethic of life." He has argued that a prolife stance consists not only of opposition to abortion, but also of opposition to the arms race and to capital punishment as well as advocacy of antipoverty efforts. It is interesting to observe how he responded to early critics (in 1984) who argued that the issue of abortion must always be a higher priority than the other issues:

> In the past year some have questioned whether the linkage of
> the right of life with other human rights may unintentionally di-
> lute our stand against abortion. On both moral and social
> grounds, I believe precisely the opposite. The credibility of our
> advocacy of every unborn child's right to life will be enhanced
> by a consistent concern for the plight of the homeless, the hun-
> gry and helpless in our nation, as well as the poor of the
> world.[120]

According to Bernardin, it is impossible to separate the issues of abortion, poverty, capital punishment, and the nuclear arms race because all concern human dignity and the value of life; and, strategically, other Americans are more likely to be convinced by a strong, consistent argument.[121] The argument includes an appeal for a more pluralist attempt to build consensus within American society, rather than reliance on uncompromising pronouncements (on abortion, especially). Bernardin has argued that it is up to individual voters, not the hierarchy, to decide on the merits of particular politicians, although it is appropriate for Catholic voters to apply the consistent ethic of life in their own evaluations of candidates.

Archbishop Rembert Weakland of Milwaukee has been one of the most prominent supporters of Bernardin's pluralist interpretation of the "consistent ethic of life." It is interesting to note that Weakland and Bernardin were, respectively, chairs of the drafting committees for *Economic Justice for All* and *The Challenge of Peace*. Weakland has been particularly willing to challenge Rome to continue decentralizing and revising doctrine at many levels in the spirit of Vatican II. He has, for example, publicly suggested that the Church ordain married men, a topic Rome considers taboo.[122] In addition to his statements in support of Bernardin's approach, Weakland promoted a somewhat less dogmatic approach to moral issues by engaging in and publicizing a series of discussions in 1990 with Catholic women in his archdiocese who disagreed with Church doctrine on abortion. Weakland's approach was to emphasize that he would uphold Church moral doctrine but felt it worthwhile to exchange views in a respectful, nonjudgmental forum. His reports on his discussions thus in a small way perhaps gave a certain legitimacy to dissent on sexual issues. (Weakland publicized, for example, that he encountered overwhelming anger over the Church prohibition of contraception.)[123] Also supportive has been Bishop Walter Sullivan of Richmond, whom we encountered earlier because of Vatican investigation of his orthodoxy.[124]

Amid the debate over the moral obligations of Catholic politicians on the issue of abortion, Weakland argued in 1990 that while the Catholic position is that all law should be moral, the Church must recognize

> that not all its moral positions will become perfectly mirrored in the legal realm, especially in a democratic and pluralist society. To change laws it knows that a consensus of the population must first be built up.

> Such moral persuasion will take much time and patience. Until that happens we will have to live with a certain ambiguity. We do so with regard to so many other issues as well....Our people here have to learn how to live in such a pluralistic society and not expect that every moral teaching will find its perfect echo in legislation....

> Those in public office do not have an easy task as we work toward a consensus. In this area I would hope that we would allow to our politicians as much latitude as reason permits,

even as we expect them to be consistent, compassionate and respectful of the dignity of life in all its aspects and developments.[125]

Although issues such as the arms race, poverty, and abortion are linked
together in the "consistent ethic," it is not entirely clear whether abortion
would still be the highest priority—that is, first issue among equals. In the
debate within the NCCB about *The Challenge of Peace* as well as during
Geraldine Ferraro's vice-presidential campaign in 1984, Bernardin fended
off attempts to specify that abortion was a greater evil than the arms
race.[126] But he has made apparently contradictory statements:

> The policy of abortion on demand needs to be resisted and re-
> versed. But this does not mean the nuclear question can be ig-
> nored or relegated to a subordinate status.[127]

> As the U.S. bishops said in 1985 as they reaffirmed the Pastoral
> Plan for Pro-Life Activities, "society's responsibility to ensure
> and protect human rights demands recognition and protection
> of the right to life as antecedent to all other rights and the nec-
> essary condition for their realization. It is unlikely that efforts
> to protect other rights will ultimately be successful if life itself is
> continually diminished in value.... That is why the church op-
> poses proposals which would cut short the lives of mentally or
> physically disabled persons on the grounds that they lack a min-
> imally acceptable 'quality of life.'"[128]

It is possible that Bernardin's use of an example of euthanasia, rather
than of abortion, in discussing the "right to life" in the second quotation
was a subtle means of avoiding identification with those bishops who
support the more Roman position of giving abortion a distinct, special
priority. Nevertheless, the second quotation would place the Church category of moral issues—which would include both abortion and euthanasia—at a higher priority than sociopolitical issues, while the first quotation
clearly would not.

Bernardin has stated that some issues are more important than others,
and he recognizes a boundary between the moral and the political.[129]
Although the location of those boundaries is not always clear, for the most
part he seems to mean that the Church takes moral positions within
Catholic dogma but never insists that they must be *implemented* dogmatically, no matter what the issue. His position, then, emphasizes persuasion
and is similar to Weakland's liberal, pluralist approach to moral issues in
the foregoing quotation.

It will be interesting to see in the coming years how the "consistent ethic
of life" develops; although almost certainly unknown to most Catholics, it

has clearly penetrated the discourse of American bishops. But many bishops, while using the "consistent ethic" language, have interpreted it in a way more consistent with current Catholic ideological structure than have its main proponents. Bernardin, Weakland, and Sullivan emphasize a *continuum* of issues in a way that downplays the distinctiveness of any one issue. But some other bishops, while accepting the notion of an ethical link among issues, continue explicitly to accord abortion a special status, emphasizing a hierarchy of priorities within that continuum.[130] Different bishops thus interpret the consistent ethic approach more or less dogmatically according to how much the continuum of issues becomes a hierarchy of issues. The more emphasis is placed on the priority of abortion, the more compatible the perspective is with Catholic ideological structure and thus with the public condemnation of particular Catholic politicians for pro-choice stands.

Future Dilemmas

Within the American episcopacy as a whole, we have seen that there is ambivalence about how to proceed in the public arena, how to further sociopolitical concerns, and how to continue constructing collegiality from the ambiguous legacy of Vatican II. The bishops clearly want to be more involved in American society and in the construction of Catholic ideology than they were before Vatican II. Indeed, they see Catholicism's development as responsive to changes in American society. And in justifying their concerns with nuclear policy and other issues, they appeal to the reformist, decentralizing images of Vatican II, such as the notion that doctrine needs to evolve with the signs of the times: "A prominent 'sign of the times' today is a sharply increased awareness of the danger of the nuclear arms race. ...The 'new moment' which exists in the public debate about nuclear weapons provides a creative opportunity and a moral imperative to examine the relationship between public opinion and public policy."[131]

A number of bishops freely admit that it was the election of Ronald Reagan, amid talk that nuclear war was winnable and that social spending had to be slashed, that precipitated the writing of their letters on peace and on the economy.[132] The peace letter points out that the moral implications of nuclear deterrence—and thus presumably of many issues of state policy—were not immediately clear in the years following the development of such weapons. Thus, the bishops argue, it became necessary to widen and develop the moral debate;[133] we cannot answer ahead of time all moral questions we will face.

Widening the moral debate cuts two ways. While it is a mechanism of increasing Church attention to, and influence on, social issues and state policy, it also easily implies that moral doctrine must develop according to the signs of the times. As long as the bishops continue to see their role as one of applying Catholic perspectives to contemporary social issues, the pressure to challenge the boundary between the moral and the political will continue, as will disagreements with Rome. Papal control over moral doctrine, claimed to be infallible and unchanging, can make it very difficult to participate in changing debates on public policy. Condemning state policies such as legal abortion by appealing to a moral law that stands above politics, an approach that many U.S. bishops indeed support, ultimately can limit episcopal freedom of movement. It leads to the need to conform to Vatican moral doctrine and restrict sociopolitical pronouncements to a subordinate status.

Within the current ideological structure of Catholicism, there are a number of issues that bishops cannot easily address. For example, despite their efforts to open the Church to new views of women, there is little they can do but register discontent; they have no power to change the Church view of this issue. Internationally, U.S. bishops have been stronger promoters than most episcopacies of an expanded role for women in the Church. Their biggest project after *Economic Justice for All* was to be a pastoral letter on the role of women in the Church, but the obstacle of Catholic ideological structure will probably make the letter a weak one, if it appears at all. The bishops' committee working on the letter has shown signs of attempting to promote the place of women as much as possible without violating Catholic doctrine. But they cannot even discuss alternatives to current Church policy on the central issues of the ordination of women, contraception, or abortion. The committee's draft report demonstrated the ambivalence on the position of women: it denounced sexism and apparently included women as much as possible in drafting the report. But the bishops have not engaged in as public a drafting procedure as they did for letters on the economy and on peace, and Catholic doctrine places rather strict limits on the ability to satisfy feminist aspirations. By 1990, dissatisfaction with the letter among bishops and among prominent American Catholic women suggested possible abandonment of the project.[134]

Bishops, then, cannot easily engage in consultation—which is essential to develop attention to and participation in their own social concerns—without occasionally hearing complaints that they are powerless to address. To address such concerns and to be influential in public policy circles, they may have to widen their own Church authority in addressing politicized issues, whether matters of individual and family morals or matters of macro policy. Given that the scope of bishops' own authority is ultimately intertwined with the subordination of sociopolitical issues to faith and morals, it is perhaps at the episcopal level where we are most likely to see the first signs of the next stage in the development of the post–Vatican II Church.

6 Radicalization at the Periphery of Power

For popes and bishops, the boundary separating faith and morals from sociopolitical issues is of crucial importance; to a great extent it defines the hierarchy's relationship to the secular world, as well as defining the limits of collegiality. However, that boundary—whether perceived as something to maintain or to challenge—is less significant for groups less committed, both institutionally and ideologically, to the status quo.

American sisters provide an important and interesting comparison with American bishops because they are at a considerably lower position in the power structure of the Church.[1] As in the case of bishops, Vatican II granted them an increased organizational autonomy (a process that for sisters began in the 1950s) but was ambiguous in identifying the new parameters of authority, if any, that those organizations would have. But as women, sisters are, unlike bishops, on the periphery of institutional power: they are excluded from ordination, the episcopacy, or comparable influence in Rome. As a result, the leadership of U.S. sisters used their newfound organizational resources and stronger collective identity to mount an ideological challenge that went much further and faster than that of U.S. bishops. They came to reject the claims of Rome and of some bishops that the hierarchical, patriarchal governance of the Catholic Church is a fundamental tenet of the faith.

There are, however, some interesting parallels in the ideological history of U.S. bishops and U.S. sisters. Remember that American bishops were rather deferential within American society throughout the period before Vatican II. In fact, they were often nationalistic. Analogously, American sisters were not rebellious in the pre–Vatican II Church. And yet American

130

bishops have become quite critical of American government policy in recent decades. And American sisters became the most rebellious group in the U.S. Church.

How could these transformations have happened? Here we must consider a point raised in chapter 1 about "negative autonomy"; within the relevant social structures—U.S. society for the bishops, the Church for sisters—each group was fairly powerless. They therefore had an autonomy from those power structures in the sense of exclusion, so that more powerful actors did not always pay great attention to them. Bishops were not an important part of American political life; their patriotism, while partly reflecting a genuine enthusiasm for American freedom of religion, also reflected caution and fear of being considered disloyal outsiders. At a time when Catholics formed a subculture of poor immigrants, American bishops sought to prove that doubts about Catholic patriotism were unfounded. Although not identical, the situation of U.S. sisters was structurally similar: they were peripheral participants within the institutional hierarchy, not people who shared in the spoils of power. They did not significantly dissent from the workings of political and ideological centralization in the Church, but neither were they directly involved.

Groups with such negative autonomy usually do not have sufficient resources to develop a great deal of ideological independence; even if they do (e.g., American bishops were somewhat strong organizationally), such independence is a very risky venture sure to elicit negative sanctions. It is rare that the situation of such excluded groups (i.e., excluded within a given social structure) suddenly improves. But Catholics' status in American society dramatically improved after World War II, and the Second Vatican Council significantly expanded the organizational autonomy of both bishops and as we shall see sisters. This happened at a time when changes within sisters' communities—such as greatly expanded educational opportunities—increased their ability to develop an independent and sophisticated worldview.

Even though groups relatively powerless in a given social structure—bishops within American society or sisters within the Church—may, then, appear to have the same ideological commitments as do more powerful groups, those commitments may not be as strong as they seem. More important, they can rapidly disintegrate when the obstacles to ideological independence weaken. As we have already seen, for example, bishops never absorbed the particulars of American secular views of economic life, never having been important economic actors in American society. Similarly, sisters rapidly rejected patriarchal, hierarchical views of the Church once conditions were right. The new, ambiguous reforms and themes of Vatican II were a crucial cause of these changes.[2]

To explain how this occurred, I first provide a summary of the changes in the 1950s that provided American sisters' communities with increased organizational resources and a greater intellectual sophistication. Following that discussion is an analysis of the effects of Vatican II on this group in terms of the council's actual pronouncements and then of the changes that resulted among communities of sisters and within their national organization, the Conference of Major Superiors of Women (CMSW). Finally, I address the routinization of ideological diversity that eventually emerged in the Church as a result of the challenge that radicalization presented to the hierarchy.

Seeds of Change before the Council

The United States has the largest contingent of women religious in the world; at the time of Vatican II, there were about 180,000. Currently there are about 100,000 American sisters, twice the number of priests.[3] Historically, they have constituted an essential component of that central institution of the U.S. Church, the Catholic school (and also have been important in missionary, nursing, and other activities). Despite performing much of the everyday social service of the Church, they have remained on the periphery of institutional power. The prerequisite to any significant access to Church inner circles is, of course, ordination, a prerogative the Vatican continues emphatically to deny women. Far from having much power, American sisters were not even a united group into the 1950s. Communities remained socially segregated, the legacy of centuries of isolation of women religious from the secular world and of different communities of women from one another. Communities had official, institutional links only to their bishops and to Rome, not to one another.

This isolation began to break down under the papacy of Pius XII. For all his emphasis on the spiritual supremacy of the Church, we have seen that Pius was interested in the Church as a spiritual *institution*. Thus despite his commitment to maintaining papal supremacy, he was at times active in identifying areas where the Church as an institution needed to update its approaches to be more effective.[4] One of those areas was the status of religious in the Church in general and the education of teaching sisters in particular. Thus he convoked a series of international congresses of religious in the 1950s.[5] Concerned that Catholic education might be unable to meet the standards of secular pedagogy, he encouraged measures to increase the educational preparation of teaching sisters. Pius originated the idea of the need for the *renewal* and *adaptation* to changed times for all nonessential aspects of religious life,[6] although neither he nor most of the hierarchy could have foreseen how differently many sisters would eventually identify those "essentials."

Initially, American sisters were enthusiastically obedient to Rome and strove to reach the goals that Pius had set, as Mary Schneider's excellent research has demonstrated.[7] To meet those goals there emerged in 1952 the Sister Formation Conference, which encouraged greater commitment to the education of sisters. (The term *formation* refers to the process of training women for the convent in the period before they take final vows, about seven years; at times it is also used to refer to the continued education and development of a sister.) The Sister Formation Conference set up training programs that could enroll only a small fraction of American sisters, but its active leadership and its widely circulated *Bulletin* ably publicized its causes. It urged communities to support their sisters' educations, rather than rush them into teaching positions unprepared; that communities seemed quite receptive to the conference's message suggests a general feeling that sisters had been pushed into teaching too soon in their careers. The conference also publicized the need for sisters to study theology and to advance their own causes.[8]

In any case, the conference helped foster an attitude of more active participation in the Church[9] and promoted the expansion of educational opportunities of American sisters. In the early 1950s, it was unusual for communities to have programs promoting college education, but according to data gathered in a sister's 1971 doctoral dissertation, by 1967, 61 percent of sisters had bachelor's degrees. In 1955, only 16 percent of sisters who began teaching had at least three years of college, but in 1964, 80 percent did.[10] The Formation Conference even developed small signs of an explicit feminism in the 1950s, as some leaders questioned the traditionally passive images of women that led to exclusion from important opportunities. Such feminism was a decade ahead of most sisters and of American society as a whole.[11] The conference also promoted contacts between U.S. and Latin American sisters;[12] together with Rome's initiation of an increased missionary presence of U.S. religious in Latin America, such contacts surely contributed to the affinity of U.S. sisters for liberation themes in their discussions of the Church in the 1970s and 1980s.

The Sister Formation Conference, then, by providing an organizational context for sisters to address their own needs, had begun to supersede Pius XII's view of adaptation and renewal, one in which the goal was to conserve the current strengths and devotion of religious. Unintentionally, Pius planted the seeds for further change as well by encouraging the founding of conferences of major superiors; thus was born in 1956 in the United States the Conference of Major Superiors of Women, which became an official ecclesiastical body in 1959. CMSW was a national organization of superiors general of communities as well as provincial and regional superiors. (Larger communities are often divided into provinces.)[13]

Like the National Catholic Welfare Conference and the National Conference of Catholic Bishops, the CMSW (and its later successor, the Leadership Conference of Women Religious, or LCWR) was the official representative of communities of sisters but could not oblige its members to abide by its decisions.[14] And under Pius XII, any meetings or new activities were to remain under the strict supervision of the Vatican's Sacred Congregation for Religious (SCR).[15] Nevertheless, the very establishment of new sisters' organizations provided resources for the development of an independent spirit to which that pope would have been thoroughly opposed. It is true that the early CMSW operated much as Rome had intended. Devotional, spiritually inspiring talks, delivered mostly by male clerics, were the main fare of its meetings.[16]

But the CMSW provided a national organization with some official status in the Church, and both the Sister Formation Conference and CMSW led to a larger sense of identification across communities. This was especially true of the leadership of the communities, who actually engaged in most of these cross-community activities. It is worth noting that a group of women religious without the organizational autonomy of sisters—American nuns—never developed a similar challenge. Rome kept tighter control over their renewal process and granted significantly less organizational autonomy to the Association of Contemplative Sisters, occasionally even forbidding its existence.[17] The male counterpart to CMSW, the Conference of Major Superiors of Men (CMSM), did go through a renewal process and had a degree of organizational autonomy equal to that of American sisters, but change was not as rapid or as radical. It appears to be the case that CMSM did develop some of the same renewal themes as the CMSW, even going to some lengths to defend the Immaculate Heart Sisters of Los Angeles as the SCR prohibited some of their renewal changes. But members of CMSM, especially those who were priests, had a significant advantage in the power structure of the Church because they were male, and so they had greater institutional access and somewhat fewer restrictions over their lives. There were some signs that the CMSM did not want to become associated too closely with the CMSW, so that, for example, it did not have as negative an image in the eyes of bishops.[18]

But there were signs of change among the leadership of American sisters as early as the 1950s. Superiors of women rejected the 1958 Vatican suggestion that the women's conference be under the supervision of the men's conference. Rome's approach probably contributed to post–Vatican II complaints that women religious were treated like children. As we see in the ensuing discussion, questioning of canon law on religious began within CMSW even before Vatican II ended. There were also significant signs of resentment of overburdened work requirements, domineering clergy, and lack of sisters' representation on bodies that made decisions affecting their lives (as well as the inability to address the Second Vatican Council itself), even if those resentments did not constitute a call for major reforms in the Church's authority structure.[19]

Unwittingly, Rome had created the conditions for consciousness-raising among American sisters (again, especially the leadership, which actively participated in the national organizations). In hindsight, we may not find it surprising that a highly educated group committed to its own organizations had the potential of using those organizations to rebel against a distribution of power in which most decisions were made for them. But that potential was not even clear to sisters themselves until Vatican II. The council, which increased the autonomy of communities of sisters and publicized a less hierarchical model of the Church, turned that potential into a reality.

Vatican II: The Message

In an ecumenical gesture, a number of prominent observers from non-Catholic faiths were invited to the Second Vatican Council. In the second session of the council, Belgian Cardinal Léon-Joseph Suenens asked why no Catholic women, who were actually members of the Church, had received such invitations. As a result, the then-chairman of the CMSW, Sister Mary Luke Tobin, S.L., was one of fifteen women who received an invitation in 1964 in time to attend part of the third council session and all of the fourth.[20] Although she would later describe the invitations as "token" but important as a first step,[21] her reaction to the council at the time was appreciative and inspired, indicative of the devotion to the hierarchy, despite occasionally differing perspectives, that then characterized CMSW. Yet she also requested greater participation of women in the Vatican II reform process, not expecting immediate success. And she was aware and in favor of the fact that the "council fathers" would expect the individual communities to develop for themselves the details of adaptation and renewal.[22]

Sister Mary Luke and other prominent American sisters were excited about the council developments in general,[23] but they naturally paid partic-ular attention to the document on religious life of both women and men,

Perfectae Caritatis ("Decree on the Appropriate Renewal of the Religious Life").[24] Although, as we have seen, the notion of renewal and updating of religious life was not completely original with the council, it was clear that Vatican II would initiate an entirely new phase.

With *Perfectae Caritatis* the council intended "to deal with the life and rules of those institutes whose members profess chastity, poverty, and obedience, and to make provisions for their needs as the tenor of the times indicates."[25] There was, then, a primary intention of updating in keeping with the general thrust of Vatican II reforms. The document itself does not specify any radical changes but gives only general principles,[26] perhaps largely for the simple reason that the council's attempt to deal with the particulars of renewal ran out of time.[27] The document emphasized the importance of the spirit of the founder of a community's particular way of religious life and of the three vows of chastity, poverty, and obedience.[28] In ways, the council's perspectives on the place of religious were quite conservative, stating that religious are excluded from the hierarchy (and thus institutional decision-making power) of the Church and actually are part of the laity, not the clergy, a passage that would come to rankle some religious.[29]

But there were a number of ways in which the document opened doors. *Perfectae Caritatis* could easily be interpreted to imply the need, and latitude, for a great deal of reform and pluralism.[30] A crucial passage states:

> The manner of living, praying, and working should be suitably adapted to the physical and psychological conditions of today's religious and also, to the extent required by the nature of each community, to the needs of the apostolate [i.e., their particular work], the requirements of a given culture, the social and economic circumstances anywhere, but especially in missionary territories.

> The way in which communities are governed should also be re-examined in the light of these same standards.

> For this reason constitutions, directories, custom books, books of prayers and ceremonies, and similar compilations are to be suitably revised and brought into harmony with the documents of this sacred Synod. This task will require the suppression of outmoded regulations.[31]

The document also implicitly promoted greater initiative and independent organization among religious, encouraging federations of similar communities and of conferences of superiors such as the CMSW.[32] Throughout, it emphasized adaptation to modern needs and social customs.[33] Communities, through their general chapters (meetings of delegates that are their supreme legislative bodies) could institute "prudent experimentation, though in all such matters...the approval of the Holy See and of local Ordinaries [i.e., bishops] must be given when it is required."[34]

It would soon become clear, however, that many communities of women would disagree with Rome about when such approval was required and also about how renewal reforms were to be "brought into harmony with the documents of" Vatican II.[35] There was an emerging tension in renewal that reflected a larger tension in the message of the council: how could modernizing reforms and decentralization take place when there were to be no specific reductions of Rome's authority?

That tension is clear in Pope Paul VI's August 1966 pronouncements (after the council had ended) on the means by which *Perfectae Caritatis* was to be implemented. Paul declared that the implementation of this and other decrees be experimental until the Code of Canon Law was revised,[36] a process expected to take years. (In fact, it was not completed until 1983.) He also stated that renewal was to be the primary responsibility of the communities themselves via ordinary or special general chapters to be held by 1969. Seeming to reduce the threat of Rome's control, he stated that experimentation contrary to a community's constitutions would be readily approved by Rome to continue through the time of two general chapters, or about ten to twelve years.[37]

Given these pronouncements, it would seem that communities could institute a great deal of independent reform, and in fact many did, quite confident that they had the council's and the pope's blessings. Yet Paul underlined the importance of episcopal authority over religious,[38] and the general tone of his and the SCR's pronouncements on the implementation of renewal belied Rome's expectations for a pious, devotional approach to reform.[39] It would be incorrect to assert that Rome wanted no reform—it in fact chided communities that were too slow in instituting renewal—but it is clear from its later disputes with some communities that it expected that women religious would concentrate on minor external changes in their habits, their daily schedules of prayer and other activities, and their relationships to the larger Catholic community. Rome expected that sisters would reaffirm commitment to the traditional interpretation of the vows of poverty, chastity, and obedience. In 1964, when some communities were just beginning renewal, a representative of the SCR instructed the CMSW, "There are essentials and there are accidentals. None of the essentials can be changed or the very nature of religious life changes. We can't change obedience and still call it obedience. The essence of religious life is already established; we can't add to or take away from that essence and still call it the religious life."[40] (His remarks are particularly interesting because "obedience" was precisely subject to a radical reinterpretation and became a major facet of ideological divergence between American sisters and Rome. Many sisters came to argue that obedience was a vow to obey God, not Rome, and that it entailed openness to the immanent inspiration of the Holy Spirit through dialogue.)

But American sisters would soon come to resent what they saw as Roman interference; they seemed particularly receptive to the decentralizing message of the council and to the emphasis on the development of doctrine in the modern world.[41] Because they could apply these themes directly to the program of renewal, this process was probably the single most important impetus for the development of an oppositional ideology among American sisters. By the end of the council, sisters had already greatly increased their communications across communities and had expanded their educational horizons; in addition, the CMSW was already well established. But the renewal process enlivened sisters at the community level and was a classic, lived instance of the confused message of Vatican II: American sisters concentrated on clear council themes to absorb a message of decentralization, while the SCR was slow to realize that these women did not accept its own more hierarchical interpretation of Vatican II, which also could be justified in a reading of the council documents. The problem was that Vatican II, having initiated but not completed decentralization, encouraged different parts of the Church to lay claim to opposing horns of an ideological and political dilemma.

The Renewal Process

Renewal was not easy for many sisters; a perusal of records and correspondence from the renewal process of a number of communities makes clear that at times there were bitter feelings between those who felt that change was going too slow and those who felt that the essentials of religious life were being lost.[42] The world looked very different when some communities experimented with members living in apartments or stopped designating individuals as superiors.[43] There were instances, it seems, of older religious and those who did not want radical change being treated with disdain. An example is a report on renewal prepared in 1969 within the Adrian (Michigan) Dominican community. After noting that younger sisters were more open than older sisters to a "person-oriented" view of religious life that emphasizes freedom, a rhetorical question (written in capitals for emphasis in the report) somewhat mocked the concerns of older religious: "Are we preserving the Adrian Congregation to provide a tranquil, secure life and retirement for the present membership, or are we building a life style that will provide the vitality and secure the growth of the community in the future?"[44] In at least some communities, superiors apparently pushed through the sweeping changes of renewal more than they responded to the desires of their communities.[45]

To some extent, friction and personal difficulties emerge with any social change, but in this instance they also reflected the fact that the post–Vatican II Church contained both an unchanged system of hierarchy and organizational and ideological conditions pulling in the opposite direction. Part of the Church's political problem with renewal was that the council produced not only the somewhat vague *Perfectae Caritatis*, but also the emphasis on collegiality, the People of God, and the signs of the times in John XXIII's speeches, in *Lumen Gentium*, and in *Gaudium et Spes*.

There was every reason for women religious to expect that *Perfectae Caritatis* would have to be interpreted in light of John's inspiration and these more major council documents. In an address that appears to have been delivered as late as 1971 or 1972, after the early struggles of renewal had already taken place, Pope Paul VI still stated that within the council documents, the basis of renewal should be, first, *Perfectae Caritatis*, "but also the others, especially the Constitutions which situate your place in the Church and in the contemporary world, *Lumen Gentium* and *Gaudium et Spes*." His words could have been taken as an encouragement of pluralism, or at least of the tendency in some communities to justify more democratic procedures as fitting the American context: "Know how to adapt yourselves to the needs of different countries by engrafting your action onto their own culture."[46]

In their efforts to decentralize the control of religious life as embodied in the code of canon law, CMSW cited *Perfectae Caritatis*'s call for adaptation to particular cultures as well as a statement of the Chairman of the Commission for the Revision of the Code, Cardinal Pericle Felici, that the law should protect human freedom and dignity.[47] And we have already seen that *Ecclesiae Sanctae*, Paul's 1966 instructions on the implementation of *Perfectae Caritatis*, emphasized experimentation and the communities' own responsibility and authority in directing renewal.

As a result, many communities weakened the wall of separation between themselves and modern, secular life.[48] Habits were often modified or done away with completely. Marie Augusta Neal found that by 1982, only 0.6 percent of U.S. sisters had no changes in their habit, 55.6 percent had major changes, and 34 percent were not wearing any form of habit.[49] The habit in general often became a controversial issue as U.S. bishops and Rome tried to prohibit the adoption of lay clothing, whereas for many communities this became a symbol of opening up the Church to the modern world.[50] Sisters were allowed more informal contact with the outside world, and such personnel procedures as psychological testing in screening applicants, or emphasis on psychology in general, became more common.[51] One community declared one of its five goals for integrating new members to be that each "deepens her understanding of self; spiritually, psychologically, socially, emotionally, sexually."[52] Some communities did away with the dowry that had formerly been required of new members while perhaps requiring greater educational preparation, such as college experience.[53] A return to given names, rather than new names on joining the community, was a common reform.[54] Neal found that in 1966 a clear majority of U.S. sisters had religious names different from their given names; in 1982, 69 percent were using their given names, and another 24 percent had the option of doing so. Given that she had a 6 percent nonresponse rate, it appears that the practice of *requiring* a change of names has all but disappeared.[55] Some communities argued that the spiritual vow of poverty did not mean that sisters and their communities should be denied fair compensation for their services.

The experiences of two communities will serve as good examples of the types of changes renewal instituted. The Sisters of Charity of Mount St. Vincent, New York, instituted in 1969 more than a hundred specified changes, many of which may initially seem trivial to an outsider. But that they involve such minute details of everyday life indicates how regimented were the lives of sisters before Vatican II over such issues as use of their time, phone calls, contact with the outside world, even the number of napkins used each week. The custom of giving a religious a new name on reception of the habit was discontinued, and in general sisters were given more freedom and autonomy. The final change listed in the community's report allowed the mother superior and her council to experiment in *any* area, emphasizing the need for charity, loyalty, and obedience in any experimentation.[56] Another report from the Sisters of Charity indicates that from questioning everyday practices of religious life beginning in 1966, this community had by 1969 come to discuss the possibility of ordination of women and thought of obedience and authority not in Rome's terms but in terms of an emphasis on dialogue.[57]

Another good example of the restrictions of pre–Vatican II community life were those of the Sisters of Mercy. Some of the changes *allowed* after their 1965–1966 General Chapter, although still only with the permission of the local superior, were traveling alone; traveling on Sundays and holidays; staying overnight in another local convent; attending *local* weddings, ordinations, and funerals; and taking nonalcoholic beverages with the laity. But after starting with these changes that outsiders might hardly consider radical, the community would by 1970 go on to question Rome's view of investing authority in a single person as superior. Distressed over Rome's obstruction of some of the desired changes, a committee focusing on formation asked the community's superior general to convey to Rome its distress that the Vatican was considering only one of two gospel traditions of authority (i.e., a hierarchical one, rather than a less authoritarian, People of God approach). "We cannot, any longer, simply accept every document that Rome issues at its face value—nor can we wait for the time when American religious women are more fully represented there."[58] Mary Jo Weaver pointed out that members of this community have included Sister Theresa Kane, then-president of the LCWR who surprised many Church officials by publicly questioning Pope John Paul II about the role of women in the Church during his 1979 visit to the United States; Sister Agnes Mary Mansour, ordered by the pope to resign her position as director of Social Service in Michigan in which she was responsible for funds to finance abortions for poor women (she reverted to lay status instead); and two other women told that holding public office was inconsistent with religious life.[59]

After renewal, in another interesting example of the deregimentation of religious life after Vatican II, the Sisters of St. Francis of the Holy Family of Dubuque were for the first time allowed to determine their own bedtime.[60] In general, there was an atmosphere of sudden liberation and reform; members of the Dominican community mentioned earlier even proposed a constitution written not as a list of rules and procedures, but as an inspirational poem in free verse![61] Referring to the regimented, hierarchical life described in the pre–Vatican II *Customs and Directives* and *Handbook for Superiors* of the School Sisters of St. Francis of Milwaukee, an adviser to the community commented, "Both are terrible, but the one for Superiors is positively frightening! As long as directives like that exist, the life of superior and subject must be awful! I pray that your Chapter will destroy this book."[62] This community was one of the three that became early rallying points for CMSW opposition to Rome and was the only one of the three that survived the fight with the SCR.

But perhaps that aspect of renewal that made the greatest contribution to rebellion was the reinterpretation of the meaning of authority and obedience so that they lost the punitive and dictatorial connotations that outsiders would generally associate with religious orders. As already mentioned, the argument was that the original monastic vow of obedience was a vow to God, not to an institutional hierarchy.[63] Writing in 1971 to the members of the School Sisters of St. Francis about the work of the community's General Legislative Assemblies, the superior general wrote, "All of us have responsibility for these decisions and for evaluating them. This is obedience. Such shared responsibility is not the obedience of a child."[64]

Reformers emphasized the need to respond to the call of the Holy Spirit and the "evolving" nature of the law of the Church in light of the principles of collegiality and subsidiarity, both of which translated into decentralization.[65] Reinforced by post–Vatican II developments in CMSW, the commitment to reinterpreting the vow of obedience to deemphasize the hierarchy's authority was profound, both in its depth of feeling and in its implications. Given the adoption of the Vatican II–inspired belief that God works through the Holy Spirit's immanent presence in the world (also a premise of the modernist theology condemned by Pius X), it followed that this presence could be discovered only through dialogue and shared authority. "Dialogue," in contrast with hierarchical decision-making, became a major emphasis of American sisters in dealing with Rome,[66] as we see further in discussing the post–Vatican II CMSW.

In general, consistent with these changed perspectives, communities democratized their systems of governance, legitimizing obedience to a superior in the style of a public servant rather than an infallible representative of God. Rome prohibited the direct election, let alone the elimination of, superiors, but some communities implemented these changes anyway.[67] Community governance became an early area of dispute with the SCR.[68]

These changes emerged from, and reflected, the process used to conduct renewal, which emphasized participation, consultation, and dialogue within the communities themselves. American sisters, used to busy daily schedules of prayer, study, and work at such professions as teaching and nursing, conducted renewal with great vigor. Self-study was a very common component of the renewal process, as individuals, study groups, and whole communities dissected the meaning and purpose of the details of their religious lives.[69]

This process of consultation, participation, and detailed analysis of the meaning and practices of religious life brings to mind the consultation processes that emerged in the National Conference of Catholic Bishops (chapter 5). But for sisters, the process began about a decade earlier (the mid-1960s rather than mid-1970s) and was much more intensive, therefore contributing to a rapid, dramatic ideological transformation. Communities' renewal processes, however, ran into a Vatican approach that at times seemed to encourage decentralization and experimentation in the renewal process and at other times insisted that Rome had the final word and need not explain its decisions. I have already noted Pope Paul's allowance of experiments, with no specified end date. The clear understanding among U.S. sisters was that any experiments, whether consistent with or contrary to the community's constitutions, were allowed and that communities were not to seek approval of changes in constitutions for over ten years, so that they could see how well the changes worked in practice.[70] And yet Paul VI's *Evangelica Testificatio* of 1971 cautioned against significant change in interpretation of the vow of obedience.[71] (But by that time, the CMSW and many, if not most, U.S. communities had rejected Rome's authority to prohibit renewal reforms.) Seeming to reverse earlier pronouncements, the secretary of the SCR insisted in 1973 that living a type of religious life outside of an order's constitutions or decisions of its General Chapter required dispensation from the vows of that community, so that the women involved would no longer be members.[72]

As previously mentioned, one of the matters that became quite controversial was that of the habits, or identifying clothing, that must be worn by a sister. The CMSW and U.S. bishops suggested, and Rome approved sometime by the late 1960s, that all regulations concerning the habit were the decision of the religious communities themselves.[73] Nevertheless, this became a major area of dispute, somewhat symbolic in the minds of both sisters and the SCR of the ultimate locus of authority over renewal. Perhaps Rome was worried about the reaction of the laity (who probably knew little about renewal but could notice that sisters who had always been covered from head to toe were suddenly wearing contemporary dress), and it had clearly expected that communities of women would make minor changes rather than, in some cases, eliminate the habit altogether.

Thus despite this matter supposedly being a matter for community control, the prefect of the SCR informed one superior in 1967 that all religious must follow the directives of the local bishop or episcopal conference on some matters, including "ecclesiastical attire."[74] The apostolic delegate to the United States (the papal representative in the United States) said in a 1972 letter to the National Conference of Catholic Bishops that the habit may not be set aside altogether. Yet he also said the habit in some circumstances or activities may be an impediment and thus the superior can permit "purely secular clothes," but such clothes should be "in some way different from the forms that are purely secular." It is no wonder that sisters had trouble deciding whether Rome permitted secular clothes![75]

The SCR's handling of renewal exemplified the strongest contradictions of Vatican II: renewal was discussed in terms that emphasized decentralization and an openness to the modern world, but in fact the SCR sent ambiguous messages about the limits of the reform process, occasionally seemed to intentionally act secretively, and then eventually decided that, most important, the authority structure of the Church must remain unchallenged. Reverend Edward Heston of the SCR emphasized in an address to the CMSW in 1969 that the needs of a religious community must be secondary to the directives of a bishop to that community. Bishops are "mainly responsible for the direction of the apostolic work of the people of God." He also stated, invoking Pius XII's model of the Church:

> With the approval of the Holy See we are enabled to work organically and in and with and for the Church—our lives and our apostolates take on authentically ecclesiastical dimensions. It is difficult to see how this collaboration, this acceptance of an integral role in implementing the program of salvation entrusted to the Church by Christ our Lord can be regarded as any infringement of either individual or community freedom, a curtailment of personal freedom of action. If we, as religious, are working in and through and for the Church and thus for the expansion of the Kingdom of God, then it is clearly our duty to pursue, not our own individual goals and interests, but rather those of the entire Mystical Body of Christ, under the guidance of legitimate authority.[76]

I cannot be sure whether Heston was aware of how hostile must have been the sentiments of the CMSW audience to such arguments.

At times renewal led to conflict not only with Rome, but also with the American episcopacy. Within the U.S. bishops' conference, there appears to have been in the early 1970s a substantial amount of criticism of some of the more radical paths of renewal. In 1971, an NCCB-CMSW liaison committee raised a number of criticisms that bishops had of the way many communities were conducting renewal and of the CMSW, among them an alleged neglect of community life (e.g., by having sisters live outside the convent) and of obedience; "a negative attitude toward and inordinate criticism of the Holy See...in liberation attitudes at times enunciated"; an emphasis on better salaries and cars that conflicted with the vow of poverty; too many independent changes without consultation of bishops; the abandonment by some communities of habits; and, most emphasized, the criticism by sisters of their teaching jobs as "slave labor," and bishops' and parishes' difficulty in planning for the needs of Catholic schools without the commitment of sisters' communities to continue staffing them. The CMSW response agreed that bishops should be notified when new works were undertaken but emphasized that the religious conception of obedience was broader than simply obedience to superiors and that dialogue and the continued development of council decrees were crucial. It also stated that disunity was not peculiar to sisters' communities but reflected society as a whole.[77]

But frustration with Rome was more prominent and ultimately more significant. Some of the inconsistency or confusion over Rome's approach to renewal may have reflected political battles within the Vatican, as Francis X. Murphy has argued.[78] The head of the SCR at the time, Cardinal Ildebrando Antoniutti, was the traditionalist alternative and runner-up in the papal conclave that elected Paul VI in 1963. Placing Antoniutti (who had been less than enthusiastic about John XXIII's approach to Vatican II) at the SCR may have been a way for Paul VI to appease traditionalists.[79]

But not too much should be placed on the shoulders of Antoniutti. The renewal process was built on ideological ambiguities and struggles that would have been present no matter who headed the SCR; communities that encountered the greatest resistance generally seem to have encountered opposition from their bishops before directly confronting the SCR. And even reform-minded members of the hierarchy would come to have difficulty with the directions taken by American sisters.

We must also remember that some of the SCR's actions, following Paul VI's instructions, were probably intended to be practical and open to reform. To want communities to live by changes for a few years before they were to be formally approved would allow the community to see whether a change was worthwhile in practice before making a permanent revision of its constitutions, which would involve the SCR's approval.[80] It is also possible that the sheer volume of revised constitutions and other documents passing through the SCR's office made it impossible for that Vatican department to keep track of the detail of changes in many communities. In any case, the message the SCR generally gave in the late 1960s and early 1970s was that it would wait until the unspecified end of the experimentation period before approving or disapproving constitutions.[81]

But in hindsight, we can see that this policy was politically and sociologically unrealistic. The problem was that Rome was reserving the right to forbid a practice that a community might have implemented, grown accustomed to, and valued over a period of several years, all along believing that it was acting perfectly legitimately. (Mary Jo Weaver, for example, noted that the Vatican rejected Carmelite nuns' constitutions that had a twenty-year history of reform within the communities.)[82]

During the renewal period, the cases of three communities of American sisters—the Immaculate Heart Sisters of Los Angeles, the Glenmary Sisters of Ohio, and the School Sisters of St. Francis of Milwaukee—became rallying points for CMSW leaders and sisters in general who felt that Rome was violating the spirit of Vatican II.[83] (Various theologians and American male religious also jumped to the defense of the Glenmary and Immaculate Heart Sisters.)[84] There was, then, a great deal of interaction between the

CMSW and individual reform-minded communities, the two allying together in struggles with Rome.

The Glenmary dispute began even before Vatican II ended.[85] Among the important issues involved, not only for the Glenmaries, but also for the other two communities, were the meaning of the vow of obedience, and, of course, the degree of independence allowed to communities to make changes they saw as appropriate and in the spirit of Vatican II.[86] Unable to resolve their differences with local bishops and with Rome, the majority of the members of the Glenmary and Immaculate Heart communities received dispensation from their vows and became lay communities in 1967 and 1970, respectively.[87] The School Sisters of St. Francis survived the conflict intact as a religious community. Part of the dispute with these Franciscan sisters was the SCR's claim that the attire worn by sisters was subject to the local bishop's or episcopal conference's approval, although the superior general claimed that she had received no specific episcopal directive. Sister Francis Borgia Rothluebber, president of the community, stated her fear of the SCR's potential actions, given what had happened to the Immaculate Heart community, and justified her own community's changes by arguing: "The new emphasis in the *Constitution on the Church* [*Lumen Gentium*] is transforming the hierarchical church into a People-of-God church. The Spirit dwells in the whole Church." She even injected a feminist note into her analysis of her problems with the SCR. Rothluebber later became president of the LCWR, just one of several indications that the leadership of American sisters supported the legitimacy of what Rome saw as a rebellion among these three communities.[88]

The disputes surrounding these three communities demonstrated that changes in CMSW very much reflected the renewal process; the superiors who constituted the conference's membership were heavily involved in their own communities' renewal. Thus many of the same themes that appeared at the community level echoed within CMSW; that the conference was the official, national organization representing sisters made ideological divergence with Rome all the more vocal.

CMSW: Consciousness-Raising and Radicalization

The transformation of American communities of sisters happened so rapidly that by 1967 (i.e., two years after Vatican II had ended), the Sacred Congregation for Religious was already showing signs of disturbance with the path CMSW was taking. At that time, the SCR directed that local ordinaries had to approve the conference's speakers and that "unqualified persons," especially laity, were not acceptable as speakers on renewal and on Vatican II.[89]

As the messages of Vatican II penetrated the U.S. Catholic Church, the CMSW did indeed develop into a flurry of activity and theological exploration. One of the earliest post–Vatican II projects sponsored by CMSW was the national Sisters' Survey, a massive study that achieved an incredible 88 percent response rate (most social science surveys soliciting mail responses achieve only one-quarter that rate), a total of almost 160,000 responses. A critic called the survey "the most comprehensive indoctrination of the American sisterhood in the nation's history."[90] If there had not been other evidence of significant change and resentments within CMSW going back into the 1950s, a charge of (attempted) indoctrination might have been persuasive. The questionnaire included such a battery of questions that simply reading its 649 items—which, on the whole, reflected an interest in a reform-minded interpretation of Vatican II—could lead a sister to wonder whether there were important aspects to religious life that she had not been considering.[91] But in isolation from other changes it is not realistic to expect that a questionnaire, no matter how publicized or interpreted, could cause a rebellion among American sisters. The Sisters' Survey was, however, one of many activities within CMSW that increased commitment to a feminist, antihierarchical worldview.

The CMSW Research Committee, which conducted the survey, was quite visible within the organization in the late 1960s, providing reports on the progress and meaning of the survey and articulating a radical view of religious life. In her presentation of the results of the survey, the chief investigator, sociologist Sister Marie Augusta Neal, emphasized "pre–Vatican II" versus "post–Vatican II" attitudes, associating with the former fear of change, closed-mindedness, and even fascist tendencies. Neal's discussion of the survey was the keynote address at this 1967 meeting, and the survey apparently also dominated the 1968 annual assembly.[92]

In the late 1960s CMSW also conducted a study of teaching sisters comparing the contribution of sisters to parochial schools to their compensation, a study that undoubtedly contributed to the growing view that sisters were an exploited labor force. There were also a series of health studies that had pre–Vatican II precedent and that seemed sparked by a view that sisters were overburdened and undercompensated (e.g., by way of inadequate health insurance). (The concern for adequate compensation for religious, adequate provisions for retirement, and so on appeared in the renewal deliberations of some individual communities as well and was the subject of a task force of the U.S. bishops' conference in the early 1970s. Retirement funding is very much a live issue, as a large number—perhaps the majority—of American sisters will reach retirement age within the next decade. The U.S. bishops' conference voted in 1987 to begin a fund drive for sisters' retirement, but a financial crisis already exists and could worsen.)[93]

But in addition to the renewal process going on in individual communities and the Sisters' Survey at the national level, the other activity that probably contributed most to the politicization of the CMSW was the study and solicitation of suggestions for revision of canon law, a revision necessitated by the council. The leaders of the CMSW thought it natural that sisters should contribute to the revision of those parts of canon law affecting them. Even before the end of Vatican II, CMSW planned to request that there be women religious on the Vatican's Canon Law Commission,[94] and it also established a canon law committee in 1964 to solicit suggestions from among American women religious.[95] Although this was only one of a number of standing CMSW committees, and it was not the sole focus of activity, the Canon Law Committee involved a vigorous solicitation of suggestions, many person-hours of work, and a great deal of commitment and energy. The committee engaged in extensive consultation with CMSW members, soliciting and reviewing their opinions in light of the committee's work and reports a total of five times in a process that lasted more than three years.[96] Thus its consciousness-raising effect on the CMSW was similar to that of self-study programs on individual communities. (The Canon Law Committee produced a number of future chairs and other officers of CMSW, indicating that canon law revision was an important concern within the organization and one that tended to involve people who remained committed to the group.)

Perhaps the most common message that emerged in that consultation process was the complaint that canon law treated religious like children not able to make their own decisions or act responsibly without supervision. To give a sense of some of the canon laws on religious before Vatican II, among the changes that were made after the council were an elimination of the requirement of legitimate birth for a woman religious to become a superior, an allowance that a superior could allow a sister to change her will (note, however, that this "adaptation" to modern times still required the superior's permission), and the end of censorship of mail.[97]

Building on the renewal experience of sisters' communities and on the CMSW's interpretation of Vatican II, the Canon Law Committee's recommendations ultimately urged a decentralization of decision-making power over the lives of religious, so that as many details of the implementation of the spirit of Vatican II, and the details of religious life in general, would be left to the individual communities. CMSW argued for "unity in diversity," with a greater variety of styles of religious life allowed,[98] and also emphasized the council notion of the development of doctrine and the need to continually adapt to changing times. Citing *Lumen Gentium, Gaudium et Spes*, and other council documents, a CMSW report on canon law revision argued:

> Because religious life partakes of the pilgrim nature of the entire Church, the guidelines established in the Code of Canon Law for living this on-the-way existence will necessarily be of a provisional rather than an absolute character. Indeed, the very subject of the decree *Perfectae Caritatis*...suggests that the norms and provisions of the 1917 Code did not encourage a constant adaptation to changing circumstances. Rather, they seem to have generated an over-cautious attitude toward suitable adaptation, which has now necessitated the call for "appropriate adaptation and renewal" of religious life in a rather far-reaching way.[99]

But despite its hopes, the Canon Law Committee, like many individual communities in the midst of renewal, encountered business as usual at the Vatican as it became increasingly clear in the late 1960s—also the period of greatest renewal activity—that Rome would ignore the committee's recommendations. There was frustration with Rome's approach to canon law revision within the CMSW by 1970, although U.S. bishops seemed more receptive to the sisters' work.[100]

Through the renewal process at the community level and CMSW activities at the national level, then, processes of reform and frustration with Rome led to a great deal of consciousness-raising. Not only did women religious, especially the leadership of communities and of CMSW, become much more attuned to thinking of their communities in terms of reforms, but they also gave a great deal of time and energy to thinking exactly what the philosophy of religious life should be, to justifying particular changes in light of their interpretations of Vatican II, and to thinking that a fundamental component of renewal is an extended process of dialogue. The old authority relations, where Rome controlled all important theological and institutional decision-making power, were not an arrangement that American sisters would ever again accept.

And yet the power structure was not simply going to disappear. Even though Vatican II provided new ideological messages, promoting decentralization and a view that doctrine evolves with the times, we have already seen that it did not actually designate specific issues that would no longer be under Rome's control. There has thus emerged a curious relationship between American sisters, especially more explicitly feminist ones, and Rome. While the papacy has attempted to retain the traditional power structure as well as the ideological structure that evolved in the period between Vatican I and Vatican II, the organization and ideology of lower levels of the Church are not consistent with such structures. There is thus a de facto institutionalization of pluralism, yet Rome does not recognize the legitimacy of such pluralism. It continues to attempt to enforce its ideological priorities.

Institutionalizing Pluralism

We have seen in this chapter that by the late 1960s many (and probably the large majority of) American sisters had rejected a power structure based on patriarchal hierarchy and a view of religious life as isolated from the secular world. The events of the years immediately following Vatican II were a fairly radical break with the past of American sisters, and events of the 1970s and 1980s followed the path whose directions we have already examined. Although it has been important to delineate above the mechanisms by which organizational resources were employed and new perspectives developed, it will suffice to mention only briefly here events in the 1970s and 1980s that continued those trends.

In 1969, CMSW officers began considering a change in the bylaws (formerly known as statutes) of the conference in response to a report from a consulting firm it hired. (Interestingly, the National Conference of Catholic Bishops later hired the same firm, Booz, Allen & Hamilton.) The consultation—which, given its timing, was probably inspired by the process of self-study that transpired in many, if not most, communities—resulted in recommendations to the 1969 National Assembly, with Reverend Edward Heston, secretary of the SCR, present. Booz, Allen & Hamilton advised a reorganization of the CMSW along more professional lines, with an expanded role for the nonelected, full-time staff, hired by the elected chairman. The most important recommendation was a reconsideration of the relationship with the SCR, with a hint that the CMSW might want to declare its independence.[101]

In fact, the revised bylaws dropped all suggestions of deference to Rome; by 1970 the dominant tendency in CMSW was a strong feeling that the days when men dictated a mandatory set of requirements for women's religious life were over. The conference had absorbed the antihierarchical view of the vow of obedience as an openness to God through dialogue, rather than subservience to the hierarchy. As the LCWR president put it in 1972, "Obedience can no longer be used to excuse ourselves from thinking, from studying our own situation, and from dialogue."[102] The organization also renamed itself the Leadership Conference of Women Religious, the argument being that the term *superior* (the "S" in CMSW) was antiquated and did not suit American conceptions of democracy and participation. Proponents argued that the call for renewal of individual communities implicitly applied to the pre–Vatican II statutes of CMSW. It justified the changes in terms of *Perfectae Caritatis*'s call for adaptation to the psychological, social, and economic circumstances of a given culture; the evolutionary nature of the Gospel mission in the world; the need for modern organizational practices (as exemplified in the Booz, Allen & Hamilton consultation); and an attempt to further democratize the conference under the principles of subsidiarity and collegiality (by increasing the legislative importance of the National Assembly). There was a clear emphasis on the need to adapt to conditions in the United States—for example, in justifying the name change. At the 1971 annual assembly, with two SCR staff members (both women religious) present, the members approved the changes 356 to 39. The name change was less popular, passing 186 to 165. The new bylaws were sent to the SCR in October, which approved them for the most part by July 1972, though it was reluctant to accept a name change which rejected the term "superior."[103]

The change in bylaws and name was the final straw for more traditionalist superiors, who broke away to form their own organization, the Consortium Perfectae Caritatis, so named because it claimed to be in true compliance with the Vatican II document.[104] LCWR officers continued to insist on unity in diversity in the Holy Spirit and emphasize the importance of dialogue, while consortium members emphasized that at some point dialogue must end and sisters must then submit to the authoritative decisions of the Church hierarchy. The consortium viewpoint resembles that of a number of traditionalist critics of U.S. sisters who have charged them with having a confused, unfaithful, or superficial approach to Vatican II.[105] LCWR and consortium members have met periodically but have never been able to surmount their differences.[106]

Ironically, the consortium, which apparently secretly hoped to replace the LCWR as the official representative of U.S. women's superiors,[107] has from its inception been at a significant disadvantage relative to the LCWR's organizational resources. Even though the group's traditionalist reading of Vatican II emphasized loyalty to Rome, and despite blessings from Rome, consortium leaders became frustrated at the lack of official recognition. Consortium leaders expected more eager support from the powers to which they precisely thought they were showing loyalty.[108] And by emphasizing traditional obedience, the consortium did not adopt the more democratic, participatory style of the LCWR and thus could not generate the type of support and leverage it would need. Nor could it escape its reputation as a small group (because it did not develop a participatory organization) dominated by priests. Even its traditionalist supporters worried about the negative image of having a priest as its main coordinator.[109] Although it still exists, the consortium is likely never to be more than an archaic example of attempts to reverse the ideological diversity of American Catholicism.

Rome's approach toward the consortium indicates why that diversity is unlikely to disappear. Rome was committed to some type of reform,[110] but by 1971 (and probably before) had already lost the ability to control how far some less privileged groups, such as American sisters, would take that reform. The groups diverging from Roman ideology had better organizational resources than those that did not: they had taken control of the everyday details of their own lives, and they had developed close relations between the LCWR and individual communities. Even though the Vatican's view of renewal was certainly more consistent with the consortium's than with the LCWR's, Rome probably held little hope that the risky strategy of decertifying the LCWR would ever be worthwhile. As Henry J. Pratt demonstrated in his study of the National Council of Churches, organizational interdependence can keep together groups that ideologically are at loggerheads.[111]

The Vatican could of course have instituted a massive purge, but only by creating enormous controversy and ill will within the Church, possibly alienating not only women religious, but also a good number of American Catholic laywomen.[112] Even if directed only at superiors, such a purge would have inflicted crippling damage on the morale and administrative abilities of sisters' communities, which, incidentally, provided an enormous supply of labor in Catholic schools, parishes, and hospitals. And there is every reason to believe that religious communities, even after a purge, would continue to produce like-minded superiors.

But the decentralizing rebellion of the LCWR, and of American sisters in general, has certainly not resulted in total victory. The Church power structure remains intact, although it has lost its control over their lives. There is little institutional power that sisters can exert outside their own communities and organizations as long as the papacy denies ordination to women and insists on hierarchical control of doctrine on faith and morals.

It is thus not surprising that active members of the LCWR have been active proponents of women's ordination, although the conference's official position on this issue is ambiguous.[113] There was a women's ordination conference in 1975 outside of Detroit at which women religious were dominant,[114] followed by a similar meeting in 1978 in Baltimore that was more explicitly feminist in tone.[115] The movement was not as visible in the 1980s, perhaps because Pope John Paul II forbade bishops even to discuss the issue with women or anyone else. It is interesting to note, however, that, apparently as a result of consideration of the ordination issue, especially with the Detroit Conference, the LCWR has adopted the term *ministry* in place of the former *apostolate*. That is, the sisters are considering their own work in the Church as part of a variety of *ministries* and thus of equal status to, if different from, ordained ministry.[116]

The problems of the movement for women's ordination serve as an example of the obstacles to the success of a rebellion by Catholic women in general; remember, for example, that some communities were forced to lose official recognition to pursue renewal as they desired. American sisters wounded the view of Catholicism that sees patriarchal hierarchy as a fundamental tenet of the faith, and so there are limits to Rome's ability to discipline. Rome is not as supreme as it used to be, but when sisters make challenges on fundamental matters of faith and morals, they are at a disadvantage in ensuing institutional power struggles. An example is the conflict surrounding two full-page ads in the *New York Times* (on 7 October 1984, and 2 March 1986) stating that there is more than one legitimate Catholic position on abortion. In the first ad, women religious formed a majority of those who signed. Rome was able to pressure most to recant formally, although its attempt to enlist the aid of women's superiors in enforcing its position failed. Furthermore, the affirmation of the Church's position signed by some was vague enough to allow them to claim that Rome's victory was an empty one. Nevertheless, Rome did eventually force two of the sisters to revert to lay status, and the whole episode demonstrates that Rome can enforce its opinions—especially if dissenters are Church personnel or depend upon, for example, speaking engagements at Catholic institutions—while sisters cannot.[117] Women can express their own opinions within their own organizations and communities, but they are at risk in publicizing those opinions beyond those confines, for they remain on the periphery of institutional power.

Nevertheless, the ads also demonstrate the de facto ideological pluralism that exists among Church personnel in the United States. The first ad appeared at a time, a month before the 1984 U.S. presidential election, when Archbishop John O'Connor was publicly critical of U.S. vice-presidential candidate (and Catholic) Geraldine Ferraro's position that the government should not outlaw abortion. The ad did not emphasize dissent from Church doctrine but instead stated that there is no one, correct Catholic opinion. Misinterpretation of exactly what the ad was trying to convey results if one does not realize that it comes from the perspective that sees the post–Vatican II Church as a People of God based on dialogue rather than hierarchical authority. That is, the perspective contains an implicit assumption that the Church is the people who belong to it, and from their lived experience arises God's truth, sometimes in plural, rather than singular, opinions. Thus the ad was not simply saying that it is legitimate for Catholics to disagree with the official teaching, but that there is no one, legitimate, official teaching.[118]

Thus there has emerged a reality of ideological pluralism in which American sisters are organizationally and ideologically autonomous of Rome. A number of U.S. sisters' organizations have emerged since the council, especially in the 1970s, including the National Association of Religious Women (which admits both women religious and laywomen), the National Coalition of American Nuns, Black Sisters, and Las Hermanas (a group of Hispanic sisters). None has the stature of the LCWR, but it appears to be the case that all groups of U.S. sisters except the consortium support a decentralizing and feminist interpretation of Vatican II.[119] It is also the case that feminist themes within the LCWR became increasingly explicit in the 1970s. The organization has continued its emphasis on dialogue and has even established a Task Force on Pluralism to foster what it sees as a healthy theological and moral pluralism.[120]

But Rome does not recognize the legitimacy of that pluralism. The two groups operate on different legacies of Vatican II, both of which are indeed legacies of the council.[121] As the passions of the late 1960s have cooled, it appears that the relationship has normalized somewhat, resulting in a routinized ideological pluralism that Rome sporadically attempts to reverse. John Paul II, who became pope in 1978, instituted a special study of American religious life.[122] But although his hopes are undoubtedly to reassert orthodoxy, such a study appears to be just another example of pressure on U.S. sisters with little probability of success. Stalemate is the legacy of a council with contradictory messages.

American Sisters and Ideological Reconstruction

Dissenting sisters see themselves as very faithful to the true spirit of Catholicism and certainly not simply as a peripheral faction. Theirs is not simply a worldview imported from outside the Church; they do not intend their perspective to be a rejection of the institution. Thus, Sister Margaret Brennan, IHM, the retiring president of the LCWR, could state at the 1973 annual meeting:

If we try to reflect on why the Church is so full of conflicting experiences today, we know it is because of differing ecclesiologies that are operative in the Church today. We know, too, that it is a necessary consequence of accepting fully the humanity and historicity of the Church as a pilgrim people of God. Assenting to this means that life in the Church—at whatever level—can no longer be a neat, easily organized, easily manageable and easily articulated reality. *And yet the unity of the Church is a sacred thing.* And it is this conviction—that the preaching of the Gospel is centered in the unity of the Church—that keeps us anguishing in faithful love of the Church.[123]

But it is clear that the Catholicism of American sisters is quite different from that of the Vatican. It is also quite different from that of most U.S. bishops. Bishops—as priests and as bishops, roles open only to men—have participated in the power structure (although they still must defer to Rome), and they have thus participated in the ideology in a much more direct way. There is the irony, then, that bishops, the group most able to further a creeping autonomy of the national Churches—although even they could fail—may be too much of a part of the Church's power structure to mount the requisite type of ideological challenge.

It is almost certain that a good number of women religious continue to hold Rome in reverence and would indeed regard the authority structure of the Church, in its general outlines, if not in its specific decisions, to be inspired by God. Conflict with the hierarchy has not been unending; by the mid-1980s, for example, the relationship between the LCWR and the NCCB had become less tense.[124] But the work of Sister Marie Augusta Neal, who has provided some of the best data on American sisters for more than two decades, indicates that sisters as a whole do not accept Rome's directives uncritically. In two very comprehensive studies of the opinions of such women, Neal found in 1966 that 62 percent thought that the directives of the SCR were a major determinant of change in their communities, while only 18.4 percent thought so in 1982. In 1966, 34.9 percent thought the ideas of the sisters were important in such change, a figure that had grown to 66.7 percent by 1982.[125]

The fact that control over such issues as religious life is justified in terms of Roman control over issues of faith (including doctrine specifying the authority structure of the Church) meant that to assert any significant independence, women religious had to challenge the fundamentals of the institutional power structure. Many sisters are quite aware of that fact. For example, in 1990, the LCWR Executive Committee urged that the NCCB abandon its proposed pastoral letter on women, despite some virtues in the letter's second draft, because

> once again, patriarchy as an embodiment of sexism is not sub-
> jected to the critique it requires. To do so would, of course,
> raise serious questions about the manner in which the church is
> institutionalized and would be self-condemnatory. Obviously,
> our church represented in our bishops is not ready for this kind
> of critical analysis. Because that is so, they will not be able to
> write a pastoral that is not intrinsically contradictory.[126]

Thus American sisters have developed a much broader critique of Church authority and ideology than have U.S. bishops. The latter have devoted much more energy to the content of sociopolitical ideology. Even though they are ambivalent about managing the boundary separating sociopolitical issues from faith and morals, the boundary remains important. It is most important, and most beneficial, to those interested in doctrinal pronouncements and management of Church affairs at the highest levels of institutional power. It is not particularly significant for groups like sisters.

Thus we find that although a number of communities as well as the CMSW stated greater commitment to social justice concerns during and after their renewal processes in the mid- and late 1960s,[127] in fact the CMSW and sisters as a whole have spent much more energy attempting to reorder their own place in the Church than they have refocusing their ministry toward work with the poor, social protest, and so forth.

Certainly sociopolitical concerns have been central for some communities, perhaps most prominently the Maryknoll Sisters, a missionary order oriented toward apostolates in the Third World and affected by Latin American liberation theology. Maryknoll's Orbis publishing house is a central source of books reflecting a leftist, politicized approach to Christianity. Indeed, liberation theology has had some effect on the thinking of American sisters for some time. At least from the time of the Sisters' Survey, Neal has publicized such a theology within the CMSW/LCWR and among American sisters in general.[128] The Vatican acted just before the council to increase the number of U.S. religious serving in Latin American missions, undoubtedly leading to the spread of new ideas in U.S. communities.[129]

Prominent members of LCWR gave addresses at the 1972, 1973, and 1975 meetings (and perhaps others) explicitly appealing to a liberation view of Catholicism. Archbishop Helder Câmara of Brazil, probably the most prominent episcopal supporter of liberation Catholicism, spoke at the 1973 meeting.[130] Since the early 1980s, sisters have also been at the center of the U.S. sanctuary movement, which challenges the morality of U.S.

policy in Central America by encouraging (primarily Salvadoran and Guatemalan) refugees to enter the United States in violation of U.S. immigration policy.[131] There is no reason for sisters to be committed ideologically to devaluing social concerns—as would be true of Rome—and so they were easily receptive to Vatican II's emphasis on social action in the modern world. Furthermore, having little power, they need not worry about the potential ideological contradictions that such an emphasis could entail (as discussed in chapter 3). But Vatican II had a much more profound meaning for their lives within Catholic ideological structure. Focusing on the content of sociological commitment, the main concern of U.S. bishops' independent initiatives, would in itself not have been enough for them to challenge patriarchal hierarchy in the Church.[132]

Of course, theirs is not the only type of radical challenge possible within contemporary Catholic ideology. While U.S. sisters to some extent simply ignore ideological boundaries separating faith and moral issues from sociopolitical issues, their more central focus has been to challenge what Rome defines as fundamental issues of faith (e.g., patriarchy within the Church and Rome's absolute primacy). Latin American liberation Catholicism instead focuses primarily on breaking down the boundary separating faith and moral issues from sociopolitical issues. Within this approach, social change is at the center, rather than the periphery, of the meaning of Catholicism, but in a context in which the People of God, not Rome, define the Church's ideological priorities.

There is a definite similarity between Latin American liberation Catholicism and the challenges presented by American sisters, which explains receptivity to liberation themes within the LCWR. Both emphasize the immanent presence of the Holy Spirit, the evolving nature of doctrine, and the opposition to hierarchy. There is a difference of emphasis, however. American sisters focus on patriarchal hierarchy, and although receptive to sociopolitical issues, they have in practice made such issues a secondary concern. Latin American liberation Catholicism has most directly questioned the subordination of sociopolitical change, and through that questioning has occasionally and less directly raised the issue of the legitimacy of Church hierarchy. Nevertheless, liberation Catholicism can sometimes be conservative on specific matters of faith and morals. The challenge liberation Catholicism presents—through questioning Catholic ideological boundaries and priorities—is indeed a radical challenge, but it is a different sort of challenge. (In some ways it might be considered "more radical" than the approach of U.S. sisters, in some ways less so.) We now turn to a consideration of the Latin American Church to understand why this different approach to Catholic ideology emerged there, rather than in the U.S. Church.

7 Catholicism and Politics
in Latin America:
A Comparative Perspective

The Catholic Church is an old and complex international institution. Because of its complexity, it is difficult, if not impossible, to examine the history of the many national branches of the Church simultaneously; thus to understand the Church's ideological structure, it has been helpful to focus on the Vatican and the U.S. Church. Nevertheless, the international character of the Church provides an opportunity for comparison, allowing insights that might otherwise be unavailable. Because the ideological transformation of the politics of religion is perhaps more striking in Latin America than anywhere else in the world, this is a particularly important region to study. Comparison raises the question of why some sectors of the Church in South and Central America have developed a more radical interpretation of the commitment to social justice than has the U.S. Church.

Comparison also allows us to see that, despite the differences between the U.S. Church and the Latin American national Churches, ideological dynamics are highly dependent on the relationship the Church has had with state and society. Central aspects of this relationship are power structures (both societal and institutional)—that is, the autonomy and resources available to different groups within the Church. Nevertheless, even though the recent history of Latin American Catholicism confirms the approach taken throughout this book, it is important to note that this chapter is perhaps more suggestive than definitive. It would be presumptuous to attempt to explain all the most important changes in Latin American Catholicism in one short chapter. It is also the case that, despite recent interest in Catholicism in Latin America, there are great gaps in social science research on the Latin American Church. There are available few recent studies of Catholicism in some Latin American nations. And we see that our knowledge of the actual composition and history of certain important phenomena, such as the "base communities," remains fragmentary.

Within these limits, this chapter first examines differences among Latin American national Churches and then moves to a discussion of post–Vatican II developments in the region as a whole. (Thus the chapter does not always follow events strictly chronologically.) This discussion of national Churches focuses on the episcopacies of the various national Churches because it is through examination of this sector of the Church that we will be able to see national differences while not hopelessly complicating discussion by attempting to simultaneously examine all aspects of all relevant national Churches.

There developed, beginning in the late nineteenth century, three basic paths of church-state relations. The first two have generally not produced many signs of liberation Catholicism in the hierarchy, for different reasons.[1] The first path is that of national Churches which have developed a fairly wide separation from the state but which have also retained strong ties to powerful and wealthy social strata. In the main examples of this path—Mexico and Venezuela—the Church has not developed an activist role.

The second path is that of the episcopacies of some of the national Churches—for example, in Argentina and Colombia—which remained allied with the state and with ruling elites (in a nonliberal relationship), producing an ideological affinity. These hierarchies have generally remained conservative and uncommitted to social reform because a liberal separation of the two never developed.

The third path has been that of alienation from the state and ruling elites. Reaching out to the poorer classes, which eventually became necessary if the Church was to retain any social base at all, was for the Brazilian hierarchy a sudden race to recover lost ground. And in the case of both Brazil and Chile, the national episcopacies needed to oppose the state in order to protect the institutional Church. It is this third path that is most likely to lead to receptivity to liberation themes and that will therefore receive the most attention. (Brazil, however, appears to be much more receptive to liberation themes than Chile, perhaps because it has had the resources and autonomy necessary to develop a pastoral outreach to the poorer classes.)

There are, of course, a few important national Churches (e.g., that of Peru) that do not fit any of these categories neatly. And there are additional factors that influenced the different ideological paths taken by different sectors of the Latin American Church, especially organizational strength.

Scott Mainwaring has observed, correctly, that there is not a simple, mechanical relationship between state repression and liberation Catholicism.[2] Nevertheless, his own analyses point out that the relationship, especially when specified as direct state repression *of the Church*, is indeed very strong.[3]

It is important to note as well that the path taken by the hierarchy was not necessarily the path taken by groups at lower positions in the institutional power structure. An important characteristic of the national Churches in El Salvador and Nicaragua, for example, has been the division between generally conservative episcopacies and other sectors of the Church, led by clergy and religious, who have espoused a liberation Catholicism. Members of the Church at less powerful positions within the institutional structure do not respond to the same constraints and influences in Church and society as do most bishops. The origins of liberation Catholicism, then, are generally not within the episcopacy (with some notable exceptions, especially in Brazil); instead the history of church-state relationships, church-society relationships, and organizational strength is commonly a history of how receptive the episcopacy becomes to liberation themes generated by other Catholics.

After discussing the various national Churches and their diverse histories, we can examine some of the dynamics and tensions that cross national boundaries. Here, the effect of Vatican II, especially as interpreted by the Latin American Episcopal Conference's meeting at Medellín, Colombia, in 1968, is of central concern. That meeting took Vatican II's concern with social justice even further than had the council itself and appeared to legitimate liberation Catholicism. Since 1968, liberation Catholics at lower levels of the Church power structure have attempted to further their cause, while both Rome and a good number of Latin American bishops have attempted to reverse what they see as a politicization of the faith.

In examining these post–Vatican II changes, we can also see clear, illuminating contrasts with the U.S. Church, a minority church that never much interacted politically with its own laity (although its *religious* ties have historically been fairly close). But in Latin America, in most countries the Catholic Church has always been a major political and social actor on the national stage. It is the case that in a number of Latin American countries, the episcopacies argue that the Church should not be involved in state or class politics. In fact, however, the Church always has been so involved in most of these nations, as many liberation theologians, and analysts of Latin American Catholicism, have pointed out.[4] At times, that involvement has been more as a passive, junior partner of the state and of wealthier social groups, but a partner nevertheless, strongly dependent on a particular political and social order. Vatican II thus led committed Catholics, often especially those outside the episcopacy, to focus on the Church's relation to state and society more than has been true in the U.S., where the focus is relatively more on internal Church issues.

In the U.S. Church, the concern with social and political issues did not arise out of an interaction with secular society; the U.S. bishops originally approached such issues as outsiders. As a minority church whose national loyalty was constantly questioned, the U.S. Church has through most of its history explicitly attempted to keep sociopolitical questions outside its institutional concerns. But most of the Latin American Churches have always been involved with such issues, and so their own approach to social and political problems, as part of their relationship to the laity, has always been a central concern. Thus there never emerged in the Latin American Church the same ideological boundary between religion and politics that was so strong in the pre–Vatican II U.S. Church.

After examining these issues, I analyze the potential political tensions within the Church that result from liberation Catholicism.

The Ideal of Church Establishment

The Latin American Catholic Church originally advanced with Spanish and Portuguese sovereignty over Central and South America. Its history of relations with the Iberian powers during the colonial period replicated and reinforced church-state relations dominant in Europe. Historians refer to the colonial period, when the Latin American Church sanctioned church-state alliance, as the age of Christendom.[5] Generally, the state selected bishops, raised the Church's revenues, and controlled communication between the colonial Churches and Rome. Christendom involved what from a contemporary point of view appear to be certain institutional weaknesses: mainly, the Church's place in society was thoroughly dependent on its ties to the state and to ruling elites. The Church was very vulnerable in the event of the breaking of those ties. Thus with the decline of Christendom, the lack of ties to the general population historically translated into the existence of a Catholicism that was often only superficially observed. As a result, Protestant evangelical missionaries have had remarkable success in some parts of Latin America. For example, in Brazil, as David Stoll reported, there may be more "real" Protestants than there are "real" Catholics.[6]

Another consequence of those weak ties is that the Latin American Churches have long encountered a low level of recruitment for the clergy and religious orders. Many Latin American Churches depend on foreigners to provide a large proportion of their priests. Phillip Berryman reported an

80 percent foreign presence in the clergy of Guatemala, Nicaragua, Honduras, Venezuela, Panama, and Bolivia;[7] approximately 50 percent of the clergy in Chile are foreign.[8] The Vatican recently reported that Latin America has the worst priest shortage in the world. With about 42 percent of the world's Catholics, the region has only 13 percent of the priests. Even with resignations and declines in recruitment in North America and Europe, those regions, with 39 percent of the world's Catholics, have 73 percent of the priests.[9]

Compounding these problems, in a number of countries, priests have also often been poorly trained and geographically isolated from their bishops and other priests. Large dioceses included areas rarely visited by the bishop or even by priests. States prevented autonomous institutional development of the Church (and thus in some countries prevented the establishment of new dioceses). Both the state's obstacles and the episcopacy's emphasis on state establishment contributed to the legacy of weak religious ties between the institutional Church and the general population. The Church functioned somewhat as does a corrupt governmental agency—with interests in its own perpetuation and ties to powerful elites despite the claim of a larger social purpose.[10] Even where the Church was institutionally strong, its association with authoritarian political and economic systems—an association that continued well into the period of independence from Spain and Portugal—often weakened what little moral authority it had.[11]

QUASI-SEPARATION

It is little wonder, then, that liberal and radical movements often saw the Church as a prime enemy. In Mexico especially, a country with a large, important national Church, Christendom came to an end with a vengeance. The Mexican Revolution, beginning in 1910, was profoundly anticlerical (and the Church profoundly antirevolutionary). The formerly sporadic conflict between the Catholic Church and the state that had begun under liberal governments by the 1830s became more or less permanently institutionalized with the Revolution.[12] But the new Mexican state's approach to the Church resembled that of France at the turn of the century more than it did a truly liberal view of church-state relations: the state sought to control the Church rather than treat it as an autonomous institution.

Meanwhile, the antirevolutionary Church maintained relationships with wealthy social sectors and some conservative political groups. Since the revolution, a true separation of functions between church and state has developed, but this is not a relationship in which the Church has the freedom to carve out its own social role without regard to government intervention. The Church does benefit from the government's inattention to constitutional restrictions on Catholic activities (e.g., the existence of private Catholic schools).[13] The Mexican Church also has the advantage that so many poorer Mexicans as well as middle- and upper-class Mexicans remain in their religion fairly conservative and devout. Nevertheless, it would be fairly risky for the hierarchy to attempt extensive and overt criticism of the Mexican state; in this sense the Church does not have the type of autonomy that the U.S. Church has.[14] Both Church and state seem wary but respectful of the other's powers and influence, fearful of backlash if relations worsened.

As a result, the contemporary Mexican episcopacy has not become socially and politically involved, despite signs that at least a few bishops are interested in issues of social and political reform.[15] Both the Church's long-standing ties to conservative groups from the wealthier classes and its particular relationship with the government have prevented it from being susceptible to the activism of liberation Catholicism.

Venezuela's church-state relations are, within Latin America, the most genuinely liberal, although there are elements of state limits on the Church's activities.[16] The Church, however, does not become involved in much activism both because it lives a secure legal existence in Venezuela and because it is fairly weak institutionally. The Church is generally unable to have much social impact, given the lack of piety in the population and the institution's own lack of financial resources and personnel.[17] The Church never regained its strength after various social, political, and economic upheavals in Venezuelan history, which ultimately made Venezuela a fairly liberal society with a social structure more fluid than that of most other Latin American nations. The solid coherence of ruling elites (as well as Christendom) has been somewhat broken, which partially accounts for the Church's fairly weak institutional and social ties to society. Nevertheless, in the absence of a complete break with secular power and privilege, the Church (especially the hierarchy) has stronger ties to upper than to lower social strata.

Furthermore, as a majority religion (at least nominally) with a stable status in society, the Venezuelan Church has little reason to take a critical view of society. Even though Daniel Levine found that its bishops are generally willing to be open-minded,[18] they are not social or political activists. The Venezuelan bishops have made statements from a social doctrine perspective, but they do not go beyond statements, perhaps because their main concern is nursing a weak institution. Even if it were to strengthen itself, the Church is unlikely in the near future to see itself as alienated from dominant political and social trends. One can almost write a recipe: that hierarchies in electoral democracies where Catholicism is the majority religion are unlikely ever to become radicalized. For it is the case that ultimately, after considerable strife, there developed in Venezuela a competitive party politics and a fairly wide separation of church and state. The Church there has in the last few decades avoided active support of particular parties, yet it need not worry about hostility from the state.

The Venezuelan case serves as an interesting contrast with the U.S. Church. Internally, the U.S. Church has historically been quite strong, with a rich institutional network of schools, hospitals, and social groups. Even with current disaffection among significant portions of the U.S. Catholic laity, levels of participation in liturgy and social identification with the faith remain high in comparison to Venezuela. Pope John Paul II's visit to Venezuela in 1987, for example, drew little enthusiasm, embarrassing devout Catholics. Further, the U.S. Church has never experienced state establishment and thus never absorbed the worldview of powerful secular elites. U.S. bishops, in fact, never absorbed the worldview of even Catholic lay elites because through most of their history they were mainly concerned not to give appearance of interest in any political or state matters, other than a vague, general patriotism.

In both Mexico and Venezuela, then, despite some important differences, the national Churches are not linked to the state, but they are somewhat closely tied to secular elites. Neither hierarchy is likely to enter on a socially activist role because of its relationship with the state and such elites and, in the case of Venezuela, because of a lack of organizational resources.

CONTINUING IN THE PATH OF CHRISTENDOM

For a different group of Latin American national Churches, the age of Christendom has not really ended, although varying measures of separation have eliminated some of the colonial excesses. These Churches constitute the second path. In Argentina and Colombia, for example, the Church has never been greatly alienated from the state or from dominant social strata, or at least not to the degree that has been true (at various times) in, for example, the United States, Italy, Brazil, or Chile.[19] It is true that even in the former countries, church-state clashes have periodically emerged (e.g., at times between Juan Perón and the Argentine hierarchy), but these have remained rivalries between partners that both have a stake in the social status quo, even if, as distinct institutions, they necessarily diverge in some of their priorities and perspectives. In the former countries, there are still elements of establishment as the official faith—for example, a formal or informal state role in the appointment of bishops or financial and legal privileges allowed Catholicism but denied to other denominations.[20]

For example, the Church actually administers quasi-civil authority in some Colombian territory and retains considerable authority over education, marriage, and divorce throughout the country. The Church is officially recognized as a central social institution.[21] Especially since Vatican II, these national Churches cannot argue that no other denominations have the right to practice, but links between the Church, on the one hand, and the state and ruling elites, on the other, remain strong. There is not much receptivity toward sociopolitical reform; thus even though Argentina went through a very repressive period of military rule in the 1970s, the episcopacy did not lead a Catholic opposition.

In some cases, the hierarchies of these nations appear to espouse a version of the ideological restructuring discussed in earlier chapters, in which sociopolitical issues involve only vague, low-priority commitments. For example, given the occasionally violent factional history of Colombian politics, Colombia's bishops, as Levine has demonstrated,[22] have in the last few decades found the best institutional strategy to be one of avoiding identification with particular parties. And, in fact, because even in the context of neo-Christendom, the Church is clearly the *junior* partner in the church-state alliance, it is sensible for the hierarchy to discourage partisan political activity by any groups (especially antigovernment groups) identifying themselves as Catholic. And so, the hierarchies of these countries generally emphasize the spiritual nature of Catholicism, discouraging (especially leftist) political activities identified with the faith as perceived by groups in lower positions in the institutional power structure.

But, in fact, the hierarchies themselves are heavily committed through social and institutional links to the politics of the status quo. Their insistence that Catholicism not be politicized is actually closer to the ideology of Pius X than of Vatican II. That is, temporal politics is an area of Catholic politics and ideology that they intend to *control* while in some sense being able to claim that they believe that politics lies outside of religion proper. By being followers of the state's lead, rather than innovators, they thus can deny their own political engagement, which might be seen as more passive than active (but which is strong nevertheless).

Peru is a somewhat special case in which the historical tendency of episcopacies to attempt to get along with governments met a "revolution from above."[23] A military regime took power in 1968 and, especially for the first few years after the takeover, implemented egalitarian reforms in a top-down fashion. In most societies, Catholic episcopal attempts at close church-state relations historically have led to a right-wing authoritarianism. But in Peru after 1968, close bonds with the government necessarily meant an openness to leftist thinking. (It is the case that Peruvian bishops of the time could also build on recent episcopal explorations in social doctrine and the activism of Catholic university intellectuals.) Thus whereas receptivity to liberation themes among Brazilian and Chilean bishops followed poor church-state relationships, in Peru such themes were, between 1968 and 1974, compatible with church-state alliance. In Peru, there was not the strong break between church and state that there had been in some countries. There was a significant change in the social role of Peruvian Catholicism, however, because alliance with the leftist orientation of the early military government led to a weakening of ties between the Church and conservative secular elites.[24] The direction of the Peruvian Church since the return to electoral politics (and increasing economic and political chaos in the late 1980s) and in the face of pressures toward Vatican views of orthodoxy remains to be determined.

In a number of these countries discussed so far—for example, in Colombia, Peru, Mexico, and Argentina (as well as in Chile)—there have emerged at various times since Vatican II groups of sisters and priests committed to liberation themes.[25] Prominent examples have been Christians for Socialism in Chile and the Movement of Priests for the Third World in Argentina. It is not surprising that there would be greater receptivity to such themes at these lower levels of the institution's power structure (although, even there, still among only a minority). Church personnel who are actively engaged in parish and missionary work with poorer, politically weak citizens or whose occupational affiliations are more academic than ecclesiastical more easily become estranged from a worldview that sees institutional and social links with powerful social forces as a natural alliance of great benefit to the Church. It is, of course, not only in these countries that many priests and religious have different outlooks from the hierarchy; in fact, it appears that only in Brazil has the hierarchy developed strong links with lower levels of the Church and liberation Catholics. But before we address that issue, it is helpful to examine the case of Chile, whose episcopacy, like Brazil's, has led an important opposition to a repressive state.

ALIENATION FROM SECULAR POWERS

Had it not been for the military coup in 1973, which placed the Church into an oppositional role, Chile's Church might have looked today much like Venezuela's. Historically it has been weak, in terms of both finances and personnel (although in recent decades it has benefited from foreign sources of Church money). Its institutional ties to the general population (which is not very devout) are likewise underdeveloped. Mass attendance historically has been less than 30 percent, at times much less, and Protestant missionaries have had some success wooing nominal Catholics.[26]

The similarity with the Venezuelan Church results not only from institutional weakness, but also from a history of church-state separation. After a strong union of church and state in the nineteenth century, Chile allowed freedom of conscience and instituted a wide church-state separation in 1925.[27] The Chilean hierarchy's decision, in the 1920s and 1930s, to support church-state separation and to avoid identification with particular political parties developed partially as a recognition of the advantages of not having the state involved in church internal decisions.[28]

Nevertheless, indirect institutional support for conservative politics persisted for several decades;[29] as in all Latin American Churches, unless prodded otherwise, Chile's bishops appeared ready to trod well-worn paths. But the Chilean Church was changing; in the period from the 1930s through the 1950s, there were among the Catholic laity groups whose politics ran from fascist to social democrat. All these groups could find some justification in social doctrine, depending on what aspects of that vague doctrine they emphasized.[30] But the openness of that doctrine combined with the changes in Chilean church-state relations does appear to have allowed the hierarchy to develop a new adaptability, so that it was not dependent only on conservative parties.

What seems to have happened in Chile over the last half century is that once church-state separation was widened, the episcopacy came to look more like the U.S. hierarchy; the ideological paths of the two groups of bishops show a number of similarities from about the 1920s to the 1960s. The Chilean bishops (who number only about thirty) gradually became more receptive to a sharper boundary separating sociopolitical issues from more fundamental religious issues. They also become more receptive to papal social doctrine and came to see temporal politics as primarily an area where they needed to assure the Church's independence. The organizational independence gained from the state after 1925 led to a greater ideological independence,[31] so that, rather than follow the lead of the state, the bishops gradually began to analyze the sociopolitical world in terms of a mildly reformist interpretation of papal social doctrine.

Not that the commitment to social reform, at least before the 1960s, was particularly strong: primarily the bishops were interested in social stability and their own autonomy. They seemed willing to accommodate and were less interested in particular policies than in political stability, which was their primary concern at least through the time of the military coup in 1973. But a number of changes led them to increase their commitment to social reform in the 1960s. First, between 1955 and 1964, there was a 50 percent turnover rate in the Chilean episcopacy; all the new appointments had close social ties with leaders of the rising Christian Democratic Party.[32] There was a general shift in Chilean politics in the early 1960s toward a greater emphasis on social reform; never eager to rock the boat unnecessarily, the bishops offered their support for such reform. In fact, with the election of a Christian Democratic president in 1964, they could find ample reason in social doctrine to support state policy. Vatican II presumably also contributed to this approach, in which the bishops, in contrast to their pronouncements in earlier decades, took a more structural view of the need for social reform.[33] It is also probably no accident that Chile and Brazil, where the episcopacies took particularly strong political stands starting in the 1970s, have until recently been the Latin American countries where Protestant missionaries have had the greatest success.[34] It is not unreasonable to think that the Chilean and Brazilian bishops worried that hostile states and Protestant citizens might eventually leave them socially irrelevant.

In any case, despite indirect support for the Christian Democrats through the 1960s, the bishops maintained some distance from the state and from party politics. It is true that in 1964 their fear of Marxism led them indirectly to endorse the Christian Democratic candidate,[35] but as Chilean politics became more volatile, they emphasized the necessity of democratic process rather than preference for a particular party.[36] They refused in 1970 to endorse or condemn any candidate, despite the real possibility (and eventual reality, under Salvador Allende) of a Socialist/Communist alliance coming to power. It appears that the bishops were quite aware that a strongly anti-Marxist position at a time of growing support for the Socialist and Communist Parties could endanger the Church. (The papacies of John XXIII and Paul VI, which allowed Christian-Marxist dialogue, and the bishops' own experiences at Vatican II may also have been factors in their approach to the 1970 election.) After the 1973 election, the episcopacy even condoned the bulk of the Allende administration's social and economic policies.[37]

Although it became clear after the 1973 military coup that a minority of bishops preferred an authoritarian social order, the majority saw electoral democracy as the best guarantee of Church autonomy. Nevertheless, historically the Church's religious autonomy (rather than democracy per se) had remained by far the primary social concern of the Chilean episcopacy, and the bishops have generally seen social stability as an important guarantee of that autonomy. A general commitment to human rights and social reform is probably second; and up until 1973 at least, support for electoral democracy may have been more a strategy (to assure Church independence) than an absolute commitment. Interestingly, then, their commitment to socioeconomic equality (as called for by social doctrine) seems a higher priority than formal democracy. They did not seem as troubled by the coup as one might have suspected; doubts emerged in response to torture, repression, and widened social inequality, but they did not denounce the regime until it attacked the institutional Church directly.[38] Their willingness to cooperate with the Allende government (1970–1973) no doubt would have diminished rapidly if Allende had ever attacked the Church.

Nevertheless, the Chilean episcopacy may be constrained by its institutional limits as much as by its ideological preferences. Up through the Allende period, the Church had trouble finding the resources for its social programs, and the population's identification with the Church remained low. Institutional weakness was reflected in the success of evangelical Protestant missionaries. It does appear that the bishops' commitment to social reform, as informed by social doctrine, is stronger than that of the general population. Furthermore, that commitment to social doctrine is probably as strong as the American episcopacy's.[39] Nevertheless, a concern with the institutional Church has always taken precedence over social commitments.

As a result, there have been changes in the Church in response to new institutional threats. The period of military rule in many Latin American republics in the 1960s and 1970s was a time of unprecedented repression, involving direct attacks not only on secular dissidents, but on sectors of the Church. This clash of church and state was an essential component in the changes that took place in the Latin American Church,[40] and Chile had among the worst experiences. It is possible that the Chilean Church will forever be changed as a result of this more recent experience; it is likely long to be suspicious of the promises of authoritarian regimes. Even though some bishops welcomed the military coup, and most seemed willing to live with it, the expectation that the Pinochet regime would respect the Church's autonomy was clearly disproved.

Consequently, the Chilean bishops eventually were willing to develop an oppositional approach to the Pinochet regime. As the Church became the only legal refuge for Chileans persecuted by a violently repressive government, the commitment to social justice became an increasingly higher priority in terms of Church resources. An official Church organization, the Vicariate of Solidarity, was the only domestic organization capable of sustained investigation and criticism of the regime's human rights violations.[41] And there were enough brave Catholics willing to risk taking on such a role.

The role thrust on the Church by military repression further alienated upper-class Chileans, already upset by the Church's social teaching during the 1960s and 1970s.[42] Circumstances may have pushed the institutional Church to widen its autonomy from wealthy, powerful elites. One might expect, then, that the Chilean episcopacy will continue to increase its commitment to social reform benefiting poorer Chileans. Even after the Chilean episcopacy's activities in the Vicariate of Solidarity, however, it is much concerned with Church unity and avoidance of what it sees as a politicization of the faith.[43] It appears unlikely that the Chilean bishops will soon be susceptible to liberation themes.[44] But we cannot be sure of the episcopacy's ultimate sentiments. While Pinochet was president, there were severe constraints on Church activity.[45] Chilean politics is now in an uncertain state, as Pinochet has ceded formal power, but an elected government still must deal with a constitution that gives the military—which remains very strong—the role of protector of order. History suggests that the Chilean Church will avoid strong sociopolitical commitments to the extent that it believes the elected government is not in danger of being overthrown. We will see in the case of Brazil that, even after strong commitment to liberation themes during times of government repression, it is likely that bishops anywhere will retreat to a more spiritual view of Catholicism when that repression ends.

Under Christendom the Church's status as the established religion was the main basis of its institutional strength. Other than ties to the state, dominant social classes, and conservative political groups, many of the national Churches had weak connections to the larger society, as in the cases of Venezuela and Chile. This has also been true of the Brazilian Church, which has long been fairly uninfluential among the general population, as there were until the last few decades weak attempts to minister to the poorer classes.[46] Traditional piety, although strong, is often far from orthodox (e.g., in the incorporation of elements from indigenous faiths). Thus in contrast to the immigrant Catholicism of the United States, popular religiosity has not been closely tied to the episcopacy—even though the parish priest has often served in a strongly paternalistic social capacity.[47]

Actually, Brazilian Catholic history has not been one of continuous Christendom. In the period between approximately 1890 and the second decade of this century, the Brazilian Church acted prudently in adapting to the emergence of a secular state, rather than face the state as an anti-republican opposition. As in Chile in 1925, the 1891 separation of Brazilian Church and state was relatively peaceful, and the Church gained certain benefits in the removal of the state from involvement in its internal affairs. This period of separation resulted in greater ties between Rome and the Brazilian Church, which in the era of Christendom had often been blocked by the state. (A similar strengthening of ties between episcopacy and papacy as a result of widened church-state separation occurred in late nineteenth-century Europe, as we saw in chapter 2.) The state's limitation of Church institutional growth could now be reversed. It is interesting to note, for example, that in 1891 there were only twelve dioceses in Brazil, all headed by bishops chosen by the state. But after that Rome named bishops; today there are more than two hundred dioceses and more than three hundred bishops.[48]

Nevertheless, as in the case of Pope Pius XI and the Chilean bishops of decades ago, the episcopacy's acceptance of church-state separation was more an act of pragmatism than conviction. Under the leadership of Sebastião Leme de Silveira Cintra, who was made bishop in 1916 and later cardinal and who died in 1942, the hierarchy took advantage of a political vacuum in the 1930s to attempt, somewhat successfully, to reestablish church-state alliance. Dom Leme, as he is sometimes known, was extremely successful in organizing Catholic groups to support the state and win concessions from Gertulio Vargas, authoritarian head of state for most of the period between 1930 and 1954. Vargas was happy to trade those concessions for such support. Dom Leme used in Brazil a strategy similar to that which Pius XI had attempted in Mussolini's Italy, but Leme was generally successful. Vargas's new constitution of 1934 recognized God, disallowed divorce, and allowed state support of the Church as well as religious education in the schools. It was also the case that Leme's successful mobilization of Catholic support for Vargas via a number of new organizations strengthened the Church institutionally.[49]

By the 1950s, however, those organizations had declined, and the Church had still failed to develop stable ties to a population that was Catholic more in name than reality.[50] Within this context of institutional weakness, however, a group of bishops in the Northeast were able to develop a new organization, the National Conference of Brazilian Bishops (Conferência Nacional dos Bispos do Brasil, or CNBB). Bishop Helder Câmara led the way in founding the CNBB in 1952, with support both from the papal nuncio and Monsignor Giovanni Battista Montini (later Pope Paul VI) of the Vatican Secretariat of State. The CNBB, which grew out of Brazilian Catholic Action, was able to speak in the name of the Brazilian Church, partly because of its support in the Vatican. But, in fact, only a minority of bishops actively supported its emphasis on sociopolitical reform as a means of attending to the needs of the poorer sectors of society.[51]

Thomas C. Bruneau noted that the CNBB was somewhat of a precursor of the message of Vatican II, but its own flexibility depended on the attitude of the Brazilian Church, which as a whole did not constrain it because the majority of bishops were not involved in the CNBB.[52] Once it did become more representative of the hierarchy, after the military coup of 1964, it turned more conservative—for example, Câmara was replaced as secretary general. But the early CNBB did serve as a model when changed circumstances, in the 1970s, led to a rapid reassessment of the Church's role in society.

But first let us examine the conditions that led to the birth of the CNBB. It appears that a number of influences—some specific to the Brazilian Church and others affecting the Church internationally—awakened the Brazilian episcopacy to the need to do something to reverse the Church's weakness in that country. First of all, despite the Leme-Vargas alliance, other religions were free to evangelize. Conditions were ripe for the Catholic Church to lose millions of nominal adherents rapidly. In fact, Brazil has seen a particularly vigorous growth of competing religions, especially African-Brazilian religions and Pentecostal Protestantism.[53] The Brazilian Catholic Church, like many of the Latin American Churches, had long been complacent about its dominance, but such competing evangelization makes clear that Catholicism's hold on society is not at all secure.

Furthermore, the 1950s were a politically and socially turbulent decade in all of Latin America, when the security of the Church's place in society (including, perhaps, the dependability of ties to authoritarian states) came into question. Bruneau pointed out that the example of Cuba appeared to the Brazilian bishops to be a very real threat; they suddenly perceived a need to strengthen Brazilian Catholic beliefs, in fact rather than only in name.[54]

With the new ecumenicism of the Second Vatican Council, the Brazilian bishops could not easily return to the strategy of demanding state establishment and the suppression of Protestantism.[55] And the Church's influence with the state, both before and after the military coup of 1964, was simply not what had it had been in Dom Leme's day. Thus to strengthen the Church in the second half of the twentieth century would mean reaching out to the large numbers of nominal Catholics. This effort would eventually emerge as an increased commitment to the political and socioeconomic welfare of poorer Brazilians because in Brazil, as elsewhere in Latin America, religious alliances had always involved political and social alliances. In the United States, religious connections with a particular social class (i.e., an immigrant working class) had historically not implied a sharing of political and socioeconomic ideology, but most sectors of the Latin American Church did not practice such a separation of religion and politics.

In addition, there were other factors making more likely a socially activist path. The papal nuncio since 1954 was decidedly in favor of this path. And it appears that he had a significant impact through his recommendations for appointments to the episcopacy, especially given that Rome considerably expanded the size of the Brazilian episcopacy during his tenure.[56] When we add in the influence of Vatican II, it appears that the rapid changes of the 1950s and 1960s led the Brazilian episcopacy to attempt to rebuild itself institutionally (with Vatican support) and reach out to the population through an advocacy of social reform. Fortunately, in doing so, the machinery of the CNBB was already available. Ultimately, the CNBB became a strong organization that, like the NCCB in the United States, gave the Brazilian bishops a stronger collective identity. The conference has been an essential component of the Brazilian episcopacy's espousal of social reform.

In the first decade of the military regime (i.e., beginning in 1964), then, the hierarchy showed sporadic interest in denouncing political injustice and social inequality; but the bishops adopted that role more wholeheartedly with the initiation of state restrictions and attacks on the institutional Church itself, starting in about 1973. The government censored Church media and apparently condoned direct attacks on prominent, outspoken Church personnel, including a bishop. As in Chile, attacks led the hierarchy to close ranks; forced into an oppositional role, the bishops became more receptive to earlier CNBB strategies to identify with the struggles of the general population. For example, the bishops were willing to look more critically at the effect of the government's capitalist economic policies on the poorer sectors of Brazilian society.[57]

Furthermore, the Brazilian episcopacy, rather than being suspicious of "base communities," has taken a positive view, incorporating them into what some have called a "people's church," but still a Church led by the bishops.[58] Base communities are communities of laypeople (often with the involvement of clergy or religious, especially in their initial formation), generally living near each other and thus of the same social class, who meet together for discussion of Bible readings. In many base communities, such discussion includes applications of Bible interpretations to their own life circumstances within a liberation perspective. This method is an application, to a liberation Catholicism approach, of Brazilian educator Paulo Freire's method of teaching literacy.[59] The base communities are partially a reaction to the scarcity of clergy and partially a social unit of liberation Catholicism.

We do not know the distribution of activities or political commitment in base communities as a whole or even how many there are. Even the socioeconomic composition of the average base community is not entirely clear.[60] But the fact that many poorer Latin Americans do encounter a new type of religious experience in these communities is probably more important than the exact class composition or even activities of base communities in the aggregate.

Brazil has had by far the largest number of base communities; there are various estimates in the fifty thousand to eighty thousand range.[61] Bruneau estimated one thousand in Chile and fewer in Paraguay and Central America.[62] There are various estimates as well of the number of people in an average community: it is certainly less than one hundred, probably less than thirty or forty.[63] These communities make up only a small fraction of the baptized Catholics in any country but are the most important organizational form of liberation Catholicism.

We do know that the Brazilian episcopacy has encouraged the base communities, in great contrast to the bishops of other nations. Colombia claims a good number of base communities, but Levine reported that this reflects simply a renaming of existing organizations that are firmly under episcopal control and do not actually fit the label.[64] In Nicaragua and El Salvador, the base communities operate independently of the hierarchy, which sees such communities as an improper politicization of the Church and a danger to ecclesiastical obedience.[65]

The Brazilian episcopacy's boldness in addressing its long-standing lack of ties to the poorer classes has been impressive. The case of Chile under Pinochet furthermore suggests that the people's Church would have had difficulty surviving under a repressive state without episcopal support.[66] This may explain why, particularly in Brazil, it appears that popular Catholic organizations, such as base communities, have valued the unity of the institution,[67] although this is probably not quite as important a value to them as to the bishops.

But even in Brazil, the episcopal commitment to liberation themes appears tenuous. There is first the problem that the Vatican under John Paul II, although occasionally vacillating in the specifics, does not approve of liberation Catholicism. Its episcopal appointments in Brazil and elsewhere have reflected the pope's emphasis on orthodoxy in faith and morals and deemphasis of liberation themes (although themes from traditional social doctrine are acceptable, even encouraged).[68] Furthermore, with the gradual transition to electoral politics in the 1980s, the Brazilian bishops appear to find less need for their own involvement in social and political activism.[69]

The history of Latin American Catholicism as well as that of U.S. Catholicism and of the papacy makes clear that for bishops, given their high position in the Church's power structure, the strength of the institution is a high priority. Nevertheless, various influences will change their perception of what needs to be done to strengthen and maintain the institutional Church. One of the biggest transitions toward a new perception, we have seen, was the development of a new relationship to the state and to dominant elites, a relationship that in some cases turned from alliance to hostility. Especially in Brazil, we can see that it is possible for bishops to change their political orientations fairly rapidly and drastically. But those political commitments have never been the primary concern of more than a handful of bishops; despite the impact that Helder Câmara has had, for example, his insistence that socialist activism is integral to Christianity is certainly a minority position among the hierarchy.

Any ideological position depends on the context of power structures. The strength of liberation Catholicism, then, is precarious: its sociopolitical themes are not a primary commitment of those who have the power—that is, bishops—to foster its growth. In Brazil, the hierarchy has already been softening some of its commitments. But it is possible that liberation Catholicism has influenced other levels of the Latin American Church enough that the Church has been fundamentally changed, just as U.S. religious life will never return to its pre–Vatican II state. To see why, we must turn to the reception of Vatican II in Latin America as a whole.

Vatican II in the Context of a Political Church

Vatican II, we have already seen, redefined the relationship between Church and society in a way that made the international Church much more compatible with the U.S. model. But the council's message was ambiguous. We have seen that it provided an unclear image of the People of God; that it accepted a widened church-state separation, yet urged a greater Church effort in social activism; and that it reaffirmed the power structure of the Church, yet left open the possibility of ideological changes in light of the signs of the times.

The impact of Vatican II has had a different history in Latin America than in the United States (although there is, of course, some important convergence); different aspects of the council's purpose and its ambiguous message appealed to the two regions because of their very different histories. In Latin America, the relationship between church and state, and between church and social justice, has been much more important because it touches on the central role of the Latin American Church in a history of authoritarian politics. Latin American Catholics, both lay and clerical, have a long history of experience with the Church as an important actor in the polity. The Church there has always favored one social sector or faction over another; part of the struggle now involves an attempt to alter the identity of that sector or faction.

In the United States, however, the bishops have never much absorbed the political outlook of any faction of its laity because they have scrupulously avoided sociopolitical issues until recently. Furthermore, the bases of institutional strength in the United States have not historically undergone radical shifts, as in, for example, Brazil. Thus for the Brazilian Church, rapid Protestant evangelization in a context of alienation from the state jolted this paper tiger of a Church into action. Having lost what social foundation it had, it scrambled to build new links to the laity. But the U.S. episcopacy had never relied on state alliance, had always been a minority among a Protestant majority, had always had stronger ties to the laity, and had based those ties much more on spiritual than sociopolitical leadership. It has always been instinctive in Brazil, but not in the United States, for the Church to link itself politically to some sector of state or society.

An ideological boundary between religion and politics can at times be useful for Latin American bishops—for example, as the Brazilian bishops deemphasized political activism in the 1980s and as the Chilean episcopacy protected its autonomy in stating in the 1970 election that the Church does not have electoral preferences. But appealing to such an ideological boundary has historically been a tactic, rather than a true commitment, among Latin America bishops, and in some countries it has never even been a tactic.

Given the weak commitment to such a boundary among even the episcopacy, then, it is not surprising to see that many Church personnel at lower levels of the power structure of the Latin American Church have not interpreted Vatican II to mean that sociopolitical issues are subordinate to faith and morals. Liberation theologians, in fact, frequently argue against a strong distinction between the spiritual and temporal purposes of the Church. They argue specifically that the Church has always been a political support for some social faction, even when it pretended to be apolitical.[70] Among some Catholic intellectuals and Church personnel, Vatican II sparked an intense reconsideration of the Church's relationship to Latin American society. They came to advocate social and political activism on behalf of the poorer sectors of Latin American society (although sometimes such commitments may have involved a romanticized and distant view of those sectors).[71] These intellectuals, sisters, and priests embraced dependency analysis, a theory of society and politics that argues that international capitalism, in alliance with domestic capitalist elites, profits through the exploitation of the masses of the Third World.

Like the United States, through most of its history Latin American Catholicism had been considered a theological backwater.[72] Liberation theologians of the region, despite their debt to modern European theology, papal social doctrine, and Vatican II, make a virtue of this history by arguing that there is a distinctive Third World theology.[73] The struggle over liberation Catholicism, then, can be seen as a struggle over the meaning of the Church's relation to society within a Latin American discourse accustomed to Church involvement in temporal politics.

This background may explain why a gathering of Latin American bishops in 1968 appeared to legitimate a new view of Catholicism without the bishops being quite aware of the potential political implications of their statements. There has generally not been the strong commitment to excluding the Church from sociopolitical questions that there has long been in the United States. Thus the tension in Vatican II between a disavowal of the ancien régime and a simultaneous call for the Church to become more involved in social reform left open the possible interpretation that the Church was not to leave politics, but to switch sides.[74] In Latin America as a whole, the seed for that interpretation was planted at the second general meeting of CELAM (Consejo Episcopal Latinoamericano, or Latin American Episcopal Conference), the regional bishops' conference, in 1968, at Medellín, Colombia. The purpose of the meeting was to implement Vatican II in Latin America. At attendance were 150 bishops (of approximately 600 in Latin America) representing all the national Churches. Following Vatican II, the conference emphasized a pastoral perspective with an openness to the signs of the times.[75] We have already seen, of course, that there were various interpretations about what it meant to implement Vatican II. CELAM's deliberations at Medellín, however, were probably the most striking episcopal interpretation of the Second Vatican Council anywhere in the world.

The Medellín meeting demonstrated the volatile ambiguity of Vatican II. It seems likely, given the evidence of later backtracking, that the assembled bishops did not quite foresee the potential meanings of the Medellín endorsement of looking at the Church in light of the signs of the times[76] and of emphasizing social justice.

It is interesting to note that the documents from the meeting did not emphasize the traditional distinctions between the clergy and laity or between spiritual and temporal responsibilities.[77] Instead, the documents straddled two different views of social change, one emphasizing gradual, developmental improvement in Latin American social conditions and the other emphasizing the necessity of working for liberation of the oppressed. The latter view emphasized solidarity of the Church with the poor and encouraged the establishment of base communities.[78]

It was, and remains, startling that a group of bishops, many of whom came from national Churches with very conservative ideologies of social order, could endorse such ideas in Latin America. How could this happen? It is difficult to answer this question definitively; but there are a number of factors that likely influenced the bishops at Medellín.

First, it is worth noting that in addition to the bishops, the meeting included a large number (about one hundred) of nonepiscopal theological experts and advisers who actually wrote and revised many of the texts. Many of these theologians were soon to initiate liberation theology. This does not mean that the bishops were simply fooled by their theologians; many deeply trusted their advisers, but it may not have been clear to either the bishops or their theologians that there was more divergence about the future goals of the Latin American Church than was obvious at Medellín itself.

There were also other influences on the direction Medellín took. For example, the Brazilian bishops—who represent by far the largest national Church in the region—were, given the existence of the CNBB, the best organized and perhaps boldest. Thus their numbers and their ideological commitments had a big impact on Medellín. It was also the case that Medellín followed the lead of Paul VI's monumental encyclical, *Populorum Progressio*,[79] which had appeared only recently. The encyclical incorporated elements of two perspectives that, we have already seen, made their way into the Medellín documents: a mainstream view that the Third World could ultimately catch up to the First, developing along similar lines, and a dependency view emphasizing First World exploitation of the Third World. And so, given that Vatican II had ended only three years before and *Populorum Progressio* had appeared in 1967, we can see that the CELAM bishops probably saw themselves as loyal supporters of the international Church's view of the role of Catholicism in the modern world.

It is also the case that the regional and international political climate of the time may have led the assembled bishops to address long-standing social grievances with proposed solutions that they normally would have rejected.[80] During the 1960s, political conservatives throughout the Americas worried about the precedent set by the Cuban Revolution. Fidel Castro's associate Che Guevara died in Bolivia in 1967 attempting to further revolution; a cleric named Camilo Torres left the priesthood in 1965 and was killed the next year fighting with leftist guerrillas in Colombia. The U.S. government's Alliance for Progress was an attempt to promote moderate social reform so as to lessen the appeal of revolutionary politics.

The most tumultuous year of the decade was 1968; by the time of Medellín (August 1968), political conservatives were on the defensive. That year student and worker rebellions erupted in France; riots followed the assassination of Martin Luther King, Jr., in the United States; there were student protests and a police riot at the U.S. Democratic Party convention in Chicago; and police shot and killed hundreds of demonstrators at a Mexico City protest gathering. The sense of an urgent need to address long-standing social grievances may have led the assembled bishops to promote solutions at variance with their history of political conservatism.

In any case, even if we take into account that Medellín was partly an attempt to follow Rome's lead, the 1968 CELAM meeting certainly produced an innovative stance. It is not that Medellín necessarily conflicted with Vatican II or with, for example, *Populorum Progressio*—it is just that the commitment to social justice was taken further than it had in any other part of the international hierarchy. And so to many Latin Americans, 1968 appeared to be a radical break, the time that the Latin American episcopacy embraced liberation. Indeed, ever since, liberation Catholics have cited Medellín as a pivotal event legitimating their cause.[81] The first treatises of liberation theology began to appear soon after the meeting.

But even though such Catholics would prefer to see Medellín as an unambiguous and irreversible commitment to social reform, battles would soon begin over its meaning and effects. We saw earlier, especially in chapter 6, that after Vatican II, Rome did not immediately perceive the problems of decentralization and of new ideological messages such as an emphasis on the People of God. Medellín paralleled the Second Vatican Council in the sense of including themes (such as the People of God and the need to increase a commitment to social justice) whose more radical readings many of the gathered bishops probably did not intend. This is not surprising because Medellín's purpose was to implement Vatican II; in implementing the council's messages, Medellín also implemented its uncertainties.[82]

When it became clear how Medellín was being interpreted, both the Vatican and more traditional bishops acted to counter the legitimation of liberation themes. One of the most important countermoves was a change in the leadership of CELAM so that the organization began to reflect a view that the Church should emphasize spiritual concerns to the exclusion of sociopolitical issues. The view of Christ as liberator and, occasionally, revolutionary came under particular attack. Interestingly, the conservatives often used the language of liberation to mean an exclusively spiritual liberation, thus excluding structural, temporal implications.[83]

It appeared by the late 1970s that the third general meeting of CELAM in Puebla, Mexico, in 1979, to be attended by the pope, would see the reversal of Medellín. The very setting of the conference—at a secluded monastery on the outskirts of the city, with no advisers permitted on the grounds—was intended to prevent the influence of liberation theologians. But the conference ended somewhat as a draw, as the more radical interpretations of Medellín were disavowed, but the Church's "preferential option for the poor" was explicitly endorsed for the first time.[84] It appears that a draw could emerge both because bishops sympathetic to liberation themes devised a clever communication system with their prohibited advisers and because John Paul II was himself somewhat unsure about his exact position on such issues.[85] The newly elected pope had been in office only a few months and so remained a somewhat unknown quantity. He did not issue the expected unequivocal condemnation of liberation, although he clearly favored a traditionalist interpretation of Vatican II. But during his travels through Mexico before the meeting opened, he seemed at times to emphasize solidarity with the poor.

Beyond the specifics of the meeting itself, structural, political forces affecting the position of the Church in Latin American society probably also had an important influence on the Puebla outcome. Marcos McGrath emphasized that a primary episcopal concern of the bishops at Puebla was freeing the Church of restraining ties with the state because states were happy to endorse Christianity only as long as the Church did not interfere with state power.[86] Repressive states' explicit claims to be defending "Christian civilization" with murderous policies appears to have helped fuel the desire of Latin American bishops for greater autonomy.[87] In any case, liberation Catholicism certainly survived Puebla.

Liberation, Power, and Ideology in the Church

It may be the case that the legacy of Vatican II and Medellín will make it difficult to control the political interpretations of modern Catholicism. It is interesting to note, for example, that Puebla followed in the footsteps of both Vatican II and Medellín in emphasizing a pastoral perspective open to the signs of the times. Liberation theologians such as Leonardo Boff can even cite the Puebla documents in support of the argument that the Church must necessarily be political.[88]

During the papacy of John Paul II, there has been a battle over liberation Catholicism. There have been clear signs of retrenchment since Puebla (even, we have seen, in Brazil). The prefect of the (Vatican's) Congregation for the Doctrine of the Faith, Cardinal Joseph Ratzinger, has been very critical of liberation themes. In 1984 his Congregation published

an instruction criticizing liberation theology in terms (concerning immanent theology) somewhat reminiscent of Pius X's condemnation of modernism.[89] John Paul II and Ratzinger's comments clearly indicate that Rome
wants to maintain a distinction between the faith and morals of individuals and families, on the one hand, and sociopolitical issues, on the
other. The subordination of sociopolitical issues is, as we have seen, of
particular interest to Rome because the papacy's power is based on
centralized control of faith and morals. Furthermore, that subordination
serves to lessen the risk of church-state conflict, but avoiding such
conflict is not a priority for those who see social activism as an integral
part of faith.

So far the conflict over liberation Catholicism has not reached crisis
proportions. This is probably because liberation Catholics, while they
do not respect the ideological boundary subordinating macropolitics
and economics, do not generally question Roman authority and opinion
on the faith and morals of individuals and families. The primary issues
of controversy in Latin American Catholicism have not involved faith
and morals (which are more usually the focus of internal conflicts in the
U.S. Church) but the relationship of the Church to the sociopolitical
world. Nevertheless, the style of disagreement with Rome can resemble
that of the Leadership Conference of Women Religious in the United
States—that is, in challenging Rome's authority indirectly by emphasizing the plural interpretations of Vatican II that can continue to develop
according to the signs of the times. For example, Juan Segundo's response to Ratzinger's criticism of liberation theology states fidelity to
the magisterium (the teaching authority of the hierarchy)[90] but insists, as
do all liberation theologians, that liberation is the faithful child of papal
social teaching, Vatican II, and Medellín. All these teachings are part of
the Church's magisterium. Segundo, like a number of Catholic theologians all over the world, explicitly emphasizes that it is not the case that
anything and everything the Vatican says is infallible.[91]

There are elements of liberation Catholicism that are a potential
challenge to the hierarchical control of ideology in the Church, but ultimately it may not quite be the challenge to orthodoxy that many of us had
expected. Let us first look at the reality and potential of challenge, followed
by discussion of the limits of that challenge.

THE POTENTIAL FOR CONFLICT

First, the emphasis on reading the gospels in a small community setting (in
base communities), allowing interpretation to develop within the group,

rather than through studying official Church doctrine, is in some ways strongly analogous to Reformation approaches to the Bible. As in the Reformation, an emphasis on Bible reading and a deemphasis of clerical supervision implicitly, and at times explicitly, questions the necessity and validity of a hierarchical institutional structure.

The base communities have been a radicalizing experience for many priests and religious (women and men) as well as lay leaders. Such communities that do involve poorer Latin Americans, even if they are a minority of all base communities, have provided an organizational base for the least powerful sectors of the Church and of society. This is a highly significant development, explaining both why liberation theology emphasizes the experience of the least advantaged social groups and why the base communities in some instances have been the only forum for political opposition under repressive governments. These communities potentially can wed sectors of the Church to political activism as well as become in themselves a new democratic experience within the Church.[92]

And, of course, with perhaps the sole exception of Brazil, base communities have reinforced an ideological divergence between the hierarchy and the significant minority of Church personnel and other committed Catholics attracted to liberation themes. Whereas the Brazilian bishops have been fairly successful in incorporating the base communities into the institutional structure,[93] in most other countries where such communities are strong (particularly in Central America), they appear to have developed independently of the hierarchy. They are fostered by sisters, brothers, priests, and lay leaders, many of whom are more committed to liberation themes than are bishops.[94]

For those involved in the base communities, especially those communities that treat liberation themes as a central concern, the Church's involvement in social and political activism is a primary mission of the Church. But sisters, priests, and laity who have identified with liberation struggles generally do so without episcopal support.[95] To the hierarchy, activism is more an occasionally useful tactic, which Rome is doing its best—through criticisms and appointments—to discourage. Usually, bishops willing to support popular movements against the state act alone, not as agents of a larger group of bishops. The most noted activist bishop of Central America, Archbishop Oscar Romero of San Salvador (who was murdered by right-wing forces in March 1982), generally acted independently of other Salvadoran bishops. The same can be said of Cardinal Miguel Obando y Bravo's opposition to Anastasio Somoza in Nicaragua; the Nicaraguan episcopacy did eventually join the opposition against Somoza, but only after considerable hesitation.[96]

Reflecting the weak episcopal support for liberation Catholicism, liberation theology sometimes strongly questions the hierarchy's authority, thus resembling the perspectives of U.S. sisters more than U.S. bishops. Emphasis on the rights of "the people" can sometimes imply a questioning of any hierarchical power structure. Thus in 1973, for example, the Chilean bishops condemned Christians for Socialism for distorting the Church's temporal role and not respecting the hierarchy's disciplinary authority.[97] This potential for conflict probably explains why Leonardo Boff has received the most intensive Vatican criticism of any liberation theologian. Boff, unlike, for example, Gustavo Gutiérrez, is persistent and explicit in his arguments that liberation requires a less hierarchical view of the Church.[98] He has argued that the Church's own internal procedures violate human rights.[99] He has extended his criticism of the Church power structure to challenge Rome's views on a number of sensitive topics, such as the ordination of women.[100] Although it is true that the Vatican investigated Gutiérrez at about the same time, Rome did not extend to Gutiérrez the order that Boff refrain from publishing and speaking on liberation theology for a year.[101]

Even if liberation Catholicism does not develop a more radical challenge of the Church's power structure (or even if Rome can control such a challenge), its emphasis on a politicized Church could create problems for the Vatican. The papacy generally avoids conflicts with states and powerful secular elites that might lead to repression of the institutional Church. But liberation Catholicism, especially as envisioned in liberation theology, sees capitalism and class inequality as inherently sinful; base-community mobilization based on liberation themes implies an ethical delegitimation of entire state structures and economic systems. But popes and bishops are hesitant to play an active oppositional role or to engage in popular mobilization unless the Church is attacked first.[102]

Yet the very structure of Catholic ideology makes it difficult to control its political applications. Given the exclusion of sociopolitical issues from the core of Church doctrine, it is not easy even for traditionalist prelates to define the signs of the times to exclude particular political options. That is, they can argue that such options are subordinate to spiritual concerns but cannot rule out Christian socialist options in a nonbinding level of doctrine. It is also the case that within an anticapitalist ideology, the "preferential option for the poor" is a sensible option indeed, especially given the secularization of the middle classes of many Catholic nations. By emphasizing the central importance of faith and morals, Rome excludes sociopolitical issues from its own ideological authority; we have already seen that the papacy had little choice but to do so. As a result, even though the Vatican critique of liberation theology argues that Catholics must not place tempo-ral social change on the same level as spiritual concerns and that the Church must avoid social division, Rome has been more hesitant to criticize the socialism of liberation Catholicism per se.

Within the ideological structure that the papacy attempts to enforce, there is significant freedom of movement around sociopolitical issues. Despite insistence by the U.S. bishops, for example, that the social teachings of the Church are a vital part of its mission, the Church does not discipline those who violate its social doctrine. It is in fact possible for Catholics to graft a variety of secular political views (within broad limits) onto the Church's view of sociopolitical issues without fearing discipline, especially given the vagueness of Church ideology on such issues.

THE POTENTIAL FOR COEXISTENCE

But there are a number of reasons to suspect that explosive conflicts between the hierarchy (whether in Rome or in the national Churches) and liberation Catholicism may be the exception rather than the norm.[103] It may be that the reality of liberation Catholicism is politically and ideologically more compatible with Roman orthodoxy than many promoters and ana-lysts imply. For one, as Mainwaring pointed out, the political nature of base communities has probably been overemphasized.[104] Luis Pásara has argued, not unconvincingly, that the political militancy and theoretical purity of liberation theology are sometimes a clerical and an intellectual affair only abstractly connected to the actual lives and experiences of socioeconomically disadvantaged Latin Americans.[105] Many discussions of base communities imply that popular religiosity is inherently highly politi-cized and even revolutionary. Historical and sociological studies have, however, cast great doubt on the assumption that in any situation, class position automatically implies a particular politics or ideology.[106]

This is certainly not to say that sisters, clerics, lay leaders, bishops, and others who promote liberation theology do so on their own or without regard to popular needs. We must remember that a significant number of such people have paid for their theology with their lives, and their approach has clearly had significant success strengthening connections between the institutional Church and the Latin American laity. By saying that bishops generally become receptive to liberation themes only after experiencing state attack on the institutional Church, I do not imply that bishops then act only in self-interest. Such attacks on the Church commonly lead to newfound commitments that are strong and genuine and that can involve significant personal risks for outspoken bishops. Although there is still a concern with the strength of the institutional Church, an episcopal commitment to liberation Catholicism means a redefinition of the needs of that institution to include greater concern with the poorer sectors of the laity.

Indeed, liberation Catholicism is an affair of the institutional Church; its origins lie in the thoughts and actions of Catholics, not of existing, secular political organizations that infiltrate the Church. (Thus the politics can sometimes be abstract, rather than pragmatic.) Proponents of liberation theology at all levels generally value their membership in that Church. As a result, they have constructed an approach that may not be as inimical to orthodoxy as some opponents and proponents have supposed.[107] With some notable exceptions, proponents of liberation Catholicism generally do not explicitly question orthodox doctrine on faith and morals.[108] (An interesting example of a liberation view deemphasizing internal Church issues was a statement by the Argentine Priests for the Third World critical of European Catholic attention to the issue of priestly celibacy.)[109] This explains why Roman approaches to and statements on liberation theology have not been entirely negative.

The commitment to Catholicism both as a belief system and as an institution is quite strong among even liberation theologians, let alone liberation Catholics not involved in the intellectual exercises of the theology.[110] The movement has not simply been an attempt to mask radical secular ideologies with a superficial layer of Christianity, as critics have often charged. The emphasis on direct reading and interpretation of scripture in base communities—while it can imply a challenge to the hierarchy's right to provide authoritative scriptural interpretation—in itself should be enough to demonstrate that liberation theology is not simply an attempt of Marxists to appropriate Christianity. Within liberation theology, there is a forcefully made argument that, when interpreted in light of lived experience, the gospels are enough in themselves to understand and change the world.[111] The starting point of such theology is clearly Christian belief; liberation theologians in fact spend little or no time defending or developing theological arguments about why one should believe. Their writings assume belief. Phillip Berryman has noted, in contrast to North American stereotypes of liberation theology, that such theologians devote remarkably little attention to discussions of Marxism or violence.[112] It is true that Marxist thinking certainly influenced liberation theology,[113] but liberation theologians can actually be quite selective in their use of Marxist concepts.[114]

Although liberation Catholicism argues that social activism is an integral part of Christian faith, even its approach to the specifics of temporal politics shows a certain similarity to that of Catholic ideological structure. That is, at least when expressed as liberation theology, the approach is quite vague; the specifics of policy do not receive the attention given to the interpretation of Catholic religious commitments. This analogy is only partly appropriate, of course, because Roman lack of specificity entails a deemphasis of sociopolitical issues, which is not true of liberation theology. But it is the case that the conceptual categories used in liberation theology divide society into simple dichotomies rather than enter detailed analysis. At its basic level, the theology posits oppressed versus oppressors, tortured versus torturers.

The roots of this approach are in the wholesale adoption of the fundamental premise of secular theories of *dependencia* (dependency). Dependency theories emphasize the exploitation of popular classes and dependent, poorer nations by international capitalism. Catholic social doctrine, I noted in chapter 2, is receptive to anticapitalist ideologies; thus Latin American leftist Catholics were quite open to the *dependencia* view. This was especially true after the more open ideological atmosphere initiated by Vatican II, allowing even experimental openings to Marxists; dependency is indeed inspired by Marxist social theories.

In some ways, the liberation view is very consistent with the occasional direction of papal social thought (especially in Paul VI's *Populorum Progressio*) toward a more critical perspective on international capitalism, while being more specific than the papacy has been. The vagueness and devaluation of papal social doctrine (relative to doctrine on faith and morals) allow the papacy to avoid alienating particular social and political factions, while liberation perspectives attempt to make Church ideology explicitly socialist and pro–Third World. By taking Catholic ideology in a more specifically leftist direction, liberation Catholicism becomes simply incompatible with right-wing interpretations of social doctrine, which were popular in some parts of Latin America at least into the 1950s.

But exactly what constitutes "socialism" and which political forces represent the "oppressed" are usually left rather vague and have elicited criticism from some analysts generally sympathetic to liberation politics. Michael Dodson argued that simplistic political categories led to a split in the Movement of Priests for the Third World; the lack of theoretical sophistication combined with a strong commitment to ending "oppression" opened the door to heated differences over the interpretation of what constitutes oppression.[115]

Indeed, a certain simplicity and vagueness in the conceptual categories of liberation theology may reflect a political and ideological distance between some proponents of that theology and the poorer classes it champions. We saw that the Church's relationship to state and society very much influenced episcopal approaches to sociopolitical issues, including the themes of liberation. Bishops did not simply decide out of nowhere that they should champion the popular classes. Even though their sentiments were genuine, those sentiments arose partly in response to forces threatening the institutional Church's place in Latin American society. It is possible that perceptions of who are the enemies have been colored as much by the threats on the Church as by any analysis of the specific problems facing a specific sector of the Latin American political economy. So for liberation bishops, the enemy was an evil state and an evil socioeconomic system. Now that the worst of Latin American dictatorship of the 1960s and 1970s is over, bishops who appealed to liberation themes (who, of course, were always very much a minority) have generally retreated from their activism. Have they done so because they are in close touch with the masses and think the masses are not as oppressed as they used to be or perhaps need a new strategy for changed times? Or have they done so because the oppressed were initially abstractly defined, to some extent, simply in opposition to the much more concrete perception of an oppressor (a hostile state)? And now that the monolith of an oppressor has weakened, is there less need to postulate the existence of a large mass of oppressed?

(Again, my rhetorical questions—used to clarify what otherwise might sound obscure—point to a social distance that exists but that should not be overemphasized. Connections with the poorer laity have definitely been strengthened, partly reversing centuries-old traditions in the Latin American Church. And it is certainly legitimate to point out that the Church's defense of the poor and defenseless was most necessary, most beneficial, and most risky during the periods of brutal dictatorship. The courage and reality of these commitments should not be forgotten.)

In the late 1980s, Latin American liberation theologians showed signs of questioning the unyielding commitment to the dichotomous categories of oppressed versus oppressors, Third World dependence versus First World avarice. The 1980s also saw some return to spiritual concerns not as explicitly politicized as in the earlier writings, most notably in the case of Gustavo Gutiérrez.[116] Liberation theology itself could easily undergo a major transformation with the decline of military dictatorships in Latin America. It is difficult at this point to say how much common ground liberation Catholicism and its successors will find with Rome; perhaps otherworldly spirituality will outlast socialist commitments so that the loyalty of liberation Catholics to the Church will prevent schism.

There will not, however, be a simple return to neo-Christendom. It may be that the historical experience of alienation from authoritarian states will lead to a sharpened boundary between sociopolitical issues and religious issues, at least in the eyes of the episcopacy.[117] Whether or not this happens, the potential for further challenges to the orthodoxies of hierarchical authority and ideological boundaries still very much exists. At the very least, some pluralism in Catholic views of sociopolitical issues is likely to continue. Too many Latin American Catholics with widely different politics are accustomed to associating religion with politics for such conflicts to disappear. Even if liberation Catholicism as a socialist ideology emphasizing base communities splits or disintegrates, leftist application of Catholicism is likely to remain an important component of that pluralism in Latin America. The noncommittal nature of Catholic ideology on sociopolitical issues allows Catholics a wide latitude in interpretation and application. By attempting to exclude sociopolitical issues from the ideological core of Catholicism, Rome has ceded control over specification to others.

8 Conclusion: The Catholic Church and Ideological Change

If we think of the Catholic Church as a building with inhabitants (or as a social structure), we can see that the modern nation-state and modern capitalism greatly upset the feudal community to which the Church had grown accustomed. Rome found itself in the midst of new neighbors it perceived as selfish and unfriendly. Of course, Catholicism was not then completely divorced from the world; it still lived in the neighborhood.

Rome did not easily accept the new arrangements; Pope Pius IX railed against the audacity of his secular neighbors. He complained that in his new isolation from temporal affairs, he was a "prisoner of the Vatican." But, in fact, he held the keys to his own jail; the Republic of Italy did not claim the right to regulate his travels. It is not clear whether Pius IX himself could see that making his home into a fortress made him more of an absolute monarch than perhaps he had ever been. With fewer intruders, or even visitors, from the world of temporal politics and economics, the pope could run his household almost any way he chose. Fortresses not only exclude intruders; they allow the inhabitants a secure and predictable existence as long as they choose to remain safely within their own walls. And within those walls, indeed, the pope could safely complain about the neighbors in a way that, had he been more involved in the community, would have been rather undiplomatic.

But, of course, the Church was more closed off from the neighborhood, so that it seemed smaller. Some of the pope's subjects, finding the fortress confining, wanted to take advantage of the neighborhood's expansion, even as the pope's little corner was no longer the center of the community. They wanted to participate in new civic organizations—such as political parties—of which the pope disapproved. They wanted their neighbors to think of them as good citizens; some, such as American bishops, resented the obstacles the papacy placed in their path.

Ultimately, despite periodic attempts to find new allies (such as Mussolini) who might be able to evict the liberal neighbors, Rome discovered the advantages of participation in the community, changed though it was. While the neighbors might ignore the pope, they saw no need to interfere in his household. Hesitantly, the papacy condoned the participation of Catholics in the modern world, often ignoring their civic activities. In the process, Rome lost the ability to control the details of Catholics' lives. The papacy and the bishops ultimately celebrated the newly legitimated place of the Church in the world; at Vatican II, they rejected the necessity of structuring the Church as if it were a besieged army that necessitated a clear hierarchy of decision-making authority to avert disaster. Some parts of the Church moved on to new pastures, certain that this was precisely what the hierarchy intended.

But the papacy still wanted to assure that when in Rome, Catholics would do as the Romans do, or as the papacy believed Romans should do. Negotiating life as if the Church consisted of several generations of an immigrant family, however, Catholics (even popes) have never been entirely sure how to reconcile old family traditions and a new civic identity. The papacy, very much perceiving itself as the traditional patriarch, reserved the right to disown other members of the family. But even that was not enough to control all the relatives, some of whom grew tired of the father's harangues; they rejected the legitimacy of patriarchy altogether. Even setting aside this problem, popes themselves did not always make clear what the house rules were.

Catholics will continue to disagree about what ultimately those rules and traditions—the true religious beliefs and moral precepts of the Catholic faith—are or should be and how comprehensive they need to be. They differ, for example, over how Catholicism relates to obligations and opportunities in the temporal world. There are many who see their faith as a spiritual devotion to the religious directives of Rome that is expressed mainly through ritual and individual conscience. Such Catholics sometimes argue, then, that liberation theologians, or sisters who promote a rebellious feminism, betray the true nature of the faith. Looking at the history of Catholic ideology, as we have done in this book, cannot tell us what are the correct theological or moral interpretations of Catholicism. But sociologically speaking, we have seen that a remarkable variety of interpretations of Catholicism have existed historically. Even the view that Catholicism should be kept distinct from temporal political agendas, a view that seems so "orthodox" today, would have been a heresy in the eyes of most nineteenth-century popes.

The various interpretations of Catholicism encountered in this book have all been sociologically and ideologically very much rooted in the Catholic Church. Even those views Rome has commonly found troublesome have their own traditions among Catholic theologians and Catholic decentralizers. That is, for example, true of a theological emphasis on an immanent view of God's presence in the Church and in the world through the Holy Spirit. Such an emphasis appeared in the modernism that Pius X condemned, was an influence on the new orthodoxy established by Vatican II, and appears very strongly in the People of God perspective of liberation theology and of American sisters. To some degree it was also true of Americanism. This is not to say that all these perspectives within the Church are equivalent. But immanence does serve as a striking example of the very Catholic origins of even those views criticized as unorthodox. Certainly, there has been influence, sometimes quite strong, from outside the Church. But that has been true not only of the dissenters; even the hierarchy at Vatican II partly incorporated liberalism into the doctrine. In all cases, however, understanding the origins of the various strands of Catholicism requires understanding how different parts of the Church contribute and react to the ideological structure of Catholicism. Even the penetration of outside ideological influences is obstructed or aided by the politics of Catholicism's ideological structure.

Different parts of the Catholic Church have influenced the direction of the Church in various ways. But no one could completely foresee or control the path of the Church. Even popes, as almighty within the Church as they may seem at times, had limited options. Pope Pius X attempted to control Catholics' party politics; he unwittingly helped push such politics out of the Church altogether. Pius XI attempted to forge a new authoritarian church-state alliance but failed somewhat miserably. Pope John Paul II attempts to maintain a strict separation between religious and political goals, the former being the more proper province of the Church. But by attempting to emphasize issues such as abortion that in some societies (including the United States) are considered eminently political, he makes that separation increasingly problematic. Thus American Catholic bishops, among others, find themselves in a dilemma. They are accused of political interference on an issue around which they allow (and they themselves have) little freedom of movement within the Church, precisely because within Catholic ideology abortion is *not* a political issue.

Meanwhile, the hierarchy has to a significant extent lost a certain amount of allegiance among some sectors of the Church, such as American sisters and, to some degree, liberation Catholics. The hierarchy can threaten and apply sanctions for overt signs of dissent on faith and moral issues, but there exists a silent pluralism nevertheless.

Such changes in the Catholic Church have been dramatic and give us much to digest. In this conclusion, I wish to ask two questions about those changes. First, what does the ideological history of Catholicism tell us about the study of ideological change in general? Second, what does the legacy suggest about the future of the Catholic Church, especially in the United States?

The Study of Ideological Change

The approach taken in this book borrows partly from new sociological emphases on the autonomy of social spheres developed by neo-Marxists,[1] among others, partly from Alexis de Tocqueville's emphasis on the importance of competing centers of social power, and perhaps even somewhat from Max Weber's and Emile Durkheim's different views of the power of religion as a motivator and social bond. There is, then, a focus on the *interaction* of power and ideology within social structures, which always contain spaces of autonomy.

Perhaps one of the strongest theoretical currents within American sociology of the last few years has been a view that we cannot explain social processes by focusing primarily on the effects of just one causal variable (religion, class, etc.), nor should we see societies as completely controlled or unified social groupings in which the dominated have no control over their own minds, bodies, and actions. This approach is quite hopeful because it makes sociologists more receptive to historical subtleties and more aware of the initiatives of millions of disadvantaged people.

There is, however, also a theoretical danger if we attempt to argue that there are no clear patterns of power and control at all. Not only would we miss another important aspect of the lives of many people, disadvantaged or not, but we would also have trouble developing much sociological insight if we imply that there is so much autonomy in society that absolutely nothing is predictable.

This book, then, has been an attempt to consider the intrinsic interaction of structural constraints with political and ideological autonomy. Autonomy is part of power. It is not the case that political power is the only influence on ideological change, but I contend that there will always be a strongly political component in any ideological change. When we think of power, we include factors such as the ability to have one's opinion heard and the ability to suppress dissent. No one ever has a monopoly on power, and so there will always be limits. But these aspects of power can translate into control over the messages children receive in their schooling, the ability to influence the framing of news stories, and the ability to define who is a radical. Power thus affects ideology, although, again, power is always partial. We saw that domination even entails some autonomy for the dominated in the negative sense that they do not fully participate in the political structures and ideologies that dominate them.

But in looking at cases other than the Catholic Church, we would have to keep in mind that ideological structures in society as a whole are likely to be more complex than in the Catholic Church. There will be many more competing centers of power; commonly, but not always, it will be more difficult for one group to define orthodoxy to the great extent that Rome is able to do so. Alternatively, in situations of great coercion, ideology may be less important in some political situations than it is in the Catholic Church. Most people are unlikely to participate in the Catholic Church if they are not to some degree participants in its ideology. Yet there are many people in the world compelled to participate in social structures in which ideology is not a significant factor in their participation; compared to modern states, the Catholic Church is a relatively noncoercive institution. Certainly Vatican investigations and condemnations can be highly intimidating, and informal social networks make it difficult for those investigated to simply "quit" the Church. And it is true that the hierarchy can in certain cases resort to economic coercion—for example, in refusing to allow a dissident theologian or priest to work within the institution. But this does not begin to compare to the economic, physical, or political coercion applied by repressive states.

Nevertheless, there are important elements of the politics of Catholic ideology that shed light on the general study of ideological change. For one, there will always be some issues and beliefs that are politically more important than others. These beliefs will usually be more specific; dissent will elicit sanctions. That beliefs are structured into different levels of significance means that those with power not only have to control the specifics of the important beliefs, but also have to keep other beliefs in their peripheral status. In a negative sense, for example, sociopolitical issues are indeed very important to Rome because Rome must prevent such issues from contaminating beliefs about the faith and morals of individuals and families. (It is not the content of sociopolitical beliefs, but their relative priority, that most concerns Rome.)

One element of the Vatican's attempt to maintain this ideological structure is the ambiguity and flexibility of doctrine on sociopolitical issues, which avoids specific policy commitments. Perhaps one of the most overlooked aspects of the study of ideology has been the importance of ambiguity. When we expect ideological change to be simply a matter of a change of content in someone's beliefs, we cannot see the importance of ambiguity. Instead, a focus on ideological structure helps us understand why the content of some beliefs are more important than others. Sometimes, for structural reasons, content does not matter; changes in ideological structure are ultimately more important than changes in content.

Ambiguity can emerge simply because certain issues are of no concern to particular groups. It also emerges as a way to avoid conflict and to avoid inflaming potential political divisions.[2] By being vague in their social pronouncements, popes could maintain ideological independence while avoiding conflict with powerful secular forces. They could make (admittedly weak) attempts to reach out to the working class without being specific enough to alienate conservative Catholics of the middle and upper classes. For the sake of the Church's reputation and the desire to reach out to poorer and reformist Catholics, popes could claim that social justice was a high priority when in fact it was not. Thus emerged the confusion that many socially minded Catholics still see in Leo XIII's founding of modern social doctrine an increased commitment, whereas in the long run, the birth of that doctrine indicated that sociopolitical issues had become a lower doctrinal priority. With a vague ideological approach to sociopolitical issues, popes were able to insist that Catholic ethical principles were relevant to social issues but that those principles did not imply specific policies. U.S. bishops have also found this ambiguity of application useful, although they have tended toward increasing specificity of ethical policy alternatives.

Within secular politics, ambiguity can emerge for much the same reasons. Those aspects of an ideology that attempt to be inclusive and to prevent conflict or division will tend to be rather vague. An example in the United States is the diverse array of regimes that some U.S. administrations have designated "democratic" to justify their status as allies. To an administration that uses the term *democracy* in a particularly vague way, democracy is in fact not a prime determinant of policy. More likely, geopolitical (or perhaps economic) concerns are a higher priority in dealing with such allies. When the specifics of the military capacity of an ally or foe draw more attention than the criteria for democracy, we can be fairly certain that security concerns are indeed a higher priority.

That ambiguity can aid in preventing conflict is amply documented in Kristin Luker's study of the political history of abortion in the United States.[3] It is interesting to note that the abortion issue could remain politically submerged from the late nineteenth century until approximately the 1950s largely because so many people misunderstood not only abortion's actual legal status, but also the extent to which it was actually practiced. This situation could emerge because the prohibition of abortion was not a high priority of the doctors who claimed it was; they were in fact more interested in having power as gatekeepers. The exact meaning, as interpreted in practice, of new laws (in the late nineteenth century) regulating abortion were ambiguous enough to give doctors greater control over this medical procedure. In practice physicians did not want to commit themselves to legislation specifically prohibiting abortion, although they claimed such prohibition was their actual intent. The emerging medical profession instead attempted to gain control of abortion as a way to increase physicians' occupational prestige. Within the medical profession, the issue of the exact moral status of abortion was (and remains), on the whole, a peripheral concern.

One of the interesting aspects of ambiguity, however, is that it involves a certain risk because it involves a delimiting of control. By avoiding specification on sociopolitical issues, Rome cannot easily restrict how Catholics use social doctrine to justify particular political programs. As long as such Catholics, especially Church personnel, do not attempt to make such issues a higher priority than faith and morals (e.g., by a priest's spending more time on political organization than on his duties as a pastor), Rome cannot easily object without calling into question its own claims that it does not favor particular policies. By the time Rome feels able and willing to rein in such personnel, it may be too late. That is, after the development of specific sociopolitical commitments, these Catholics may strongly resist the papal attempt to maintain the strict boundary separating temporal issues from faith and morals. Similarly, doctors had obscured the question of the moral status of abortion and as a result lost control of that issue. As prochoice and prolife groups reshaped the issue of abortion, doctors became secondary players in the debate.

One might argue that ambiguity is also an important factor in social change in a different way. The negative ideological autonomy that people have from social structures in which they are not important participants could be described as a somewhat more ambiguous, diffuse commitment than would be true of the commitment of central participants. Thus although American bishops through most of their history have displayed a strong patriotism, that patriotism has perhaps been somewhat diffuse because the same bishops avoided involvement in specific public policy debates. Similarly, although American sisters in the pre–Vatican II period certainly were quite devout, they were not involved in the intricacies of institutional decision-making or socialized into the theological underpinnings of Church hierarchy to the extent that some other Church personnel would have been. Thus after Vatican II, they did not belabor the various legitimations of hierarchy and patriarchy that were such important components of the faith to bishops and curial officials. They quickly adopted a quite different view of the meaning of participation in the Church.

The Future of Catholicism

AN IDEOLOGICAL LEGACY

What does the future hold for the Catholic Church, especially in the United States? There are a number of directions we might expect the Church to take, beginning with the legacy of the last century or so, that should inform our expectations. It is important to note that one cannot predict this future with certainty, not only because the predictions of sociologists, like those of anyone else, may unwittingly overlook certain factors. It is also the case that the future of the Catholic Church, like any social institution, very much depends on how its members attempt to defend or expand their autonomy and power within the institution.

For example, consider two very different scenarios for the Latin American Church. First, imagine that liberation Catholics continue to value the hierarchical traditions of the Church and access to institutional resources. Then they would likely continue to avoid challenging matters of faith and morals and instead gently pressure the hierarchy to continue addressing sociopolitical issues and support their efforts to build base communities, strengthen ties with labor and peasant organizations, and so on. Then Rome, while depending on its own nuances to explain the goals and actions of liberation Catholicism, could tolerate such an approach and attempt to reconcile it with its own social doctrine. Alternatively, imagine that liberation theologians, building on directions Leonardo Boff has already taken, spearhead an explicit rejection of the right of Rome to define the bounds of political involvement among liberation Catholics in Nicaragua and elsewhere. They go on to question the legitimacy of papal supremacy as a whole. In that case, Rome could easily perceive all liberation Catholicism— even as espoused by people quite loyal to the hierarchy—as a threat that had to be eliminated once and for all. Even though I believe that the former path is more likely, each scenario is possible (and so are others). The path taken could depend to a significant degree on the choices of a relatively small number of influential Latin American Catholics as well as on the perceptions and policies of a few men in Rome, especially Pope John Paul II and Cardinal Joseph Ratzinger.

No matter what sectors of the Church we examine, Catholic ideological structure will be an essential component of our analysis and our ability to predict the likely directions of Catholicism. The history of the Catholic Church demonstrates that ideological change does not entail automatic functional adaptations, does not involve simply an absorption of secular ideas, and is not simply a case of the Church absorbing or espousing the views of obvious or hidden constituencies (e.g., the laity or a dominant social class).[4] All these factors matter at times, but whether and when they matter depend on the ideological structure in which Catholics operate. They act within a structure that they themselves influence but that no group in the Church fully controls. It is appropriate to think of ideologies as having a structural component not only because no one is in full control, but because participants commonly do not fully understand the dynamics and constraints within which they operate. Thus their intentions can backfire if they futilely attempt to fight against impossible structural odds of which they are unaware.

As we have seen, the occupant of the papal office has more latitude to influence that structure than do other Catholics. Nevertheless, popes always find some paths more manageable than others and cannot always predict the ultimate effects of their initiatives. We encountered in chapter 2, then, a number of instances where papal attempts to continue or restore an ancien régime approach to church-state relations very much backfired.

To the extent that issues and disputes can be contained within the institutional Church itself, the papacy has somewhat more ideological control than it would over church-state conflicts, for example. The future of groups such as American sisters depends not only to a great degree on their own actions, but also on Rome's responses and initiatives. Even though American sisters have managed to institute a de facto pluralism within the Church, their current status is probably at least partly unsatisfactory to many. They did not create a Church of dialogue in which women are central participants. Instead, they encounter more of a polite standoff in which they do not have the power to move further, and Rome is unwilling to move further or allow bishops to do so. The weakness of an ideological structure from the point of those who are most powerful is that less powerful groups do not fully participate in the ideology and can come to reject much of it. There are always spaces of political and ideological autonomy. But from the perspective of less powerful groups, the price of that autonomy can be a certain amount of exclusion. Sisters can expect significant gains only with a decentralization of power in the Church.

And whether there is further political decentralization of the Church depends on how future popes and bishops approach faith and morals.

Should the specification of doctrine on such matters continue to be the ideological property of Rome, with sociopolitical issues defined as subordinate concerns, the pace of change will not match that of the 1960s.

The world changes, however, even when the Catholic Church does not. It was not only papal initiative that led to the birth of social doctrine; there was also a transformation in the de facto church-state relationship, pressuring the papacy into some kind of response. Leo XIII's response was certainly not the only conceivable response, and the papacy might have chosen to make no response at all, although it would have suffered the consequences. That is, the pressure on the Church would have still been there. Similarly, the fact that the patriarchal worldview informing Catholic views of morality is controversial today, while it would not have been in the nineteenth century, creates certain difficulties for Catholic ideology. Rome does not *have* to change the ideological structure in response to those pressures, but it pays a price in the form of public controversy as long as it resists. It was nineteenth-century controversy that bequeathed the most significant aspect of the ideological structure of twentieth-century Catholicism: the sharpened boundary subordinating sociopolitical issues to faith and morals.

But powerful groups do not usually dramatically undermine the basis of their own power, which Rome would have to do if it wanted to avoid controversy by relaxing moral doctrine. Within an ideological structure, some issues are higher priorities than others because they form an important basis of power.

Understanding the internal politics of the Church depends on an understanding of the history of Catholic ideological structure. To argue, for example, that the Catholic Church has always been involved in temporal politics and so always intertwines its religious and political views (as many analysts of liberation Catholicism argue)[5] is to pursue a half-truth that cannot account for major changes in the nature of the Catholic Church in this century. (It is more true of the Latin American Church but cannot explain the directions of the papacy or the comparative differences of the U.S. Church.) Within an ideological structure, some issues allow more freedom of movement than others.

By focusing on ideological structure, we can also explain why the social and political opinions of the laity, and even their religious opinions, are at most a weak, indirect constraint on the hierarchy. In discussing my research with various audiences, I have occasionally come across the strongly voiced objection that I do not take into account the Church's need to respond to lay opinions. This (functionalist) perspective emphasizes that the Church will need to make doctrinal changes—on, for example, birth control, priestly celibacy, or the ordination of women—to deal with the decline of allegiance among the American Catholic laity. The Church, the argument continues, needs to deal with declining Mass attendance and personnel crises in the Church—namely, precipitous drops in entrance levels to seminaries and convents. In fact, there is almost no evidence of such trends having a major effect on papal ideology, and bishops are affected only under certain circumstances.

To deal first with Rome: southern Europe and Latin America, traditionally very "Catholic," have long had lower Mass attendance than the United States, sometimes abysmally low. And Latin America as well as other parts of the world has long had much more serious shortages of Church personnel than the United States has today. It is true that Rome attempted a quarter century ago to increase the missionary presence of U.S. religious in Latin America. But over several centuries, the papacy has not usually made such problems a high priority or much of a priority at all. The Vatican has certainly not considered democratizing the Church as a solution. (Note that American bishops were a decentralizing force at Vatican II, and yet the American laity attended Mass and participated in the Church at a much higher level than the laities of many other national Churches at the time.) As the preceding pages have made clear, and even a superficial consideration of lay opinion (e.g., in the United States) on such issues as birth control and papal infallibility indicates, the papal worldview is not much influenced by the mass of Catholic opinion, as Rome itself likes to point out when it makes unpopular pronouncements.

The hierarchy has historically focused on institutional strength and ideological continuity, reforming not in response to the aggregate opinions of the laity, but to the views and actions of powerful secular forces that can support or threaten the institution. Doctrine that the Church itself is a divine institution legitimates this approach. Thus popes have at times presented the principle of the need to maintain the institutional Church as legitimation in itself for various policies and pronouncements.[6] That has meant that a working relationship with states—and, until relatively recently, establishment as the official state religion—has historically been a primary goal of the hierarchy.

National Churches accustomed to strong alliance with the state commonly become "lazy monopolies," out of touch with the laity.[7] In Latin America, despite centuries of Catholicism supposedly being the religion of the vast majority of the population, large numbers of "Catholics" in fact have never been much ministered to and have been taught little Catholic doctrine. There have historically been few priests or women religious to perform such tasks, yet only in recent decades, and in only a few countries, is there any sign that Latin American bishops have found such realities problematic enough to require a new approach to the laity. As a general trend, Latin American episcopacies are more likely to reach out actively to the laity in countries where the Church has lost its former privileged alliance with the state and finds itself without much of a social base of influence at a time when Protestant evangelization has made great inroads, drawing away nominal Catholics.

Different social conditions will vary in the pressures they place on churches to respond to the laity. For example, internationally the Catholic Church has had very close ties with the laity when the Church was alienated from a repressive state and was one of the few strong organizations that could therefore become identified with the populace (e.g., the Irish under British rule and the Polish under a succession of governments until the fall of the communists in 1989–1990). Frequently in such situations, Catholicism suffered enough repression to be a victim, and to be perceived as such, but not enough actually to destroy the institution.

Close ties can also result from experience as a minority religion, as in the American case. As Roger Finke and Rodney Stark have demonstrated, denominational competition is likely to make churches more responsive to the laity.[8] I add, however, that the ideological history of a national church will determine to what types of lay issues an episcopacy responds. Bishops often reproduce ideological boundaries in their relationships with the laity. In the United States, a close relationship has been based on religious, rather than sociopolitical, issues. Thus even though clerics are free to disagree with each other on sociopolitical issues, it has been the case that the strongest Catholic opposition to *The Challenge of Peace* and *Economic Justice for All* has come from prominent lay Catholics of the right, such as Michael Novak, former Treasury secretary William Simon, and columnist Patrick Buchanan.

THE FUTURE

Nevertheless, the constraints on Church ideology may be changing. It is possible that we can gain insight into the future by noting the parallel between Leo XIII's attempt (although perhaps a weak one) to reach out to the European working class and the receptivity of some Brazilian bishops to liberation themes beginning in the 1950s. In both cases, the Church had lost some of its ability to depend on state alliance to maintain the presence of the institution in society. Although the hierarchy, most likely, will always concern itself primarily with the strength of the institution, it is possible that through fits and starts the Catholic Church has begun to reconstruct the basis of that strength to depend more on ties to its own laity.

It is unlikely, however, that any such process will develop rapidly or dramatically within the Church as a whole. There is too much at stake. Within contemporary Catholic ideology, the hierarchical control of faith and morals is a central component of the political structure of the Church. Although attempts to rebuild the strength of the institution more on its own laity are possible, they depend primarily on the hierarchy's initiative. More likely to force changes are constraints from outside the Church that the hierarchy cannot easily avoid. The Catholic Church has found its ideological structure pressured by liberalism for well over a century, and, barring unforeseen dramatic changes in international politics and economics, the Church continues to face difficulties in its resistance to further liberalization.

Catholics and others might disagree about whether further liberalization of the ideology is desirable, but it is indeed the case that the Church has difficulty maintaining its particular boundary between morals and politics. This boundary represents a significant accommodation of liberal political relationships with a simultaneous resistance to liberal views of morality. At the very least, non-Catholics and even many Catholics have trouble understanding that boundary because in the United States and elsewhere, Church boundaries are at variance with generally accepted civil boundaries.

Granted, in the United States issues such as abortion, or First Amendment questions on the relationship between religion and public life, raise boundary questions for many denominations and many Americans, not just Catholics. But the questions are of a different nature than those that exist within Catholicism. Catholic ideology attempts to maintain that moral advocacy is *distinct* from political advocacy, while the more common framing of debates such as that over abortion involves the question of how and how much to *apply* morals to politics. I suspect it unlikely that many persons involved in the debate over abortion—that is, those who are not Catholic bishops—would argue that abortion is not a political issue. Within American politics, it clearly is. There may be many Americans who would like religious morality to be *less* involved in political questions, but few would maintain, as Catholic ideology does, that religious morality is not already so involved.

Within American Catholicism, abortion is the most prominent issue in which binding, high-priority moral doctrine has implications for an issue that is popularly defined as political but that is not "political" within Catholic ideology. Sociopolitical issues, the concerns of Church social doctrine, are, however, issues that the Church can agree are not purely religious issues but also matters of public policy. Nevertheless, the disjuncture between secular and Catholic boundaries, including on issues such as abortion, also creates problems for social doctrine. Specifically, the higher priority of abortion within Catholic ideology is likely to present the bishops with two problems as they advance sociopolitical concerns. The first already has begun: bishops participate in undermining their own claims that social issues, the ethics of government economic policies, and so on are important concerns of the Church. Even when only a few bishops go so far as to excommunicate prochoice political candidates or proclaim from the pulpit that Catholics must not vote for such candidates, the fact that such bishops can point to Catholic doctrine as strong support for their positions has a constraining effect on the public priorities of all bishops. Quite conspicuously, Rome has prevented the bishops from going too far in implying that there are binding Catholic doctrines on sociopolitical policies, and no bishop is likely at this point to excommunicate a public official or candidate who disagrees with anything stated in *The Challenge of Peace* or *Economic Justice for All*. This would be true even of the supposedly binding general moral principles that inform those pastoral letters because the principles are sufficiently broad to allow many interpretations; in any case, the Church does not attempt to enforce those principles as it does doctrine on abortion.

It is quite clear, then, that abortion is indeed currently a higher Church priority than, for example, social reform. Because they participate in the current ideological structure, bishops participate in the undermining of their own emphasis of sociopolitical issues. (That also means they participate in a centralization of Church authority that reserves the most important issues for Rome.) Yes, they also challenge that structure, but only occasionally and cautiously.

The second problem that I expect the higher priority of such issues as abortion will present to the bishops would exist even if the NCCB manages simultaneously to treat moral doctrine on abortion as binding and social doctrine as nonbinding. The problem is that this particular approach will make it difficult for Americans to understand the bishops' social doctrine. I already touched on this problem: from an American secular perspective (or any American non-Catholic perspective), the hierarchy's boundary between the moral and the political can easily appear unintelligible. Americans will continue to be confused about why bishops discuss the sociopolitical issues that they do and about why bishops can claim that their pronouncements on such issues are not meant to be binding religious pronouncements. Many Americans will expect that because bishops denounce opposition on (what is from a secular perspective) one political issue, that of abortion, that all of their social and political statements are made in the same spirit. Stated another way, the bishops, and their Church, draw the ideological boundary between church and state in a way that does not make much sense to most Americans. There are many Americans who think that religion does not belong in politics, and there are many who think that it does; but neither group is likely to defend its views by arguing that the use of religious doctrine to criticize public policies is sometimes (on sociopolitical issues) a political act and other times (on moral issues) is not.[9]

The Catholic ideological boundary between morals and politics, given the secular political contexts in which the Church operates, also causes distortions within the Church itself that apparently remain undetected. Perhaps because so many people are accustomed to the Catholic Church having strong opinions, authoritatively handed down, on many issues, there is little notice of the anomaly that the hierarchy in effect treats public policy on central moral issues like abortion as more important than beliefs in Jesus Christ or in the legitimacy of the Catholic Church. With *Dignitatis Humanae* (Vatican II's Declaration on Religious Freedom) as well as in other pronouncements at the council, the hierarchy abandoned the view that the Catholic Church should depend on state enforcement as a means of maintaining and spreading the Catholic faith. Yet on what the Church defines as moral issues, governments are obliged to follow the Catholic view. Popes, bishops, and some theologians might counter that the Church expects compliance only on natural moral law—morals present in the nature of the world whose legitimacy can be clear to any moral person, regardless of his or her particular religious beliefs. Natural law theology is indeed a fundamental component of Catholic moral doctrine. But there is the problem that the Church recognizes only its own authority to pronounce what those natural laws are. And many people disagree with the pronouncements, including people that the Church would be hesitant to condemn (at least publicly) as unequivocally immoral.

Before Vatican II, or at least before Leo XIII, faith and morals could generally be considered a single category that was a matter of Vatican control and that, according to doctrine, was to be favored by governments, in opposition to Protestant and other alternatives. But with the council, the Church accepted a more liberal view of church-state relations and religious freedom. The public controversy of the Church's view of the relationship between its authority on faith issues and temporal political life was more or less settled to the satisfaction of a great many non-Catholics as well as Catholics. The Declaration on Religious Freedom was such a striking change that even long-standing critics of Catholicism reacted to John XXIII and Vatican II with wonder and some admiration. But the view of morals had changed little, somewhat making morals a category with different status than issues of faith. As we saw in chapter 3, the council required that governments not violate what the Catholic Church considered divine, objective moral law.

It may be that the contemporary hierarchy indeed prefers an ideological structure in which "objective" morals are a higher priority than belief in the divinity of Jesus Christ or in the authority of the papacy. Although there are, as always, tensions and ambiguities within that structure, that does seem to be the set of priorities bequeathed by Vatican II. Thus the council could pronounce that there is something of value, some divine inspiration, in all cultures and in non-Catholic religions; with such a statement the Church accepted a more tolerant approach to other faiths. There would presumably be limits; for example, atheism would not be acceptable in any circumstance. Since the natural moral law is divinely granted and since that which is of value in non-Catholic religions is the spiritual belief in God, a basic spirituality (which is not necessarily Catholic or even Christian) would be a higher priority than, and necessary component of, a moral life. But when it comes to specific beliefs, the Church insists that binding moral doctrine must be enforced; that is not the case with issues of faith.

But the ideological priority of morals over faith does seem to have some strange implications, at least from the vantage point of this author. This is, after all, an institution that claims to be the sole divine Church established directly by Jesus Christ. Is the status of that Church as a whole less important than its hierarchy's interpretation of divine intentions on the morals of individuals and families? Does the hierarchy really want to imply that a devout Catholic politician who feels that outlawing abortion would be an undemocratic imposition of her own morality is an unequivocally evil person, while a rabidly anti-Catholic prolife activist is closer to God (as long, perhaps, as that activist is not an atheist)?

The point here, of course, is not to state that one position or another is theologically preferable, but to point to likely foci of change, political tension, and even stability in the Catholic Church. I very much suspect that the hierarchy will continue to encounter public confusion about, and resistance to, its ideology as long as it continues its current approach to moral issues. Cardinal Joseph Bernardin's "consistent ethic of life" approach, popular with a minority of U.S. bishops, would reduce much of that controversy by allowing more flexibility in interpretation of the implications and requirements of Catholic morals for public policy. The hierarchy would then likely continue to take controversial positions on a variety of issues, given Church political and ideological autonomy from secular politics, but the controversy would be of a more manageable sort. That is, it would probably involve less confusion and fewer accusations that the Church refuses to play by democratic rules or violates the separation of church and state. The Church would probably also have more success having its views heard; unless there is movement toward Bernardin's approach, the current abortion controversy could conceivably repeat the paths of Pius IX and Pius X, in which papal attempts to retain control of Catholics' political choices ironically reduced Catholic influence in secular politics. Pius IX ordered that Catholics not vote in Italian elections after the Italian republic took away his temporal kingdom, with the result that those Catholics most sympathetic to the pope's views were not an electoral force. Pius X was averse to allowing Catholic parties not under episcopal control, especially if those parties had a progressive orientation. The result, again, was a reduction in Catholic political participation. The current position of the Catholic hierarchy on abortion makes it difficult for American politicians to identify with the Church. This is especially true if, as recent American politics suggests, a Catholic prolife stand is a liability at the ballot box. Catholic influence might suffer in one of two ways. First, public episcopal criticisms of Catholic politicians often draw media attention. Such politicians will have to tone down their public identity as Catholics to avoid the appearance of obeying political directives from the pulpit. No matter what the candidate does, there could be significant electoral costs: as a *New York Times* editorial of 17 June 1990 argued, neither appearing to reject one's religious identity nor being seen as a bishop's political mouthpiece is likely to be consistently popular within American politics.

Of course, in some cases, such controversy may actually help the candidate because the episcopal attacks appear in the American context to be out of line, to be violations of the church-state boundary. Then, in this second scenario, episcopal credibility and prestige would suffer both within the Church and within American society.

And so there are various possible directions for the Catholic Church. Because ideological tensions are so closely related to power structures, and because the Catholic Church is operated as a monarchy, much will depend on who is pope at a particular time, as I have already mentioned. The particular political and ideological structure of the Church makes gradual ideological change unlikely; instead, conservatism versus dramatic reform is the more likely alternative. And it is unlikely there will be dramatic change in the ideological structure of the Catholic Church as long as John Paul II remains the pope. He has indeed generally acted to make more solid (or rigid, depending on one's point of view) the centralization of authority over faith and morals.

In closing, however, I should note that the preceding discussion may focus too much on tensions and problems. We might expect that John Paul II's attempts to maintain a Catholic boundary between morals and politics in a world that draws the boundary differently is doomed to fail. We might then think that the Catholic Church, as exemplified by Pius IX's approach to Italian republicanism and Pius XI's attempt to rebuild an ancien régime alliance, has a history of constructing unattainable, contradictory goals. The laity's lack of power within the Church, which translates into weak ideological influence, could be interpreted as further evidence of a Church political structure unable to address pressing problems. Without a greater attempt at involving the laity, can the hierarchy expect to reverse the decline in the numbers of sisters and priests, declining Mass attendance, and the inroads of Protestant missionaries into parts of the world previously thought to be bastions of Catholicism?

But things looked pretty bad 100 or 125 years ago as well. When the papacy lost its kingdom in central Italy, eventually losing even most of Rome itself to the Italian republic, devout European Catholics had reason to be very pessimistic. They had argued, with nineteenth-century popes, that retention of the Papal States was an essential guarantee of the pope's independence and authority. Yet looking back, we can say with confidence that they were quite wrong. No, the pope could no longer depose monarchs, but he had not been able to do that for some time. Yes, having his kingdom reduced to the size of a neighborhood seemed threatening in those turbulent times. But losing the Papal States was one of the best things that ever happened to the Catholic Church. Although readjustment took some time, Rome became much more ideologically independent and could eventually renounce the need for embarrassing alliances with authoritarian regimes. Its increase autonomy meant that it could make decisions and pronouncements based more on institutional ideology and internal concerns than on the need to placate one or another European government that had helped suppress rebellion in the Papal States or that threatened the Church's political prerogatives. In the United States, bishops could eventually forsake the difficult balancing act of attempting to argue for church-state separation at home without provoking Rome's wrath over fundamental doctrine. Internationally, cynicism about the pope's true intentions as he wrapped himself in the cloak of divine morality probably declined (although this is difficult to measure).

The ideological and political changes in the Church initiated at Vatican II certainly began with more optimism than did the forced widening of the distinction between religion and politics in the nineteenth century. Nevertheless, predictions and possible signs of decline very much emerged at both times. Institutional decline was possible then and is possible now; but it is far from inevitable.

Indeed, as I write in 1991, Vatican officials concerned with the Catholic Church in Eastern Europe have much reason to be optimistic.[10] The Church may not always obtain quite the place in society it would like (as the Polish electorate's resistance to efforts of their country's bishops to dictate laws on abortion in mid-1991 suggest), but it will surely be on a much more solid footing than it was under Soviet-style communism. By 1990, the Vatican had reestablished diplomatic relations with most countries in the region, and relations with even the Soviet Union itself had greatly improved. With lightning speed in 1989 and 1990, building on a process at most a decade old, the prospects for the Catholic Church vastly improved in European societies that had at times in the past been major centers of international Catholicism. And had not the pope's influence in Poland been central to such changes? The pope who so strongly opposed communism as an atheistic menace ultimately prevailed.

One might also argue that the Church's continued presence internationally is a great testament to the success of the ideological reconstruction of the last century. It is true that reconstruction had a somewhat difficult birth. It was not always intentionally arrived at and has not been to everyone's liking, but the Church's ideological structure does have a certain genius to it. Rome's strategy of emphasizing individual faith and morals not only avoids conflict with states; it also allows the Church to maintain unity by avoiding some issues that could divide Catholics along class lines and other political lines. Even within the hierarchy, it is quite possible for one bishop to agree with another on faith and moral issues and have quite different politics on more obviously temporal issues.[11] Even though there is a general tendency for more politicized members of the hierarchy to emphasize a People of God model of the Church, it is not unusual for a bishop to accept traditional religious doctrines yet see it as necessary that the Church more actively promote ethical economic and social policies. We saw, for example, that this is a common perspective in the U.S. hierarchy. Berryman pointed out that many Latin American Catholics committed to temporal liberation are actually quite conservative theologically; indeed, the faith and morals of individuals and families are not usually the main issues of contention in Latin American Catholicism.[12]

It may be the case that the Catholic Church will become increasingly liberalized by, for example, accepting the "consistent ethic" approach to moral issues. No matter what direction the Church takes, there will be tensions between its ideological boundaries and the boundaries defined by liberal societies. We can end this discussion, then, by asking whether the Catholic Church's conflict with as well as absorption of liberalism is still in its middle stages. If so, it has been a long and interesting beginning.

Notes

1. Please see the Glossary for definitions and explanations of the terminology used in this book, including those to whom I refer as the "personnel" and "hierarchy" of the Catholic Church. It is worth noting here that it is unavoidable to use terms that for some people could be ideologically charged. I do not mean implicitly to take sides but instead use terms that seem best to clarify the actual organizational and power structure of the Catholic Church.

2. James Hitchcock, *The Decline and Fall of Radical Catholicism* (New York: Herder and Herder, 1971), pp. 20–22; Msgr. George A. Kelly, *The Battle for the American Church* (Garden City, N.Y.: Doubleday/Image, 1981), p. vii; Malachi Martin, *The Jesuits: The Society of Jesus and the Betrayal of the Roman Catholic Church* (New York: Simon and Schuster/Linden, 1987), pp. 260–271, 310.

3. Vatican II, an ecumenical council (see the Glossary), addressed a host of issues within the Church, from particulars about the mass such as the use of the vernacular, rather than Latin, to a general philosophy about what it meant to be a Catholic. Vatican II is most commonly considered the Church's opening to the modern world, although that characterization can be quite vague. Indeed, much of the legacy of that council remains ambiguous, as we see in chapter 3.

4. Eric O. Hanson, *The Catholic Church in World Politics* (Princeton, N.J.: Princeton University Press, 1987), pp. 101–104.

5. I am using the term *ideology*, rather than the term *belief systems*, because I want to stress the sociological tradition emphasizing structural influences, which tends to use the former term. My use, however, does not imply that ideology is a "false" system of beliefs (Karl Mannheim, *Ideology and Utopia*, trans. Louis Wirth and E. A. Shils [New York: Harcourt Brace Jovanovich, 1936]), only that one can understand it in the context of given

social structures. I do, however, mean to speak broadly of the various components of belief systems, e.g., values, insofar as they have relevance to social interaction and social change.

6. *Oxford English Dictionary*, 2d ed. (Oxford: Clarendon Press, 1989), vol. 2, p. 1036; vol. 8, p. 798.

7. See the Glossary entry for *liberalism*.

8. Anthony Giddens, *The Constitution of Society: Outline of the Theory of Structuration* (Berkeley and Los Angeles: University of California Press, 1984), pp. 169–174.

9. Stephen D. Krasner, "Review Article: Approaches to the State," *Comparative Politics* 16 (1984): 223–246, following Sidney Verba ("Sequences and Development," in *Crises and Sequences in Political Development*, ed. Leonard Binder et al. [Princeton, N.J.: Princeton University Press, 1971], p. 308), made similar points in his "branching tree" metaphor for structures, emphasizing that past choices constrain future choices. That metaphor, however, does not adequately emphasize that we can—albeit by incurring costs—sometimes remake structures. One can also think of structures as rules (see, e.g., Giddens, *The Constitution of Society*).

10. Steven Lukes, "Power and Structure," in *Essays in Social Theory* (London: Macmillan, 1977), pp. 3–29.

11. Max Weber, *The Theory of Social and Economic Organization*, ed. Talcott Parsons (New York: Free Press, 1964), p. 152.

12. Peter Bachrach and Morton S. Baratz, *Power and Poverty: Theory and Practice* (New York: Oxford University Press, 1970); Steven Lukes, *Power: A Radical View* (London: Macmillan, 1974), pp. 16–20.

13. Lukes, "Power and Structure."

14. Of course, even the U.S. government's autonomy—in the positive sense of having the ability to change the constraints on other people's lives—is empirically limited. To have total autonomy would mean to have unlimited power. But U.S. government officials can face resistance, the threat of loss at election time, etc. They have more autonomy than do private citizens or city officials, but within empirical limits.

15. Otto Maduro, *Religion and Social Conflicts*, trans. Robert R. Barr (Maryknoll, N.Y.: Orbis, 1982), p. 75.

16. John W. Kingdon, *Agendas, Alternatives, and Public Policies* (Boston: Little, Brown, 1984); Stephen Hilgartner, "Constructing the Public Agenda" (Paper presented at the annual meeting of the American Sociological Association, August 1990).

17. See Weber, *The Theory*, p. 148.

18. This is a point Steven Lukes made in emphasizing that power includes the "mobilisation of bias"—i.e., controlling socialization so that potential opponents do not even think of offering resistance. See Lukes, "Power and Structure"; also see Steven Lukes, "Political Ritual and Social Integration," *Sociology* 9 (1975): 289–308.

19. Lukes, *Power: A Radical View*; Lukes, "Political Ritual and Social Integration," pp. 298–305; Michael Mann, "The Social Cohesion of Liberal Democracy," *American Sociological Review* 35 (1970): 423–439.

20. See the Glossary entry for *canon law*.

21. See George Cheney, *Rhetoric in an Organizational Society: Managing Multiple Identities* (Columbia: University of South Carolina Press, 1991). Cheney's book was published too late for me to discuss it at any length in this book. While he began from somewhat different premises, he was the first to provide any detailed analysis of the conflicting pressures that have affected American bishops in recent years. Thus to a certain extent my discussion in chapter 5 repeats points he has made. However, he does not address the question of why some issues become higher priorities than others, or why certain groups, including bishops, will choose not to commit themselves on some issues.

22. The classic example of such an approach was Parsonianism's use of pattern variables and focus on the "I" and "L" functions (integrative and latent pattern maintenance). Some modern studies of political culture empirically demonstrate the existence of certain belief patterns much more effectively but too easily fall into an analysis that sees those beliefs as purely causal variables, organizing all social and political life according to the logic of abstract beliefs: e.g., Lynn Hunt, *Politics, Culture, and Class in the French Revolution* (Berkeley and Los Angeles: University of California Press, 1984); Said Amir Arjomand, "Iran's Islamic Revolution in Comparative Perspective," *World Politics* 38 (1986): 383–414; John Boli-Bennett and John W. Meyer, "The Ideology of Childhood and the State: Rules Distinguishing Children in National Constitutions, 1870–1970," *American Sociological Review* 43 (1978): 797–812; John W. Meyer, Francisco O. Ramirez, Richard Rubinson, and Boli-Bennett, "The World Educational Revolution, 1950–1970," *Sociology of Education* 50 (1977): 242–258. Meyer and his colleagues have been very attentive to empirical demonstration of their idealist arguments, but the evidence is sometimes of questionable relevance (see, e.g., Ronnie Steinberg Ratner and Paul Burstein, "Ideology, Specificity, and the Coding of Legal Documents: What Do Measures of Constitutional Content Measure?" *American Sociological Review* 45 [1980]: 522–525). A more recent article (John Boli, Francisco O. Ramirez, and John W. Meyer, "Explaining the Origins and Expansion of Mass Education," *Comparative Education Review* 29 [1985]: 145–170) emphasizes more of an interaction between institutional factors and ideology. Nevertheless, their approach suffers two problems common to world-systems perspectives: first, it is too eclectic to be easily generalized to other issues in the study of ideology—the "world system" too easily expands conceptually to include a grab bag of causal variables (see especially p. 169). Second, their explanation of the process of ideological change—a central focus in this book—is occasionally functionalist, despite their own

criticisms of functionalist theories (pp. 156–158: the world system needs individualism and so has no trouble institutionalizing a pervasive ideology of individualism).

23. William H. Sewell, Jr., "Ideologies and Social Revolutions: Reflections on the French Case," *Journal of Modern History* 57 (1985): 57–85.

24. Ibid.

25. Paul M. Harrison, *Authority and Power in the Free Church Tradition* (Carbondale: Southern Illinois University Press, 1959); Henry J. Pratt, *The Liberalization of American Protestantism: A Case Study in Complex Organizations* (Detroit: Wayne State University Press, 1972).

26. Robert Wuthnow, *Communities of Discourse: Ideology and Social Structure in the Reformation, the Enlightenment, and European Socialism* (Cambridge, Mass.: Harvard University Press, 1989).

27. Thomas F. Gieryn, "Boundary-Work and the Demarcation of Science from Non-Science: Strains and Interests in Professional Ideologies of Scientists," *American Sociological Review* 48 (1983): 781–795; Thomas F. Gieryn, George M. Bevins, and Stephen C. Zehr, "Professionalization of American Scientists: Public Science in the Creation/Evolution Trials," *American Sociological Review* 50 (1985): 392–495.

28. James R. Wood, *Leadership in Voluntary Organizations: The Controversy over Social Action in Protestant Churches* (New Brunswick, N.J.: Rutgers University Press, 1981).

29. See Pratt, *The Liberalization of American Protestantism.*

30. Wood, *Leadership in Voluntary Organizations*, pp. 14–15.

31. Michael Hornsby-Smith and Raymond M. Lee, *Roman Catholic Opinion: A Study of Roman Catholics in England and Wales in the 1970s* (Guildford: University of Surrey, 1979), pp. 73, 211; Michael Hornsby-Smith, Raymond M. Lee, and Peter A. Reilly, "Social and Religious Change in Four English Roman Catholic Parishes," *Sociology* 18 (1984): 362.

32. I regret, then, that, with the possible exception of chapter 6, this study does not help to correct an increasingly noticed bias in Catholic historiography—i.e., an overemphasis on higher officials of the Church. One of the more important studies of lay Catholicism is Jean-Guy Vaillancourt, *Papal Power: A Study of Vatican Control over Lay Catholic Elites* (Berkeley and Los Angeles: University of California Press, 1980). For interesting studies of lay interpretations of Catholicism that have implicitly or explicitly challenged the hierarchy, see Ann Taves, "Context and Meaning: Roman Catholic Devotion to the Blessed Sacrament in Mid-Nineteenth-Century America," *Church History* 54 (1985): 482–495; John J. Bukowczyk, "Mary the Messiah: Polish Immigrant Heresy and the Malleable Ideology of the Roman Catholic Church, 1880–1930," *Journal of American Ethnic History* 4, 2 (Spring 1985): 5–32; Ralph Della Cava, *Miracle at Joseiro* (New York: Columbia University Press, 1970).

33. Nevertheless, the laity are passively affected by such ideological tendencies; for example, after a long history of receiving the message that sociopolitical issues are not the Church's concern, the U.S. laity are apparently baffled by and unreceptive to American bishops' more recent attempts to address such issues.

34. There is a distinction to be made between Catholic doctrine and Catholic ideology. My focus is on the latter; it is the case that Catholic ideology on sociopolitical, or "temporal," issues came to avoid specific, binding directives, in contrast to ideology of the faith and morals of individuals and families. But ideological distinctions do not always translate neatly into doctrinal distinctions, though there is a rough correspondence. All social doctrine falls under the nonbinding level of ideology dealing with macro issues, but there is also other doctrine that falls under that level of ideology. The only important examples relevant to this discussion are certain moral principles associated with the just war doctrine, addressed in chapter 5. These are apparently considered part of moral doctrine, but they are vague principles not easily translated into condemnations of specific state actions; historically, they have been vague enough to allow bishops from opposing nations in the same war each to declare their own country's cause just.

Catholic ideology, we see later, is still adjusting from the changes forced on it in the last century. The exact boundary between moral doctrine and social doctrine is not always clear.

35. For an analogous argument about the relationship between specificity and the exercise of power, see Alan Wolfe, *Whose Keeper? Social Science and Moral Obligation* (Berkeley and Los Angeles: University of California Press, 1989), pp. 231–232. Cf. also Robert K. Merton and Elinor Barber, "Sociological Ambivalence," in Merton, *Sociological Ambivalence and Other Essays* (New York: Free Press, 1976), pp. 3–31. Even though I owe a debt to Merton's conception of "ambivalence," my own approach does not assume the central importance of socially encompassing normative systems.

36. Alexis de Tocqueville, *Democracy in America* (New York: Vintage/Knopf, 1945), vol. 1, pp. 319–326; vol. 2, p. 28. The French original of volume 1 was published in 1835 and volume 2 in 1840.

CHAPTER TWO

1. Madonna Kolbenschlag, ed., *Between God and Caesar: Priests, Sisters and Political Office in the United States* (New York: Paulist Press, 1985).

2. See the Vatican II documents, *Gaudium et Spes* and *Ad Gentes*, in *The Documents of Vatican II*, ed. Walter M. Abbott, S.J. (Piscataway, N.J.: New Century, 1966), pp. 287–289, 599. It is customary to refer to Church documents by a brief title taken from the first few words of the document

in the language of the official text, usually Latin. *Gaudium et Spes* is the "Pastoral Constitution on the Church in the Modern World"; *Ad Gentes*, the "Decree on the Church's Missionary Activity." Within Catholic documents and scholarship, references are commonly made to numbered sections of the documents; each section can be anywhere from a sentence to many paragraphs long. I occasionally refer to such numbered sections when that helps identify the location of particular passages.

3. In Claudia Carlen, IHM, ed., *The Papal Encyclicals. Vol. 1: 1740–1878* (Wilmington, N.C.: McGrath Publishing, 1981), p. 383. Most of the papal encyclicals cited in this book appear in this very useful, five-volume collection.

4. It is important to remember that this book is making an argument about the structure of Catholic ideology, not about Catholic doctrine per se. I refer the reader to note 35 in chapter 1.

5. The *Syllabus* is reproduced in Henry Denzinger, ed., *The Sources of Catholic Dogma*, trans. Roy J. Defarrari (St. Louis: Herder, 1957), pp. 433–442.

6. Thomas F. Gieryn, "Boundary-Work and the Demarcation of Science from Non-Science: Strains and Interests in Professional Ideologies of Scientists," *American Sociological Review* 48 (1983): 781–795; Thomas F. Gieryn, George M. Bevins, and Stephen C. Zehr, "Professionalization of American Scientists: Public Science in the Creation/Evolution Trials," *American Sociological Review* 50 (1985): 392–495.

7. Otto Maduro, "New Marxist Approaches to the Relative Autonomy of Religion," *Sociological Analysis* 38 (1977): 362–363, made somewhat similar points but assumed a class reductionism that cannot recognize the Church's newfound autonomy.

8. Owen Chadwick, *The Popes and European Revolution* (Oxford: Clarendon, 1981), pp. 253–341; Robert A. Graham, S.J., *Vatican Diplomacy: A Study of Church and State on the International Plane* (Princeton, N.J.: Princeton University Press, 1959), pp. 17–18, 107.

9. Graham, ibid., p. 141.

10. Ibid., pp. 158, 175–177.

11. In Carlen, ed., *The Papal Encyclicals. Vol. 1: 1740–1878*, p. 382.

12. Joseph N. Moody, "From Old Regime to Democratic Society," in *Church and Society*, ed. Joseph N. Moody (New York: Arts, 1953), pp. 95–186; Margaret M. O'Dwyer, *The Papacy in the Age of Napoleon and the Restoration* (Lanham, Md.: University Press of America, 1985).

13. Moody, ibid., p. 111.

14. A. C. Jemolo, *Church and State in Italy, 1850–1950*, trans. David Moore (Philadelphia: Dufour, 1960), pp. 4–6; Graham, *Vatican Diplomacy*, p. 134.

15. Lillian Parker Wallace, *Leo XIII and the Rise of Socialism* (Durham, N.C.: Duke University Press, 1966), p. 18; the encyclical can be

found in Carlen, ed., *The Papal Encyclicals. Vol. 1: 1740–1878*, pp. 235–241.

16. Richard L. Camp, *The Papal Ideology of Social Reform: A Study in Historical Development, 1878–1967* (Leiden: Brill, 1969), p. 7; Jemolo, *Church and State in Italy*, p. 2.

17. Wallace, *Leo XIII and the Rise of Socialism*, p. 19.

18. Camp, *The Papal Ideology of Social Reform*, p. 8.

19. In Carlen, ed., *The Papal Encyclicals. Vol. 1: 1740–1878*, pp. 277–284.

20. E. E. Y. Hales, *Pio Nono* (London: Eyre, 1954), pp. 58–67; S. William Halperin, *Italy and the Vatican at War: A Study of Their Relations from the Outbreak of the Franco-Prussian War to the Death of Pius IX* (Chicago: University of Chicago Press, 1939); Graham, *Vatican Diplomacy*, pp. 136–139.

21. Joseph N. Moody, "The Church and the New Forces in Western Europe and Italy," in *Church and Society*, ed. Moody, pp. 21–92; Halperin, *Italy and the Vatican at War*.

22. Wallace, *Leo XIII and the Rise of Socialism*, p. 260.

23. Carlen, ed., *The Papal Encyclicals. Vol. 1: 1740–1878*, pp. 381–386.

24. Francis X. Murphy, C.SS.R., *The Papacy Today* (New York: Macmillan, 1981), p. 9.

25. Halperin, *Italy and the Vatican at War*, chs. 2–4; Jemolo, *Church and State in Italy*, ch. 2.

26. Marvin R. O'Connell, "Ultramontanism and Dupanloup: The Compromise of 1865," *Church History* 53 (1984): 200–217.

27. James L. Heft, S.M., "From the Pope to the Bishops: Episcopal Authority from Vatican I to Vatican II," in *The Papacy and the Church in the United States*, ed. Bernard Cooke (New York: Paulist Press, 1989), p. 65.

28. John Courtney Murray, S.J., "Leo XIII on Church and State: The General Structure of the Controversy," *Theological Studies* 14 (1953): 8.

29. O'Connell, "Ultramontanism and Dupanloup," p. 201.

30. See, e.g., Jerome G. Kerwin, *Catholic Viewpoint on Church and State* (Garden City, N.Y.: Hanover House/Doubleday, 1960), pp. 15–52; Sidney Z. Ehler and John B. Morrall, trans. and eds., *Church and State Through the Centuries* (Westminster, Md.: Newman, 1954); Gregory XVI, *Commissum Divinitus*, nos. 4–7, in *The Papal Encyclicals. Vol. 1: 1740–1878*, ed. Carlen, p. 254.

31. As Pius IX noted—see Carlen, ed., *The Papal Encyclicals. Vol. 1: 1740–1878*, p. 279; the council declaration can be found in Denzinger, ed., *The Sources of Catholic Dogma*, pp. 455–457.

32. See, e.g., Leo XIII, *Sapientiae Christianae*, 1890, nos. 28–29, in *The Papal Encyclicals. Vol. 2: 1878–1903*, ed. Carlen, pp. 217–218; in it, he discussed the difference between civil rule and "the kingdom of Christ." He distinguished between "holy and inviolate" morals and religious duties

from "the fleeting exigencies of politics" where there may be ample grounds for "legitimate difference of opinion." Cf. also Murray, "Leo XIII on Church and State," pp. 15–18.

33. E. E. Y. Hales, *The Catholic Church in the Modern World* (London: Eyre and Spottiswoode, 1958), pp. 141–156.

34. See, e.g., W. E. Gladstone, *The Vatican Decrees in Their Bearing on Civil Allegiance* (New York: Harper and Brothers, 1875); Cuthbert Butler, *The Vatican Council: The Story Told from Inside in Bishop Ullathorne's Letters*, vol. 2 (London: Longmans, Green, 1930); Carlen, ed., *The Papal Encyclicals. Vol. 1: 1740–1878*, p. 396.

35. Friedrich Engel-Janosi, "Austria and the Conclave of 1878," *Catholic Historical Review* 39 (1953): 142–166.

36. Oscar L. Arnal, "Why the French Christian Democrats Were Condemned," *Church History* 49 (1980): 201.

37. Pope Leo XIII, *Social Wellsprings: Fourteen Epochal Documents by Pope Leo XIII*, ed. Joseph Husslein, S.J. (Milwaukee: Bruce, 1940), pp. 129–130, 239; cf. also no. 21 of Leo XIII, *Immortale Dei*, in *The Papal Encyclicals. Vol. 2: 1878–1903*, ed. Carlen, p. 112.

38. John Tracy Ellis, "Review Article: From the Enlightenment to the Present: Papal Policy Seen through the Encyclicals," *Catholic Historical Review* 69 (1983): 55; Leo XIII, *Social Wellsprings*, pp. 68, 74–77, 81–82, 127–128.

39. Camp, *The Papal Ideology of Social Reform*, p. 11; Carlo Falconi, *The Popes in the Twentieth Century: From Pius X to John XXIII*, trans. Muriel Grindrod (Boston: Little, Brown, 1967), p. 5.

40. Gabriel Daly, O.S.A., *Transcendence and Immanence: A Study in Catholic Modernism and Integralism* (Oxford: Clarendon, 1980), pp. 9–10, 18–19; cf. no. 17 of Leo XIII, *Providentissimus Deus*, in *The Papal Encyclicals. Vol. 2: 1878–1903*, ed. Carlen, p. 334.

41. O'Connell, "Ultramontanism and Dupanloup," p. 208; Wallace, *Leo XIII and the Rise of Socialism*, p. 81.

42. Robert Emmett Curran, S.J., "The McGlynn Affair and the Shaping of the New Conservatism in American Catholicism," *Catholic Historical Review* 66 (1980): 184–204; Thomas T. McAvoy, "Americanism, Fact and Fiction," *Catholic Historical Review* 31 (1945): 133–153; Elwyn A. Smith, "The Fundamental Church-State Tradition of the Catholic Church in the United States," *Church History* 38 (1969): 495–496; Carlen, ed., *The Papal Encyclicals. Vol. 2: 1878–1903*, pp. 364–365.

43. Wallace, *Leo XIII and the Rise of Socialism*, pp. 277–308.

44. Leo XIII, *Social Wellsprings*, pp. 3, 7–8, 79; Jemolo, *Church and State in Italy*, p. 54.

45. Leo XIII, ibid., pp. 167–204.

46. Richard A. McCormick, S.J., "*Laborem Exercens* and Social Morality," *Theological Studies* 43 (1982): 99.

47. See, e.g., Joseph N. Moody, "Leo XIII and the Social Crisis," in *Leo XIII and the Modern World*, ed. Edward T. Gargan (New York: Sheed and Ward, 1961), p. 73; Leslie Griffin, "The Integration of Spiritual and Temporal: Contemporary Roman Catholic Church-State Theory," *Theological Studies* 48 (1987): 227.

48. To point out that social doctrine deals with politics and economics at the societal level is all that needs to be said for this discussion here because the main issue here is the structure, not the content, of Catholic ideology. The content of social doctrine is dealt with in a separate section because the particulars are more relevant to an analysis of the medieval heritage that remained with Catholic thought as it reacted against liberalism.

49. Charles E. Curran, "The Changing Anthropological Bases of Catholic Social Ethics," in *Directions in Social Ethics* (Notre Dame, Ind.: Notre Dame University Press, 1985), pp. 5–42; Donal Dorr, *Option for the Poor: A Hundred Years of Vatican Social Teaching* (Maryknoll, N.Y.: Orbis, 1983), p. 9.

50. See, e.g., McCormick, "*Laborem Exercens* and Social Morality," p. 100.

51. Leo XIII, *Social Wellsprings*, p. 182; Carlen, ed., *The Papal Encyclicals. Vol. 2: 1878–1903*, p. 52.

52. Leo XIII, ibid., pp. 232, 234; Raymond H. Schmandt, "The Life and Work of Leo XIII," in *Leo XIII and the Modern World*, ed. Gargan, pp. 30–31.

53. Carlen, ed., *The Papal Encyclicals. Vol. 3: 1903–1939*, pp. 71–98; Falconi, *The Popes in the Twentieth Century*, pp. 32–71; Daly, *Transcendence and Immanence*; Lester R. Kurtz, "The Politics of Heresy," *American Journal of Sociology* 88 (1983): 1085–1115; Lester R. Kurtz, *The Politics of Heresy: The Modernist Crisis in Roman Catholicism* (Berkeley and Los Angeles: University of California Press, 1986).

54. Stephen G. Lyng and Lester R. Kurtz, "Bureaucratic Insurgency: The Vatican and the Crisis of Modernism," *Social Forces* 63 (1985): 906.

55. Falconi, *The Popes in the Twentieth Century*, pp. 11–23, 74, 79; Peter Hebblethwaite, *In the Vatican* (Bethesda, Md.: Adler and Adler, 1986), pp. 26–27.

56. Arnal, "Why the French Christian Democrats Were Condemned," pp. 193–196; Sandor Agócs, "Christian Democracy and Social Modernism in Italy During the Papacy of Pius X," *Church History* 42 (1973): 77–78; Camp, *The Papal Ideology of Social Reform*, p. 35.

57. Arnal, ibid., pp. 189, 197; Falconi, *The Popes in the Twentieth Century*, p. 57; Jemolo, *Church and State in Italy*, p. 119.

58. Charles Breunig, "The Condemnation of the *Sillon*: An Episode in the History of Christian-Democracy in France," *Church History* 26 (1957): 240.

59. Camp, *The Papal Ideology of Social Reform*, pp. 13–14; Friedrich Engel-Janosi, "The Roman Question in the First Years of Benedict XV," *Catholic Historical Review* 40 (1954): 271.

60. Quotation is from Jemolo, *Church and State in Italy*, p. 85; see also pp. 100, 109, 112; Agócs, "Christian Democracy and Social Modernism," pp. 76–77.

61. Jemolo, ibid., p. 112; Falconi, *The Popes in the Twentieth Century*, pp. 21–25; Camp, *The Papal Ideology of Social Reform*, p. 15.

62. Jemolo, ibid., pp. 114–115, 170; John A. Coleman, *The Evolution of Dutch Catholicism, 1958–1974* (Berkeley and Los Angeles: University of California Press, 1978).

63. Jemolo, ibid., p. 168; Falconi, *The Popes in the Twentieth Century*, p. 127.

64. Falconi, ibid., pp. 161–162, 187; Pope Pius XI, *Social Wellsprings. Vol. 2: Eighteen Encyclicals of Social Reconstruction by Pope Pius XI*, ed. Joseph Husslein, S.J. (Milwaukee: Bruce, 1942), p. 171.

65. Jemolo, *Church and State in Italy*, p. 232; Anthony Rhodes, *The Vatican in the Age of the Dictators, 1922–1945* (London: Hodder and Stoughton, 1973), p. 46.

66. Rhodes, ibid., pp. 37–52; Falconi, *The Popes in the Twentieth Century*, pp. 289–292; Jean-Guy Vaillancourt, *Papal Power: A Study of Vatican Control over Lay Catholic Elites* (Berkeley and Los Angeles: University of California Press, 1980), p. 248.

67. Falconi, ibid., p. 189.

68. His administration seemed more realistic in negotiating with Germany. There the Church signed a concordat with a government whose good faith was questionable from the beginning, but it was fairly clear that refusal to sign would have meant unrelenting persecution. William M. Harrigan, "Nazi Germany and the Holy See, 1933–1936: The Historical Background of *Mit brennender Sorge*," *Catholic Historical Review* 47 (1961): 166–198; George O. Kent, "Pope Pius XII and Germany: Some Aspects of German-Vatican Relations," *American Historical Review* 70 (1964): 59–78.

69. Falconi, *The Popes in the Twentieth Century*, pp. 197–198.

70. Pius XI, *Social Wellsprings*, pp. 178–234.

71. Carlo Falconi, *The Silence of Pius XII* (Boston: Little, Brown, 1970); Saul Friedlander, *Pius XII and the Third Reich* (New York: Knopf, 1966); Joseph L. Lichten, *A Question of Judgement: Pius XII and the Jews* (Washington, D.C.: National Catholic Welfare Conference, 1963); Guenther Lewy, "Pius XII, the Jews and the German Catholic Church," in *The Storm over "The Deputy*," ed. Eric Bentley (New York: Grove Press, 1964), pp. 195–217; Rhodes, *The Vatican in the Age of the Dictators*, pp. 337–352; Vaillancourt, *Papal Power*, pp. 293–295; Gordon Zahn, *German Catholics and Hitler's War* (New York: Sheed and Ward, 1962).

72. In Carlen, ed., *The Papal Encyclicals. Vol. 4: 1939–1958*, pp. 37–63.

73. See, e.g., ibid., p. 27.

74. Dorr, *Option for the Poor*, pp. 84–86.

75. Carlen, ed., *The Papal Encyclicals. Vol. 4: 1939–1958*, p. 368.

76. Falconi, *The Popes in the Twentieth Century*, pp. 282–283. *Humani generis* is found in Carlen, ed., *The Papal Encyclicals. Vol. 4: 1939–1958*, pp. 175–184.

77. Ibid., pp. 175, 180.

78. Ibid., pp. 178–179.

79. Ibid., p. 43.

80. Ibid., p. 180.

81. See, e.g., Dorr, *Option for the Poor*, pp. 76–86.

82. Jemolo, *Church and State in Italy*, pp. 278–319.

83. Murphy, *The Papacy Today*, p. 120.

84. Carlen, ed., *The Papal Encyclicals. Vol. 4: 1939–1958*, pp. 39, 53, 65, 109, 179, 370.

85. Mary Fulbrook, *Piety and Politics: Religion and the Rise of Absolutism in England, Württemberg and Prussia* (Cambridge: Cambridge University Press, 1983).

86. Leo XIII, *Social Wellsprings*, pp. 3, 7–8, 79.

87. After Vatican II, the priority of sociopolitical issues became more complex, as we see in later chapters.

88. A. R. Vidler, *A Century of Social Catholicism, 1820–1920* (London: S.P.C.K., 1964), pp. 125–129.

89. Wallace, *Leo XIII and the Rise of Socialism*, pp. 262–267; Moody, "Leo XIII and the Social Crisis," pp. 78–79.

90. Falconi, *The Popes in the Twentieth Century*, pp. 15–16; Schmandt, "The Life and Work of Leo XIII," p. 33.

91. Leo XIII, *Social Wellsprings*, pp. 195–198; Rev. John J. Pawlikowski, "Introduction to Rerum Novarum," in *Justice in the Marketplace: Collected Statements of the Vatican and the United States Catholic Bishops on Economic Policy, 1891–1984*, ed. David M. Byers (Washington, D.C.: United States Catholic Conference, 1985), p. 11.

92. Wallace, *Leo XIII and the Rise of Socialism*, pp. 80, 91, 278–279; Leo XIII, *Social Wellsprings*, pp. 49–62, 86–87.

93. *Rerum Novarum*, in Leo XIII, ibid., p. 168.

94. See, e.g., no. 217 of Pope John XXIII, *Mater et Magistra*, 1961, in *The Papal Encyclicals. Vol. 5: 1958–1981*, ed. Carlen, p. 83.

95. *Rerum Novarum*, pp. 175, 183, 203–204; see also *Graves de Communi*, in Leo XIII, *Social Wellsprings*, pp. 234–235.

96. *Rerum Novarum*, p. 178.

97. Ibid., pp. 192–194.

98. Ibid., pp. 168, 180.

99. Ibid. p. 180; Leo XIII, *Social Wellsprings*, p. 237.

100. *Rerum Novarum*, pp. 177, 182; ibid., pp. 176–177; Camp, *The Papal Ideology of Social Reform*, pp. 30–32; Wallace, *Leo XIII and the Rise of Socialism*, pp. 113, 272; cf. also his *Graves de Communi*, p. 233.

101. *Rerum Novarum*, pp. 189–190.

102. Camp, *The Papal Ideology of Social Reform*, p. 116.

103. In Pius XI, *Social Wellsprings*, pp. 178–234.

104. Ibid., pp. 179, 229 (on charity), 187 (on unions).

105. Ibid., p. 200.

106. Ibid., pp. 214–215.

107. Ibid., p. 181.

108. Ibid., pp. 182, 188, 224.

109. Ibid., p. 230.

110. Ibid., pp. 182, 185, 211.

111. Ibid., p. 190.

112. Ibid., pp. 193–196 (on property as social benefit), 220 (on control of property to avoid social harm).

113. Ibid., p. 201.

114. Ibid., p. 196.

115. Pius XI, *Quadragesimo Anno*, in *Social Wellsprings*, pp. 196–199, 203. John Paul II's argument may be found in the encyclical *Laborem Exercens*, in *The Papal Encyclicals. Vol. 5: 1958–1981*, ed. Carlen, p. 312.

116. Ibid., pp. 201, 203–204.

117. Ibid., pp. 192–193.

118. Ibid., pp. 207, 212.

119. Ibid., p. 202.

120. Ibid., p. 213.

121. Ibid., p. 206.

122. Ibid., pp. 209, 211.

123. Kurtz, "The Politics of Heresy"; Kurtz, *The Politics of Heresy*; Lyng and Kurtz, "Bureaucratic Insurgency."

CHAPTER THREE

1. *Dignitatis Humanae*, no. 12, in *The Documents of Vatican II*, ed. Walter M. Abbott, S.J. (Piscataway, N.J.: New Century, 1966), pp. 692–693.

2. See, e.g., Pius IX's 1864 usage in *Quanta Cura*, in *The Papal Encyclicals. Vol. 1: 1740–1878*, ed. Claudia Carlen, IHM (Wilmington, N.C.: McGrath Publishing, 1981), p. 382; and Leo XIII in his *Humanum Genus*, 1884, in Carlen, ed., *The Papal Encyclicals. Vol. 2: 1878–1903*, p. 95.

3. On Protestant religions, see *Unitatis Redintegratio*, no. 4, in *The Documents of Vatican II*, ed. Abbott, p. 349; *Lumen Gentium*, no. 15, in *The Documents of Vatican II*, ed. Abbott, pp. 33–34. On non-Christian religions, see *Ad Gentes*, no. 9, in *The Documents of Vatican II*, ed. Abbott, pp. 595–596; *Nostra Aetate* ("Decree on the Relationship of the

Church to Non-Christian Religions"), in ibid., pp. 660–668. This latter document, even though many non-Catholics might argue that it does not go far enough, was a dramatic opening when considered in light of previous Church approaches to other religions. (See the commentaries on the document by Robert A. Graham, S.J., and Claud Nelson, in ibid., pp. 656–659, 669–671.)

4. *Lumen Gentium*, no. 15, p. 33.

5. As with much of the history of the Catholic Church, I will address the history of Vatican II only insofar as it relates to the issues at hand. For a more general description of the council, see such works as E. E .Y. Hales, *Pope John and His Revolution* (Garden City, N.Y.: Doubleday, 1965); and Xavier Rynne, *Vatican Council II* (New York: Farrar, Straus, and Giroux, 1968). The doctrinal implications of the council have been a primary concern of most important theological and social writings of Catholics ever since, so that giving a few specific references is pointless. The easiest way to begin, however, is by examining the conciliar documents themselves in Abbott, ed., *Documents of Vatican II*; or Austin P. Flannery, ed., *Vatican Council II: The Conciliar and Post Conciliar Documents* (Grand Rapids, Mich.: William B. Eerdmans, 1984). John A. Coleman's *The Evolution of Dutch Catholicism, 1958–1974* (Berkeley and Los Angeles: University of California Press, 1978) examines, in the context of the Dutch Catholic Church, many of the changes I focus on in this chapter. Coleman, as well as John Seidler and Katherine Meyer in *Conflict and Change in the Catholic Church* (New Brunswick, N.J.: Rutgers University Press, 1989), uses a quite different theoretical framework to investigate these changes than I do.

There were some important changes instituted by Vatican II that are not dealt with in this book because, compared to the changes that are discussed here, they were ultimately of much greater relative ideological importance for the laity than for the Church personnel who are the focus of the following chapters. The council instituted a great number of liturgical reforms, in the Mass and other ritual, such as the use of the vernacular (the language of the society) rather than Latin, the priest's facing the congregration as he said Mass rather than having his back to them, and so on. Such changes were certainly very much related to a more democratic and participatory image of the Church evoked by the image of the Church as the "People of God," which is discussed below. They were also the result of international liturgical reform movements and Church researchers' findings on the practices of the early Church. And, given the importance of the ritual expression of faith, these issues were undoubtedly important in the mind of most council participants. In addition to the general turmoil that affected the nuns and priests with whom they interacted, the laity probably experienced the council most directly and most immediately through these changes in the liturgy. For many members of the laity, indeed, such changes required some adjustment in ritual experience that was at the center of how they identified as practicing Catholics. For some, the changes were even quite disturbing, as these people had been socialized for decades into thinking that the Church does not change because it possesses eternal truth. However, beyond participation in the liturgy itself, such reforms do not seem to have had many implications for the way Church personnel interacted with each other, and it was the more general "People of God" image, rather than anything specifically liturgical, that affected the political and ideological structure of the Church. Even with the important conciliar concern with liturgy, I would argue that such reform in itself did not touch the fundamental beliefs of most of the hierarchy, even if within the perspective of some Catholics the changes were indeed radical.

6. See *Origins*, 4 August 1988, pp. 149, 151–152.

7. Carlen, ed., *The Papal Encyclicals. Vol. 5: 1958–1981*, p. 3; Francis X. Murphy, C.SS.R., *The Papacy Today* (New York: Macmillan, 1981), p. 76; Peter Hebblethwaite, *Pope John XXIII: Shepherd of the Modern World* (Garden City, N.Y.: Doubleday, 1985), p. 274.

8. Pius was, however, occasionally very concerned with updating the internal strength of the institutional Church, as we see in chapter 6. In fact, the notion of updating, or *aggiornamento*, so strongly associated with John XXIII, actually originated under Pius XII (Sr. Mary Margaret Modde, OSF, "A Canonical Study of the Leadership Conference of Women Religious of the United States of America" [Ph.D. diss., Catholic University of America, 1977], pp. 53, 57–59, 62). Hebblethwaite, *Pope John XXIII*, p. 310, reported that archival records show that Pius XII even considered calling an ecumenical council, one of whose purposes would be *aggiornamento* and reform of the Code of Canon Law. Nevertheless, John did take the process a quantum leap further, and we can be quite sure that a council under Pius would have been a much more conservative affair. It is appropriate, then, to associate *aggiornamento* more with John than with Pius.

9. Hebblethwaite, ibid., pp. 260–261, 469; Murphy, *The Papacy Today*, p. 123; Carlo Falconi, *The Popes in the Twentieth Century: From Pius X to John XXIII*, trans. Muriel Grindrod (Boston: Little, Brown, 1967), pp. 309, 323.

10. George Bull, *Vatican Politics: At the Second Vatican Council, 1962–5* (London: Oxford University Press, 1966), pp. 34–50; Hales, *Pope John and His Revolution*, pp. 95–160; Rynne, *Vatican Council II*, pp. 3–23.

11. Some traditionalists argued that John ultimately became disenchanted with the direction of the council, but there is at least as much evidence that he became disenchanted with the traditionalists. Initially he seemed to condone dominance of the agenda by curial conservatives, but once the council opened, he intervened in a way that undermined their position. See Bull, ibid., pp. 35–39, 44–50; Hebblethwaite, *Pope John*

XXIII, pp. 400–405, 448–458, 491; Murphy, *The Papacy Today*, pp. 80–81.

As pointed out in chapter 1, more powerful persons will have significantly greater ability to change social structures, including ideological structures, than less powerful persons. In the Catholic Church, the typical pope—elected by cardinals who are, in turn, chosen by previous popes—is not a radical innovator. But should he choose to be innovative, he often has room to do so. Even so, there are limits. For example, even though Leo XIII and John XXIII were particularly innovative, temporal, structural realities favored abandonment of the ancien régime model—thus the failure of Pius XI's policy toward Mussolini. (Incidentally, it seems to me quite likely that Vatican II was partially a reaction against the distasteful association of Catholicism with totalitarian government and intolerance fostered by Pius XI's dealings with Mussolini and Pius XII's debated approach toward the Holocaust. But such a hypothesis seems unverifiable because it would require extended knowledge of the motivations of the prelates who met and debated at the council.)

In any case, however, Leo and John initiated important changes; other men, had they been popes, might have steered the Church in at least slightly different directions. Even a reaction against the papacies of Pius XI and Pius XII certainly did not have to take the exact form of Vatican II.

12. Falconi, *The Popes in the Twentieth Century*, pp. 335–336; quotation from Abbott, ed., *The Documents of Vatican II*, p. 712.

13. In Abbott, ibid., p. 716.

14. John was elected in October 1958 and first expressed the idea of a council in January 1959.

15. Hebblethwaite, *Pope John XXIII*, p. 281.

16. Falconi, *The Popes in the Twentieth Century*, p. 330.

17. In *Dignitatis Humanae*, pp. 675–696. To be specific, *Dignitatis Humanae* argues that individuals have a *moral* obligation to follow the one true faith, i.e., Catholicism. But no one is to be coerced, externally or psychologically, to practice or believe any faith.

18. *Ad Gentes*, no. 12, p. 599.

19. *Gaudium et Spes*, no. 73, pp. 282–283.

20. See, e.g., Leo XIII, *Diuturnum*, no. 7, in *The Papal Encyclicals. Vol. 2: 1878–1903*, ed. Carlen, p. 52.

21. *Dignitatis Humanae*, no. 6, p. 685.

22. *Gaudium et Spes*, no. 21, p. 219.

23. Thomas T. Love, *John Courtney Murray: Contemporary Church-State Theory* (Garden City, N.Y.: Doubleday, 1965).

24. *Gaudium et Spes*, no. 87, p. 302.

25. Ibid., no. 74, pp. 284–285.

26. *Dignitatis Humanae*, no. 7, p. 686.

27. *Gaudium et Spes*, no. 76, p. 289; for a similar passage see no. 24 of *Apostolicam Actuositatem*, in *The Documents of Vatican II*, ed. Abbott, p. 514.

28. Abbott, ed., *The Documents of Vatican II*, p. 673.

29. Quoted in Cuthbert Butler, *The Vatican Council: The Story Told from Inside in Bishop Ullathorne's Letters*, vol. 2 (London: Longmans, Green, 1930), p. 267.

30. *Dignitatis Humanae*, no. 12, p. 692.

31. John's comments in Abbott, ed., *The Documents of Vatican II*, p. 704; the document in question is *Gaudium et Spes*, no. 4, p. 201.

32. No. 13, in *The Papal Encyclicals. Vol. 5: 1958–1981*, ed. Carlen, p. 185.

33. No. 10, in National Conference of Catholic Bishops, *Economic Justice for All: Pastoral Letter on Catholic Social Teaching and the U.S. Economy* (Washington, D.C.: United States Catholic Conference, 1986), p. 6; Charles E. Curran, "The Moral Methodology of the Bishops' Pastoral," in *Catholics and Nuclear War*, ed. Philip J. Murnion (New York: Cross-road, 1983), pp. 45–56.

34. See Abbott, ed., *The Documents of Vatican II*, p. 695fn.

35. *Lumen Gentium*, nos. 18–29, pp. 37–56.

36. Ibid., nos. 9–17, pp. 24–37; National Conference of Catholic Bishops, *To Do the Work of Justice* (Washington, D.C.: United States Catholic Conference, 1978), p. 22; Coleman, *The Evolution of Dutch Catholicism*, p. 168.

37. Tobin made her comments at the Annual Assembly of the (U.S.) Conference of Major Superiors of Women (CMSW); CMSW, *Proceedings of the Annual Assembly*, August 1966, Milwaukee, pp. 75–83, Leadership Conference of Women Religious Collection, University of Notre Dame Archives, Box 10, Folder 11. For another example of an expanded notion of collegiality among American sisters (in a community of which Tobin was a member), see (Sisters of Loretto), "Government Structure," (approx. 1967–1969), p. 2, Paul Boyle, CP, Papers, University of Notre Dame Archives, Box 79, Folder 1.

38. Phillip Berryman, *Liberation Theology: Essential Facts about the Revolutionary Movement in Latin America—and Beyond* (Philadelphia: Temple University Press, 1987), p. 52; Msgr. George A. Kelly, *The Battle for the American Church* (Garden City, N.Y.: Doubleday/Image, 1981), p. 27.

39. Eric R. Wolf, *Peasant Wars of the Twentieth Century* (New York: Harper and Row, 1969), pp. 71–73; and Theda Skocpol, *States and Social Revolutions* (Cambridge: Cambridge University Press, 1979), pp. 90, 95, discussed a similar situation in nineteenth- and early-twentieth-century Russia. The tsarist regime created rural representative bodies, known as *zemstvos*, that were supposed to control local decision-making but that in fact had little real authority. They became to some extent meeting places

and platforms from which some citizens demanded an extension of representative government.

40. No. 25, in *The Documents of Vatican II*, ed. Abbott, p. 48.

41. Ibid., no. 25, p. 49.

42. Ibid., pp. 97–101; see also p. 49fn.

43. Ibid., no. 12, p. 29.

44. See the Glossary entry for *ethics*. The Church actually uses the term *morals* to refer both to the morals of individuals and families and the ethics informing ideology on sociopolitical issues. To prevent confusion, I use "morals" only to refer to individual and family issues.

But the very use of the term *morals* in both contexts points to the difficulty of completely separating the two levels of ideology. Yet the hierarchy continually distinguishes "faith and morals" from "political" issues. Nevertheless, the fact that the Catholic boundary is difficult to maintain in a liberal world does not mean that the Catholic boundary is inherently less logical than other boundaries. It is almost impossible to imagine anyone unambiguously separating all "religious" issues from all sociopolitical issues. But remember that liberalism attempts to draw its own boundary, even though we all know that people's religion can affect their politics.

45. And, indeed, post–Vatican II popes would continue to exhibit at least occasional interest in sociopolitical issues themselves. The most important postconciliar encyclical on such issues was Paul VI, *Populorum Progressio,* in *The Papal Encyclicals. Vol. 5: 1958–1981,* ed. Carlen, pp. 183–275. Even John Paul II, who often attempts to prohibit Church personnel from social activism, has shown clear sympathy for traditional social doctrine (see *Laborem Exercens* in *The Papal Encyclicals. Vol. 5: 1958–1981,* ed. Carlen, pp. 299–326; and *Sollicitudo Rei Socialis* in *Origins,* 3 March 1988, pp. 641, 643–660).

46. Abbott, ed., *The Documents of Vatican II,* p. 199fn.

47. Ibid., no. 2, p. 200.

48. Ibid., no. 33, p. 232.

49. *Lumen Gentium,* no. 31, p. 57.

50. *Gaudium et Spes,* no. 62, pp. 268–270.

51. In this context, it is interesting to note a sociologist's recent characterization of the Church's approach toward abortion as continuous with doctrinal preferences of centuries ago, in great contrast to other issues explored in ecumenical efforts with Protestants: James Kelly, "Ecumenism and Abortion: A Case Study of Pluralism, Privatization and the Public Conscience," *Review of Religious Research* 30 (1989): 225–235.

52. Pre–Vatican II popes saw Freemasonry as a vast conspiracy out to destroy the Church: see Pius VIII's *Traditi Humilitati* of 1829, nos. 6–7, in *The Papal Encyclicals. Vol. 1: 1740–1878,* ed. Carlen, pp. 222–223; Pius IX, *Qui Pluribus,* 1846, in *The Papal Encyclicals. Vol. 1: 1740–1878,* ed.

Carlen, pp. 277–284; Pius IX, *Esti Multa*, 1873, no. 28, in *The Papal Encyclicals. Vol. 1: 1740–1878*, ed. Carlen, p. 433; Pius XI, *Caritate Christi Compulsi*, 1932, no. 7, in *The Papal Encyclicals. Vol. 3: 1903–1939*, ed. Carlen, p. 477; also Gerald P. Fogarty, S.J., *The Vatican and the American Hierarchy from 1870 to 1965* (Stuttgart: Anton Hiersemann, 1982), p. 134. Leo XIII was particularly obsessed with Freemasonry; see the discussion of the proposed condemnation of the Knights of Labor in chapter 4. On Pius XII and communism, see Murphy, *The Papacy Today*, pp. 62–64.

53. No. 21, in *The Papal Encyclicals. Vol. 5: 1958–1981*, ed. Carlen, p. 61.

54. In ibid., pp. 107–129.

55. No. 9, in ibid., p. 108.

56. Nos. 26 and 58, in ibid., pp. 188, 194.

57. Cf. Jean-Guy Vaillancourt, *Papal Power: A Study of Vatican Control over Lay Catholic Elites* (Berkeley and Los Angeles: University of California Press, 1980), esp. pp. 283–284.

58. *Humanae Vitae*, in *The Papal Encyclicals. Vol. 5: 1958–1981*, ed. Carlen, pp. 223–236.

59. Daniel Callahan, ed., *The Catholic Case for Contraception* (London: Macmillan, 1969); Maurice J. Moore, *Death of a Dogma? The American Catholic Clergy's Views of Contraception* (Chicago: Community and Family Study Center, University of Chicago, 1973); Murphy, *The Papacy Today*, pp. 128–131.

60. On an issue also linked to sexuality but probably more a "faith" issue than a "moral" issue, Paul VI reaffirmed the traditional teaching on clerical celibacy about the same time as *Humanae Vitae*; *Sacerdotalis Caelibatus*, in *The Papal Encyclicals. Vol. 5: 1958–1981*, ed. Carlen, pp. 203–221.

61. See, for example, John XXIII, *Mater et Magistra*, no. 20, in *The Papal Encyclicals. Vol. 5: 1958–1981*, ed. Carlen, p. 61; Paul VI, *Populorum Progressio*, no. 33, in *The Papal Encyclicals. Vol. 5: 1958–1981*, ed. Carlen, p. 33; John Paul II, *Laborem Exercens*, no. 83, p. 316.

62. No. 84, in *The Documents of Vatican II*, ed. Abbott, pp. 288–289; no. 78, in *The Papal Encyclicals. Vol. 5: 1958–1981*, ed. Carlen, p. 197. Paul VI also showed strong support for the United Nations in a speech there in October 1965, while Vatican II was in session (Xavier Rynne, *The Fourth Session: The Debates and Decrees of Vatican Council II* [New York: Farrar, Straus and Giroux, 1966], pp. 102–109, 285–291). For similar sentiments, see also John Paul II, *Laborem Exercens*, no. 81, p. 316; National Conference of Catholic Bishops, *Economic Justice for All*, no. 261, p. 126.

63. Rev. Roger Heckel, S.J., *The Social Teaching of John Paul II*, vol. 1 (Vatican City: Pontifical Commission "Iustitia et Pax," 1980); *New York Times*, 9 and 12 May 1988.

64. No. 41, in *Origins*, 3 March 1988, p. 655.

65. Madonna Kolbenschlag, ed., *Between God and Caesar: Priests, Sisters and Political Office in the United States* (New York: Paulist Press, 1985); Eric O. Hanson, *The Catholic Church in World Politics* (Princeton, N.J.: Princeton University Press, 1987), pp. 95–97, 243–244.

66. Quotation from Hanson, ibid., p. 227; *New York Times*, 16 August 1989; Heckel, *The Social Teaching of John Paul II*, vol. 8, pp. 7, 10–11.

67. See Abbott, ed., *The Documents of Vatican II*, p. 202fn.

CHAPTER FOUR

1. This chapter cannot delve into all the subtleties or the complete history of changes in the pre–Vatican II U.S. Church but instead focuses only on aspects of that history most relevant to the issues of ideological boundaries and power structures. Readers interested in more detail on the general history and social context should consult some of the works on which this chapter draws, such as Aaron I. Abell, *American Catholicism and Social Action: A Search for Social Justice, 1865–1950* (Garden City, N.Y.: Doubleday, 1960); Robert D. Cross, *The Emergence of Liberal Catholicism in America* (Cambridge, Mass.: Harvard University Press, 1958); John Tracy Ellis, *American Catholicism* (Chicago: University of Chicago Press, 1956); and James Hennesey, S.J., *American Catholics: A History of the Roman Catholic Community in the United States* (New York: Oxford University Press, 1981). James Edmund Roohan, *American Catholics and the Social Question, 1865–1900* (New York: Arno, 1976), gave a particularly interesting account of the approach the Church took toward labor questions in the late nineteenth century because he gave a good flavor of events beyond just the hierarchy and officially Catholic organizations. Mel Piehl's essay on the differing political conditions under which Protestantism and Catholicism met American social issues is especially perceptive and eloquent (*Breaking Bread: The Catholic Worker and the Origin of Catholic Radicalism in America* [Philadelphia: Temple University Press, 1982], pp. 25–55). On the hierarchy, I have relied a good deal on Fogarty's impressive, very complete account, based on extensive archival research (Gerald P. Fogarty, S.J., *The Vatican and the American Hierarchy from 1870 to 1965* [Stuttgart: Anton Hiersemann, 1982]). Readers not already familiar with much of the history and the workings of Church bureaucracy, however, will find at least some of Fogarty's text difficult to follow: the author frequently made reference to terms and events not explained in the book itself.

2. Elwyn A. Smith, "The Fundamental Church-State Tradition of the Catholic Church in the United States," *Church History* 38 (1969): 486–487.

3. Hennesey, *American Catholics*, pp. 284–285.

4. See, e.g., Jay P. Dolan, *The American Catholic Experience: A History from Colonial Times to the Present* (Garden City, N.Y.: Doubleday, 1985), pp. 201–203, 295–297.

5. Fogarty, *The Vatican and the American Hierarchy*, p. 18.

6. Ibid., pp. xvi, 31–34, 45–64, 115–118, 223.

7. James Hennesey, S.J., *The First Council of the Vatican: The American Experience* (New York: Herder and Herder, 1963), pp. 17, 23–25.

8. Fogarty, *The Vatican and the American Hierarchy*, p. 105.

9. Ibid., pp. 1–2, 6; Hennesey, *The First Council of the Vatican*; Abell, *American Catholicism and Social Action*, pp. 101–102, 110.

10. See, e.g., Abell, ibid., pp. 97–98.

11. Fogarty, *The Vatican and the American Hierarchy*, pp. 15–18, 27, 107.

12. Smith, "The Fundamental Church-State Tradition," pp. 487–491.

13. David J. O'Brien, *American Catholics and Social Reform: The New Deal Years* (New York: Oxford University Press, 1968), p. 30.

14. Ibid., p. 44; Abell, *American Catholicism and Social Action*, p. 225; Smith, "The Fundamental Church-State Tradition," p. 499; Roohan, *American Catholics and the Social Question*, pp. 29–30.

15. Fogarty, *The Vatican and the American Hierarchy*, pp. 65–80.

16. O'Brien, *American Catholics and Social Reform*, p. 46.

17. Hennesey, *The First Council of the Vatican*.

18. As noted in earlier chapters, there had always been some distinction between religious and temporal concerns but a narrower distinction than would develop in papal ideology after the late nineteenth century. Given Vatican I and papal pronouncements on temporal issues, nineteenth-century references to "faith and morals" were probably meant at times to be broader than they would be today.

19. Cross, *The Emergence of Liberal Catholicism*, p. 182.

20. In the last few decades, the U.S. Church most probably has provided the single largest financial contribution to Rome; Jean-Guy Vaillancourt, *Papal Power: A Study of Vatican Control over Lay Catholic Elites* (Berkeley and Los Angeles: University of California Press, 1980), p. 318.

21. Cross (*The Emergence of Liberal Catholicism*, pp. 178–180) believed nearly all American bishops opposed this move. See also Hennesey, *American Catholics*, pp. 198–201; Robert Emmett Curran, S.J., "The McGlynn Affair and the Shaping of the New Conservatism in American Catholicism," *Catholic Historical Review* 66 (1980): 199–201; Aaron I. Abell, "The Reception of Leo XIII's Labor Encyclical in America, 1891–1919," *Review of Politics* 7 (1945): 96, 478.

22. Fogarty, *The Vatican and the American Hierarchy*, p. 129.

23. Curran, "The McGlynn Affair."

24. Fogarty, *The Vatican and the American Hierarchy*, pp. 131, 140–141.

25. In Claudia Carlen, IHM, ed., *The Papal Encyclicals. Vol. 2: 1878–1903* (Wilmington, N.C.: McGrath Publishing, 1981), pp. 363–370.

26. No. 12, in ibid., p. 366.

27. No. 6, in ibid., pp. 364–365.

28. Quoted in John Tracy Ellis, "Review Article: From the Enlightenment to the Present: Papal Policy Seen through the Encyclicals," *Catholic Historical Review* 69 (1983): 55.

29. Fogarty, *The Vatican and the American Hierarchy*, pp. 143–151, 160.

30. Ibid., pp. 151–152.

31. On the details of the Americanism controversy, see Margaret Mary Reher, "Leo XIII and Americanism," *Theological Studies* 34 (1973): 679–689; Thomas T. McAvoy, *The Great Crisis in American Catholic History, 1895–1900* (Chicago: Regnery, 1957); Thomas T. McAvoy, "Americanism, Fact and Fiction," *Catholic Historical Review* 31 (1945): 133–153; Smith, "The Fundamental Church-State Tradition," pp. 495–496.

32. Fogarty, *The Vatican and the American Hierarchy*, pp. 170–183.

33. Ibid., pp. 172–173; Hennesey, *American Catholics*, p. 197.

34. Ireland was himself an example of the standard American ideological package: theologically very conservative and committed to papal supremacy, while diverging ideologically from Rome on church-state issues, as Neil T. Storch pointed out in "John Ireland and the Modernist Controversy," *Church History* 54 (1985): 353–365. (See also Fogarty, *The Vatican and the American Hierarchy*, p. 148, for an example of Ireland distinguishing faith and morals from other issues.) Despite his involvement in Americanism, Ireland seemed to have been sincerely and forcefully opposed to the theological questioning of orthodoxy associated with European modernism, arguing that above all else the authority of the hierarchy must be maintained.

35. Fogarty, ibid., pp. 185–190.

36. Ibid., pp. 45, 151–176, 189–194, 346; Hennesey, *American Catholics*, pp. 202–203, 217.

37. Cross, *The Emergence of Liberal Catholicism*, pp. 204–205.

38. Fogarty, *The Vatican and the American Hierarchy*, pp. 195–207.

39. Ibid., pp. 195–209, 218.

40. See, e.g., ibid., pp. 135–136.

41. See the Glossary entry for *primate*.

Gibbons was the second American cardinal and the most prominent one in the late nineteenth and early twentieth centuries; the Vatican usually communicated with the American episcopacy through Gibbons. His long tenure meant that he was the senior American cardinal for thirty-five years, from 1886 until his death in 1921 (Fogarty, *The Vatican and the American Hierarchy*, pp. 38, 218, 220).

42. All encyclicals noted here are in Carlen, ed., *The Papal Encyclicals. Vol. 2: 1878–1903: Humanum Genus*, 1884, pp. 91–101; *Dall'Alto*

230 / Notes to Pages 84-86

dell'Apostolico Seggio, 1890, pp. 225–232; *Inimica Vis*, 1892, pp. 297–299; *Custodi di Quella Fede*, 1892, pp. 301–305. See also Leo XIII, *Quod Apostolici Muneris*, 1878, no. 3, p. 12; *Officio Sanctissimo*, 1887, no. 12, pp. 153–154; John Courtney Murray, S.J., "Leo XIII on Church and State: The General Structure of the Controversy," *Theological Studies* 14 (1953): 1–7.

43. Fogarty, *The Vatican and the American Hierarchy*, pp. 86–92.

44. For the text of Gibbons's appeal to Rome see Henry J. Browne, *The Catholic Church and the Knights of Labor* (New York: Arno Press, 1976), pp. 365–378. For the history of the Church's approach to the Knights of Labor, see Browne; Abell, *American Catholicism and Social Action*, pp. 67–71; and Fogarty, *The Vatican and the American Hierarchy*, pp. 86–92.

45. Abell, "The Reception of Leo XIII's Labor Encyclical," p. 469; Piehl, *Breaking Bread*, p. 35.

46. Abell, *American Catholicism and Social Action*, pp. 62–66; Curran, "The McGlynn Affair"; Fogarty, *The Vatican and the American Hierarchy*, pp. 92–99.

47. Abell, ibid., p. 72; Fogarty, ibid., pp. 99–103.

48. Fogarty, ibid., pp. 93, 96, 98; Curran, "The McGlynn Affair," pp. 190–201.

49. Fogarty, ibid., p. 114; Cross, *The Emergence of Liberal Catholicism*, pp. 120–123; Roohan, *American Catholics and the Social Question*, pp. 332–383.

50. Fogarty, ibid., pp. 82, 109–114; Abell, *American Catholicism and Social Action*, p. 80.

51. Ibid., p. 92.

52. Ibid., pp. 92, 131–132, 139.

53. Ibid., p. 100; Roohan, *American Catholics and the Social Question*, pp. 332–383.

54. Archbishop Ireland is often thought of as a prominent example of episcopal interest in the rights of workers and in social reform. But Ireland, a Republican Party enthusiast, was basically socially conservative and had occasional antilabor tendencies. Abell, *American Catholicism and Social Action*, pp. 86, 138, 152; O'Brien, *American Catholics and Social Reform*, p. 36.

55. Fogarty, *The Vatican and the American Hierarchy*, pp. 96–98.

56. Abell, *American Catholicism and Social Action*, p. 173.

57. See, e.g., the discussion of Pope Pius X in chapter 2.

58. Fogarty, *The Vatican and the American Hierarchy*, p. 104.

59. Neil Betten, *Catholic Activism and the Industrial Worker* (Gainesville: University Presses of Florida, 1976), pp. 12–13.

60. An exception was their consistent, even paranoid, anticommunism; but here they did not need to worry about alienating Rome or Americans.

And, like Rome, they could argue that anticommunism had a strong religious basis, given "godless" Marxism, and thus was not in the same category as other sociopolitical issues.

61. In Rev. Peter Guilday, ed., *The National Pastorals of the American Hierarchy (1792–1919)* (Westminster, Md.: Newman Press, 1954), p. 192; and Hugh J. Nolan, ed., *Pastoral Letters of the American Hierarchy, 1792–1970* (Huntington, Ind.: Our Sunday Visitor, 1971), pp. 230, 333, 378–379.

62. See the 1866 pastoral letter in Guilday, ed., ibid., pp. 205–206; or the 1951 statement that "no state...may reject a truth of the moral order to suit the claim of convenience" (in Nolan, ed., ibid., p. 457).

63. Elizabeth McKeown, "The National Bishops' Conference: An Analysis of its Origins," *Catholic Historical Review* 66 (1980): 565–583.

64. Fogarty, *The Vatican and the American Hierarchy*, pp. 34, 50.

65. Abell, *American Catholicism and Social Action*, p. 224; Elizabeth McKeown, "Apologia for an American Catholicism: The Petition and Report of the National Catholic Welfare Council to Pius XI, April 25, 1922," *Church History* 43 (1974): 514–528; McKeown, "The National Bishops' Conference"; Fogarty, *The Vatican and the American Hierarchy*, pp. 214–228.

66. Fogarty, ibid., pp. xvi, xviii, 241–242.

67. See, e.g., their 1919 pastoral letter in Nolan, ed., *Pastoral Letters*, p. 230.

68. The document may be found in Raphael M. Huber, S.T.D., O.F.M.Conv., ed., *Our Bishops Speak, 1919–1951* (Milwaukee: Bruce, 1952), pp. 243–260.

69. John A. Ryan, *A Living Wage: Its Ethical and Economic Aspects* (New York: Macmillan, 1906).

70. Neil A. Wynn, *From Progressivism to Prosperity: World War I and American Society* (New York: Holmes and Meier, 1986), pp. 196–225.

71. I am indebted to Fred Block for this possible explanation. We see in chapter 7 that there may have been an analogous situation affecting the Latin American Church in 1968.

72. Paul Sigmund, "The Catholic Tradition and Modern Democracy," in *Religion and Politics in the American Milieu*, ed. Leslie Griffin (Notre Dame, Ind.: Review of Politics and Office of Policy Studies, University of Notre Dame, n.d.), pp. 15–16; Francis L. Broderick, "But Constitutions Can Be Changed...," *Catholic Historical Review* 49 (1963): 390–393; Francis L. Broderick, "The Encyclicals and Social Action: Is John A. Ryan Typical?" *Catholic Historical Review* 55 (1969): 1–6; John A. Ryan, *Social Doctrine in Action: A Personal History* (New York: Harper and Brothers, 1941), pp. 80–81.

73. O'Brien, *American Catholics and Social Reform*, p. 45.

74. Hennesey, *American Catholics*, p. 252.

75. Smith, "The Fundamental Church-State Tradition," pp. 500–501.

76. Abell, *American Catholicism and Social Action*, pp. 240–242; Fogarty, *The Vatican and the American Hierarchy*, pp. 237–245, 251–252, 277–278.

77. Cross, *The Emergence of Liberal Catholicism*, p. 208.

78. Interesting examples emerged at least by 1905 (*Rerum Novarum* appeared in 1891) in a work by the bishop of Fall River, Massachusetts (Rt. Rev. William Stang, *Socialism and Christianity* [New York: Benziger Brothers, 1905]). Other examples are works by the bishop of Omaha (Rt. Rev. James O'Connor, *Socialism* [Philadelphia: Catholic Truth Society, n.d]), which seems to have appeared about 1903; by Bishop Fulton J. Sheen (*Liberty, Equality, and Fraternity* [New York: Macmillan, 1938]; and *Communism and the Conscience of the West* [Indianapolis and New York: Bobbs-Merrill, 1948]); and by various other Catholic writers (John A. McClorey, S.J., *The Catholic Church and Bolshevism* [St. Louis: Herder, 1931]; Sodality Union of Washington, D.C., *Wolves in Sheep's Clothing* [Washington, D.C.: Sodality Union, 1937]; F. J. Sheed, *Communism and Man* [New York: Sheed and Ward, 1939]; Augustine J. Osgniach, O.S.B., *Must It Be Communism? A Philosophical Inquiry into the Major Issues of Today* [New York: Joseph F. Wagner, 1950]). Sheen, of course, was well known for his popular religious broadcasts, starting on radio in 1930 and airing on television from 1951 to 1957 (Jay P. Dolan, *The American Catholic Experience* [Garden City, N.Y.: Doubleday, 1985], p. 393).

Although Sheen's and Sheed's works demonstrate considerable learning, the most striking thing about these various writings that appeared over a half century is their lack of originality. There are minor differences in their recommendations and analyses, but for the most part they borrow their views of capitalism and communism straight from Leo XIII and Pius XI.

79. Abell, *American Catholicism and Social Action*, pp. 49–51, 137–188, 211.

80. O'Brien, *American Catholics and Social Reform*, pp. 35–36, 42; Abell, *American Catholicism and Social Action*, pp. 80–83.

81. O'Brien, ibid., pp. 48–49.

82. Ibid., p. 53; Abell, *American Catholicism and Social Action*, p. 248.

83. Fogarty, *The Vatican and the American Hierarchy*, pp. 230–235.

84. Ibid., pp. 248–315; George Q. Flynn, "Franklin Roosevelt and the Vatican: The Myron Taylor Appointment," *Catholic Historical Review* 58 (1972): 171–194.

85. O'Brien, *American Catholics and Social Reform*.

86. Ibid., pp. 43–44, 49–50, 58–60; Abell, *American Catholicism and Social Action*, p. 228; Hennesey, *American Catholics*, p. 233.

87. Abell, ibid., p. 225; Hennesey, ibid., p. 248.

88. On Spain, see, O'Brien, *American Catholics and Social Reform*, p. 67. The concern with Mexico began in the 1910s—i.e., the period of the

Mexican Revolution (O'Brien, *American Catholics and Social Reform*, p. 45; Hennesey, *American Catholics*, p. 223). Examples of such concern are the numerous pastoral letters and statements on the situation of the Church in Mexico by the U.S. episcopacy in Huber, ed., *Our Bishops Speak*: from the years 1926 (pp. 66–97, 188–189, 268–270), 1933 (pp. 201–202), 1934 (pp. 205–209), 1935 (pp. 307–309), and 1936 (pp. 212–214). The 1935 statement was explicitly devoted to taking the U.S. government to task, insisting that it "be consistent and live up to its own set policy" of expecting religious freedom in Mexico. A 1950 resolution (pp. 238–239) expressed dismay over the alleged apathy of Western nations toward religious persecution behind the "Iron Curtain."

89. In Nolan, ed., *Pastoral Letters*, pp. 338–353.

90. Abell, *American Catholicism and Social Action*, pp. 264, 280.

91. Abell, "The Reception of Leo XIII's Labor Encyclical," pp. 486–487.

92. It of course makes sense that priests such as Peter Dietz (see Henry J. Browne, "Peter E. Dietz, Pioneer Planner of Catholic Social Action," *Catholic Historical Review* 33 [1948]: 448–456) and McGlynn, who interacted daily with lay Catholics, would be more oriented toward their everyday concerns and less oriented toward purely institutional needs than would be bishops. But this was a relative difference only; evidence suggests that American priests as well as religious in the pre–Vatican II period emphasized pious devotion, not social change. But we do not have much systematic research on the political views and activities of priests and religious in this period. See, however, Ronald W. Schatz, "American Labor and the Catholic Church, 1919–1950," *U.S. Catholic Historian* 3 (1983): 178–190; Dolan, *The American Catholic Experience*, pp. 337–340, 402–403, 406, 415, 446.

93. For Coughlin, see Hennesey, *American Catholics*, pp. 274–275; cf. O'Brien, *American Catholics and Social Reform*, pp. 61–62. For McCarthy, see Vincent P. De Santis, "American Catholics and McCarthyism," *Catholic Historical Review* 51 (1965): 1–30. For Franco, see Hennesey, *American Catholics*, pp. 272–274. Cf. O'Brien, *American Catholics and Social Reform*, pp. 86–87, 89. For the CIO, see Hennesey, *American Catholics*, p. 263; Abell, *American Catholicism and Social Action*, p. 257.

94. O'Brien, *American Catholics and Social Reform*, p. 34.

95. Hennesey, *American Catholics*, p. 244.

96. Ibid., p. 232.

97. The bishops' statement is in Huber, ed., *Our Bishops Speak*, pp. 113–114. Also see Hennesey, *American Catholics*, pp. 277, 285, 305.

98. Ibid., p. 288.

99. In Nolan, *Pastoral Letters*, pp. 453–458.

100. In ibid., pp. 487–491.

101. In ibid., pp. 506–510.

102. In ibid., pp. 520–523.

CHAPTER FIVE

1. For De Soto's views, see his *El otro sendero*, 2d ed. (Lima: Editorial el Barranco, 1986).

2. Norval D. Glenn and Ruth Hyland, "Religious Preference and Worldly Success: Some Evidence from National Surveys," *American Sociological Review* 32 (1967): 73–85; Andrew Greeley, *American Catholics Since the Council* (Chicago: Thomas More Press, 1985), pp. 26–34.

3. Lawrence H. Fuchs, *John F. Kennedy and American Catholicism* (New York: Meredith, 1967); Eric O. Hanson, *The Catholic Church in World Politics* (Princeton, N.J.: Princeton University Press, 1987), pp. 167, 172.

4. Paul M. Harrison, *Authority and Power in the Free Church Tradition* (Carbondale: Southern Illinois University Press, 1959), provided an interesting study of a somewhat opposite process within the American Baptist Convention. In that case, organizational centralization partly undermined a doctrinal emphasis on the autonomy of individual congregations.

5. *Christus Dominus*, no. 42, in *Vatican Council II: The Conciliar and Post Conciliar Documents*, ed. Austin P. Flannery (Grand Rapids, Mich.: Eerdmans, 1984), p. 589.

6. Ibid., no. 37, p. 587.

7. There are actually two separate organizations with the same membership (all American bishops)—the National Conference of Catholic Bishops (NCCB) and the United States Catholic Conference (USCC). The former is the body with canonical status in the Church, whereas the latter is incorporated within the United States as a civil organization. In theory, the NCCB embodies the bishops' teaching authority within the Church, while the USCC deals with civil matters affecting the Church. The fact that the USCC has its own full-time staff (of nonbishops) devoted to applying Catholic ethics to social and political issues has made the bishops' commitment to such issues more vocal, e.g., at congressional hearings.

In any case, the distinction between the two organizations is somewhat artificial, perhaps reflecting the fact that matters of social doctrine are considered as much religious as civil in nature. For example, the presidency of the two organizations is a joint position always held by one individual. The bishops' letters on nuclear strategy and on the economy are in theory written by the NCCB and published by the USCC. Although the distinction between the two organizations can be important for those focusing more on the internal details of the Church bureaucracy than is necessary here, for my purposes it is more confusing than helpful. I, therefore, generally refer only to the NCCB, for simplicity's sake.

8. *Christus Dominus*, p. 587.

9. Ibid., no. 38, p. 587.

10. Hanson, *The Catholic Church in World Politics*, p. 76.

11. Congregation for Bishops, "Draft Statement on Episcopal Conferences," *Origins*, 7 April 1988, pp. 731–737; quotation from *Origins*, 8 November 1990, pp. 355–356; *New York Times*, 3 and 17 November 1988.

12. Eugene Kennedy, *Re-Imagining American Catholicism: The American Bishops and Their Pastoral Letters* (New York: Vintage, 1985), pp. 12–19.

13. Interview with Thomas J. Gumbleton, Auxiliary Bishop of Detroit, 22 August 1987; Kennedy, *Re-Imagining American Catholicism*, pp. 17–18, 34–36.

14. Hans Küng made a similar point in "Cardinal Ratzinger, Pope Wojtyla, and Fear at the Vatican: An Open Word After a Long Silence," in *The Church in Anguish: Has the Vatican Betrayed Vatican II?* ed. Hans Küng and Leonard Swidler (San Francisco: Harper and Row, 1987), pp. 71–72.

15. In Claudia Carlen, IHM, ed., *The Papal Encyclicals. Vol. 5: 1958–1981* (Wilmington, N.C.: McGrath Publishing, 1981), pp. 223–236.

16. See Küng, "Cardinal Ratzinger, Pope Wojtyla, and Fear at the Vatican."

17. Hanson, *The Catholic Church in World Politics*, p. 82.

18. Charles E. Curran, *Faithful Dissent* (Kansas City: Sheed and Ward, 1986); *New York Times*, 16 March 1986.

19. Hanson, *The Catholic Church in World Politics*, pp. 80–81.

20. See the Vatican's public chronology of the Hunthausen case and Hunthausen's response in *Origins*, 6 November 1986, pp. 361, 363–365; also *New York Times*, 28 October 1986, 10, 11, and 15 November 1986, 30 January 1987, 28 May 1987, 13 and 25 April 1989. Exactly why Hunthausen was singled out remains unclear, although there is no real evidence to support speculation that Hunthausen's activism in antinuclear protests and opposition to U.S. Central America policy was an important reason. After his disciplining, Hunthausen declined interviews (*New York Times*, 14 November 1986; Very Rev. Michael G. Ryan [Vicar General and Chancellor, Archdiocese of Seattle] to author, 4 December 1987). See also *New York Times*, 10 November 1986.

21. Hanson, *The Catholic Church in World Politics*, p. 82; Curran, *Faithful Dissent*, p. 28.

22. *New York Times*, 23 December 1986, 9 October 1986, 24 December 1986, 17 November 1987; *Origins*, 27 December 1990, pp. 461, 463–467.

23. Nos. 181–182, in *Pastoral Letters of the American Hierarchy, 1792–1970*, ed. Hugh J. Nolan (Huntington, Ind.: Our Sunday Visitor, 1971), pp. 658–659.

24. Hanson, *The Catholic Church in World Politics*, pp. 84–85.

25. Msgr. George A. Kelly, *The Battle for the American Church* (Garden City, N.Y.: Doubleday/Image, 1981), pp. 347–408.

26. *New York Times*, 11 March 1987; "Public Policy and Reproductive Technology," *Origins*, 30 July 1987, pp. 143–144. The Vatican prohibition follows from the view that sexuality, a family matter in Catholic ideology, must be open to its "natural" purpose—reproduction within a marriage. See "Instruction on Respect for Human Life in Its Origin and on the Dignity of Procreation," *Origins*, 19 March 1987, pp. 697, 699–711.

27. See, e.g., *New York Times*, 24 September 1986, and 9 October 1986, concerning Archbishop Rembert Weakland's questioning of methods of discipline; and the comments of Bishop James Malone, then-president of the NCCB, on the Hunthausen affair (*New York Times*, 11 November 1986).

28. *New York Times*, 31 October 1987; *Philadelphia Inquirer*, 30 October 1987, 31 October 1987.

29. Joseph P. Brennan, "Women in the Seminary: A Roman Catholic Perspective," *Theological Education* 11 (Winter 1975): 96; *1984 Catholic Almanac*, ed. Felician A. Foy, O.F.M. (Huntington, Ind.: Our Sunday Visitor, 1983), pp. 63–64; "Priests vs. Authority," *Christian Century*, 27 August 3–September 1986, p. 736.

30. *New York Times*, 13 November 1986, 27 May 1987.

31. See, e.g., *New York Times*, 17 November 1987.

32. Nolan, ed., *Pastoral Letters*, pp. 571–725.

33. Hanson, *The Catholic Church in World Politics*, p. 179; Patrick H. McNamara, "American Catholicism in the Mid-Eighties: Pluralism and Conflict in a Changing Church," *Annals of the American Academy of Political and Social Science* 480 (1985): 70. In 1966, they hoped for nonmilitary means to resolve the issues but trusted the good faith efforts of the U.S. government. J. Brian Benestad and Francis J. Butler, eds., *Quest for Justice: A Compendium of Statements of the United States Catholic Bishops on the Political and Social Order, 1966–1980* (Washington, D.C.: United States Catholic Conference, 1981), pp. 51–55; James Finn, "American Catholics and Social Movements," in *Contemporary Catholicism in the United States*, ed. Philip Gleason (Notre Dame, Ind.: University of Notre Dame Press, 1969), pp. 127–146.

34. Kristin Luker, *Abortion and the Politics of Motherhood* (Berkeley and Los Angeles: University of California Press, 1984).

35. Nolan, ed., *Pastoral Letters*, pp. 600–603, 679–705, 709–710, 721–722, 731, 747, 748.

36. Luker, *Abortion and the Politics of Motherhood*.

37. In Benestad and Butler, eds., *Quest for Justice*, p. 155.

38. Ibid., pp. 153–169; *Origins*, 21 March 1974, pp. 601, 603–606; *Origins*, 28 March 1974, pp. 620–627.

39. NCCB, "A Review of the Principal Trends in the Life of the Catholic Church in the United States," *Origins*, 4 July 1974, pp. 93–96.

40. Hanson, *The Catholic Church in World Politics*, pp. 186–188.

41. For example, ibid., pp. 178–179.

42. "U.S. Bishops' Conferences File Suit on Abortion Benefits," *Origins*, 5 July 1979, pp. 97, 99–103; Hanson, *The Catholic Church in World Politics*, p. 81.

Interestingly, in 1980 prochoice groups sued the bishops' conference, claiming that the bishops' political activity in opposition to abortion violated their tax-exempt status as a religious organization (*New York Times*, 6 December 1987). The Supreme Court determined the prochoice groups did not have standing to bring the suit (*New York Times*, 1 May 1990).

43. Joseph A. Varacalli, *Toward the Establishment of Liberal Catholicism in America* (Lanham, Md.: University Press of America, 1983), provided a detailed account of the Call to Action, although his view of the program as a watershed liberalization of American Catholicism greatly exaggerates its significance. See also NCCB, *To Do the Work of Justice* (Washington, D.C.: United States Catholic Conference, 1978).

44. Hanson, *The Catholic Church in World Politics*, pp. 182–183.

45. NCCB, *To Do the Work of Justice*, p. 23. In an interview I conducted with Cardinal Dearden in 1987, he maintained that simply because certain Church positions are not subject to change does not mean that Catholics cannot discuss them—i.e., the discussions that emerged in the Call to Action were healthy. (John Paul II would not agree.) He remained quite positive in his assessment of the Call to Action program. Interview with Cardinal John Dearden, Emeritus Archbishop of Detroit, 17 August 1987. (Dearden died in August 1988.)

46. Joseph A. Varacalli, "Social Change in the American Catholic Church," *Free Inquiry in Creative Sociology* 10, 2 (1982): 204.

47. National Conference of Catholic Bishops, *The Challenge of Peace: God's Promise and our Response* (Washington, D.C.: United States Catholic Conference, 1983); and National Conference of Catholic Bishops, *Economic Justice for All: Pastoral Letter on Catholic Social Teaching and the U.S. Economy* (Washington, D.C.: United States Catholic Conference, 1986).

48. See, for example, the list of those who testified during hearings on the letter on the U.S. economy between November 1981 and July 1984 in *Origins*, 15 December 1984, pp. 381–383. Individual lay Catholics, or anyone for that matter, were of course able to write and comment on the letter, but there was no systematic attempt to solicit the average American Catholic's opinion.

49. Kennedy, *Re-Imagining American Catholicism*, p. 129; McNamara, "American Catholicism in the Mid-Eighties," pp. 70–71.

50. See, for example, the discussion of such critics in ibid., pp. 97–110; Andrew M. Greeley's, Robert J. Samuelson's, and Philip F. Lawler's contributions in Robert Royal, ed., *Challenge and Response: Critiques of the Catholic Bishops' Draft Letter on the U.S. Economy* (Washington, D.C.: Ethics and Public Policy Center, 1985); J. Brian Benestad, *The Pursuit of a Just Social Order: Policy Statements of the U.S. Catholic Bishops, 1966–80* (Washington, D.C.: Ethics and Public Policy Center, 1982).

51. Nevertheless, as noted in chapter 3, Vatican II did not absolutely rule out Church establishment; some national Churches do not accept liberal arrangements (see chapter 7). The Polish Catholic Church, for example, as of early 1991, had not only attempted to write its view of abortion and education into law; it also wanted recognition as the official church. Ironically, this path may ultimately backfire and strengthen Polish lay commitments to liberal politics, echoing the failures of earlier papal attempts to oppose church-state separation (discussed in chapter 2).

52. See, e.g., Gerald Mara, "Poverty and Justice: The Bishops and Contemporary Liberalism," in *The Deeper Meaning of Economic Life*, ed. R. Bruce Douglass (Washington, D.C.: Georgetown University Press, 1986), pp. 157–178.

53. "Church and Social Order," in *Pastoral Letters*, ed. Nolan, pp. 338–353; "Man's Dignity," in *Pastoral Letters*, ed. Nolan, pp. 475–480.

54. "Church and Social Order," no. 10, p. 339.

55. Ibid., no. 41, p. 346.

56. NCCB, *Economic Justice for All*, no. 28, p. 15.

57. Ibid., no. 143, p. 73.

58. Ibid., no. 140, p. 71.

59. Ibid., no. 273, p. 132.

60. Ibid., no. 189, p. 93.

61. Ibid., nos. 193–194, pp. 95–97.

62. Ibid., no. 94, pp. 48–49; nos. 134–135, p. 68; no. 258, p. 124.

63. Ibid., p. ix.

64. Ibid., no. 115, p. 58.

65. Ibid., p. xii.

66. Hanson, *The Catholic Church in World Politics*, p. 169; Gerald P. Fogarty, S.J., *The Vatican and the American Hierarchy from 1870 to 1965* (Stuttgart: Anton Hiersemann, 1982), p. 162.

67. Hanson, ibid., pp. 169–170.

68. In Nolan, ed., *Pastoral Letters*, pp. 467–474, 492–495, 496–497, 504, 515–519.

69. *Pacem in Terris*, in *The Papal Encyclicals. Vol. 5: 1958–1981*, ed. Carlen, pp. 107–129; *Gaudium et Spes*, nos. 79–82, in *The Documents of Vatican II*, ed. Walter M. Abbott, S.J. (Piscataway, N.J.: New Century, 1966), pp. 291–297.

70. David Hollenbach, "*The Challenge of Peace* in the Context of Recent Church Teachings," in *Catholics and Nuclear War*, ed. Philip J. Murnion (New York: Crossroad, 1983), pp. 3–15; George Weigel, *Tranquillitas Ordinis: The Present Failure and Future Promise of American Catholic Thought on War and Peace* (Oxford: Oxford University Press, 1987), pp. 82–103.

71. See, e.g., the testimony of Rev. J. Bryan Hehir, of the USCC Office of International Peace and Justice, before a subcommittee of the U.S. House of Representatives Foreign Affairs Committee: "USCC Opposes Military Aid to El Salvador," *Origins*, 11 March 1982, pp. 615–619. Also, *New York Times*, 20 November 1987.

72. Jim Castelli, *The Bishops and the Bomb* (Garden City, N.Y.: Doubleday/Image, 1983), p. 19.

73. In Carlen, ed., *The Papal Encyclicals. Vol. 5: 1958–1981*, pp. 183–201.

74. Hanson, *The Catholic Church in World Politics*, p. 179.

75. See also David J. O'Brien, "American Catholics and American Society," in *Catholics and Nuclear War*, ed. Murnion, pp. 16–29.

76. See, e.g., Charles Krauthammer's and George Will's contributions to Royal, ed., *Challenge and Response*. This seems somewhat to be the perspective of Archbishop Philip Hannan of New Orleans, one of the most vocal opponents within the episcopacy of the letter on peace and one of only nine bishops to vote against the final draft (as opposed to 238 votes in favor). Telephone interview with Philip Hannan, 17 November 1987; Castelli, *The Bishops and the Bomb*, p. 177.

Some critics see the bishops' conference's staff as the source of a 1960s radicalism. Nevertheless, although some members of the staff (especially Rev. J. Bryan Hehir) may be influential, it is unlikely the bishops are simply being manipulated by the staff, as some critics charge (Weigel, *Tranquillitas Ordinis*, p. 314; Kelly, *The Battle for the American Church*, p. 370). The process of extensive debate about pastoral letters, for example, would make it unlikely that staff could force the conference to take a position toward which the bishops were not already inclined.

77. NCCB, *The Challenge of Peace*, p. vi; nos. 131–132, p. 42.

78. Ibid., p. v.

79. Ibid., no. 193, p. 61.

80. Ibid, nos. 27–55, pp. 9–18.

81. Ibid., no. 28, pp. 9–10; no. 55, p. 17.

82. Ibid., no. 99, p. 31. For a more detailed discussion of the just war tradition, see, e.g., Weigel, *Tranquillitas Ordinis*; or the bishops' letter itself, especially fn. 31 on p. 27.

83. NCCB, *The Challenge of Peace*, p. vi; no. 72, p. 23; no. 97, p. 30; no. 241, p. 75; nos. 264–269, pp. 81–83.

84. Ibid., nos. 178–188, pp. 56–59.

85. Ibid., pp. iii, vi; no. 10, pp. 4–5; no. 138, p. 43; no. 188, p. 59; no. 191, p. 60; no. 217, p. 68; nos. 282–283, p. 87; no. 318, p. 95.

86. See, e.g., ibid., nos. 88–89, p. 28; nos. 107–109, p. 34.

87. Ibid., no. 132, p. 42; no. 281, p. 87.

88. Ibid., nos. 237–239, p. 74.

89. Ibid., nos. 163–166, pp. 51–52; nos. 206–208, pp. 65–66.

90. Ibid., p. iv; nos. 175–177, pp. 55–56.

91. Ibid., no. 221, p. 69; see also no. 332, p. 101.

92. Ibid., nos. 120–121, p. 37.

93. *Gaudium et Spes*, nos. 78–79, in *The Documents of Vatican II*, ed. Abbott, pp. 290–293.

94. Finn, "American Catholics and Social Movements"; Patricia F. McNeal, *The American Catholic Peace Movement, 1928–1972* (New York: Arno Press, 1978).

95. McNeal, ibid.

96. Robert Rizzo, "Moral Debate on the Arms Race and Its Economic Implications," *International Journal of Social Economics* 14, 12 (1987): 19.

97. Interview, 22 August 1987.

98. "Battle of the Bishops: Should Church Oppose Nuclear Arms?" *U.S. News & World Report*, 20 December 1982, p. 47.

99. NCCB, *The Challenge of Peace*, no. 89, p. 28.

100. *New York Times*, 5 November 1986.

101. Michael Novak, *Moral Clarity in the Nuclear Age* (Nashville: Thomas Nelson, 1983), pp. 27–28.

102. Ibid., pp. 39, 59.

103. Bishop Walter Sullivan is an interesting example: Arthur Jones, "Bishops Tell How Views on Nuclear Arms Formed," *National Catholic Reporter*, 11 December 1981, p. 6.

104. Novak, *Moral Clarity in the Nuclear Age*, p. 59.

105. Weigel, *Tranquillitas Ordinis*, p. 287; Thomas C. Fox, "Catholics Debate Papal Nuclear Shift," *Bulletin of the Atomic Scientists* 44, 4 (1988): 30–31.

106. See Patty Edmonds and Steve Askin, "Meetings Tense; Views Divided," *National Catholic Reporter*, 22 April 1983, p. 7; also *Origins*, 7 April 1983, pp. 690–696; Castelli, *The Bishops and the Bomb*, pp. 130–134; Weigel, *Tranquillitas Ordinis*, pp. 275–280.
It is interesting to note that through the 1980s European episcopacies had been more hesitant to address nuclear strategy as specifically or in such strong moral terms as were the U.S. bishops, apparently because of the perceived need to defer to their governments, given the proximity to the Soviet bloc (Francis X. Winters, S.J., "Nuclear Deterrence Morality: Atlantic Community Bishops in Tension," *Theological Studies* 43 [1982]: 428–446; James V. Schall, S.J., ed., *Out of Justice, Peace: Joint Pastoral Letter of the West German Bishops. Winning the Peace: Joint Pastoral Letter of*

the French Bishops [San Francisco: Ignatius Press, 1984]). Perhaps that will change given the disintegration of Eastern European communism. Of course, the Catholic Church as a whole, from the Vatican down, may have less difficulty approving of (presumably softened) nuclear policies with these changes in the European political landscape.

107. Castelli, ibid.; Novak, *Moral Clarity in the Nuclear Age*, pp. 109–110.

108. NCCB, *The Challenge of Peace*, no. 144, p. 45; no. 181, p. 57.

109. Ibid., no. 178, p. 56; no. 187, pp. 58–59.

110. NCCB, *Economic Justice for All*, no. 135, p. 68.

111. In March 1987 the Congregation for the Doctrine of the Faith distinguished the moral status of various birth technologies, providing a level of detail that it would discourage on most matters of social and political policy; *New York Times*, 11 March 1987, 12 March 1987.

112. Bishop John Meyers, "Obligations of Catholics and Rights of Unborn Children," *Origins*, 14 June 1990, p. 72; Cardinal John O'Connor, "Abortion: Questions and Answers," *Origins*, 28 June 1990, pp. 108–109; Msgr. Robert Lynch, "The Bishops' Pro-Life Public-Relations Campaign," *Origins*, 30 August 1990, p. 191.

113. *Philadelphia Inquirer*, 4 December 1989; on the case in the diocese of San Diego, see *Origins*, 14 December 1989, pp. 457–458. For a view strongly circumscribing Catholics' moral options in voting, see Meyers, ibid., pp. 65, 67–72. A considerably less dogmatic statement that nevertheless states that it is fundamentally immoral to vote for a prochoice candidate came from the bishops of Pennsylvania: "The Church, Public Policy and Abortion," *Origins*, 17 May 1990, pp. 14–15.

O'Connor has occasionally sounded conciliatory, focusing on persuasion (*Origins*, 12 April 1990, p. 742; *New York Times*, 22 April 1990). But he also speaks of excommunication (*New York Times*, 15 June 1990) and has strongly supported Bishop Austin Vaughan's harsh judgment of Cuomo (*New York Times*, 1 June 1990).

114. Interview with William Weigand, Bishop of Salt Lake City, 9 December 1987; David J. O'Brien, "The Economic Thought of the American Hierarchy," in *The Catholic Challenge to the American Economy*, ed. Thomas M. Gannon, S.J. (New York: Macmillan, 1987), p. 41.

115. *New York Times*, 15 April 1988, 13 November 1990; *Origins*, 29 November 1990, pp. 397, 399–400.

116. See NCCB, *Building Economic Justice: The Bishops' Pastoral Letter and Tools for Action* (Washington, D.C.: United States Catholic Conference, 1987).

117. *Origins*, 21 June 1990, p. 87; Eugene Kennedy, "Catholic Bishops' Big P.R. Blunder," *New York Times*, 19 April 1990; *New York Times*, 20 November 1990.

118. Kenneth R. Overberg, *An Inconsistent Ethic? Teachings of the American Catholic Bishops* (Lanham, Md.: University Press of America, 1980).

119. "The Many Faces of AIDS," *Origins*, 24 December 1987, pp. 486–487. Other sources of the discussion of the statement, in this and the following paragraph, are "Reaction to AIDS Statement," *Origins*, 24 December 1987, pp. 489–493; *New York Times*, 14, 29, and 30 December 1987, 7 January 1988, 28 June 1988; *Philadelphia Inquirer*, 31 December 1987; "Cardinal Ratzinger's Letter on AIDS Document," *Origins*, 7 July 1988, pp. 117–118; "Called to Compassion and Responsibility: A Response to the HIV/AIDS Crisis," *Origins*, 30 November 1989, pp. 421, 423–434.

120. From an address at Georgetown University on 25 October 1984, reproduced in "Religion and Politics: The Future Agenda," *Origins*, 8 November 1984, pp. 321, 323–328; quotation from p. 326.

121. In addition to those speeches cited elsewhere in this section, see especially the following, all in *Origins*: "Consistent Ethic of Life: 'Morally Correct, Tactically Necessary,'" 12 July 1984, pp. 120–122; "The Consequences of a Consistent Ethic of Life," 20 March 1986, pp. 655–658; "The Consistent Ethic of Life After Webster," 12 April 1989, pp. 741, 743–748.

122. Rembert Weakland, "From Dream to Reality to Vision," *Origins*, 11 October 1990, pp. 289–293; *New York Times*, 9 January 1991.

123. *Origins*, 31 May 1990, p. 39; 7 June 1990, p. 50.

124. Bishop Walter Sullivan, "Abortion Strategy," *Origins*, 21 June 1990, pp. 87–88.

125. Rembert Weakland, "Listening Sessions on Abortion: A Response," *Origins*, 31 May 1990, p. 39.

126. Hanson, *The Catholic Church in World Politics*, pp. 188–190; Castelli, *The Bishops and the Bomb*.

127. "Religion and Politics: The Future Agenda," *Origins*, 8 November 1984, p. 326.

128. From an 8 August 1988 address to an annual meeting of diocesan prolife directors, reproduced in "Voters and the Consistent Ethic of Life," *Origins*, 1 September 1988, pp. 186–189; quotation from p. 187. See also Kennedy, *Re-imagining American Catholicism*, pp. 134–142.

129. Kennedy, ibid., pp. 137, 140.

130. See, e.g., statements by the bishops of Maine, Vermont, Massachusetts, and New Hampshire, "Not a Single-Issue Church, Bishops Say," *Origins*, 20 September 1984, pp. 217–218; by Albany Bishop Howard Hubbard, *Origins*, 21 December 1989, pp. 474–476; and by the bishops of Wisconsin in "A Consistent Ethic of Life," *Origins*, 28 December 1989, pp. 461–465. See also the 10 December 1989 newspaper editorial by the bishops of Montana, reproduced in *Origins*, 14 December 1989, pp.

458–459, which they issued amid their publicly taking to task various Montana Catholic politicians (same issue of *Origins*, pp. 457–458).

131. NCCB, *The Challenge of Peace*, nos. 125, 140, pp. 40, 44.

132. It was just weeks after Reagan's election, at the annual Washington meeting of the NCCB, that the bishops voted to write the pastoral letters that would become *The Challenge of Peace* and *Economic Justice for All*. The vote was a conscious reaction to Reagan's economic and nuclear policy views (Castelli, *The Bishops and the Bomb*, pp. 14–15, 18; interview with Thomas Gumbleton, Auxiliary Bishop of Detroit, 21 August 1987; interview with William Weigand, Bishop of Salt Lake City, 9 December 1987).

133. NCCB, *The Challenge of Peace*, nos. 167–170.

134. See, e.g., *New York Times*, 12 April 1988, 19 May 1990; and the critique from the Leadership Conference of Women Religious, *Origins*, 30 August 1990, pp. 185, 187. The second draft of the letter, "One in Christ Jesus," appears in *Origins*, 5 April 1990, pp. 717, 719–740.

CHAPTER SIX

1. See the Glossary entries for *sisters, women religious, religious*, and *community*. One of the main issues addressed in this chapter—the increased organizational autonomy granted to sisters' communities under renewal and the resultant rebellion against hierarchical control—owes much to Mary Jo Weaver's excellent analysis, *New Catholic Women: A Contemporary Challenge to Traditional Religious Authority* (New York: Harper and Row, 1985). On the general history, Msgr. George A. Kelly, *The Battle for the American Church* (Garden City, N.Y.: Doubleday/Image, 1981), pp. 253–302; and Sr. Mary Margaret Modde, OSF, "A Canonical Study of the Leadership Conference of Women Religious of the United States of America" (Ph.D. diss., Catholic University of America, 1977), are informative. I am also greatly indebted to the many sister scholars who have written about the changes in their communities, which have gone generally unnoticed by other historians and social scientists.

In this chapter's notes, I abbreviate references to the following collections from the University of Notre Dame Archives: Rev. Paul Boyle, CP, Papers, hereafter the Boyle Collection; Sr. Rose Eileen Masterman, CSC, Collection, hereafter Masterman Collection; the Leadership Conference of Women Religious Collection, hereafter LCWR Collection.

2. The resource mobilization approach to the study of social movements and rebellions, to which my approach is partly indebted, could explain why greater organizational autonomy (i.e., organizational resources) led to rebellion. But it could not explain why there was so little sign of rebellion in either group before Vatican II. Within the resource mobilization approach, dominated groups are unable to rebel not for ideological

reasons, but because they do not have adequate resources. But the evidence certainly does not support the view that bishops and sisters had the same ideological commitments in 1940 that they have today and simply lacked resources to put those commitments into practice.

3. Elizabeth Kolmer, ASC, *Religious Women in the United States* (Wilmington, Del.: Michael Glazier, 1984), p. 41; "General Summary," *Official Catholic Directory 1990* (Wilmette, Ill.: P. J. Kenedy and Sons, 1990), p. 40. The precipitous drop in the number of women joining religious orders in the last two decades has been the topic of much research but is not relevant to the discussion in this book.

4. Modde, "A Canonical Study of the Leadership Conference of Women Religious," pp. 53, 57–59, 62.

5. Ibid., pp. 49, 56, 67.

6. Ibid., pp. 54, 62, 70.

7. Mary Schneider, "The Transformation of American Women Religious: The Sister Formation Conference as Catalyst for Change (1954–1964)," Working Paper Series 17, no. 1 (Notre Dame, Ind.: University of Notre Dame, Cushwa Center for the Study of American Catholicism, 1986), pp. 7, 9.

8. Ibid., pp. 6–14, 18–20.

9. Ibid.

10. Sr. Regina Clare Salazar, CSJ, "Changes in the Education of Roman Catholic Religious Sisters in the United States from 1952 to 1967" (Ph.D. diss., University of Southern California, 1971), pp. 25–27.

11. Schneider, "The Transformation of American Women Religious," p. 33.

12. Ibid., p. 25.

13. The exact titles of superiors varied and probably varies even more today. To orient the reader, it may be worth mentioning that CMSW had 623 members in 1969, a figure, I would guess, that had not changed much since the organization's founding; Booz, Allen and Hamilton, *Survey of Objectives, Programs, Organization, Administration, and Financing* [of CMSW], 2 August 1969, pp. 2–3, in Boyle Collection, Box 43, Folder 1. The 1987–1988 *Membership Directory* (Silver Spring, Md.: LCWR) lists 740 members.

14. Modde, "A Canonical Study of the Leadership Conference of Women Religious," pp. 63–68; CMSW, "Bylaws," n.d., pp. 1–2, Boyle Collection, Box 41, Folder 3.

15. It seems that before Vatican II the CMSW needed approval from the SCR even to hold workshops for religious. P. Philippe, OP (Secretary, SCR) to Mother M. Florence, SL, 11 April 1962, LCWR Collection, Box 1, Folder 17.

16. See, e.g., Memo, Sr. M. Rose Emmanuella, SNJM (Executive Secretary, CMSW) to Members of CMSW, 9 October 1965, Boyle Collec-

tion, Box 41, Folder 6. Men continued to dominate meetings as late as 1966, even though by then there was already a clear ferment of change within CMSW. See the list of speakers in CMSW, *Proceedings of the Annual Assembly,* August 1966, Milwaukee, LCWR Collection, Box 10, Folder 11.

17. (All materials cited in this note are from the Boyle Collection.) See the series of letters from 1965 between the Chairman of CMSW and Rev. Paul Boyle in Box 41, Folder 5; the letters from John Joseph Cardinal Carberry of 3 August 1970, and 14 August 1970, in Box 41, Folder 3; and documents on the Association for Contemplative Sisters in Box 70, Folders 5–7.

18. (All documents cited here are from the Boyle Collection.) See Paul M. Boyle, CP (President, CMSM) to CMSM members, 18 August 1969, and 22 September 1969, Box 43, Folder 2; Boyle to Ildebrando Cardinal Antoniutti (Prefect, SCR), 31 October 1969, Box 43, Folder 2; Bro. William Quinn, FSC (Assistant to the President, CMSM) to Very Rev. Paul M. Boyle, CP, 21 May 1970, Box 43, Folder 3; CMSM Canon Law Committee, Annual Report, June 1966, Box 41, Folder 2; the September and October 1973 letters between Francis X. Gokey, SSE (Executive Secretary, CMSM) and Sr. M. Thomas Aquinas, RSM, Box 42, Folder 10; Sr. M. Thomas Aquinas, RSM (President, LCWR) to Rev. Paul M. Boyle, CP, 29 September 1971, Box 42, Folder 11; Boyle to Rev. Francis Gokey, SSE (Permanent Secretary, CMSM), 5 October 1971, Box 42, Folder 11.

19. For example, the chairman of CMSW sought out a speaker on the need for reform of canon law for religious when arranging the 1965 CMSW annual meeting. Sr. Mary Luke, SL, to Rev. Paul M. Boyle, CP, Boyle Collection, Box 41, Folder 5.

On Vatican efforts in the late 1950s to have the women's conference under the control of the men's (the SCR stated that in most countries the two were in one organization), see Thomas More Page (of the CMSM-LCWR Liaison Committee), memo to LCWR/CMSM staff giving a tentative outline of the history of the relationship between LCWR and CMSM, 2 November 1976, LCWR Collection, Box 6, Folder 7. The memo stated that relations between the women's and men's conferences improved after the 1960s.

For evidence of resentments expressed before and during Vatican II, see Mother Mary Consolatrice, BVM (Chairman, CMSW) to "Dear Reverend Mother" (members, National Executive Committee, CMSW), 23 July 1960, LCWR Collection, Box 1, Folder 16; "Problems Proposed for Discussion, [CMSW] Annual Conference, 1965" (probably written by CMSW's executive secretary), 1-page mimeo, Boyle Collection, Box 41, Folder 6; CMSW, 4-page mimeo on requests of matters for consideration by the ecumenical council, untitled, n.d., LCWR Collection, Box 1, Folder 20.

20. At the time the head of CMSW was indeed known as the "chairman." Using the term is not only historically accurate, but makes the point that in the early 1960s, in their own language, as in their actions, feminism among women religious was at most incipient. With the 1971 changes in the organization, addressed later in this chapter, the head became known as the "president." It is interesting to note that an LCWR document probably produced in 1972 lists former heads of the CMSW as "chairwomen," although at the time they had been known as "chairmen." "Getting to Know You," 4-page mimeo, Boyle Collection, Box 42, Folder 10.

Tobin left for Rome early in 1965 and again on 6 September 1965. Rev. Paul M. Boyle, CP, to Rev. Sr. Mary Luke, SL, 10 February 1965; Sr. Rose Alma, SL, to Boyle, 11 Sept 1965; both letters in Boyle Collection, Box 41, Folder 5; LCWR, "Getting to Know You," 4-page mimeo, n.d., Boyle Collection, Box 42, Folder 10.

21. Mary Luke Tobin, SL, "Women in the Church: Vatican II and After," *The Ecumenical Review* 37, 3 (1985): 295–296.

22. See the Memo of Sr. M. Rose Emmanuella, SNJM, Executive Secretary of CMSW, to Members of CMSW, 9 October 1975, Boyle Collection, Box 41, Folder 6; Sr. Mary Luke Tobin, SL, to "Dear Mothers" (members, CMSW), 22 Sept 1965 (written from Rome), Boyle Collection, Box 41, Folder 6; Tobin, ibid.

23. The more reforming circles of superiors, and of sisters in general, were strongly influenced by theologians whose ideas found their way into council documents, and later interpretations of the council, proclaiming a more modern and less centralized model of the Church: e.g., Yves Congar, Hans Küng, Richard McBrien, Karl Rahner, Edward Schillebeeckx, Cardinal Suenens, and Tielhard de Chardin. (See, e.g., memo of Sr. M. Rose Emmanuella, SNJM [Executive Secretary, CMSW], to Members of the CMSW, 9 October 1965, Boyle Collection, Box 41, Folder 6; Schneider, "The Transformation of American Women Religious," p. 19; Transcription of Tape and Notes, Meeting of Administrative Board of Consortium Perfectae Caritatis and Executive Committee of LCWR, 15 March 1972, Washington, D.C., Masterman Collection, Box 2, Folder 29; Sr. Nadine Foley, O.P., "...And Miles to Go," address to LCWR Assembly, 26 August 1975, St. Paul, Minn., Masterman Collection, Box 3, Folder 7.) Some of the same theologians, whose ideas have some similarity to those of turn-of-the-century modernists condemned by Pius X, also influenced Latin American liberation theology.

24. In Walter M. Abbott, S.J., ed., *The Documents of Vatican II* (Piscataway, N.J.: New Century, 1966), pp. 466–482.

25. Ibid., no. 1, p. 466.

26. Ibid., no. 1, p. 467.

27. Modde, "A Canonical Study of the Leadership Conference of Women Religious."

28. On the founder's spirit, see no. 2, in *The Documents of Vatican II*, ed. Abbott, p. 468; on the three vows, see nos. 12–14, *The Documents of Vatican II*, ed. Abbott, pp. 474–477.

29. On the exclusion of religious, see *Lumen Gentium*, no. 44, in ibid., p. 75; on the religious as part of the laity, see *Perfectae Caritatis*, no. 10, in ibid., p. 473.

30. *Perfectae Caritatis*, no. 8, p. 472.

31. Ibid., no. 3, p. 469.

32. Ibid., nos. 22–23, p. 480.

33. Ibid., no. 2, p. 468; no. 18, p. 479; no. 20, p. 480.

34. Ibid., no. 4, p. 470.

35. Ibid., no. 3, p. 469.

36. *Ecclesiae Sanctae I*, in *Vatican Council II: The Conciliar and Post Conciliar Documents*, ed. Austin P. Flannery (Grand Rapids, Mich.: Eerdmans, 1984), p. 592.

37. Ibid., nos. 1, 3, and 6, pp. 624–625.

38. Ibid., nos. 22–40, pp. 604–609.

39. In addition to Paul's *Ecclesiae Sanctae*, already cited, see the SCR's *Renovationis Causam*, January 1969, in ibid., pp. 634–655, which mostly concerns formation, and its *Evangelica Testificatio*, June 1971, in ibid., pp. 680–706.

40. "Remarks of Father Ransing at the Meeting of the Executive Committee of the CMSW—August 1964," 2-page mimeo (attached to minutes of the meeting), LCWR Collection, Box 10, Folder 9.

See also Ildebrando Cardinal Antoniutti (Prefect, SCR) to "Dear Reverend Mothers" (i.e., members of CMSW at their annual meeting), 6 August 1965, LCWR Collection, Box 10, Folder 10.

41. See, e.g., Mother Mary Consolatrice, BVM (National Chairman, CMSW), "Welcome and Introductory Remarks" to CMSW National Conference and the address of Sr. M. Francine, OSF, in the Program, CMSW National Conference, August 1964, Cincinnati, LCWR Collection, Box 10, Folder 9; Sr. Helen Marie, OSU, to Rev. Paul M. Boyle, CP, 21 May 1965, Boyle Collection, Box 84, Folder 12; "Problems Proposed for Discussion, [CMSW] Annual Conference, 1965," 1-page mimeo, Boyle Collection, Box 41, Folder 6; Sr. Rose Emmanuella, SNJM, summary of "Panels on Impact of Vatican II on Content and Structure of General Chapters," 2-page typescript, CMSW National Meeting, August 1965, Denver, LCWR Collection, Box 10, Folder 10; "Proposals Accepted by Vote of the Chapter," attached to Sr. Mary Luke to "Dear Sisters" (members, Sisters of Loretto), 18 June 1969, Boyle Collection, Box 79, Folder 1. See also the five reports of various regional subcommittees of the CMSW Canon Law Committee, showing agreement about the general, decentralizing thrust of reform, in Boyle Collection, Box 41, Folder 1. (These reports are not dated but were apparently written for a 1 December 1966 deadline.)

42. See, e.g., the letter from Sr. Celestine Schall to Boyle, 4 October 1969, Boyle Collection, Box 74, Folder 9; Sr. M. Francis Borgia, OSF, to Rev. Edward Heston, CSC (of the SCR), 15 December 1970, Boyle Collection, Box 75, Folder 1; Sr. Eileen Burtle to "Dear Father" (Rev. Paul M. Boyle, CP), 27 December 1970, Boyle Collection, Box 73, Folder 10; Sr. Helen Marie, OSU, to Boyle, 21 May 1965, 20 October 1965, and 4 January 1966, Boyle Collection, Box 84, Folder 12; Sr. Grace Swift to Boyle, 26 February 1966, Boyle Collection, Box 84, Folder 12; Paul M. Boyle, C.P., "Presidential Report, CMSM Activities," 1970, Boyle Collection, Box 42, Folder 1; Joan Chittister, OSB, et al., *Climb Along the Cutting Edge: An Analysis of Change in Religious Life* (New York: Paulist Press, 1977), p. 19. In a community that had a major dispute with the SCR, it seemed that, based on a questionnaire on responses to a letter from the SCR, a solid block of 10–20 percent strongly questioned the directions the community was taking. School Sisters of St. Francis, Milwaukee, *Response in Faith and Hope*, Boyle Collection, Box 75, Folder 2.

43. Members of the Generalate Commission on Basic Formation and Continuing Development to Sr. M. Regina Cunningham, RSM (Superior General), 17 May 1970, Boyle Collection, Box 79, Folder 12; Sr. Dorothy Coons, BVM, *Apartment Living: A Study in Life Styles*, July 1969, Boyle Collection, Box 72, Folder 13; see also the articles by Sr. Francis Borgia Rothluebber, OSF ("Experiments in Living"), and Father Paul Boyle, CP ("Small Community Experiences"), in Canadian Religious Conference, Bureau of Religious Affairs, *Living in Fraternity*, 28 April 1971, in Boyle Collection, Box 64, Folder 7.

44. Quotation from Adrian Dominican Congregation, *Outlook: Hope*, 1969, p. 3, Boyle Collection, Box 73, Folder 6; see also Sr. Mary Jeanne Salois, RSM, *Pilot Study of Local Community Experimentation in the Generalate of the Sisters of Mercy of the Union, U.S.A., 1969–1970* (Bethesda, Md.: Sisters of Mercy Generalate, 1970), in Boyle Collection, Box 79, Folder 13.

Concern over resources to provide for retirement was, however, a concern of the Adrian Dominican Congregation a few years later; the earlier quotation may reflect more of an attitude than an actual financial decision. See Adrian Dominican Sisters, "Resources for Ministry," Spring 1972, Boyle Collection, Box 73, Folder 6.

45. See, e.g., Sr. Helen Marie, OSU, to Rev. Paul M. Boyle, CP, 21 May 1965 and 20 October 1965, Boyle Collection, Box 84, Folder 12.

46. "Address of the Pope to the Union of Major Superiors," n.d., Boyle Collection, Box 41, Folder 3.

47. CMSW, "Proposed Revision of Canon Law," n.d., p. 9, Boyle Collection, Box 40, Folder 7.

48. Weaver, *New Catholic Women*, pp. 89–105, provided a perceptive analysis, to which this discussion is deeply indebted, of the relationship

between renewal and the development of feminism among sisters. I know of no published histories of the renewal process among American women religious as a whole, although there is an extended analysis of a federation of Benedictine convents, from an insider's point of view (Chittister et al., *Climb Along the Cutting Edge*). Kelly, *The Battle for the American Church*, provided quite a bit of historical information, and some sociological insights compatible with my argument, in the context of criticizing the direction of renewal from a traditional point of view. Otherwise, renewal receives only short treatment in various community histories, which do not provide enough to really understand the dynamics or the details: e.g., Sr. Mary Assumption Ahles, OSF, *In the Shadow of His Wings: A History of the Franciscan Sisters* (St. Paul: North Central Publishing, 1977); Sr. M. Francis Cooke, OSF, *His Love Heals: A History of the Hospital Sisters of the Third Order of St. Francis, Springfield, Illinois, 1875–1975* (Chicago: Franciscan Herald Press, 1977); Sr. Lois Curry, OP, *Women After His Own Heart: The Sisters of Saint Dominic of the American Congregation of the Sacred Heart of Jesus, Caldwell, New Jersey, 1881–1981* (New York: New City Press, 1981); Sr. M. DeChantal, CSFN, *Out of Nazareth: A Centenary of the Sisters of the Holy Family of Nazareth in the Service of the Church* (New York: Exposition Press, 1974); Sr. Mary Camilla Koester, PCC, *Into This Land: A Centenary History of the Cleveland Poor Clare Monastery of the Blessed Sacrament* (Cleveland: Robert J. Liederbach, 1980); Susan Carol Peterson, "The Presentation Sisters in South Dakota, 1880–1976" (Ph.D. diss., Oklahoma State University, 1979).

My own treatment benefits from these other works but is heavily based on the papers of Rev. Paul M. Boyle, CP, a canon lawyer heavily involved in advising many communities during their renewal processes. It is possible there is a bias in these papers (in the University of Notre Dame Archives) toward communities in favor of more extensive reform than average. Nevertheless, included are documents on a variety of communities that altogether constitute at least a significant minority of all American sisters. That the same changes in outlook developed at the national level, in CMSW, suggests that the majority of communities took similar paths. By the early 1970s, if not before, the CMSW/LCWR could certainly be considered an organization representative of sisters in general as much as any elected organization because the selection of superiors had become increasingly democratized with the renewal process. There are, moreover, data from Marie Augusta Neal, SND de N, *Catholic Sisters in Transition: From the 1960s to the 1980s* (Wilmington, Del.: Michael Glazier, 1984), that suggest that extensive reform was the norm, not the exception. Even if reformers were only a minority, they were enough to provide a thorough ideological and political challenge to the hierarchy.

49. Neal, *Catholic Sisters in Transition*, p. 48.

50. See, e.g., (Sisters of the Precious Blood) Coordinating Habit Committee Report to Special General Chapter, August 1969, Boyle Collection, Box 82, Folder 6; Chittister et al., *Climb Along the Cutting Edge*, pp. 24–25; Peterson, "The Presentation Sisters in South Dakota," p. 108; Weaver, *New Catholic Women*, p. 106.

51. There had been signs of increasing concern for mental health issues before the council as well: Schneider, "The Transformation of American Women Religious," pp. 19, 22, 23; Program, National Congress of Religious, University of Notre Dame, 16–19 August 1961, LCWR Collection, Box 10, Folder 5; Program, CMSW Workshops for Major Superiors, Summer 1962, LCWR Collection, Box 10, Folder 6; Sr. Mary Carita Pendergast, SC, "Assessment of a Psychological Screening Program for Candidates to a Religious Congregation of Women" (Ph.D. diss., Fordham University, 1968), p. 4.

A 1-page mimeo, probably prepared by CMSW's executive secretary, titled "Problems Proposed for Discussion, Annual Conference, 1965" (Boyle Collection, Box 41, Folder 6), stated concerns over presentation of "essential attitudes & practices such as mortification, penance, self-sacrifice in such a way as to avoid psychologically harmful effects." On the general emphasis of psychological screening and adapting to the psychological needs of sisters after Vatican II, see, e.g., *Seventh General Chapter, Sisters of Mercy of the Union*, Second Session, 14–23 May 1966, in Boyle Collection, Box 79, Folder 15; "Report of the General Government to the General Chapter of the Sisters of St. Joseph," July 1974, p. 35, Boyle Collection, Box 76, Folder 14; Adrian Dominican Congregation, *Outlook: Hope*, p. 6, Boyle Collection, Box 73, Folder 6; (Sisters of the Precious Blood) *Perspectives #5* (Ordinances of the Special General Chapter, August 1969), p. 14, Boyle Collection, Box 82, Folder 9; CMSW, "Proposed Revision of Canon Law," n.d., p. 9, Boyle Collection, Box 40, Folder 7; Paul M. Boyle, CP, "New Directions in Canon Law for Religious," n.d., p. 22, Boyle Collection, Box 40, Folder 1; Salazar, "Changes in the Education of Roman Catholic Religious Sisters," p. 127. Neal, *Catholic Sisters in Transition*, p. 38, found that in 1982, 55.8 percent of communities required consultation with a professional psychologist as a requirement for admission, compared to 29.1 percent in 1966.

It appears that some of this emphasis on psychology was a response to a passage in *Perfectae Caritatis*, no. 3, p. 469, quoted elsewhere in this chapter.

The archbishop who disputed with the Glenmary Sisters, one of three communities that became rallying points for those opposing hierarchical control (addressed later in this chapter), warned women religious in his diocese to be wary of psychologists and sociologists, in a letter of 11 May 1965, Boyle Collection, Box 75, Folder 5. Likewise, the prefect of the SCR, Cardinal Antoniutti, in 1970 warned against "sensitivity training" as incompatible "with every form of consecrated life" (John Joseph Cardinal Carberry to "Your Excellency" [presumably sent to all U.S. bishops], 14 August 1970, Boyle Collection, Box 41, Folder 3).

52. School Sisters of St. Francis, Milwaukee, *Response in Faith and Hope* (January 1971), Boyle Collection, Box 75, Folder 2.

53. On the doing away with the dowry, see "Propositions Accepted by Vote of the Chapter," attached to Sr. Mary Luke to "Dear Sisters" (Sisters of Loretto), 18 June 1969, Boyle Collection, Box 79, Folder 1; on the education requirement, see Adrian Dominican Congregation, *Outlook: Hope*, p. 10, Boyle Collection, Box 73, Folder 6. In general, communities require more preparation of candidates than they used to; Neal, *Catholic Sisters in Transition*, p. 37, found that in 1982, 63.7 percent required some kind of work experience (in 1966, only 8.7 percent did) and 42.1 percent some college (3.1 percent in 1966). It was still the case that only a minority (9.6 percent in 1982, 0.7 percent in 1966) required a bachelor's degree, but 41 percent of candidates actually did have such a degree in 1982.

54. See, e.g., Adrian Dominican Congregation, ibid.; Sisters of Charity of Mount St. Vincent, "Report to the Chapter of Affairs, 1969, on the Chapter Enactments of 1966–1969," Boyle Collection, Box 72, Folder 8.

55. Neal, *Catholic Sisters in Transition*, p. 48.

56. Sisters of Charity, "Report to the Chapter of Affairs, 1969, on the Chapter Enactments of 1966–1969."

57. Sisters of Charity, "Official Report to the Community of the Chapter of Affairs, 1969," Boyle Collection, Box 72, Folder 6.

58. "Norms and Determinations Approved by the Seventh General Chapter [1965–1966] of the Sisters of Mercy in the Union in the United States of America," 19-page photocopy, Boyle Collection, Box 79, Folder 14; Members of the Generalate Commission on Basic Formation and Continuing Development to Sr. M. Regina Cunningham, RSM (Superior General), 17 May 1970, Boyle Collection, Box 79, Folder 12. The quotation is from this letter.

59. Weaver, *New Catholic Women*, pp. 97–101.

60. "Summary of Steps Toward Renewal and Adaptation—1965–1966"; "Summary of Steps Toward Renewal and Adaptation—1966–1967"; both in Boyle Collection, Box 74, Folder 2.

61. (Adrian Dominican Congregation), "Proposed Constitution," n.d., Boyle Collection, Box 73, Folder 8.

62. The comments on the *Customs* and *Handbook* are from Boyle in a letter of 8 February 1966; all materials in Boyle Collection, Box 74, the booklets in Folder 3 and Boyle's letter in Folder 9.

63. See Sr. Mary Jeanne Salois, RSM, *Pilot Study of Local Community Experimentation in the Generalate of the Sisters of Mercy of the Union, U.S.A., 1969–1970* (Bethesda, Md.: Sisters of Mercy Generalate, 1970), Boyle Collection, Box 79, Folder 13. The author noted, from survey results,

that sisters professed twenty-five or more years saw the superior as representing God, while the younger ones generally did not.

For further examples of the new view of obedience, see Adrian Dominican Congregation, *Outlook: Hope*, p. 6; Sisters of St. Joseph of the Third Order of St. Francis, "Report of Government Committee," 12-page mimeo, August 1967, Boyle Collection, Box 61, Folder 3; Chittister et al., *Climb Along the Cutting Edge*, pp. 15, 192–193, 223–224. A 1974 survey within Chittister's Benedictine federation is particularly interesting because 72 percent of respondents agreed that religious "owe their obedience to a duly chosen superior," but only 32 percent accepted that the "Holy See [i.e., Rome] has the right to interpret the norms of religious life for the universal Church and within each diocese" (p. 223).

64. Sr. Francis Borgia, OSF, to sisters of School Sisters of St. Francis, 20 September 1971, Boyle Collection, Box 74, Folder 9.

65. Sr. M. Joel, OSF, to Fr. Paul M. Boyle, CP, 10 February 1966, Boyle Collection, Box 74, Folder 9; Sr. Helen Marie, OSU, to Rev. Paul M. Boyle, CP, 21 May 1965, Boyle Collection, Box 84, Folder 12; "Propositions Accepted by Vote of the Chapter (cited n. 53)."

66. See, e.g., the Sisters of Charity, "Official Report to the Community of the Chapter of Affairs, 1969"; Sr. Francis Borgia, OSF, to sisters of School Sisters of St. Francis, 20 September 1971, Boyle Collection, Box 74, Folder 9; Generalate Commission on Basic Formation and Continuing Development (of the Sisters of Mercy of the Union) to Sr. M. Regina Cunningham, RSM (Superior General), 17 May 1970, Boyle Collection, Box 79, Folder 12. See also letters of 25ʳMay 1970, and 31 January 1972 from individual members of the Sisters of Mercy, in the same folder.

67. Peterson, "The Presentation Sisters in South Dakota," p. 109.

68. Sr. Rose Emmanuella, SNJM, summary of "Panels on Impact of Vatican II on Content and Structure of General Chapters," 2-page typescript, CMSW National Meeting, August 1965, Denver, LCWR Collection, Box 10, Folder 10; Sisters of St. Joseph of the Third Order of St. Francis, "Report of Government Committee," 12-page mimeo, August 1967, Boyle Collection, Box 61, Folder 3.

69. See, e.g., Adrian Dominican Congregation, *Outlook: Hope*, pp. 1–5, concerning an August 1969 self-study, Boyle Collection, Box 73, Folder 6; Sr. Mary Anthonita Hess, CPPS (Superior General), untitled address to General Chapter, 4 August 1969, Boyle Collection, Box 82, Folder 5; Emmanuella, ibid.; "Self-Study Programs of Religious Communities," pp. 41–59 of CMSW, *Proceedings of the Annual Assembly* (cited n. 16); Chittister et al., *Climb Along the Cutting Edge*, p. 52; Sr. Marie Augusta Neal, "Implications of the Sisters' Survey for Structural Renewal," in *Proceedings* (of the 1967 CMSW Annual Assembly) (Washington, D.C.: CMSW, 1968), pp. 16–17, in LCWR Collection, Box 10, Folder 12.

70. See, e.g., Rev. Paul M. Boyle, CP, to Sr. Mary Cephas Wichman, RSM, 6 November 1973, Boyle Collection, Box 79, Folder 11; *Chapter Materials* of the Sisters of Charity, n.d., p. 18, Boyle Collection, Box 72, Folder 14; Edigio Vagnozzi (Apostolic Delegate to the United States) to Mother M. Luke, SL, 11 April 1967, LCWR Collection, Box 1, Folder 22. Also noteworthy was the SCR's *Renovationis Causam*, pp. 636–655, which relaxed the juridical norms on formation, allowing individual communities greater autonomy in the selection and training of candidates.

71. In Flannery, ibid., pp. 680–706; see esp. nos. 25–28.

72. Augustine Mayer to Rev. Mother M. Augustilde, SCC, 23 June 1973, Boyle Collection, Box 72, Folder 1.

73. See Sr. Mary Luke, SL, to Rev. Paul Boyle, CP, 27 June 1966, Boyle Collection, Box 41, Folder 5; Paul M. Boyle, CP, "New Directions in Canon Law for Religious," Boyle Collection, Box 40, Folder 1. This latter document is a summary of a U.S. bishops' subcommittee report dealing with the revision of canon law for religious in light of Vatican II, apparently written about 1969.

74. I. Cardinal Antoniutti to Francis Borgia, OSF, 21 November 1967, Boyle Collection, Box 74, Folder 10.

75. Luigi Raimondi (Apostolic Delegate to the United States) to John Cardinal Krol (President, NCCB), 28 January 1972, Masterman Collection, Box 2, Folder 23.

76. Rev. Edward Heston, "Religious Life in the Church" (first quotation, p. 16, second quotation, p. 19) opening address to Annual Meeting of the CMSW, 18–22 September 1969, Boyle Collection, Box 41, Folder 4. See also, e.g., Br. William Quinn, FSC (Assistant to the President, CMSM), to Very Rev. Paul M. Boyle, CP, 11 February 1970, Boyle Collection, Box 42, Folder 4; Weaver, *New Catholic Women*, pp. 105–108.

77. NCCB Liaison Committee, "Points Submitted by Various Bishops for the Consideration of the CMSW," 25 April 1971; CMSW, "Comments on Points Submitted by Various Bishops for the Consideration of the CMSW (April 25, 1971)." Both documents attached to Sr. Ann V. Bowling (of CMSW) to Rev. Paul Boyle, CP (President, CMSM), 17 June 1971, Boyle Collection, Box 42, Folder 11. See also LCWR 1972 National Assembly, "Official Minutes of Business Meetings," 28 pp., p. 12, Boyle Collection, Box 42, Folder 10.

In the interpretation of the bishops' concern with the supply of teachers, it is worth noting that in 1966, 72 percent of American sisters were teachers, the majority (70 percent of those who were teachers) in elementary schools, which were probably almost all parish schools. Sr. Marie Augusta Neal, SND de N, "Implications of the Sisters' Survey for Structural Renewal" (cited n. 69).

78. Francis X. Murphy, C.SS.R., *The Papacy Today* (New York: Macmillan, 1981), pp. 134, 249.

79. Ibid., pp. 106–107, 116, 134.

80. Rev. Paul M. Boyle, CP, to Sr. M. Giovanni, OSU, 29 September 1966, Boyle Collection, Box 84, Folder 11.

81. Cardinal Antoniutti (Prefect, SCR) to Most Rev. Leo A. Pursley, 5 February 1972, Masterman Collection, Box 2, Folder 29.

82. Weaver, *New Catholic Women*, p. 232n.

83. On the Immaculate Heart Sisters, see Sarah Bentley Doely, ed., *Women's Liberation and the Church: The New Demand for Freedom in the Life of the Church* (New York: Association Press, 1970), pp. 70–76.

84. Weaver, *New Catholic Women*, pp. 93–95.

85. Ibid., pp. 92–93; "An Account of Events Concerning Development of the Glenmary Sisters Community During the Months of July and August, 1965," Boyle Collection, Box 75, Folder 5.

86. See, e.g., Karl Alter (Archbishop of Cincinnati, who was at the center of the dispute with the Glenmary Sisters), "To All Members of Religious Institutes [in the Cincinnati archdiocese]," 11 May 1965, Boyle Collection, Box 75, Folder 5; cover letter for "Statement Concerning the Goals...," Boyle Collection, Box 75, Folder 5; letter of Mother Mary Catherine to Archbishop, 5 January 1967, Boyle Collection, Box 75, Folder 5; Auxiliary Bishop to Boyle, 5 September 1968, Boyle Collection, Box 75, Folder 8.

87. Sr. Mary Catherine (Superior General, Glenmary Sisters) to members of the CMSW, 20 July 1967, LCWR Collection, Box 1, Folder 22; Doely, ed., *Women's Liberation and the Church*, pp. 70–76; Weaver, *New Catholic Women*, pp. 93–94.

88. Quotation from Sr. Francis Borgia, OSF, to membership, 5 July 1969. See also the letter from I. Cardinal Antoniutti (Prefect, SCR) to Sr. Francis Borgia, OSF, 21 Nov 1967; Borgia to Boyle, 11 Dec 1967. All in Boyle Collection, Box 74, Folder 10.

89. Edigio Vagnozzi (Apostolic Delegate to the United States) to Mother Mary Luke, SL, 12 January 1967, LCWR Collection, Box 1, Folder 22.

90. Sr. Joan Tabat, OSF, "A Brief History of the Conference of Major Religious Superiors of Women's Institutes in the United States of America," Boyle Collection, Box 41, Folder 3, p. 9. See also Kelly, *The Battle for the American Church*, pp. 257–260.

91. "Sister's Survey" (mimeo), Annual Assembly of the Major Superiors of Women's Institutes in the U.S.A., 24–28 September 1967, Boyle Collection, Box 40, Folder 3; Research Committee of CMSW, *Sisters' Survey* (questionnaire booklet), 1 April 1967, Boyle Collection, Box 40, Folder 3.

92. Neal, "Implications of the Sisters' Survey for Structural Renewal"; Sr. M. Rose Emmanuella (Executive Secretary, CMSW), memo to CMSW members, 30 October 1967, LCWR Collection, Box 1, Folder 22.

93. On teaching and compensation, see Booz, Allen and Hamilton, *Survey of Objectives, Programs, Organization, Administration, and Financing*. For a pre–Vatican II health survey, see CMSW, "Status of Health Care of Religious Women, 1962 Survey," 13-page mimeo, LCWR Collection, Box 1, Folder 18. Health and health insurance seem to have been a major concern of the pre–Vatican II CMSW. Sr. Mary Luke, SL (National Chairman, CMSW), to CMSW membership, 16 February 1965, LCWR Collection, Box 1, Folder 20.

For individual community discussions of inadequate compensation and provisions for retirement, see, e.g., Adrian Dominican Sisters, "Resources for Ministry," Spring 1972, Boyle Collection, Box 73, Folder 6. On the U.S. bishops' Task Force, see Sister Dorothy Kammerer, C.PP.S., to Monsignor Olin J. Murdick (Chairman, Religious Retirement Task Force), 29 October 1973, Boyle Collection, Box 83, Folder 4. On more recent dimensions of the problem of funding retirement, see *Wall Street Journal*, 19 May 1986, and 18 November 1987.

94. Sr. Mary Luke, SL, to Rev. Paul M. Boyle, CP, 30 August 1965, Boyle Collection, Box 41, Folder 5. See also the newspaper clippings in LCWR Collection, Box 10, Folder 10: Wes French, "Nuns Ask Church for Women Voice," *Rocky Mountain News* (Denver), 28 August 1965; Rev. Vincent Lovett, "Nuns Ask Voice in Church Bodies," *National Catholic Reporter*, 1 September 1965.

95. CMSW, "Proposed Revision of Canon Law," n.d., Boyle Collection, Box 40, Folder 7; Sr. Mary Luke, SL, to Rev. Paul M. Boyle, CP, 1 February 1965, Boyle Collection, Box 41, Folder 5; Boyle to Rev. Sister Mary Luke, 10 February 1965, Boyle Collection, Box 41, Folder 5.

The committee may have been established as a result of the suggestions of Rev. Paul M. Boyle, CP. Boyle (President, Canon Law Society of America) to "Dear Reverend Mother" (presumably sent to many or all CMSW members), 16 January 1965, Boyle Collection, Box 41, Folder 6; Mother Timothy Marie Flaherty, (proposed) "Preface" to "Proposed Norms for Consideration in the Revision of Canon Law," April 1968, Boyle Collection, Box 40, Folder 1.

96. CMSW, "Proposed Revision of Canon Law"; Mother Mary Omer, SC (National Chairman, CMSW), "Foreword," p. iii in CMSW, *Proposed Norms for Consideration in the Revision of the Code of Canon Law* (Washington, D.C.: CMSW National Secretariat, April 1968), in LCWR Collection, Box 16, Folder 20. In explaining the purpose of preparing the proposed norms, Omer cited "the words of the Council Fathers that the faithful make known their needs (*Lumen Gentium*, 37)...."

Clearly there was great interest in the Canon Law Committee's work among U.S. sisters; after selling thirteen hundred copies of their "Proposed Norms for Consideration in the Revision of the Code of Canon Law," which apparently was the committee's final report, the committee decided it would need to print another two thousand. Sr. Angelita Myerscough to CMSW Canon Law Committee members, 4 June 1969, Boyle Collection, Box 41, Folder 1.

97. Paul M. Boyle, CP, "New Directions in Canon Law for Religious," pp. 11–12, Boyle Collection, Box 40, Folder 1; Edigio Vagnozzi (Apostolic Delegate to the United States) to Mother M. Luke (Tobin), SL, 11 April 1967, LCWR Collection, Box 1, Folder 22.

On the issue of being treated as adults, see Sr. Mary Luke (Tobin), SL, to Rev. Paul M. Boyle, CP, 23 March 1965, Boyle Collection, Box 41, Folder 5; "Reform of Law for Renewal of Religious Life," a press release by Rev. James C. McDonald (Publicity Director, Canon Law Society of America), 13 September 1965, Boyle Collection, Box 41, Folder 6; CMSW, "Proposed Revision of Canon Law," n.d., p. 9, Boyle Collection, Box 40, Folder 7; "Report: Canon Law Committee," 19 August 1966, LCWR Collection, Box 10, Folder 11.

98. "Introductory Commentary for the CMSW Proposed Canons on Religious Life," in CMSW, "Proposed Revision of Canon Law," pp. 5–6, Boyle Collection, Box 40, Folder 7.

99. Ibid., p. 7. See also Canon Law Committee Report to CMSW National Assembly, 9–13 September 1970, Boyle Collection, Box 41, Folder 1.

100. A member of the Canon Law Committee wrote to others in 1969, "Recent brief news releases, as you are probably aware, quoted Cardinal Felici [chairman of Rome's Commission for the Revision of the Code] as saying that the revision work was rather far toward completion and that the work had been done more or less in secret because it was too technical to be of general interest....The fact of secrecy is something which I know some members of the American hierarchy and canonists deplore"—Sr. Angelita Myerscough, ASC, to CMSW Canon Law Committee members, 4 June 1969, Boyle Collection, Box 41, Folder 1. See also Myerscough, untitled report of Canon Law Committee, pp. 103–104, in *Proceedings* of the Annual Assembly 1969 and Special Assembly 1970 (Washington, D.C.: CMSW, 1970), in LCWR Collection, Box 10, Folder 15; "Additional Resolutions Proposed by Region IX[?]" of CMSW, 1970, Boyle Collection, Box 41, Folder 3; Sr. Rosalie Murphy, SND, to Rev. Paul Boyle, CP, 30 April 1970, Boyle Collection, Box 41, Folder 3.

101. LCWR, "Rationale for Revision of Statutes," n.d., 4-page mimeo, Boyle Collection, Box 42, Folder 10; LCWR, "Chronology: Revision of *Statutes* of the Leadership Conference of Women Religious of the United States of America," 8-page mimeo, n.d., Boyle Collection, Box 42, Folder 10.

102. Quotation from Sr. M. Thomas Aquinas Carroll, RSM (President, LCWR), memo to "Major Superiors Requesting Reflections...on Letter of January 28, 1972 Relative to Religious Habit," p. 2, 22 February 1972, Masterman Collection, Box 2, Folder 23. See also, e.g., Sr. Adrienne

Ellis, "Search for Unity," (keynote) address to Annual Assembly of CMSW, St. Louis, 10 September 1970, Boyle Collection, Box 41, Folder 7.

103. The revision began with the work of the CMSW Statutes Committee, and in 1970 and 1971 the proposed revisions were sent to all CMSW members for comments. In the (July) 1971 mailing, CMSW officers informed members that the proposed bylaws would be considered by the September National Assembly, the officers having received assurance from the SCR that this would be the proper procedure. LCWR, "Rationale for Revision of Statutes"; "Bylaws of the Leadership Conference of Women Religious in the United States of America (LCWR)," 12-page photocopy, Boyle Collection, Box 42, Folder 10; LCWR, "Chronology"; Memo, Sr. Mary Daniel (Executive Director, LCWR) to LCWR members, 8 November 1972 (attached to Sr. Margaret Brennan, IHM, to members, 8 November 1972), Boyle Collection, Box 42, Folder 10; Sr. Joan Tabat, OSF, "A Brief History of the Conference of Major Superiors of Women's Institutes in the United States of America," 25-page manuscript, Boyle Collection, Box 41, Folder 3.

104. The roots of the split seem to go back to 1970. See the following materials in the booklet on the Charter Meeting of the Consortium in Masterman Collection, Box 2, Folder 26: Memo to CMSW Membership, 1-page mimeo, n.d.; "Statement" (on religious life, St. Louis Workshop), 1970, 5-page mimeo; Sr. M. Eucharia Malone, proposed draft of letter to "Dear Sister," n.d.

105. See, e.g., Kelly, *The Battle for the American Church*, pp. 253–302; the 1967 exchange of letters between Boyle and a Jesuit college rector in Boyle Collection, Box 41, Folder 1; James Hitchcock, *The Decline and Fall of Radical Catholicism* (New York: Herder and Herder, 1979).

106. See in the Masterman Collection the interesting transcripts of the 1972 (Box 2, Folder 29) and 1975 (Box 3, Folder 7) meetings between LCWR and consortium officers trying to resolve their differences. There was also a meeting in 1974 (Sr. M. Francine Zeller to Sr. Mary Elise, SND, 11 March 1975, Masterman Collection, Box 3, Folder 7), and there have been occasional meetings since then. Interestingly, it seems that the LCWR has been more anxious to continue meeting than has the consortium; the LCWR's position is that all superiors should participate in the officially recognized organization ("Transcription of Dialogue CPC-LCWR," Chicago, 3 September 1975, Masterman Collection, Box 3, Folder 7; interview with Sr. Janet Roesener, CSJ [Executive Director, LCWR], 10 December 1987, Washington, D.C.).

107. (All documents in this note in Masterman Collection, Box 2, Folder 23.) Sr. Mary Elise, SND, to Sr. Rose Eileen (CSC), Easter Sunday, 1978. Although consortium leaders tried to present a public image that would counter the reputation of being an ultraconservative organization competing with the LCWR, they in fact had a hostile view of the LCWR.

Sr. Mary Elise, SND, to Sr. Rose Eileen, 10 September 1975; Sr. M. Rose Eileen Masterman, CSC, to Sr. M. Ines, OCD, 31 October 1975; Masterman to Sr. Mary Elise, 5 November 1975.

108. All the following documents are in the Masterman Collection, Box 2: Consortium Perfectae Caritatis, untitled pamphlet, n.d., Folder 29; Cardinal Antoniutti (Prefect, SCR) to "Dear Members of the Consortium 'Perfectae Caritatis,'" 18 August 1972, Folder 28; Basil Heiser (Secretary, SCR), "To Whom It May Concern," 19 December 1973, Folder 28; Rev. James A. Viall (Coordinator, Consortium) to Most Rev. Augustine Mayer, OSB (Secretary, SCR), 20 November 1975, Folder 23; Sr. Mary Elise, SND, to Sr. Rose Eileen (CSC), Easter Sunday, 1978, Folder 23; Augustine Mayer (Secretary, SCR) to Rev. James A. Viall, 7 May 1979, Folder 23. In their inability to gather official recognition, the consortium's leaders also apparently became frustrated with the U.S. bishops' conference. Sr. Rose Eileen Masterman, CSC, 4 December 1975, Folder 23.

109. See the following materials in the Masterman Collection, Box 2, Folder 26: Rev. James A. Viall, untitled address, Chardon, Ohio, 7 October 1970; Rev. John A. Hardon, SJ, "Rome and the Religious Life," address at Chardon, Ohio, 7 October 1970; Hardon, "The Religious Woman in America Today," 2 December 1970; Edigio Cardinal Vagnozzi (Prefect of the Economic Affairs of the Holy See [and, 1959–1967, Apostolic Delegate to the United States]), "Renewal According to the Second Vatican Council," 2 December 1970; Fr. John W. Mole, OMI, "Two Opposing Ideals of Religious Community Life," 2 December 1970; Hardon, untitled address to charter meeting of Consortium Perfectae Caritatis, 28 January 1971, Arlington, Va.; Mother Claudia, IHM, "The Reform of Renewal," address to charter meeting of Consortium Perfectae Caritatis, 27–29 January 1971, Alexandria, Virginia. See also Consortium Perfectae Caritatis, *Proceedings: Third National Assembly*, 1972, Washington, D.C., Masterman Collection, Box 2, Folder 29. Concern over leadership by priests, rather than sisters, even came from the apostolic delegate to the United States (Jean Jadot [Apostolic Delegate to the United States] to Rev. James A. Viall, 2 October 1974, Masterman Collection, Box 2, Folder 23) and from within the consortium itself (Sr. Mary Elise, SND, to Sr. Rose Eileen [CSC], Easter Sunday, 1978, Masterman Collection, Box 2, Folder 23).

It is difficult to state how large the consortium has been over the years. There was a 1977 claim of eighty major superior members (at the time the LCWR probably had about six hundred), but because it tried to maintain a public image of a communications group, rather than a formal organization in competition with the LCWR, it had a loose organizational structure in which the definition of "membership" was not always clear. Minutes of the Exploratory Meeting held in Alhambra (California) for a group of Communities interested in the Consortium, 18 January 1977, presided by Mother Mary Elise, SND (Executive Director, Consortium), Masterman

Collection, Box 2, Folder 23. Incidentally it appears that consortium members, at least in the 1970s, continued to attend LCWR meetings, at the advice of the SCR, to present their viewpoint. Sr. Rose Eileen Masterman, CSC, to Sr. Mary Elise, 5 November 1975, Masterman Collection, Box 2, Folder 23.

On the LCWR perspective on the consortium, see Sr. Margaret Mary Brennan, IHM (President, LCWR), to LCWR members, 8 November 1972, Boyle Collection, Box 42, Folder 10.

110. See, e.g., Cardinal Antoniutti to "Dear Members of the Consortium 'Perfectae Caritatis' "(cited in n. 108).

111. Henry J. Pratt, *The Liberalization of American Protestantism: A Case Study in Complex Organizations* (Detroit: Wayne State University Press, 1972).

112. The SCR continued to show concern about negative attitudes toward itself displayed within LCWR. See, e.g., Sr. Margaret Mary Brennan, IHM (President, LCWR), to LCWR members, 8 November 1972.

113. Cf. Weaver, *New Catholic Women*, p. 112; and Sr. Barbara Thomas, SCN (President, LCWR), to Sr. Myra Mahoney, OP, 7 January 1976, Masterman Collection, Box 2, Folder 28. Cf. Sr. Margaret Brennan, IHM (President, LCWR), to all U.S. bishops, 28 September 1972, with attached "The Recent Apostolic Letters on Ministries: A Response," Boyle Collection, Box 42, Folder 10. The LCWR's critique of the NCCB's proposed pastoral letter on women implied strong support for women's ordination (*Origins*, 30 August 1990, 187).

114. Anne Marie Gardiner, S.S.N.D., ed. *Women and Catholic Priesthood: An Expanded Vision. Proceedings of the Detroit Ordination Conference* (New York: Paulist Press, 1976). See also Women's Ordination Conference, news release, "Ordination Conference Leadership Selected," 6 June 1976, Masterman Collection, Box 2, Folder 16.

115. Weaver, *New Catholic Women*, p. 114.

116. Doris Gottemoeller, RSM, and Rita Hofbauer, GNSH, *Women and Ministry: Present Experience and Future Hopes* (Washington, D.C.: Leadership Conference of Women Religious, 1981); interview with Sr. Janet Roesener, CSJ (Executive Director, LCWR), 10 December 1987, Silver Spring, Maryland.

117. "Most Women Religious Resist Vatican's Retraction Demand," *National Catholic Reporter*, 28 December 1984, p. 1; *New York Times*, 2 March 1986, 22 July 1986, 6 June 1988; Brett Harvey, "Sisterhood Is Subversive," *Village Voice*, 27 January 1987; and *Origins*, 23 June 1988, pp. 91–92.

The LCWR position on the ad was that it will aid any member of the conference that asks its support, without necessarily supporting their particular opinions. Of course, not all signers were members because only officers (known as provincial and major superiors, presidents, or other titles, depending on the community) of communities are members of the LCWR. Interview with Sr. Janet Roesener, CSJ, 10 December 1987, Silver Spring, Maryland.

118. For an example of a misinterpretation of the ad's claims, see the editorial in *National Catholic Reporter*, 28 December 1984, p. 10.

119. Patricia Wittberg, "Feminist Consciousness Among American Nuns: Patterns of Ideological Diffusion," *Women's Studies International Forum* 12 (1989): 529–537.

120. On the growth of feminist themes in the LCWR, see, e.g., Sr. Marion L. Carr, PVBM (Communications Director, LCWR), to members of LCWR, 6 March 1974, Boyle Collection, Box 42, Folder 10; Weaver, *New Catholic Women*, pp. 83–89. On the Task Force, see LCWR, *1987 Conference Report* (Silver Spring, Md.: LCWR), pp. 9, 19.

121. An interesting example appeared when the SCR published Paul's 1971 *Evangelica Testificatio*, which clearly intended to prohibit some of the more far-reaching interpretations of renewal. The LCWR replied with a book of essays titled *Widening the Dialogue* (1974), the title and content a clear statement that the conference would accept papal statements affecting women religious not as the end of discussion, but only the beginning.

122. Weaver, *New Catholic Women*, pp. 106–107.

123. Boyle Collection, Box 71, Folder 3.

124. LCWR, *1987 Conference Report*; interview with Bishop William K. Weigand, 9 December 1987, Washington, D.C.

125. Neal, *Catholic Sisters in Transition*, p. 65.

126. *Origins*, 30 August 1990, p. 187.

127. See, e.g., the political resolutions of the LCWR 1972 Annual Assembly, "Official Minutes of Business Meetings," 28 pages, Boyle Collection, Box 42, Folder 10. For some community examples of social justice concerns, see Sisters of the Precious Blood (based in Dayton, Ohio), "Perspectives #5" (Ordinances of the Special General Chapter, August 1969), Boyle Collection, Box 82, Folder 9; Sr. Mary Therese McCarthy to "Dear Sisters" (members of the Adrian Dominicans), 26 April 1972, and McCarthy, "Apostolic Program," 11 August 1970, both in Boyle Collection, Box 73, Folder 6; "Report of the General Government to the General Chapter of the Sisters of St. Joseph [of Brentwood, New York]," pp. 45, 51–52, July 1974, Boyle Collection, Box 76, Folder 14.

128. See, e.g., Marie Augusta Neal, SnD de N, "A Theoretical Analysis of Renewal in Religious Orders in the U.S.A.," *Social Compass* 18, 1 (1971): 7–25.

129. The Pontifical Commission on Latin America proposed that all religious communities of the United States work in the 1960s toward contributing up to 10 percent of their members to Latin American missions. Between 1961 and 1964, the number of U.S. sisters in Latin America had increased 55 percent, although it still represented less than 2 percent of all

American sisters. CMSW, "Latin America Survey, 1963–64," 2-page mimeo, LCWR Collection, Box 10, Folder 9. See also three 1961 letters from Mother M. Florence, SL (Executive Secretary, CMSW), LCWR Collection, Box 1, Folder 16.

130. Sr. Nadine Foley, OP, "...And Miles to Go"; Sr. Barbara Thomas, SCN, "Living the Promises," address to LCWR National Assembly, August 1975, St. Paul, Minn., Masterman Collection, Box 3, Folder 7; Sr. Mary Daniel Turner, SND de N, "Promises to Keep," address to LCWR Assembly, August 1975, St. Paul, Minnesota, Masterman Collection, Box 3, Folder 7.

The 1973 addresses by Câmara and the retiring and incoming presidents (Sr. Margaret Brennan, IHM, and Sr. Francis Borgia Rothluebber, OSF, respectively), all addressing liberation themes, are in the Boyle Collection, Box 41; Câmara's and Brennan's are in Folder 3, Rothluebber's in Folder 4. Rothluebber made reference to a presentation on women and oppression at the 1972 assembly that contained similar liberation themes.

131. R. Lorentzen, "Women in the Sanctuary Movement: A Case Study in Chicago," presented at the joint annual meeting of the Society for the Scientific Study of Religion and Religious Research Association, Salt Lake City, Utah, 1989.

132. See Neal, *Catholic Sisters in Transition*, p. 27; Sr. Marie Augusta Neal, SND de N, "Implications of the Sisters' Survey for Structural Renewal."

CHAPTER SEVEN

1. See the Glossary entry for *liberation Catholicism*. There are, of course, many Catholics, both laity and Church personnel, who are receptive to some liberation themes but not others or who support the politics but do not support or understand the theology. For sociological purposes, liberation is best thought of as a new set of themes, and a new activism, that has penetrated different sectors of the Latin American Church to varying degrees. It is certainly not the dominant perspective there.

2. Scott Mainwaring, "Grass-Roots Catholic Groups and Politics in Brazil," in *The Progressive Church in Latin America*, ed. Scott Mainwaring and Alexander Wilde (Notre Dame, Ind.: University of Notre Dame Press, 1989), pp. 160–161.

3. Scott Mainwaring and Alexander Wilde, "The Progressive Church in Latin America: An Interpretation," in ibid., pp. 13–14, 26.

4. While there are a number of different religious ideas grouped together as "liberation theology" (see, e.g., Deane William Ferm, *Third World Liberation Theologies: An Introductory Survey* [Maryknoll, N.Y.: Orbis, 1986]), the theological distinctions are not important for the purposes of this book.

5. See, e.g., Enrique Dussel, *A History of the Church in Latin America: Colonialism to Liberation* (Grand Rapids, Mich.: Eerdmans, 1981); Phillip Berryman, *Liberation Theology: Essential Facts About the Revolutionary Movement in Latin America—and Beyond* (Philadelphia: Temple University Press, 1987); Thomas C. Bruneau, *The Church in Brazil: The Politics of Religion* (Austin: University of Texas Press, 1982).

6. David Stoll, *Is Latin America Turning Protestant? The Politics of Evangelical Growth* (Berkeley and Los Angeles: University of California Press, 1989), p. 6.

7. Berryman, *Liberation Theology*, pp. 11–12; see also Brian H. Smith, *The Church and Politics in Chile: Challenges to Modern Catholicism* (Princeton, N.J.: Princeton University Press, 1982), p. 61.

8. Smith, *The Church and Politics in Chile*, p. 55.

9. *Origins*, 28 March 1991, p. 683. For some other factors that may also have contributed to low recruitment of clergy and religious, see Ralph Della Cava, "Catholicism and Society in Twentieth-Century Brazil," *Latin American Research Review* 11 (1976): 7–50; Scott Mainwaring, *The Catholic Church and Politics in Brazil, 1916–1985* (Stanford, Calif.: Stanford University Press, 1986), p. 25; and Penny Lernoux, *Cry of the People* (Harmondsworth: Penguin, 1982), pp. 388–389.

Pope John XXIII attempted to deal with the problem by calling for U.S. religious orders to send up to 10 percent of their personnel to Latin America, but only a small fraction of that number were ever sent (Della Cava, "Catholicism and Society," pp. 23–24; see also the discussion on this point in chapter 6 of this book). The *Origins* article cited previously suggests Rome will make a new effort focusing on priests.

10. Bruneau, *The Church in Brazil*, pp. 12–14.

11. Ivan Vallier, *Catholicism, Social Control, and Modernization in Latin America* (Englewood Cliffs, N.J.: Prentice-Hall, 1970), pp. 23–28; Smith, *The Church and Politics in Chile*, p. 68.

12. J. Lloyd Mecham, *Church and State in Latin America: A History of Politico-Ecclesiastical Relations*, rev. ed. (Chapel Hill: University of North Carolina Press, 1966), p. 348ff.; Dussel, *A History of the Church in Latin America*, p. 103.

13. Mecham, ibid., pp. 410–414; *New York Times*, 15 February 1990, 6 May 1990. There are signs that Mexico's current president, Carlos Salinas de Gortari, will attempt to institutionalize a more truly liberal church-state relationship.

14. There are, of course, other examples (e.g., Guatemala and Paraguay) where, even if other conditions were right, historically it would have been very risky for the hierarchy to attempt too strident and sustained a criticism of the government.

15. Lernoux, *Cry of the People*, pp. 353–356.

16. Daniel H. Levine, *Religion and Politics in Latin America: The Catholic Church in Venezuela and Colombia* (Princeton, N.J.: Princeton University Press, 1981).

17. Ibid., pp. 56–72, 159–161. Another national Church that appears to be institutionally weak and therefore fairly inactive is the Bolivian Church. There is a contrast, however, in that the Bolivian Church has not experienced quite the degree of church-state separation as has Venezuela's (Mecham, *Church and State in Latin America*, pp. 179–190).

18. Levine, ibid.

19. Mecham, *Church and State in Latin America*, pp. 160–178, 225–251; Pablo Richard, *Death of Christendoms, Birth of the Church*, trans. Phillip Berryman (Maryknoll, N.Y.: Orbis, 1987), pp. 92–107.

20. Smith, *The Church and Politics in Chile*, p. 69.

21. Levine, *Religion and Politics in Latin America*, pp. 70–71.

22. Ibid.

23. Ellen Kay Trimberger, *Revolution from Above: Military Bureaucrats and Development in Japan, Turkey, Egypt and Peru* (New Brunswick, N.J.: Transaction, 1978).

24. Catalina Romero, "The Peruvian Church: Change and Continuity," in *The Progressive Church in Latin America*, ed. Mainwaring and Wilde, pp. 253–275; Luis Pásara, "Peru: The Leftist Angels," in *The Progressive Church in Latin America*, ed. Mainwaring and Wilde, pp. 276–325.

25. Berryman, *Liberation Theology*, p. 21; Michael Dodson, "Commentary on Mainwaring: Comparing the 'Popular Church' in Nicaragua and Brazil," *Journal of Interamerican Studies and World Affairs* 26 (1984): 131–136.

26. Smith, *The Church and Politics in Chile*, pp. 54–61, 98–99; Brian H. Smith, "Chile: Deepening the Alliance of Working-Class Sectors to the Church in the 1970s," in *Religion and Political Conflict in Latin America*, ed. Daniel H. Levine (Chapel Hill: University of North Carolina Press, 1986), p. 161; Edward L. Cleary, O.P., *Crisis and Change: The Church in Latin America Today* (Maryknoll, N.Y.: Orbis, 1985), p. 128.

27. Mecham, *Church and State in Latin America*, pp. 201–224.

28. It is interesting to note, however, that the avoidance of identification with particular parties in particular was also due to Vatican directive. Pope Pius XI and his secretaries of state, including the future Pius XII, had apparently learned from experiences such as in Mexico that attempting to retain church-state alliance was often counterproductive. Nevertheless, the Vatican told the Chilean government that in principle the Church was opposed to church-state separation. Remember that at this time as well, Pius XI was encouraging Catholic Action movements (rather than the Catholic parties that were less subject to hierarchical control), and he hoped for a reestablishment of church-state alliance under Italian fascism.

Not being a proponent of liberal democracy, he was quite happy to avoid and discourage Church identification with particular political parties (Smith, *The Church and Politics in Chile*, pp. 70–81).

29. Ibid., pp. 70–83.

30. Ibid., pp. 98–105.

31. Virginia Marie Bouvier, *Alliance or Compliance: Implications of the Chilean Experience for the Catholic Church in Latin America* (Syracuse, N.Y.: Maxwell School of Citizenship and Public Affairs, Syracuse University, 1983), p. 23.

32. Smith, *The Church and Politics in Chile*, pp. 111–112.

33. Ibid., pp. 93, 106–111, 133.

34. Stoll, *Is Latin America Turning Protestant?* pp. 8–9.

35. Smith, *The Church and Politics in Chile*, p. 111.

36. Bouvier, *Alliance or Compliance*, p. 35.

37. Smith, *The Church and Politics in Chile*, pp. 134–135, 147–148, 174, 186–196.

38. Ibid., p. 287ff.

39. Ibid., pp. 137, 142, 148; Cleary, *Crisis and Change*, pp. 127–128.

40. Daniel H. Levine, "Religion, Society, and Politics: States of the Art" (Review Essay), *Latin American Research Review* 16, 3 (1981): 186, 188.

41. Smith, "Chile," pp. 163–166.

42. Ibid., p. 173.

43. Smith, *The Church and Politics in Chile*, p. 33.

44. Ibid., pp. 341–342.

45. Smith, "Chile," pp. 176–179.

46. Bruneau, *The Church in Brazil*; Bruneau, "Brazil: The Catholic Church and Basic Christian Communities," in *Religion and Political Conflict in Latin America*, ed. Levine, pp. 106–107; Mecham, *Church and State in Latin America*, pp. 270, 280.

47. For a fascinating, if extreme, example of loyalty to the local priest over the episcopacy in the Brazilian Northeast in the late nineteenth century, see Ralph Della Cava, *Miracle at Joseiro* (New York: Columbia University Press, 1970).

48. Bruneau, *The Church in Brazil*, pp. 17, 93.

49. Ibid., pp. 19–20; Della Cava, "Catholicism and Society," pp. 13–15.

50. Bruneau, ibid., pp. 47–48; Della Cava, ibid., p. 15.

51. Bruneau, ibid., pp. 50–51; Della Cava, ibid., pp. 32–33, 35–36; Mainwaring, *The Catholic Church and Politics in Brazil*, pp. 19, 48. It is interesting to note that according to a Vatican report in 1991, the Brazilian Northeast has the worst priest shortage in the world, suggesting a history of particularly weak Church ties to the population (*Origins*, 28 March 1991, p. 683).

52. Bruneau, ibid., p. 52.

53. Bruneau, *The Church in Brazil*; Mecham, *Church and State in Latin America*, pp. 270, 280–282; Cleary, *Crisis and Change*, pp. 127–128; Stoll, *Is Latin America Turning Protestant?* pp. 8–9.

54. Bruneau, ibid., p. 49.

55. Della Cava, "Catholicism and Society," p. 28.

56. Ibid., pp. 37–38.

57. Bruneau, *The Church in Brazil*, pp. 69–76; Mainwaring, *The Catholic Church and Politics in Brazil*, p. 15.

58. Ralph Della Cava, "The 'People's Church,' the Vatican and the Abertura" (unpublished paper, 1985).

59. Paolo Freire, *Pedagogy of the Oppressed* (New York: Continuum, 1970).

60. W. E. Hewitt, "The Influence of Social Class on Activity Preferences of Comunidades Eclesiais de Base (CEBs) in the Archdiocese of Sao Paulo," *Journal of Latin American Studies* 19 (1987): 141–156; Bruneau, *The Church in Brazil*.

61. Thomas C. Bruneau, "Basic Christian Communities in Latin America: Nature and Significance (especially in Brazil)," in *Churches and Politics in Latin America*, ed. Daniel H. Levine (Beverly Hills, Calif.: Sage, 1980), p. 225; Berryman, *Liberation Theology*, p. 63.

62. Bruneau, ibid., p. 225.

63. See, e.g., Smith, "Chile," p. 160; Mainwaring and Wilde, "The Progressive Church in Latin America," p. 6.

64. Levine, *Religion and Political Conflict in Latin America*, p. 199.

65. Mainwaring, *The Catholic Church and Politics in Brazil*, p. 16.

66. Ibid., p. 15.

67. Ibid., p. 21.

68. *New York Times*, 12 November 1989, 13 May 1990.

69. Mainwaring, *The Catholic Church and Politics in Brazil*, pp. 237–253; Della Cava, "The 'People's Church,' the Vatican and the Abertura."

70. See, e.g., Gustavo Gutiérrez, *A Theology of Liberation*, trans. and ed. Sr. Caridad Inda and John Eagleson (Maryknoll, N.Y.: Orbis, 1973), pp. 269–270; Juan Luis Segundo, *Liberation of Theology* (Maryknoll, N.Y.: Orbis, 1976), pp. 71–73; Leonardo Boff, *Church: Charism and Power*, trans. John W. Diercksmeier (New York: Crossroad, 1985), p. 27.

71. Paul Sigmund, *Liberation Theology at the Crossroads* (New York: Oxford University Press, 1990); Pásara, "Peru," pp. 291–312.

72. Levine, "Religion, Society, and Politics," p. 186.

73. Cleary, *Crisis and Change*, pp. 55–63; Dussel, *A History of the Church in Latin America*, p. 18.

74. Levine, *Religion and Politics in Latin America*, p. 30.

75. Archbishop Marcos McGrath, CSC, "The Puebla Final Document: Introduction and Commentary," in *Puebla and Beyond*, ed. John Eagleson and Philip Scharper (Maryknoll, N.Y.: Orbis, 1979), pp. 87–110.

76. Gutiérrez, *A Theology of Liberation*, pp. 8–9.

77. Smith, *The Church and Politics in Chile*, p. 26.

78. Berryman, *Liberation Theology*, p. 77.

79. In Claudia Carlen, IHM, ed., *The Papal Encyclicals. Vol. 5: 1958–1981* (Wilmington, N.C.: McGrath Publishing, 1981) pp. 183–201.

80. Berryman, *Liberation Theology*, p. 22.

81. See, e.g., Cleary, *Crisis and Change*, pp. 92–95; Ferm, *Third World Liberation Theologies*, pp. 7, 10–11; Gutiérrez, *A Theology of Liberation*, pp. 35, 134–135.

82. Levine, *Religion and Politics in Latin America*, p. 176; Berryman, *Liberation Theology*, pp. 22–24.

83. Berryman, ibid., pp. 98–99; Ferm, *Third World Liberation Theologies*, pp. 54–55; Lernoux, *Cry of the People*, pp. 413–414; Mainwaring, *The Catholic Church and Politics in Brazil*, pp. 243–244; Smith, *The Church and Politics in Chile*, pp. 249–253.

84. John Eagleson and Philip Scharper, eds., *Puebla and Beyond* (Maryknoll, N.Y.: Orbis, 1979).

85. On the communication scheme, see McGrath, "The Puebla Final Document."

86. Ibid., pp. 101–102.

87. Levine, "Religion, Society, and Politics," p. 192.

88. Boff, *Church: Charism and Power*, pp. 26–27.

89. Reprinted in Juan Luis Segundo, *Theology and the Church: A Response to Cardinal Ratzinger and a Warning to the Whole Church* (Minneapolis: Winston/Seabury, 1985), pp. 169–188.

90. Ibid., p. 154.

91. Ibid., pp. 4–5.

92. Bruneau, "Basic Christian Communities in Latin America"; Bruneau, *The Church in Brazil*, pp. 127–145; Leonardo Boff, *Ecclesiogenesis: The Base Communities Reinvent the Church*, trans. Robert R. Barr (Maryknoll, N.Y.: Orbis, 1986).

93. Della Cava, "The 'People's Church,' the Vatican and the Abertura."

94. Smith, *The Church and Politics in Chile*, p. 42; Dodson, "Commentary on Mainwaring," p. 33; Phillip Berryman, "Commentary on Mainwaring: Basismo and the Horizon of Change," *Journal of Interamerican Studies and World Affairs* 26 (1984): 125–129; Bouvier, *Alliance or Compliance*, pp. 21–22.

95. Dodson, ibid.

96. A useful source of information on the Nicaraguan episcopacy's stance during the revolution is Michael A. Gismondi, "Transformations in the Holy: Religious Resistance and Hegemonic Struggles in the Nicaraguan Revolution," *Latin American Perspectives* 13, 3 (1986): 13–36. See, however, my critique of his theoretical approach in chapter 8, note 4.

97. Smith, *The Church and Politics in Chile*, pp. 253–257.

98. Boff, *Church: Charism and Power* and *Ecclesiogenesis*.

99. Boff, *Church: Charism and Power*, pp. 32–46.

100. Boff, *Ecclesiogenesis*, pp. 76–97; Leonardo Boff, *The Maternal Face of God*, trans. Robert R. Barr and John W. Diercksmeier (San Francisco: Harper and Row, 1987).

101. Richard, *Death of Christendoms*, pp. 158–159.

102. Smith, *The Church and Politics in Chile*, pp. 30–33, 39–43, 140; Sr. Katherine Anne Gilfeather, MM, "Women Religious, the Poor, and the Institutional Church in Chile," in *Churches and Politics in Latin America*, ed. Levine, pp. 198–224.

103. On relations between the Vatican and liberation theologians, see Sigmund, *Liberation Theology at the Crossroads*, pp. 154–175.

104. Mainwaring, "Grass-Roots Catholic Groups," p. 157; see also Mainwaring and Wilde, "The Progressive Church in Latin America," p. 6.

105. Pásara, "Peru."

106. See, e.g., Craig Calhoun, *The Question of Class Struggle* (Chicago: University of Chicago Press, 1981); Ernesto Laclau and Chantal Mouffe, *Hegemony and Socialist Strategy* (London: Verso, 1985); Mark Traugott, *Armies of the Poor* (Princeton, N.J.: Princeton University Press, 1985); Ira Katznelson and Aristide R. Zolberg, eds., *Working-Class Formation* (Princeton, N.J.: Princeton University Press, 1986); Stoll, *Is Latin America Turning Protestant?* pp. 310–314.

107. See, e.g., Pásara, "Peru," p. 312.

108. Phillip Berryman (personal communication, 5 May 1988) believes that there was in the early 1970s a conscious decision within the network that would become "liberation theologians" to avoid the type of internal Church battles (e.g., over priestly celibacy and decentralization of the hierarchical structure) that threatened to divide the North American and European Churches. Effort could then be directed more exclusively toward advocacy for poor people. Berryman is one of the most knowledgeable North American observers of (and participants in) Latin American Catholic involvement in politics.

109. In Gutiérrez, *A Theology of Liberation*, pp. 122–123.

110. Mainwaring and Wilde, "The Progressive Church in Latin America," pp. 5, 19.

111. Juan Luis Segundo, *The Hidden Motives of Pastoral Action* (Maryknoll, N.Y.: Orbis, 1978).

112. Berryman, *Liberation Theology*, pp. 8, 141; see also Mainwaring and Wilde, "The Progressive Church in Latin America," pp. 8–9.

113. Gutiérrez, *A Theology of Liberation*, pp. 9–10, 104, 136–137; Ferm, *Third World Liberation Theologies*, pp. 34–35.

114. See, e.g., Ferm, ibid., pp. 35–36, 112–113; Segundo, *Liberation of Theology*, pp. 57–62.

115. Michael Dodson, "Liberation Theology and Christian Radicalism in Contemporary Latin America," *Journal of Latin American Studies* 11 (1979): 203–222; Pásara, "Peru."

116. Gustavo Gutiérrez, *Beber en su propio pozo* (Lima: CEP, 1983); Sigmund, *Liberation Theology at the Crossroads*, pp. 176–198.

117. See, e.g., Consejo Episcopal Latinoamericano, *Relaciones Iglesia-Estado* (Quito: Ediciones de la Pontificia Universidad Católica del Ecuador, 1987).

CHAPTER EIGHT

1. See, especially, Otto Maduro, *Religion and Social Conflicts* (Maryknoll, N.Y.: Orbis, 1982). I, however, reject a major assumption of Maduro's approach—that modes of production are necessarily a major determinant of ideological dynamics. My approach borrows more from Anthony Giddens, *The Constitution of Society: Outline of the Theory of Structuration* (Berkeley and Los Angeles: University of California Press, 1984).

2. Alan Wolfe developed a similar argument in *Whose Keeper? Social Science and Moral Obligation* (Berkeley and Los Angeles: University of California Press, 1989), pp. 231–232, although the argument is not a central component of his analysis.

3. Kristin Luker, *Abortion and the Politics of Motherhood* (Berkeley and Los Angeles: University of California Press, 1984),

4. For an example of the problems of attempting to explain religious ideology as a reflection of class interest, see Michael A. Gismondi, "Transformations in the Holy: Religious Resistance and Hegemonic Struggles in the Nicaraguan Revolution," *Latin American Perspectives* 13, 3 (1986): 13–36. Such an approach, which becomes functionalist, avoids explaining exactly why different contexts will lead religious groups at one time to uphold ruling class or state interests and other times to attack them. Gismondi attempted to explain such phenomena as hegemonic crises within Nicaraguan society. This explanation, besides being nonfalsifiable (because it finds evidence for class hegemony in both church-state alliance and church-state conflict), leaves unclear why the state would ever alienate a hierarchy whose ideology, he also claimed, is bourgeois.

Similarly, Michael Kearney ("Religion, Ideology, and Revolution in Latin America," *Latin American Perspectives* 13, 3 [1986]: 3–12) argued in functionalist fashion that "liberal secular reforms during this period [the mid-nineteenth century] were intended not to destroy the church as an institution but to reduce its power as an economic competitor while allowing it to fulfill its ideological functions as a mainstay of capitalist relations" (p. 6). Kearney did not explain why the Church should necessarily function as the ideological mainstay of powers that have precisely attacked the Church's privileges. His assumption that the hierarchy identifies with the bourgeois class is empirically wrong in a number of countries, as we have seen.

5. See, e.g., Scott Mainwaring and Alexander Wilde, "The Progressive Church in Latin America: An Interpretation," in *The Progressive Church in Latin America*, ed. Scott Mainwaring and Alexander Wilde (Notre Dame, Ind.: University of Notre Dame Press, 1989), p. 19.

6. See, e.g., Leo XIII, *Satis Cognitum*, in *The Papal Encyclicals. Vol. 2: 1878–1903*, ed. Claudia Carlen, IHM (Wilmington, N.C.: McGrath Publishing, 1981), pp. 388–389; and Leo XIII, *Divinum Illud Munus*, in *The Papal Encyclicals. Vol. 2: 1878–1903*, ed. Carlen, p. 412.

7. R. Stephen Warner, "Change and Continuity in the U.S. Religious System: Perspectives from Sociology" (Paper presented at Princeton Theological Seminary, Princeton, New Jersey, 6 February 1989); John Seidler and Katherine Meyer, *Conflict and Change in the Catholic Church* (New Brunswick, N.J.: Rutgers University Press, 1989), pp. 139–142.

8. Roger Finke and Rodney Stark, "Religious Economies and Sacred Canopies: Religious Mobilization in American Cities, 1906," *American Sociological Review* 53 (1988): 41–49.

9. A. M. Rosenthal, "The Cardinal's Crusade," *New York Times*, 17 June 1990.

10. See *New York Times*, 1 October 1989, 22 and 23 April 1990, 10 May 1990.

11. See, e.g., Daniel H. Levine, *Religion and Politics in Latin America: The Catholic Church in Venezuela and Colombia* (Princeton, N.J.: Princeton University Press, 1981).

12. Phillip Berryman, *Liberation Theology: Essential Facts About the Revolutionary Movement in Latin America—and Beyond* (Philadelphia: Temple University Press, 1987).

Glossary

Note: I indicate in this Glossary when terms are my own constructions—i.e., not to be found in official Catholic Church terminology.

canon law: Catholic Church rules about internal institutional processes; e.g., disciplinary procedures for all Church personnel.

Church: when capitalized, refers specifically to the Catholic Church. I capitalize for ease and clarity of reference and imply nothing about the Catholic Church's status relative to other churches.

clergy: ordained Catholic Church personnel (priests, bishops, cardinals, and popes). Although from many perspectives it is reasonable to consider "Catholic Church personnel" to be equivalent to "Catholic clergy," I do not mean the terms to be synonymous. The Second Vatican Council appeared to exclude all women—even women religious—from the "clergy." This terminology is useful for my purposes, especially for chapter 6, because it emphasizes the boundary that denies certain Church privileges to all women.

community: the term I use to refer to a group of women religious who live under the same constitutions; i.e., the rules governing daily life in their community, their type of work (e.g., teaching, nursing, missionary), and their relationship to the hierarchy. Women may be members of the same community, yet live in different convents or even different countries. Two sisters may also both be members of a historically identified order (e.g., the Franciscans), have the same initials after their names (e.g., for Franciscans, OSF), yet be members of different communities because they belong to different federations of Franciscan convents, with different constitutions.

ecumenical council: a meeting of the world's Catholic bishops that can make official doctrinal pronouncements. Such councils often signal important developments or crises within the Church and/or attempts by a pope (who has the authority to call a council) to mobilize support for his positions. They are rare events, averaging about one a century; the most recent have been the First Vatican Council (1869–1870) and the Second Vatican Council (1962–1965), more commonly known as Vatican I and Vatican II.

employees: the term I use to refer to persons who earn salaries or wages from the Church much as they might in any secular job. That is, they could leave their jobs without having to renounce vows. Among those included are consultants, administrators, and secretaries. (Cf. *personnel.*)

episcopacy: those bishops who work within dioceses (thus for example, excluding bishops who work in the Vatican bureaucracy). Thus "episcopacy" is a subset of "hierarchy," which is a subset of "clergy," which is a subset of "Catholic Church personnel."

ethics: the term I use to refer to the moral principles that guide sociopolitical pronouncements from popes and bishops. Popes and bishops themselves indeed refer to these as moral principles, but confusion results from the fact that the hierarchy also uses the term *faith and morals*, which excludes sociopolitical issues. Thus I refer to the ethical, not the moral, principles of sociopolitical pronouncements.

faith and morals: Catholic ideology concerning the faith and morals of individuals and families. (Cf. *ethics.*)

hierarchy: bishops (including assistant bishops and similar offices), top officials of the Vatican bureaucracy (who are almost always also bishops of at least honorary, i.e., "titular," status), and popes. (Cf. *episcopacy, clergy.*)

liberalism: a general perspective and/or social system emphasizing separation of powers and individual autonomy. Throughout this book, I use the term *liberalism* not in its contemporary sense of a moderately left-of-center perspective, but in its classical sense. Liberalism was not simply one movement, but a number of more or less similar trends associated with the rise of bourgeois classes and modern states, which affected the Catholic Church throughout Europe. Liberal economics (in the form of capitalism), liberal politics (especially republican forms separating church and state), and liberal ideology (e.g., freedom of conscience, freedom of religious practice) all threatened the ancien régime privileges of the Church.

liberation Catholicism: my term to identify a perspective that interprets Catholic beliefs to necessitate a commitment to leftist social activism (i.e., praxis), popular especially in Latin America; equivalent to what some call the "progressive Church." More commonly people speak of "liberation theology," but many of the relevant Catholic activists are not interested in abstract theology. Those who are indeed so interested I of course refer to as liberation theologians.

liberation theology/theologians: see *liberation Catholicism.*

national Church: a branch of the Catholic Church in a particular country; e.g., the U.S. Catholic Church or the Brazilian Catholic Church.

nuns: see *sisters.*

personnel: the term I use to refer to those Catholics who explicitly take formal vows that pledge their entire lives toward participation in the Catholic Church; e.g., members of religious orders, priests, bishops. (Cf. *employees, clergy.*)

primate: the officially recognized leader of the episcopacy, and thus of the Church, in a particular country. Not all countries have or ever have had primates. The United States has never had an official primate.

religious: used as a noun or an adjective to refer to all women and men in religious orders; e.g., the Benedictines, Franciscans, Jesuits. This includes all sisters and all nuns. Male religious can be priests or (nonordained) brothers. Religious priests are a minority among American priests; most U.S. priests are "secular" in Church terminology, mainly indicating that they work in dioceses and are under the direct jurisdiction of their bishop only, not of the superiors of a religious order.

sisters: those women who have taken vows within the Church (or intend to take vows) and are not in contemplative orders but instead are engaged in teaching, nursing, parish administration, etc. Sisters are commonly known as "nuns," but I follow official Church terminology in which nuns are those women who belong to contemplative orders. (Cf. *women religious.*)

sociopolitical issues: my term to refer to issues of macropolitics and economics; i.e., issues most commonly thought of as matters of state policy. They are generally less binding within Catholic doctrine. I refer to them also as "temporal issues."

temporal issues: see *sociopolitical issues.*

women religious: a term, commonly used among Catholic Church personnel but not among the laity, that includes both sisters and nuns. (Note, however, that U.S. sisters' national organizations generally include in their names the term *women religious* even when the organizations represent only sisters.)

Bibliography

SERIALS

Christian Century
National Catholic Reporter
New York Times
Origins
Philadelphia Inquirer
Wall Street Journal

ARCHIVAL COLLECTIONS

Rev. Paul Boyle, CP, Papers, Archives of the University of Notre Dame
Leadership Conference of Women Religious Collection, Archives of the University of Notre Dame
Sr. Rose Eileen Masterman, CSC, Collection, Archives of the University of Notre Dame

BOOKS AND ARTICLES

Abbott, Walter M., S.J., ed. *The Documents of Vatican II*. Piscataway, N.J.: New Century, 1966.
Abell, Aaron I. *American Catholicism and Social Action: A Search for Social Justice, 1865–1950*. Garden City, N.Y.: Doubleday, 1960.
———. "The Reception of Leo XIII's Labor Encyclical in America, 1891–1919." *Review of Politics* 7 (1945): 464–495.
Agócs, Sandor. "Christian Democracy and Social Modernism in Italy During the Papacy of Pius X." *Church History* 42 (1973): 73–88.
Ahles, Sr. Mary Assumption, OSF. *In the Shadow of His Wings: A History of the Franciscan Sisters*. St. Paul, Minn.: North Central Publishing, 1977.
Arjomand, Said Amir. "Iran's Islamic Revolution in Comparative Perspective." *World Politics* 38 (1986): 383–414.
Arnal, Oscar L. "Why the French Christian Democrats Were Condemned." *Church History* 49 (1980): 188–202.

Bachrach, Peter, and Morton S. Baratz. *Power and Poverty: Theory and Practice.* New York: Oxford University Press, 1970.

Benestad, J. Brian. *The Pursuit of a Just Social Order: Policy Statements of the U.S. Catholic Bishops, 1966–80.* Washington, D.C.: Ethics and Public Policy Center, 1982.

Benestad, J. Brian, and Francis J. Butler, eds. *Quest for Justice: A Compendium of Statements of the United States Catholic Bishops on the Political and Social Order, 1966–1980.* Washington, D.C.: United States Catholic Conference, 1981.

Berryman, Phillip. "Commentary on Mainwaring: Basismo and the Horizon of Change." *Journal of Interamerican Studies and World Affairs* 26 (1984): 125–129.

———. *Liberation Theology: Essential Facts About the Revolutionary Movement in Latin America—and Beyond.* Philadelphia: Temple University Press, 1987.

Betten, Neil. *Catholic Activism and the Industrial Worker.* Gainesville: University Presses of Florida, 1976.

Boff, Leonardo. *Church: Charism and Power,* trans. John W. Diercksmeier. New York: Crossroad, 1985.

———. *Ecclesiogenesis: The Base Communities Reinvent the Church,* trans. Robert R. Barr. Maryknoll, N.Y.: Orbis, 1986.

———. *The Maternal Face of God,* trans. Robert R. Barr and John W. Diercksmeier. San Francisco: Harper and Row, 1987. (Originally published in Portuguese in 1979.)

Boli, John, Francisco O. Ramirez, and John W. Meyer. "Explaining the Origins and Expansion of Mass Education." *Comparative Education Review* 29 (1985): 145–170.

Boli-Bennett, John, and John W. Meyer. "The Ideology of Childhood and the State: Rules Distinguishing Children in National Constitutions, 1870–1970." *American Sociological Review* 43 (1978): 797–812.

Bouvier, Virginia Marie. *Alliance or Compliance: Implications of the Chilean Experience for the Catholic Church in Latin America.* Syracuse, N.Y.: Maxwell School of Citizenship and Public Affairs, Syracuse University, 1983.

Brennan, Joseph P. "Women in the Seminary: A Roman Catholic Perspective." *Theological Education* 11 (Winter 1975): 96–100.

Breunig, Charles. "The Condemnation of the *Sillon*: An Episode in the History of Christian-Democracy in France." *Church History* 26 (1957): 227–244.

Broderick, Francis L. "But Constitutions Can Be Changed...." *Catholic Historical Review* 49 (1963): 390–393.

———. "The Encyclicals and Social Action: Is John A. Ryan Typical?" *Catholic Historical Review* 55 (1969): 1–6.

Browne, Henry J. *The Catholic Church and the Knights of Labor.* New York: Arno, 1976. (Originally Washington, D.C.: Catholic University Press, 1949.)

———. "Peter E. Dietz, Pioneer Planner of Catholic Social Action." *Catholic Historical Review* 33 (1948): 448–456.

Bruneau, Thomas C. "Basic Christian Communities in Latin America: Their Nature and Significance (Especially in Brazil)." In *Churches and Politics in Latin America,* ed. Daniel H. Levine, pp. 225–237. Beverly Hills, Calif.: Sage, 1980.

———. "Brazil: The Catholic Church and Basic Christian Communities." In *Religion and Political Conflict in Latin America,* ed. Daniel H. Levine, pp. 106–123. Chapel Hill: University of North Carolina Press, 1986.

———. *The Church in Brazil: The Politics of Religion.* Austin: University of Texas Press, 1982.

Bukowczyk, John J. "Mary the Messiah: Polish Immigrant Heresy and the Malleable Ideology of the Roman Catholic Church, 1880–1930." *Journal of American Ethnic History* 4, 2 (Spring 1985): 5–32.

Bull, George. *Vatican Politics: At the Second Vatican Council, 1962–65.* London: Oxford University Press, 1966.

Butler, Cuthbert. *The Vatican Council: The Story Told from Inside in Bishop Ullathorne's Letters,* vol. 2. London: Longmans, Green, 1930.

Calhoun, Craig. *The Question of Class Struggle.* Chicago: University of Chicago Press, 1981.

Callahan, Daniel, ed. *The Catholic Case for Contraception.* London: Macmillan, 1969.

Camp, Richard L. *The Papal Ideology of Social Reform: A Study in Historical Development, 1878–1967.* Leiden: Brill, 1969.

Carlen, Claudia, IHM, ed. *The Papal Encyclicals,* 5 vols. Wilmington, N.C.: McGrath Publishing, 1981.

Carson, Clayborne. *In Struggle: SNCC and the Black Awakening of the 1960s.* Cambridge, Mass.: Harvard University Press, 1981.

Castelli, Jim. *The Bishops and the Bomb.* Garden City, N.Y.: Doubleday/Image, 1983.

Chadwick, Owen. *The Popes and European Revolution.* Oxford: Clarendon, 1981.

Chittister, Joan, OSB, et al. *Climb Along the Cutting Edge: An Analysis of Change in Religious Life.* New York: Paulist Press, 1977.

Cleary, Edward L., O.P. *Crisis and Change: The Church in Latin America Today.* Maryknoll, N.Y.: Orbis, 1985.

Coleman, John A. *The Evolution of Dutch Catholicism, 1958–1974.* Berkeley and Los Angeles: University of California Press, 1978.

Consejo Episcopal Latinoamericano (CELAM). *La iglesia en la actual transformación de América Latina a la luz del concilio.* Bogotá: CELAM, 1969.

———. *Relaciones Iglesia-Estado.* Quito: Ediciones de la Pontificia Universidad Católica del Ecuador, 1987.

Cooke, Sr. M. Francis, OSF. *His Love Heals: A History of the Hospital Sisters of the Third Order of St. Francis, Springfield, Illinois, 1875–1975.* Chicago: Franciscan Herald Press, 1977.

Cross, Robert D. *The Emergence of Liberal Catholicism in America.* Cambridge, Mass.: Harvard University Press, 1958.

Curran, Charles E. *American Catholic Social Ethics: Twentieth-Century Approaches.* Notre Dame, Ind.: University of Notre Dame Press, 1982.

———. "The Changing Anthropological Bases of Catholic Social Ethics." In Charles E. Curran, ed., *Directions in Social Ethics,* pp. 5–42. Notre Dame, Ind.: Notre Dame University Press, 1985.

———. *Faithful Dissent.* Kansas City, Mo.: Sheed and Ward, 1986.

———. "The Moral Methodology of the Bishops' Pastoral." In *Catholics and Nuclear War,* ed. Philip J. Murnion, pp. 45–56. New York: Crossroad, 1983.

Curran, Robert Emmett, S.J. "The McGlynn Affair and the Shaping of the New Conservatism in American Catholicism." *Catholic Historical Review* 66 (1980): 184–204.

Curry, Sr. Lois, OP. *Women After His Own Heart: The Sisters of Saint Dominic of the American Congregation of the Sacred Heart of Jesus, Caldwell, New Jersey, 1881–1981.* New York: New City Press, 1981.

Daly, Gabriel, O.S.A. *Transcendence and Immanence: A Study in Catholic Modernism and Integralism.* Oxford: Clarendon, 1980.

De Santis, Vincent P. "American Catholics and McCarthyism." *Catholic Historical Review* 51 (1965): 1–30.

De Soto, Hernando. *El otro sendero.* 2d ed. Lima: Editorial el Barranco, 1986.

DeChantal, Sr. M., CSFN. *Out of Nazareth: A Centenary of the Sisters of the Holy Family of Nazareth in the Service of the Church.* New York: Exposition Press, 1974.

Della Cava, Ralph. "Catholicism and Society in Twentieth-Century Brazil." *Latin American Research Review* 11 (1975): 7–50.

———. *Miracle at Joseiro.* New York: Columbia University Press, 1970.

———. "The 'People's Church,' the Vatican and the Abertura." Unpublished paper, 1985.

Denzinger, Henry, ed. *The Sources of Catholic Dogma*, trans. Roy J. Defarrari. St. Louis: Herder, 1957.

Dodson, Michael. "Commentary on Mainwaring: Comparing the 'Popular Church' in Nicaragua and Brazil." *Journal of Interamerican Studies and World Affairs* 26 (1984): 131–136.

———. "Liberation Theology and Christian Radicalism in Contemporary Latin America." *Journal of Latin American Studies* 11 (1979): 203–222.

Doely, Sarah Bentley, ed. *Women's Liberation and the Church: The New Demand for Freedom in the Life of the Church.* New York: Association Press, 1970.

Dolan, Jay P. *The American Catholic Experience.* Garden City, N.Y.: Doubleday, 1985.

Dorr, Donal. *Option for the Poor: A Hundred Years of Vatican Social Teaching.* Maryknoll, N.Y.: Orbis, 1983.

Dussel, Enrique. *A History of the Church in Latin America: Colonialism to Liberation.* Grand Rapids, Mich.: Eerdmans, 1981.

Eagleson, John, and Philip Scharper, eds. *Puebla and Beyond.* Maryknoll, N.Y.: Orbis, 1979.

Ehler, Sidney Z., and John B. Morrall, trans. and eds. *Church and State Through the Centuries.* Westminster, Md.: Newman, 1954.

Ellis, John Tracy. *American Catholicism.* Chicago: University of Chicago Press, 1956.

———. "Review Article: From the Enlightenment to the Present: Papal Policy Seen Through the Encyclicals." *Catholic Historical Review* 69 (1983): 51–58.

Engel-Janosi, Friedrich. "Austria and the Conclave of 1878." *Catholic Historical Review* 39 (1953): 142–166.

———. "The Roman Question in the First Years of Benedict XV." *Catholic Historical Review* 40 (1954): 269–285.

Evans, Sara M., and Harry C. Boyte. *Free Spaces: The Sources of Democratic Change in America.* New York: Harper and Row, 1986.

Falconi, Carlo. *The Popes in the Twentieth Century: From Pius X to John XXIII*, trans. Muriel Grindrod. Boston: Little, Brown, 1967.

———. *The Silence of Pius XII.* Boston: Little, Brown, 1970.

Ferm, Deane William. *Third World Liberation Theologies: An Introductory Survey.* Maryknoll, N.Y.: Orbis, 1986.

Finke, Roger, and Rodney Stark. "Religious Economies and Sacred Canopies: Religious Mobilization in American Cities, 1906." *American Sociological Review* 53 (1988): 41–49.

Finn, James. "American Catholics and Social Movements." In *Contemporary Catholicism in the United States*, ed. Philip Gleason, pp. 127–146. Notre Dame, Ind.: University of Notre Dame Press, 1969.

Flannery, Austin P., ed. *Vatican Council II: The Conciliar and Post Conciliar Documents*. Grand Rapids, Mich.: Eerdmans, 1984.

Flynn, George Q. "Franklin Roosevelt and the Vatican: The Myron Taylor Appointment." *Catholic Historical Review* 58 (1972): 171–194.

Fogarty, Gerald P., S.J. *The Vatican and the American Hierarchy from 1870 to 1965*. Stuttgart: Anton Hiersemann, 1982.

Fox, Thomas C. "Catholics Debate Papal Nuclear Shift." *Bulletin of the Atomic Scientists* 44, 4 (1988): 30–31.

Freire, Paulo. *Pedagogy of the Oppressed*. New York: Continuum, 1970.

Friedlander, Saul. *Pius XII and the Third Reich*. New York: Knopf, 1966.

Fuchs, Lawrence H. *John F. Kennedy and American Catholicism*. New York: Meredith, 1967.

Fulbrook, Mary. *Piety and Politics: Religion and the Rise of Absolutism in England, Württemberg and Prussia*. Cambridge: Cambridge University Press, 1983.

Gardiner, Anne Marie, S.S.N.D., ed. *Women and Catholic Priesthood: An Expanded Vision: Proceedings of the Detroit Ordination Conference*. New York: Paulist Press, 1976.

Gargan, Edward T., ed. *Leo XIII and the Modern World*. New York: Sheed and Ward, 1961.

Giddens, Anthony. *The Constitution of Society: Outline of the Theory of Structuration*. Berkeley and Los Angeles: University of California Press, 1984.

Gieryn, Thomas F. "Boundary-Work and the Demarcation of Science from Non-Science: Strains and Interests in Professional Ideologies of Scientists." *American Sociological Review* 48 (1983): 781–795.

Gieryn, Thomas F., George M. Bevins, and Stephen C. Zehr. "Professionalization of American Scientists: Public Science in the Creation/Evolution Trials." *American Sociological Review* 50 (1985): 392–495.

Gilfeather, Sr. Katherine Anne, MM. "Women Religious, the Poor, and the Institutional Church in Chile." In *Churches and Politics in Latin America*, ed. Daniel H. Levine, pp. 198–224. Beverly Hills, Calif.: Sage, 1980.

Gismondi, Michael A. "Transformations in the Holy: Religious Resistance and Hegemonic Struggles in the Nicaraguan Revolution." *Latin American Perspectives* 13, 3 (1986): 13–36.

Gitlin, Todd. *The Whole World Is Watching: Mass Media in the Making and Unmaking of the New Left*. Berkeley and Los Angeles: University of California Press, 1980.

Gladstone, W. E. *The Vatican Decrees in Their Bearing on Civil Allegiance*. New York: Harper and Brothers, 1875.

Glenn, Norval D., and Ruth Hyland. "Religious Preference and Worldly Success: Some Evidence from National Surveys." *American Sociological Review* 32 (1967): 73–85.

Gottemoeller, Doris, RSM, and Rita Hofbauer, GNSH. *Women and Ministry: Present Experience and Future Hopes.* Washington, D.C.: Leadership Conference of Women Religious, 1981.

Graham, Robert A., S.J. *Vatican Diplomacy: A Study of Church and State on the International Plane.* Princeton, N.J.: Princeton University Press, 1959.

Greeley, Andrew. *American Catholics Since the Council.* Chicago: Thomas More Press, 1985.

Griffin, Leslie. "The Integration of Spiritual and Temporal: Contemporary Roman Catholic Church-State Theory." *Theological Studies* 48 (1987): 225–257.

Guilday, Rev. Peter, ed. *The National Pastorals of the American Hierarchy (1792–1919).* Westminster, Md.: Newman Press, 1954. (Originally published 1923.)

Gutiérrez, Gustavo. *Beber en su propio pozo.* Lima: CEP, 1983. (English translation: *We Drink from Our Own Wells.* Maryknoll, N.Y.: Orbis, 1984.)

———. *A Theology of Liberation,* trans. and ed. Sr. Caridad Inda and John Eagleson. Maryknoll, N.Y.: Orbis, 1973.

Hales, E. E. Y. *The Catholic Church in the Modern World.* London: Eyre and Spottiswoode, 1958.

———. *Pio Nono.* London: Eyre, 1954.

———. *Pope John and His Revolution.* Garden City, N.Y.: Doubleday, 1965.

Halperin, S. William. *Italy and the Vatican at War: A Study of Their Relations from the Outbreak of the Franco-Prussian War to the Death of Pius IX.* Chicago: University of Chicago Press, 1939.

Hanna, Mary T. *Catholics and American Politics.* Cambridge, Mass.: Harvard University Press, 1979.

Hanson, Eric O. *The Catholic Church in World Politics.* Princeton, N.J.: Princeton University Press, 1987.

Harrigan, William M. "Nazi Germany and the Holy See, 1933–1936: The Historical Background of *Mit brennender Sorge.*" *Catholic Historical Review* 47 (1961): 166–198.

Harrison, Paul M. *Authority and Power in the Free Church Tradition.* Carbondale: Southern Illinois University Press, 1959.

Hebblethwaite, Peter. *In the Vatican.* Bethesda, Md.: Adler and Adler, 1986.

———. *Pope John XXIII: Shepherd of the Modern World.* Garden City, N.Y.: Doubleday, 1985.

Heckel, Rev. Roger, S.J. *The Social Teaching of John Paul II,* vols. 1 and 8. Vatican City: Pontifical Commission "Iustitia et Pax," 1980.

Heft, James L., S.M. "From the Pope to the Bishops: Episcopal Authority from Vatican I to Vatican II." In *The Papacy and the Church in the United States,* ed. Bernard Cooke, pp. 55–78. New York: Paulist Press, 1989.

Hennesey, James, S.J. *American Catholics: A History of the Roman Catholic Community in the United States.* New York: Oxford University Press, 1981.

———. *The First Council of the Vatican: The American Experience.* New York: Herder and Herder, 1963.

Hewitt, W. E. "The Influence of Social Class on Activity Preferences of Comunidades Eclesiais de Base (CEBs) in the Archdiocese of Sao Paulo." *Journal of Latin American Studies* 19 (1987): 141–156.

Hilgartner, Stephen. "Constructing the Public Agenda." Paper presented at the annual meeting of the American Sociological Association, Washington, D.C., August 1990.

Hitchcock, James. *Catholicism and Modernity: Confrontation or Capitulation?* New York: Seabury, 1979.

———. *The Decline and Fall of Radical Catholicism.* New York: Herder and Herder, 1971.

Hoffman, Pat. *Ministry of the Dispossessed: Learning from the Farm Worker Movement.* Los Angeles: Wallace Press, 1987.

Hollenbach, David. "*The Challenge of Peace* in the Context of Recent Church Teachings." In *Catholics and Nuclear War*, ed. Philip J. Murnion, pp. 3–15. New York: Crossroad, 1983.

Hornsby-Smith, Michael P., and Raymond M. Lee. *Roman Catholic Opinion: A Study of Roman Catholics in England and Wales in the 1970s.* Guildford: University of Surrey, 1979.

Hornsby-Smith, Michael P., Raymond M. Lee, and Peter A. Reilly. "Social and Religious Change in Four English Roman Catholic Parishes." *Sociology* 18 (1984): 353–365.

Huber, Raphael M., S.T.D., O.F.M.Conv., ed. *Our Bishops Speak, 1919–1951.* Milwaukee: Bruce, 1952.

Hunt, Lynn. *Politics, Culture, and Class in the French Revolution.* Berkeley and Los Angeles: University of California Press, 1984.

Jablonski, Carol J. "Rhetoric, Paradox, and the Movement for Women's Ordination in the Roman Catholic Church." *Quarterly Journal of Speech* 74 (1988): 164–183.

Jemolo, A. C. *Church and State in Italy, 1850–1950*, trans. David Moore. Philadelphia: Dufour, 1960.

Johnson, Paul. *Pope John Paul II and the Catholic Restoration.* New York: St. Martin's Press, 1981.

Jones, Gareth Stedman. *Languages of Class: Studies in English Working Class History, 1832–1932.* Cambridge: Cambridge University Press, 1983.

Katznelson, Ira, and Aristide R. Zolberg, eds. *Working-Class Formation.* Princeton, N.J.: Princeton University Press, 1986.

Kearney, Michael. "Religion, Ideology, and Revolution in Latin America." *Latin American Perspectives* 13, 3 (1986): 3–12.

Kelly, Msgr. George A. *The Battle for the American Church.* Garden City, N.Y.: Doubleday/Image, 1981.

Kelly, James. "Ecumenism and Abortion: A Case Study of Pluralism, Privatization and the Public Conscience." *Review of Religious Research* 30 (1989): 225–235.

Kennedy, Eugene. *Re-Imagining American Catholicism: The American Bishops and Their Pastoral Letters.* New York: Vintage, 1985.

Kent, George O. "Pope Pius XII and Germany: Some Aspects of German-Vatican Relations." *American Historical Review* 70 (1964): 59–78.

Kerwin, Jerome G. *Catholic Viewpoint on Church and State.* Garden City, N.Y.: Hanover House/Doubleday, 1960.

Kingdon, John W. *Agendas, Alternatives, and Public Policies.* Boston: Little, Brown, 1984.

Koester, Sr. Mary Camilla, PCC. *Into This Land: A Centenary History of the Cleveland Poor Clare Monastery of the Blessed Sacrament.* Cleveland: Robert J. Liederbach, 1980.

Kolbenschlag, Madonna, ed. *Between God and Caesar: Priests, Sisters and Political Office in the United States.* New York: Paulist Press, 1985.

Kolmer, Elizabeth, ASC. *Religious Women in the United States: A Survey of Influential Literature from 1950 to 1983.* Wilmington, Del.: Michael Glazier, 1984.

Krasner, Stephen D. "Review Article: Approaches to the State." *Comparative Politics* 16 (1984): 223–246.

Küng, Hans. "Cardinal Ratzinger, Pope Wojtyla, and Fear at the Vatican: An Open Word After a Long Silence." In *The Church in Anguish: Has the Vatican Betrayed Vatican II?* ed. Hans Küng and Leonard Swidler, pp. 58–74. San Francisco: Harper and Row, 1987.

Kurtz, Lester R. "The Politics of Heresy." *American Journal of Sociology* 88 (1983): 1085–1115.

———. *The Politics of Heresy: The Modernist Crisis in Roman Catholicism.* Berkeley and Los Angeles: University of California Press, 1986.

Laclau, Ernesto, and Chantal Mouffe. *Hegemony and Socialist Strategy.* London: Verso, 1985.

Leadership Conference of Women Religious. *Widening the Dialogue: Reflection on "Evangelica Testificatio."* Ottawa: Canadian Religious Conference and Washington, D.C.: Leadership Conference of Women Religious, 1974.

Leo XIII, Pope. *Social Wellsprings: Fourteen Epochal Documents by Pope Leo XIII,* ed. Joseph Husslein, S.J. Milwaukee: Bruce, 1940.

Lernoux, Penny. *Cry of the People.* Harmondsworth: Penguin, 1982.

Levine, Daniel H. *Religion and Politics in Latin America: The Catholic Church in Venezuela and Colombia.* Princeton, N.J.: Princeton University Press, 1981.

———. "Religion, Society, and Politics: States of the Art" (Review Essay). *Latin American Research Review* 16, 3 (1981): 185–209.

———, ed. *Churches and Politics in Latin America.* Beverly Hills, Calif.: Sage, 1980.

———, ed. *Religion and Political Conflict in Latin America.* Chapel Hill: University of North Carolina Press, 1986.

Lewy, Guenther. "Pius XII, the Jews and the German Catholic Church." In *The Storm over "The Deputy,"* ed. Eric Bentley, pp. 195–217. New York: Grove Press, 1964.

Lichten, Joseph L. *A Question of Judgement: Pius XII and the Jews.* Washington, D.C.: National Catholic Welfare Conference, 1963.

Lorentzen, R. "Women in the Sanctuary Movement: A Case Study in Chicago." Paper presented at the joint annual meeting of the Society for the Scientific Study of Religion and Religious Research Association, Salt Lake City, Utah, 1989.

Love, Thomas T. *John Courtney Murray: Contemporary Church-State Theory.* Garden City, N.Y.: Doubleday, 1965.

Luker, Kristin. *Abortion and the Politics of Motherhood.* Berkeley and Los Angeles: University of California Press, 1984.

Lukes, Steven. "Political Ritual and Social Integration." *Sociology* 9 (1975): 289–308.

———. *Power: A Radical View.* London: Macmillan, 1974.

———. "Power and Structure." In *Essays in Social Theory,* pp. 3–29. London: Macmillan, 1977.

Lyng, Stephen G., and Lester R. Kurtz. "Bureaucratic Insurgency: The Vatican and the Crisis of Modernism." *Social Forces* 63 (1985): 901–922.

Maduro, Otto. "New Marxist Approaches to the Relative Autonomy of Religion." *Sociological Analysis* 38 (1977): 359–367.

———. *Religion and Social Conflicts*, trans. Robert R. Barr. Maryknoll, N.Y.: Orbis, 1982.

Mainwaring, Scott. *The Catholic Church and Politics in Brazil, 1916–1985.* Stanford, Calif.: Stanford University Press, 1986.

———. "Grass-Roots Catholic Groups and Politics in Brazil." In *The Progressive Church in Latin America*, ed. Scott Mainwaring and Alexander Wilde, pp. 151–192. Notre Dame, Ind.: University of Notre Dame Press, 1989.

Mainwaring, Scott, and Alexander Wilde. "The Progressive Church in Latin America: An Interpretation." In *The Progressive Church in Latin America*, ed. Scott Mainwaring and Alexander Wilde, pp. 1–37. Notre Dame, Ind.: University of Notre Dame Press, 1989.

———, eds. *The Progressive Church in Latin America.* Notre Dame, Ind.: University of Notre Dame Press, 1989.

Mann, Michael. "The Social Cohesion of Liberal Democracy." *American Sociological Review* 35 (1970): 423–439.

Mannheim, Karl. *Ideology and Utopia*, trans. Louis Wirth and E.A. Shils. New York: Harcourt Brace Jovanovich, 1936.

Mara, Gerald. "Poverty and Justice: The Bishops and Contemporary Liberalism." In *The Deeper Meaning of Economic Life*, ed. R. Bruce Douglass, pp. 157–178. Washington, D.C.: Georgetown University Press, 1986.

Martin, Malachi. *The Jesuits: The Society of Jesus and the Betrayal of the Roman Catholic Church.* New York: Simon and Schuster/Linden, 1987.

Marx, Karl. *The Marx-Engels Reader*, ed. Robert Tucker, 2d ed. New York: Norton, 1978.

McAvoy, Thomas T. "Americanism, Fact and Fiction." *Catholic Historical Review* 31 (1945): 133–153.

———. *The Great Crisis in American Catholic History, 1895–1900.* Chicago: Regnery, 1957.

McClorey, John A., S.J. *The Catholic Church and Bolshevism.* St. Louis: Herder, 1931.

McCormick, Richard A., S.J. "*Laborem Exercens* and Social Morality." *Theological Studies* 43 (1982): 92–103.

McGrath, Archbishop Marcos, CSC. "The Puebla Final Document: Introduction and Commentary." In *Puebla and Beyond*, ed. John Eagleson and Philip Scharper, pp. 87–110. Maryknoll, N.Y.: Orbis, 1979.

McKeown, Elizabeth. "Apologia for an American Catholicism: The Petition and Report of the National Catholic Welfare Council to Pius XI, April 25, 1922." *Church History* 43 (1974): 514–528.

———. "The National Bishops' Conference: An Analysis of Its Origins." *Catholic Historical Review* 66 (1980): 565–583.

McNamara, Patrick H. "American Catholicism in the Mid-Eighties: Pluralism and Conflict in a Changing Church." *Annals of the American Academy of Political and Social Science* 480 (1985): 63–74.

McNeal, Patricia F. *The American Catholic Peace Movement, 1928–1972*. New York: Arno Press, 1978.

Mecham, J. Lloyd. *Church and State in Latin America: A History of Politico-Ecclesiastical Relations*, rev. ed. Chapel Hill: University of North Carolina Press, 1966.

Meconis, Charles A. *With Clumsy Grace: The American Catholic Left, 1961–1975*. New York: Seabury Press, 1979.

Merton, Robert K., and Elinor Barber. "Sociological Ambivalence." In Robert K. Merton, *Sociological Ambivalence and Other Essays*, pp. 3–31. New York: Free Press, 1976.

Meyer, John W., Francisco O. Ramirez, Richard Rubinson, and John Boli-Bennett. "The World Educational Revolution, 1950–1970." *Sociology of Education* 50 (1977): 242–258.

Modde, Sr. Mary Margaret, OSF. "A Canonical Study of the Leadership Conference of Women Religious of the United States of America." Ph.D. diss., Catholic University of America, 1977.

Moody, Joseph N. "The Church and the New Forces in Western Europe and Italy." In *Church and Society*, ed. Joseph N. Moody, pp. 21–92. New York: Arts, 1953.

———. "Leo XIII and the Social Crisis." In *Leo XIII and the Modern World*, ed. Edward T. Gargan, pp. 65–86. New York: Sheed and Ward, 1961.

———. "From Old Regime to Democratic Society." In *Church and Society*, ed. Joseph N. Moody, pp. 95–186. New York: Arts, 1953.

Moore, Maurice J. *Death of a Dogma? The American Catholic Clergy's Views of Contraception*. Chicago: Community and Family Study Center, University of Chicago, 1973.

Murnion, Philip J., ed. *Catholics and Nuclear War*. New York: Crossroad, 1983.

Murphy, Francis X., C.SS.R. *The Papacy Today*. New York: Macmillan, 1981.

Murray, John Courtney, S.J. "Leo XIII on Church and State: The General Structure of the Controversy." *Theological Studies* 14 (1953): 1–30.

National Conference of Catholic Bishops. *Building Economic Justice: The Bishops' Pastoral Letter and Tools for Action*. Washington, D.C.: United States Catholic Conference, 1987.

———. *The Challenge of Peace: God's Promise and Our Response*. Washington, D.C.: United States Catholic Conference, 1983.

———. *To Do the Work of Justice: A Plan of Action for the Catholic Community in the United States*. Washington, D.C.: United States Catholic Conference, 1978.

———. *Economic Justice for All: Pastoral Letter on Catholic Social Teaching and the U.S. Economy*. Washington, D.C.: United States Catholic Conference, 1986.

Neal, Marie Augusta, SND de N. *Catholic Sisters in Transition: From the 1960s to the 1980s*. Wilmington, Del.: Michael Glazier, 1984.

———. "A Theoretical Analysis of Renewal in Religious Orders in the U.S.A." *Social Compass* 18, 1 (1971): 7–25.

1984 Catholic Almanac, ed. Felician A. Foy, O.F.M. Huntington, Ind.: Our Sunday Visitor, 1983.

Nolan, Hugh J., ed. *Pastoral Letters of the American Hierarchy, 1792–1970*. Huntington, Ind.: Our Sunday Visitor, 1971.

Novak, Michael. *Moral Clarity in the Nuclear Age*. Nashville: Thomas Nelson, 1983.

O'Brien, David J. "American Catholics and American Society." In *Catholics and Nuclear War*, ed. Philip J. Murnion, pp. 16–29. New York: Crossroad, 1983.

———. *American Catholics and Social Reform: The New Deal Years*. New York: Oxford University Press, 1968.

———. "The Economic Thought of the American Hierarchy." In *The Catholic Challenge to the American Economy*, ed. Thomas M. Gannon, S.J., pp. 27–41. New York: Macmillan, 1987.

O'Connell, Marvin R. "Ultramontanism and Dupanloup: The Compromise of 1865." *Church History* 53 (1984): 200–217.

O'Connor, Rt. Rev. James. *Socialism*. Philadelphia: Catholic Truth Society, n.d.

O'Dwyer, Margaret M. *The Papacy in the Age of Napoleon and the Restoration*. Lanham, Md.: University Press of America, 1985.

Osgniach, Augustine J., O.S.B. *Must It Be Communism? A Philosophical Inquiry into the Major Issues of Today*. New York: Joseph F. Wagner, 1950.

O'Toole, James M. "'That Fabulous Churchman': Toward a Biography of Cardinal O'Connell." *Catholic Historical Review* 70 (1984): 28–44.

Overberg, Kenneth R. *An Inconsistent Ethic? Teachings of the American Catholic Bishops*. Lanham, Md.: University Press of America, 1980.

Pásara, Luis. "Peru: The Leftist Angels." In *The Progressive Church in Latin America*, ed. Scott Mainwaring and Alexander Wilde, pp. 276–325. Notre Dame, Ind.: University of Notre Dame Press, 1989.

Pawlikowski, Rev. John J. "Introduction to Rerum Novarum." In *Justice in the Marketplace: Collected Statements of the Vatican and the United States Catholic Bishops on Economic Policy, 1891–1984*, ed. David M. Byers, pp. 9–12. Washington, D.C.: United States Catholic Conference, 1985.

Pendergast, Sr. Mary Carita, SC. "Assessment of a Psychological Screening Program for Candidates to a Religious Congregation of Women." Ph.D. diss., Fordham University, 1968.

Peterson, Susan Carol. "The Presentation Sisters in South Dakota, 1880–1976." Ph.D. diss., Oklahoma State University, 1979.

Piehl, Mel. *Breaking Bread: The Catholic Worker and the Origin of Catholic Radicalism in America*. Philadelphia: Temple University Press, 1982.

Pius XI, Pope. *Social Wellsprings. Vol. 2: Eighteen Encyclicals of Social Reconstruction by Pope Pius XI*, ed. Joseph Husslein, S.J. Milwaukee: Bruce, 1942.

Pratt, Henry J. *The Liberalization of American Protestantism*. Detroit: Wayne State University Press, 1972.

Ratner, Ronnie Steinberg, and Paul Burstein. "Ideology, Specificity, and the Coding of Legal Documents: What Do Measures of Constitutional Content Measure?" *American Sociological Review* 45 (1980): 522–525.

Reese, Thomas J., ed. *Episcopal Conferences: Historical, Canonical, and Theological Studies*. Washington, D.C.: Georgetown University Press, 1989.

Reher, Margaret Mary. "Leo XIII and Americanism," *Theological Studies* 34 (1973): 679–689.

Rhodes, Anthony. *The Vatican in the Age of the Dictators, 1922–1945*. London: Hodder and Stoughton, 1973.

Richard, Pablo. *Death of Christendoms, Birth of the Church*, trans. Phillip Berryman. Maryknoll, N.Y.: Orbis, 1987.

Rizzo, Robert F. "Moral Debate on the Arms Race and Its Economic Implications." *International Journal of Social Economics* 14, 12 (1987): 19–30.

Romero, Catalina. "The Peruvian Church: Change and Continuity." In *The Progressive Church in Latin America*, ed. Scott Mainwaring and Alexander Wilde, pp. 253–275. Notre Dame, Ind.: University of Notre Dame Press, 1989.

Roohan, James Edmund. *American Catholics and the Social Question, 1865–1900.* New York: Arno Press, 1976.

Royal, Robert, ed. *Challenge and Response: Critiques of the Catholic Bishops' Draft Letter on the U.S. Economy.* Washington, D.C.: Ethics and Public Policy Center, 1985.

Ryan, John A. *A Living Wage: Its Ethical and Economic Aspects.* New York: Macmillan, 1906.

———. *Social Doctrine in Action: A Personal History.* New York: Harper and Brothers, 1941.

Rynne, Xavier. *The Fourth Session: The Debates and Decrees of Vatican Council II.* New York: Farrar, Straus and Giroux, 1966.

———. *Vatican Council II.* New York: Farrar, Straus and Giroux, 1968.

Salazar, Sr. Regina Clare, CSJ. "Changes in the Education of Roman Catholic Religious Sisters in the United States from 1952 to 1967." Ph.D. diss., University of Southern California, 1971.

Sanders, Thomas G. "The Politics of Catholicism in Latin America" (Review Essay). *Journal of Interamerican Studies and World Affairs* 24 (1982): 241–258.

Schall, James V., S.J., ed. *Out of Justice, Peace: Joint Pastoral Letter of the West German Bishops. Winning the Peace: Joint Pastoral Letter of the French Bishops.* San Francisco: Ignatius Press, 1984.

Schatz, Ronald W. "American Labor and the Catholic Church, 1919–1950." *U.S. Catholic Historian* 3 (1983): 178–190.

Schmandt, Raymond H. "The Life and Work of Leo XIII." In *Leo XIII and the Modern World*, ed. Edward T. Gargan, pp. 15–48. New York: Sheed and Ward, 1961.

Schneider, Mary. "The Transformation of American Women Religious: The Sister Formation Conference as Catalyst for Change (1954–1964)." Working Paper Series 17, no. 1. Notre Dame, Ind.: University of Notre Dame, Cushwa Center for the Study of American Catholicism, 1986.

Segundo, Juan Luis. *The Hidden Motives of Pastoral Action.* Maryknoll, N.Y.: Orbis, 1978.

———. *Liberation of Theology.* Maryknoll, N.Y.: Orbis, 1976.

———. *Theology and the Church: A Response to Cardinal Ratzinger and a Warning to the Whole Church.* Minneapolis: Winston/Seabury Press, 1985.

Seidler, John, and Katherine Meyer. *Conflict and Change in the Catholic Church.* New Brunswick, N.J.: Rutgers University Press, 1989.

Sewell, William H., Jr. "Ideologies and Social Revolutions: Reflections on the French Case." *Journal of Modern History* 57 (1985): 57–85.

Sheed, F. J. *Communism and Man.* New York: Sheed and Ward, 1939.

Sheen, Fulton J. *Communism and the Conscience of the West.* Indianapolis: Bobbs-Merrill, 1948.

———. *Liberty, Equality, and Fraternity.* New York: Macmillan, 1938.

Sigmund, Paul E. "The Catholic Tradition and Modern Democracy." In *Religion and Politics in the American Milieu*, ed. Leslie Griffin, pp. 3–21. Notre Dame, Ind.: Review of Politics and Office of Policy Studies, University of Notre Dame, n.d.

———. *Liberation Theology at the Crossroads: Democracy or Revolution?* New York: Oxford University Press, 1990.

Skocpol, Theda. "Cultural Idioms and Political Ideologies in the Revolutionary Reconstruction of State Power: A Rejoinder to Sewell." *Journal of Modern History* 57 (1985): 86–96.

———. "Rentier State and Shi'a Islam in the Iranian Revolution." *Theory and Society* 11 (1983): 265–283.

———. *States and Social Revolutions*. Cambridge: Cambridge University Press, 1979.

Smith, Brian H. "Chile: Deepening the Alliance of Working-Class Sectors to the Church in the 1970s." In *Religion and Political Conflict in Latin America*, ed. Daniel H. Levine, pp. 156–186. Chapel Hill: University of North Carolina Press, 1986.

———. *The Church and Politics in Chile: Challenges to Modern Catholicism*. Princeton, N.J.: Princeton University Press, 1982.

Smith, Elwyn A. "The Fundamental Church-State Tradition of the Catholic Church in the United States." *Church History* 38 (1969): 486–505.

Sodality Union of Washington, D.C. *Wolves in Sheep's Clothing*. Washington, D.C.: Sodality Union, 1937.

Stang, Rt. Rev. William. *Socialism and Christianity*. New York: Benziger Brothers, 1905.

Stoll, David. *Is Latin America Turning Protestant? The Politics of Evangelical Growth*. Berkeley and Los Angeles: University of California Press, 1989.

Storch, Neil T. "John Ireland and the Modernist Controversy." *Church History* 54 (1985): 353–365.

Swidler, Ann. "Culture in Action: Symbols and Strategies." *American Sociological Review* 51 (1986): 273–286.

Taves, Ann. "Context and Meaning: Roman Catholic Devotion to the Blessed Sacrament in Mid-Nineteenth-Century America." *Church History* 54 (1985): 482–495.

Tobin, Mary Luke, SL. "Women in the Church: Vatican II and After." *The Ecumenical Review* 37, 3 (1985): 295–305.

Tocqueville, Alexis de. *Democracy in America*, 2 vols. New York: Vintage/Knopf, 1945.

Traugott, Mark. *Armies of the Poor*. Princeton, N.J.: Princeton University Press, 1985.

Trimberger, Ellen Kay. *Revolution from Above: Military Bureaucrats and Development in Japan, Turkey, Egypt and Peru*. New Brunswick, N.J.: Transaction, 1978.

Vaillancourt, Jean-Guy. *Papal Power: A Study of Vatican Control over Lay Catholic Elites*. Berkeley and Los Angeles: University of California Press, 1980.

Vallier, Ivan. *Catholicism, Social Control, and Modernization in Latin America*. Englewood Cliffs, N.J.: Prentice-Hall, 1970.

Varacalli, Joseph A. "Social Change in the American Catholic Church." *Free Inquiry in Creative Sociology* 10, 2 (1982): 202–206.

———. *Toward the Establishment of Liberal Catholicism in America*. Lanham, Md.: University Press of America, 1983.

Verba, Sidney. "Sequences and Development." In *Crises and Sequences in Political Development*, ed. Leonard Binder et al., pp. 283–316. Princeton, N.J.: Princeton University Press, 1971.

Vidler, A. R. *A Century of Social Catholicism, 1820–1920.* London: S.P.C.K., 1964.

Wallace, Lillian Parker. *Leo XIII and the Rise of Socialism.* Durham, N.C.: Duke University Press, 1966.

Warner, R. Stephen. "Change and Continuity in the U.S. Religious System: Perspectives from Sociology." Paper presented at Princeton Theological Seminary, Princeton, N.J., 6 February 1989.

Weaver, Mary Jo. *New Catholic Women: A Contemporary Challenge to Traditional Religious Authority.* New York: Harper and Row, 1985.

Weber, Max. *The Theory of Social and Economic Organization*, ed. Talcott Parsons. New York: Free Press, 1964.

Weigel, George. *Tranquillitas Ordinis: The Present Failure and Future Promise of American Catholic Thought on War and Peace.* Oxford: Oxford University Press, 1987.

Winters, Francis X., S.J. "Nuclear Deterrence Morality: Atlantic Community Bishops in Tension." *Theological Studies* 43 (1982): 428–446.

Wittberg, Patricia. "Feminist Consciousness Among American Nuns: Patterns of Ideological Diffusion." *Women's Studies International Forum* 12 (1989): 529–537.

———. "The Problem of Generations in Religious Life." *Review for Religious* (November–December 1988): 901–912.

Wolf, Eric R. *Peasant Wars of the Twentieth Century.* New York: Harper and Row, 1969.

Wolfe, Alan. *Whose Keeper? Social Science and Moral Obligation.* Berkeley and Los Angeles: University of California Press, 1989.

Wood, James R. *Leadership in Voluntary Organizations: The Controversy over Social Action in Protestant Churches.* New Brunswick, N.J.: Rutgers University Press, 1981.

Wuthnow, Robert. *Communities of Discourse: Ideology and Social Structure in the Reformation, the Enlightenment, and European Socialism.* Cambridge, Mass.: Harvard University Press, 1989.

———. *Meaning and Moral Order: Explorations in Cultural Analysis.* Berkeley and Los Angeles: University of California Press, 1987.

———. "State Structures and Ideological Outcomes." *American Sociological Review* 50 (1985): 799–821.

Wynn, Neil A. *From Progressivism to Prosperity: World War I and American Society.* New York: Holmes and Meier, 1986.

Zahn, Gordon. *German Catholics and Hitler's War.* New York: Sheed and Ward, 1962.

Zaret, David. *The Heavenly Contract: Ideology and Organization in Pre-Revolutionary Puritanism.* Chicago: University of Chicago Press, 1985.

Index

Abortion: binding doctrine on, 54, 63–64, 70; and boundary between moral and political, 19, 68, 71, 99, 120, 126–27, 191, 201–2; and Catholic politicians, 120–21, 125–26, 202, 205; history of, in U.S., 105–6, 194–95; as priority of U.S. bishops, 122, 124; and sisters, 141, 153–54; U.S. bishops' orthodoxy on, 103, 105–6, 125, 128

Acquired immune deficiency syndrome (AIDS), 123

Action Française, 33

Adrian Dominican community, 138–39, 141

Allende, Salvador, 168–69

Ambiguity: and autonomy within power structures, 195–96; and bishops' autonomy, 195; bishops' specification to eliminate, 109–11, 116–17, 118–19, 194; bishops' use of, to avoid conflict, 59–60, 114–15; and development of doctrine, 71; and ideological diversity, 23, 167, 184, 194–96; and Latin American Catholicism, 165, 175, 177, 179, 186; to maintain Church unity, 62, 207; and papacy's hesitancy toward ideological reconstruction, 5; papal use of, to avoid conflict, 18, 23, 45, 59–60, 114–15, 186; political conditions resulting in, 48, 71, 193, 194–95; and sisters' autonomy, 195–96; and subordination of sociopolitical issues, 32, 42, 44, 59, 60, 61–62, 186; of Vatican II, ideological reconstruction and, 18, 23, 48–49, 58, 62, 100; of Vatican II, liberation Catholicism and, 175, 177, 179; of Vatican II, sisters and, 130, 132, 138, 149, 154. *See also* Social doctrine; Sociopolitical issues

Americanism: "new," 123–27; and modernism, 82, 191; "political" vs. "religious," 81–82, 89–90; at time of Leo XIII, 31, 72, 76, 81–82, 89–90

Antonelli, Cardinal Giacomo, 26, 29

Antoniutti, Cardinal Ildebrando, 145

Compositor:	Printed Page Productions
Text:	10 / 13 Aldus
Display:	Aldus
Printer:	Maple-Vail Book Mfg. Group
Binder:	Maple-Vail Book Mfg. Group

Sometimes as we go through life
we master our experiences
Sometimes we don't

pathological emotions   { Extent
    — vast shifts   { severity
    — fixation on polarities   { duration

enabler: actually do things, out of misguided
    love, to save addict, excuse, even
    forgive 'enabling' addict to continue
    — learning to set limits
    — tough love — allowing person to experience
        pain, consequences, etc.